# POLITICAL SPEECHES

MARCUS TULLIUS CICERO (106–43 BC) was the son of a Roman *eques* from Arpinum, some 70 miles south-east of Rome. He rose to prominence through his skill in speaking and his exceptional success in the criminal courts, where he usually spoke for the defence. Although from a family that had never produced a Roman senator, he secured election to all the major political offices at the earliest age permitted by law. His consulship fell in a year (63) in which a dangerous insurrection occurred, the Catilinarian conspiracy; by his persuasive oratory and his controversial execution of five confessed conspirators, he prevented the conspiracy from breaking out at Rome and was hailed as the father of his country. Exiled for the executions by his enemy Clodius in 58 but recalled the following year, he lost his political independence as a result of the domination of politics by the military dynasts Pompey and Caesar. His governorship of Cilicia (51–50) was exemplary in its honesty and fairness. Always a firm republican, he reluctantly supported Pompey in the Civil War, but was pardoned by Caesar. He was not let into the plot against Caesar, but was in a sense its inspiration, being seen by now as a symbol of the republic. After Caesar's assassination (44), he supported the young Octavian (the future emperor Augustus) and led the senate in its operations against Mark Antony. When Octavian and Antony formed the 'second triumvirate' with Lepidus in 43, Cicero was their most prominent victim; he met his end with great courage.

Cicero's speeches are models of eloquence and persuasion; and together with his letters they form the chief source for the history of the late republic. His philosophical treatises, written in periods when he was deprived of his political freedom, are the main vehicle by which Hellenistic philosophy was transmitted to the west. His prose style raised the Latin language to an elegance and beauty that was never surpassed.

D. H. BERRY is Senior Lecturer in Classics at the University of Leeds. He has published an edition of and commentary on Cicero's *Pro Sulla* (Cambridge Classical Texts and Commentaries, 1996) and a translation *Cicero: Defence Speeches* (Oxford World's Classics, 2000), to which this book is a companion volume. He lives in Leeds and the Scottish Borders.

D0840105

## OXFORD WORLD'S CLASSICS

*For over 100 years Oxford World's Classics have brought readers closer to the world's great literature. Now with over 700 titles—from the 4,000-year-old myths of Mesopotamia to the twentieth century's greatest novels—the series makes available lesser-known as well as celebrated writing.*

*The pocket-sized hardbacks of the early years contained introductions by Virginia Woolf, T. S. Eliot, Graham Greene, and other literary figures which enriched the experience of reading. Today the series is recognized for its fine scholarship and reliability in texts that span world literature, drama and poetry, religion, philosophy and politics. Each edition includes perceptive commentary and essential background information to meet the changing needs of readers.*

OXFORD WORLD'S CLASSICS

# CICERO

# *Political Speeches*

Translated with Introductions and Notes by
D. H. BERRY

OXFORD
UNIVERSITY PRESS

# OXFORD
## UNIVERSITY PRESS

Great Clarendon Street, Oxford OX2 6DP

Oxford University Press is a department of the University of Oxford.
It furthers the University's objective of excellence in research, scholarship,
and education by publishing worldwide in

Oxford  New York

Auckland  Cape Town  Dar es Salaam  Hong Kong  Karachi
Kuala Lumpur  Madrid  Melbourne  Mexico City  Nairobi
New Delhi  Shanghai  Taipei  Toronto

With offices in

Argentina  Austria  Brazil  Chile  Czech Republic  France  Greece
Guatemala  Hungary  Italy  Japan  Poland  Portugal  Singapore
South Korea  Switzerland  Thailand  Turkey  Ukraine  Vietnam

Oxford is a registered trade mark of Oxford University Press
in the UK and in certain other countries

Published in the United States
by Oxford University Press Inc., New York

British Library Cataloguing in Publication Data

Data available

Library of Congress Cataloging in Publication Data

Cicero, Marcus Tullius.
[Speeches. Selections. English]
Political speeches/Cicero; translated with introductions and notes by D. H. Berry.
p. cm.—(Oxford world's classics)
Includes bibliographical references (p. ).
1. Cicero, Marcus Tullius—Translations into English.  2. Speeches,
addresses, etc., Latin—Translations into English.  3. Rome—Politics
and government—265–30 B.C.—Sources.  I. Berry, D. H.  II. Title.
III. Series: Oxford world's classics (Oxford University Press)
PA6307.A4B474 2006   875'.01—dc22   2005020919

Typeset in Ehrhardt
by RefineCatch Limited, Bungay, Suffolk
Printed in Great Britain by
Clays Ltd., St. Ives plc

ISBN 0–19–283266–2   978–0–19–283266–5

2

*To my father*

# CONTENTS

*Acknowledgements*      ix

*Abbreviations*      x

*Introduction*      xi

*Note on the Translation*      xxvi

*Note on the Latin Text*      xxxi

*Select Bibliography*      xxxiv

*Chronology*      xxxix

*Maps*      xli

## POLITICAL SPEECHES      1

In Verrem ('Against Verres') I      3

In Verrem ('Against Verres') II.5      30

De imperio Cn. Pompei ('On the command of Gnaeus Pompeius')      102

In Catilinam ('Against Catiline') I      134

In Catilinam ('Against Catiline') II      170

In Catilinam ('Against Catiline') III      181

In Catilinam ('Against Catiline') IV      193

Pro Marcello ('For Marcellus')      204

Philippic II      222

*Explanatory Notes*      271

*Glossary*      340

# ACKNOWLEDGEMENTS

THIS book has long been overdue to my patient publisher. That I have finally had time to write it, and with the care that it required, is due entirely to the generosity of two bodies: the University of Leeds, which granted me a University Study Leave Award in the Humanities from September 2003 to January 2004, and the Arts and Humanities Research Board, which granted me a Research Leave Award from February to May 2004. I am deeply grateful to both of them for effectively giving me the year I needed to bring this project to completion.

I am also grateful to Professor Andrew R. Dyck for letting me see his list of textual readings and his appendix on the date of *In Catilinam* I from his forthcoming Cambridge edition of the *Catilinarians*. It should perhaps be pointed out that I have not seen his edition and he has not seen this book; readers who use both works together will no doubt discover important differences of opinion between us. On the subject of editions, I should mention that I have profited enormously from those of W. K. Lacey, D. R. Shackleton Bailey, and, especially, J. T. Ramsey on the *Second Philippic*. If works of this quality were available for Cicero's other speeches, my task would have been much easier—though also perhaps less necessary.

I have often thought while writing this book how lucky I am to be able to read Cicero in Latin, and to have studied Latin continuously since the age of 9. It was my father who paid for my education, and it is therefore fitting that I dedicate this book to him, with love.

# ABBREVIATIONS

| | |
|---|---|
| Asc. | Asconius |
| Cic. *Arch.* | Cicero, *Pro Archia* |
| *Att.* | *Epistulae ad Atticum* |
| *Brut.* | *Brutus* |
| *Cael.* | *Pro Caelio* |
| *Cat.* | *In Catilinam* |
| *Clu.* | *Pro Cluentio* |
| *Div. Caec.* | *Divinatio in Caecilium* |
| *Fam.* | *Epistulae ad familiares* |
| *Flac.* | *Pro Flacco* |
| *Imp.* | *De imperio Cn. Pompei* (*Pro lege Manilia*) |
| *Marc.* | *Pro Marcello* |
| *Mur.* | *Pro Murena* |
| *Off.* | *De officiis* |
| *Orat.* | *Orator* |
| *Phil.* | *Orationes Philippicae* (*Philippics*) |
| *Pis.* | *In Pisonem* |
| *Scaur.* | *Pro Scauro* |
| *S. Rosc.* | *Pro Roscio Amerino* |
| *Sul.* | *Pro Sulla* |
| *Ver.* | *In Verrem* |
| Plin. *Nat.* | Pliny the Elder, *Natural History* |
| Plut. *Ant.* | Plutarch, *Life of Antony* |
| *Caes.* | *Life of Caesar* |
| *Cat. Mi.* | *Life of Cato the Younger* |
| *Cic.* | *Life of Cicero* |
| *Luc.* | *Life of Lucullus* |
| *Pomp.* | *Life of Pompey* |
| Quint. *Inst.* | Quintilian, *Institutio oratoria* |
| Sal. *Cat.* | Sallust, *Catilina* |

Note: *Ver.* 56 denotes § 56 of *In Verrem* I (the first *actio* or 'hearing'); *Ver.* 2.5.56 denotes § 56 of *In Verrem* II.5 (the fifth speech of the second *actio*).

| | |
|---|---|
| *AJP* | *American Journal of Philology* |
| *CJ* | *Classical Journal* |
| *CP* | *Classical Philology* |
| *CQ* | *Classical Quarterly* |
| *JRS* | *Journal of Roman Studies* |
| *TAPA* | *Transactions of the American Philological Association* |

# INTRODUCTION

MARCUS TULLIUS CICERO was the greatest orator of the ancient world. His dates were 106–43 BC: so he lived through the fall of the Roman republic. This was a period of national instability and unprecedented political competition, and the power of persuading others through speech became as important as it has ever been. Cicero rose to prominence not because of his birth (his non-aristocratic, Italian origin was a severe handicap to him), but because of his ability. He could persuade the ordinary citizens of Rome to vote down proposals that were in their interest, and he could (it seems) persuade just about any jury that black was white. In a gesture of triumph he published his speeches for his contemporaries and posterity to admire and imitate. Fifty-eight of these still survive today in whole or part. They are in every sense classics—works which have been read, enjoyed, quoted from, studied, and imitated by people in western societies, off and on, for two millennia. And in a world in which mass communication becomes ever more important, they retain their interest, relevance, and vibrancy.

Cicero excelled in both of the two main types of oratory, 'forensic' (the oratory of the forum, i.e. of the law courts, also known as 'judicial') and 'deliberative' (the oratory of the political assemblies). A third type, 'epideictic' (the oratory of display, or of praise and blame—more technically, 'panegyric' and 'invective'), was less important at the higher political level in Cicero's time, though from the 40s BC it started to take the place vacated by deliberative oratory, as senators' freedom of action and expression was progressively removed. Cicero's *Defence Speeches*,[1] to which this book is a companion, contains five forensic speeches, all speeches for the defence, and all except one to some degree (like virtually all of Cicero's speeches, in fact) connected with politics. This volume, on the other hand, presents a more diverse collection: two further forensic speeches, both speeches for the prosecution, four deliberative ones, and three epideictic ones (counting *In Catilinam* I, which does not fit easily into any scheme of classification, as an epideictic speech, and

---

[1] Oxford World's Classics, 2000.

*In Catilinam* II–IV as deliberative speeches). All these speeches are
strongly political, and the volume has therefore been called *Political
Speeches*. (Incidentally, the term 'political' is used by some scholars
as a synonym for 'deliberative', and so it should be pointed out that
though all the speeches in this volume are 'political' in the normal
sense, only a minority would be classed as 'political' in the sense of
'deliberative'.) *In Verrem* ('Against Verres') I and II.5 are a prosecution of a corrupt governor of Sicily, and are concerned with Roman
provincial government, and with the question whether senators
deserve the exclusive right to sit on juries. *De imperio Cn. Pompei*
('On the command of Gnaeus Pompeius') is a classic deliberative
speech recommending the appointment of Pompey (as Pompeius is
known in English) to an important military command in Asia Minor;
it also is concerned with Roman government, while at the same time
giving us a clear view of the way politics worked at Rome, and the
way magistrates presented themselves to their electors. *In Catilinam*
('Against Catiline') I–IV are a set of speeches originally delivered at
four separate moments during the Catilinarian conspiracy of 63 BC,
when Cicero was consul: the first is a denunciation of Catiline in the
senate, the second and third are reports to the people on the situation and the action Cicero has taken, and the fourth is Cicero's
contribution to the famous debate in the senate on the punishment
of the conspirators. *Pro Marcello* ('For Marcellus') is an epideictic
speech from the period of Caesar's dictatorship: Cicero offers Caesar
effusive thanks for permitting the return to Rome of his most
implacable republican enemy. Finally, *Philippic* II is another epideictic speech, but from the period following Caesar's assassination:
this famous invective is the devastating attack on Mark Antony
which was ultimately to cost Cicero his life. All these nine speeches
have been consistently viewed as masterpieces of oratory since they
were first written. At the beginning of the second century AD, Taci-
tus (*Dialogus* 37.6) singled out for special praise the speeches in
which Cicero defended Milo and attacked Catiline, Verres, and
Antony—a selection which includes seven of our speeches. But all
the speeches presented here rank among the most celebrated works
of Latin literature; and together they occupy an important place in
western intellectual culture.

## Cicero's Public Career

Thanks to his voluminous writings, particularly his letters, we know more about Cicero than about any other person in ancient history. He was the elder son of a wealthy *eques* from Arpinum, a town about 70 miles south-east of Rome that had possessed full Roman citizenship since as early as 188 BC; his younger brother Quintus was also to pursue a public career with distinction, and share his brother's brutal end. Arpinum was notable for being the home town of Gaius Marius, the seven-times consul and in 102 and 101 the saviour of Rome from the northern invaders; Cicero's paternal grandmother was in fact a relation of Marius by marriage. In *c*.95 the Ciceros bought a house in Rome so that the two boys should have the best education possible, and Cicero studied rhetoric under the two most famous orators of the day, Lucius Licinius Crassus (consul in 95) and Marcus Antonius (consul in 99); both men were later rewarded by being given parts in one of Cicero's mature rhetorical works, *De oratore* ('On the orator', 55 BC). During the Social War, Cicero saw military service: in 89 he served under Pompey's father Gnaeus Pompeius Strabo, and in 88 he served under Sulla. In 87 Marius occupied Rome and murdered his opponents, including Antonius. During the Cinnan regime which followed, Cicero continued his studies at Rome, studying rhetoric and, less usually, philosophy. In 82 Sulla recaptured the city, had himself appointed dictator, and 'proscribed' his enemies by posting in the forum lists of those to be killed. It was now (81), at the age of 25, that Cicero undertook his first court case, a civil case for Publius Quinctius afterwards published as *Pro Quinctio* ('For Quinctius'). He lost; but he lost to the most distinguished advocate in Rome, Quintus Hortensius Hortalus.

The next year (80) he undertook his first criminal case, *Pro Roscio Amerino* ('For Roscius of Ameria'). This was a defence of a man, Sextus Roscius, who had been charged with the murder of his father. The trial became sensational when Cicero boldly exposed the unscrupulous profiteering of one of Sulla's cronies, the freedman Chrysogonus, who was behind the prosecution; he won his case and became famous overnight. Among the briefs which came to him as a result of this success was the politically sensitive defence of the freedom of a woman from Arretium (a town in Etruria). This time Cicero argued successfully that Sulla had not been justified in stripping Arretium of its citizen rights. Both these cases helped Cicero to win the support of the Italians on whom he relied throughout his political career.

From 79 to 77 he studied abroad. The many cases which he had taken on immediately after the Roscius case had damaged his health (oratory was physically very demanding), and his defence of the woman from Arretium may also have made his absence from Rome politically expedient. The two brothers travelled to Greece, Rhodes, and Asia Minor (to which Quintus, who was also to pursue a political career, would later return as governor). They studied philosophy in Athens, and Cicero studied rhetoric under Molon of Rhodes. Molon, he later maintained, helped him to make his oratory a little more restrained, less 'Asianist' (elaborate and florid) in style. This toning down of his oratorical style was in keeping with the direction in which taste at Rome was moving, and it was also sensible in view of the risk to his health.

In 76 he was elected quaestor at Rome, and he served his term of office in western Sicily the following year. Election to the quaestor-ship brought life membership of the senate, and Cicero was the first member of his family to attain this distinction; thus he became in Roman terms a 'new man' (*novus homo*, the first man of a family to reach the senate).

This success was followed up in 70 by his election as plebeian aedile for 69. But, more significantly, he decided in 70 to undertake a prosecution: having served as an honest quaestor in Sicily five years earlier, he was only too happy to help the Sicilians by bringing a charge of extortion against the rapacious governor, Gaius Verres, who had systematically fleeced the province from 73 to 71. Verres' defence, however, was undertaken by Hortensius, who was to be consul in 69, and he was also aided by one of the leading families in Rome, the Metelli. One Metellus had become Verres' successor in Sicily, and made it difficult for Cicero to collect evidence; another was to be Hortensius' consular colleague the following year; and a third would be praetor in charge of the court if, as the defence hoped, the case could be prolonged into 69. But in the event Cicero overcame all these obstacles. He collected his evidence quickly, delivered a brief opening speech, and then brought out his witnesses. In his speech he dwelt upon the political aspect of the case: if some-one as obviously guilty as Verres were let off, the people would judge the exclusively senatorial juries (prescribed by a law of Sulla's) to be unfit to try cases, and a law would be passed handing the courts over to the *equites* instead. Once this speech had been given and the evidence presented, Verres went into exile, without waiting to hear more; and Cicero then published the speeches he would have gone on to deliver—*In Verrem* ('Against Verres') or, in English, the *Verrines*, a damning and sometimes hilarious exposé of Verres' crimes. With this success Cicero took Hortensius' place as Rome's foremost advocate: Hortensius all but abandoned the courts, returning only when Cicero had reached the consulship, and then as his partner, not his opponent.

Cicero's irresistible rise continued. In 67 he was elected praetor, by all the centuries (voting units in the centuriate assembly), three times over (because the election had to be repeated), and at the earliest age permitted by law (he was by now 39). He served his year of office as praetor in charge of the extortion court, the scene of his success against Verres; and in 66 he also gave his first deliberative speech, *De imperio Cn. Pompei* ('On the command of Gnaeus Pompeius'), alternatively known as *Pro lege Manilia* ('For the Manilian law'). Rome had recently suffered a serious reverse in the Third Mithridatic War (73–63). Public opinion wanted the command of the Roman forces, which since the beginning of the war had been held by Lucullus, to be given to Pompey, who had just enjoyed a spectacular success in wiping out the pirates of the Mediterranean, and was already on the scene; the traditionalists in the senate, however, such as Hortensius, did not wish to see Pompey's career advanced any further. The tribune Gaius Manilius proposed a bill to have the command transferred to Pompey, and invited Cicero to support it. As a praetor, Cicero could not avoid expressing an opinion—and yet he did not wish to alienate either the senate or the people, given that he would shortly be standing for the consulship. His solution was to give the bill his enthusiastic support, while also taking care to compliment Lucullus. The bill was passed, Cicero published his speech, and Pompey concluded the war in 63. A non-political speech, but a celebrated one, was also delivered in 66, *Pro Cluentio* ('For Cluentius'). This was an oratorical triumph in which Cicero, as he afterwards boasted, 'threw dust in the eyes of the jury' (Quint. *Inst.* 2.17.21).

In 64 he was elected to the consulship for 63, again at the earliest age permitted by law (he was 43 in 63). With this success his family entered the ranks of the nobility (a 'noble' was a direct descendant of a consul through the male line). It was certainly unusual for new men to rise as high as the consulship: the last one to do so had been Gaius Norbanus twenty years previously. Cicero's consulship was an eventful one, and one that afforded further scope for the exercise of his oratorical talents. It began with his four speeches *De lege agraria* ('On the agrarian law'), in which he successfully opposed the land redistributions proposed by the tribune Publius Servilius Rullus; the speeches demonstrate Cicero's ability to persuade the people to vote down a proposal that was in their interest. He claimed to be a popular consul acting in the people's interest, but was actually taking a conservative line. Now that he had reached the highest place in the 'sequence of offices' (*cursus honorum*), he was always to follow the conservative, traditional, and republican line which by nature he preferred. Having been allowed to join the club, he would defend its rules to the death.

But the major event of Cicero's consulship, and indeed of his life, was his controversial suppression of the Catilinarian conspiracy. The conspirators were a small group of failed politicians some of whom had ruined themselves financially in their attempts to secure political advancement and live up to their social status; some, in marked contrast to Cicero, were high-ranking aristocrats. Led by the patrician Lucius Sergius Catilina ('Catiline' in English), they hoped, by assassinations, arson, and a march on Rome, to seize power; then they would reward themselves with political office and put forward legislation for a general cancellation of debts (there is no evidence of any plans for wider reform, or of any genuine social concern). The conspiracy began in earnest with Catiline's failure to be elected consul in July, and by mid-November he had thrown in his lot with an agrarian rising in Etruria led by one Gaius Manlius, a former Sullan centurion. Cicero's vigilance and prompt action saved his own life from an assassination attempt and prevented the conspiracy from breaking out at Rome—but at the cost of executing without trial five leading conspirators (including one ex-consul, Publius Cornelius Lentulus Sura), who had been arrested and had confessed their guilt. His illegal execution of the five men on 5 December had the explicit backing of the senate and overwhelming public support (on Cato's motion, he was voted father of his country by the people), and probably saved a great many lives. Nevertheless, it was to lay him open to attack for years afterwards, and required him constantly to be justifying the action that he had taken (something which has unfairly caused him to be perceived as boastful and vain). His publication in 60 of his four magnificent speeches against Catiline (*In Catilinam* ('Against Catiline') or, in English, the *Catilinarians*) was a major exercise in self-justification. The effectiveness of his attack ensured that Catiline's name was blackened for all time. Catiline himself, together with his army, was destroyed in the field by Cicero's colleague as consul, Gaius Antonius Hybrida, at the beginning of 62.

In the midst of the Catilinarian crisis (in November) Cicero also found time to undertake the defence of one of the consuls-elect for 62, Lucius Licinius Murena, who had been prosecuted for electoral malpractice by one of the unsuccessful candidates; the law under which the case was brought was Cicero's own bribery law, the *lex Tullia de ambitu*, which he had successfully carried earlier in the year. Together with Hortensius and Crassus, he secured his acquittal, arguing that, in the face of the danger from Catiline, the necessity of having as consul an experienced military man such as Murena overrode all other considerations. *Pro Murena* ('For Murena') is Cicero's funniest and most enjoyable speech (unless one prefers *Pro Caelio*). Much of it is taken up with making fun of the prosecutors, the lawyer Servius Sulpicius Rufus and the Stoic philosopher Marcus Porcius Cato, both men for whom Cicero had in reality a considerable regard.

Cicero's suppression of the Catilinarian conspiracy won him enormous prestige, and on 1 January 62 he was the first senator to be asked for his opinion in the senate: he was viewed as the leading senator present (Pompey was still in the east). We have two speeches of his from this year, *Pro Sulla* ('For Sulla') and *Pro Archia* ('For Archias'). *Pro Sulla* is a defence of a wealthy aristocrat, the nephew of the dictator Sulla (and probably the brother-in-law of Pompey), on a charge of participation in the conspiracy; Cicero secured his acquittal by arguing that he of all people would hardly have undertaken his defence if he had believed him to be guilty. In this speech we see Cicero seeking to present himself as a mild and compassionate person, to counteract his enemies' portrayal of him as cruel and vindictive in his execution of the conspirators. *Pro Archia*, by contrast, is one of the least political of Cicero's forensic speeches. A defence not of a Roman aristocrat but of a Syrian poet, Cicero's old teacher, on a charge of illegally assuming Roman citizenship, it contains not just a legal defence of Archias' claim, but a lengthy encomium of literature. This is of great interest to literary historians, and shows the degree to which Cicero had to go to present Archias' profession to a Roman jury in a favourable light. Archias was acquitted.

At the end of the year a scandal occurred at Rome which was to have disastrous consequences for Cicero. A young aristocrat, Publius Clodius Pulcher, was discovered to have dressed up in women's clothes and attended the festival of the Bona Dea, to which only women were admitted, and which was being held at the house of Caesar, the *pontifex maximus*. The suggestion was that he had taken advantage of Caesar's absence from his house to commit adultery with his wife. Caesar divorced his wife on the grounds that 'Caesar's wife must be above suspicion' (Plut. *Caes.* 10.6). At Clodius' trial for sacrilege in May 61, Cicero gave evidence which disproved his alibi. Nevertheless, Clodius managed to bribe his way to an acquittal; and he was henceforward to be a far more troublesome enemy to Cicero than Catiline had been.

At the end of 60, Caesar, who was consul-elect for the following year, formed a political alliance with Pompey and Crassus conventionally known as the 'first triumvirate'. He tried to persuade Cicero to join the alliance: Cicero would have lost his political independence, but would have been protected from Clodius and from the increasing attacks on his execution of the Catilinarians. He preferred to keep his independence—and was to pay for it. In 59 Caesar sanctioned Clodius' adoption into a plebeian family (he was of patrician birth), thus enabling him to stand for election to the tribunate of the plebs, the office traditionally sought by popular politicians who wished to propose radical legislation or, in conservative eyes, to stir up trouble. Clodius was duly elected and, as tribune in 58, he proposed a bill outlawing anyone who had put a Roman citizen to death without trial. The senate put on mourning for Cicero and the towns of Italy passed resolutions in his favour. But Clodius, who had earlier carried a law to provide the people with free grain for the first time, had the support of the urban plebs. More importantly, he also had the tacit support of the triumvirs, who were angered at Cicero's rejection of their advances and worried that he might lead the conservatives in the senate in an attack on their position. The consuls Piso and Gabinius did as the triumvirs wanted, and instructed the senate to resume normal dress. Cicero's support melted away, and he himself left for exile in Macedonia on the day that Clodius' law was passed. His house in Rome was plundered and burned, and Clodius consecrated the site as a shrine to Libertas ('Liberty'), in order to portray Cicero as a tyrant and to prevent rebuilding.

Cicero's exile, which lasted almost eighteen months, was the biggest disaster of his life. He had saved Rome, and had been exiled for his pains. The charge was executing citizens without trial; yet he had been denied a trial himself. In his despair he thought of suicide. Publicly he represented his departure as a deliberate act of self-sacrifice, intended to save Rome from the likelihood of civil war—the second time he had saved the city. But privately he felt he should have stood his ground. He was recalled to Rome the following year, when the triumvirs concluded that Clodius had become an obstacle to their plans. His actual return was glorious and gratifying. On Pompey's motion the senate passed a decree, unanimous with the single exception of Clodius, describing Cicero as the saviour of his country; and the people passed a bill authorizing his recall. His journey through Italy resembled a triumphal procession: towns passed resolutions honouring him, and he was escorted by cheering crowds. But he never recovered from the blow to his pride; and, as the price of his recall, he had had to assure the triumvirs that in future he would serve their interests.

The speeches he gave in 57 and 56 are known as the *Post reditum* ('After his return') speeches. *Post reditum in senatu* ('in the senate', 57) and *Post reditum ad quirites* ('to the citizens', 57) offered thanks for his restoration. *De domo sua* ('On his house', 57) and *De haruspicum responsis* ('On the answers of the omen-interpreters', 56) dealt with the religious aspects of his feud with Clodius; he successfully persuaded the pontiffs that Clodius' consecration of the site of his house in Rome had been invalid, and he secured compensation to enable him to rebuild. Other speeches of this period included defences of people who had campaigned for his recall and opposed Clodius. Publius Sestius and Titus Annius Milo were tribunes in 57 who had used violence against Clodius and worked tirelessly for Cicero's recall. Sestius was prosecuted in 56 by dependants of Clodius, was defended by Hortensius, Crassus, and Cicero (the same

team that had defended Murena in 63), and was unanimously acquitted. Cicero's *Pro Sestio* ('For Sestius') contains a full exposition of
the orator's own political standpoint: the state can be divided into
patriots and traitors, with Sestius and Milo and the majority of
Roman citizens of all classes belonging to the former category, and
Clodius, Piso, and Gabinius to the latter.

A month later Cicero was to revenge himself on Clodius in a more
personal way. A former friend of Clodius', Marcus Caelius Rufus,
was prosecuted on an array of charges: violence, murder, and the
attempted poisoning of Clodius' sister, Clodia Metelli, with whom
Caelius had previously had an affair. Caelius had originally been a
pupil of Cicero's, before switching allegiance to the Clodii, and now
that he had broken with the Clodii he was to become a friend of
Cicero's again. In taking on his defence, Cicero saw his chance to
hurt Clodius by publicly humiliating his sister, whom he had reasons
for hating: she had persecuted his family during his exile. In *Pro
Caelio* ('For Caelius') the charges are largely ignored, and Cicero
instead focuses on Caelius' affair with Clodia, portraying her as a
common prostitute (she was a high-ranking society lady) and holding her up to ridicule. Ingeniously, he manages to do this while
exempting Caelius from moral blame. The speech is wonderfully
funny, and very cruel: Cicero won his case by avoiding the issue and
making the jury laugh at his enemy. After the trial, Clodia (who has a
one-in-three chance of being the same person as Catullus' 'Lesbia')
disappears from history.

Cicero owed his recall from exile to Pompey's influence, and in
return he had reluctantly undertaken to give the triumvirs his political support. But he soon detected an apparent rift between Pompey
and Caesar (who was absent in Gaul from 58 to 49), and decided to
drive the two men further apart by opposing Caesar. First he published an attack on Publius Vatinius which he had made at the time
of Sestius' trial (*In Vatinium*, 'Against Vatinius'): Vatinus was a legate of Caesar's who as tribune in 59 had procured for him his Gallic
command. Secondly, he put a motion before the senate calling for
discussion of Caesar's controversial agrarian law of 59. This challenge to Caesar's position did not split the triumvirate as Cicero had
hoped: instead it drove the three men closer together. They reaffirmed their alliance, and Pompey and Crassus held a second joint
consulship in 55 (they had held the consulship together in 70), with

commands for each of them to follow afterwards. Caesar's command in Gaul was extended for a further five years.

Cicero now realized that resistance to the triumvirs would be futile, and in any case he needed their protection against Clodius' continuing attacks; he also felt that the conservatives in the senate, such as Hortensius, were failing to give him their full support. He therefore publicly declared his allegiance to the triumvirs: in *De provinciis consularibus* ('On the consular provinces', 56) he lavishes praise on Caesar and advocates the extension of his Gallic command.

The later 50s were unhappy years for Cicero. In 54 he had to defend Vatinius; although he won, he apparently chose not to publish his defence. Soon afterwards (in 54 or 53) he was compelled to defend Gabinius, the consul of 58 who had allowed Clodius to exile him; at least this time he had the satisfaction of losing. In his private moments he consoled himself by starting to write a series of philosophical treatises in which he explained the various philosophical systems of the Greeks (he was the first person to do this in Latin; the work involved formulating a Latin philosophical vocabulary, which then became standard). At the same time he began a series of treatises on oratory and rhetoric; some of these works also explore, in theoretical terms, his own political philosophy. In 53 (or 52) he was gratified to receive, on Hortensius' nomination, an important political honour: he was elected to a place in the College of Augurs, in succession to Crassus' son, who had been killed with his father at Carrhae.

Clodius during these years had become a powerful independent force in Rome with a large popular following. He had assembled a gang of thugs and used it to attack his enemies, most of all Cicero, and to terrorize the city. His chief opponent was Titus Annius Milo, who used similar tactics against him in return. The increasing willingness of politicians to resort to violence to achieve their ends was a symptom of the collapse of the republic; in the next decade, urban violence would be superseded by civil war. Clodius and Milo had fought numerous battles against each other, Milo defending Cicero's interests; and in one such battle outside Rome on 18 January 52 Clodius was accidentally wounded, and then killed on Milo's orders. Cicero must have been overjoyed. Amid the chaotic scenes which followed, Clodius' supporters cremated his body in the senate-house, which was burned down. Pompey was appointed sole consul to restore order (the violence in Rome had prevented the elections for 52 from taking place), and Milo was put on trial and defended by Cicero. The evidence for his guilt was unimpeachable, and Pompey wanted him removed from public life, so Cicero's defence stood no chance of success: he was convicted, and went into exile at Massilia (Marseilles). But later in the year public opinion swung against Pompey and the Clodians, and in Milo's favour. Milo's accomplices were tried and acquitted, whereas Clodius' supporters, who were put on trial for the burning of the senate-house, were convicted. Cicero, who had played a leading part in these trials, now regarded himself and Milo as having been vindicated, and he wrote and published a new, more confident version of his unsuccessful defence. This is our *Pro Milone* ('For Milo'), which has always been accepted as the oratorical masterpiece that Cicero intended it to be.

During his consulship in 52 Pompey had legislation passed which ruled that consuls and praetors should have to wait at least five years before going out to govern their provinces (the purpose of the law was to discourage electoral bribery by delaying the period at which a magistrate would be able to recoup the money he had spent when standing for office). This created a short-term shortage of provincial governors, and as Cicero had not previously held a provincial governorship he was made to serve for a year (51–50) as governor of Cilicia, on the south-east coast of Asia Minor (the province also included Cyprus). He was very distressed at having to be away from the political scene at Rome: his governorship seemed like a second exile, and his greatest fear was that his term of office might be extended. But he resolved to make the best of the situation by acting as a model provincial governor—no easy matter, when fairness to the provincials ran directly counter to the financial interests of prominent men at Rome. He also led a successful campaign against the brigands of the interior; but on his return to Rome the impending civil war prevented him from obtaining the triumph he had hoped for.

At the outbreak of the Civil War in 49 Cicero agonized over what to do. He was put in charge of the Campanian coast, but, being unable to raise recruits in any number, soon gave up and retired to one of his villas. Caesar repeatedly tried to win him over to his side, even coming to visit him at home: to win the endorsement of such a senior republican would serve to legitimize his position. But Cicero could not in conscience give his support to a man who had invaded

Italy and declared war on his country. On the other hand, he had little confidence in Pompey, the man into whose hands the republic had been placed: Pompey's decision to abandon Italy and cross over to Greece seemed to Cicero a catastrophic misjudgement, and he was disgusted by the motives and behaviour of Pompey's followers. Eventually he concluded, despairingly, that his duty was to join Pompey in Greece. He crossed over to him in June 49; but once in Pompey's camp he declined to accept a command, and irritated the Pompeian leaders with his criticisms. He was not present at Pompey's defeat at Pharsalus in August 48, and after Pompey's flight and murder he was invited to assume command of the surviving republican forces, but declined. In October 48 he returned to Brundisium in Italy, but it was not until September 47 that he was pardoned by Caesar and allowed to move on to Rome.

Under Caesar's dictatorship there was no free political debate in which he could participate, and in any case his advice on political matters was not sought; he attended meetings of the senate, but without speaking. It was now that he found time to resume work on his many philosophical and rhetorical treatises, the bulk of which were written during this period; and he also taught rhetoric to aristocratic pupils. These activities helped take his mind off the fall of the republic, Caesar's increasing autocracy, and (in 45) the death of his beloved daughter Tullia. In September 46 he broke his silence in the senate. Caesar had unexpectedly agreed to pardon an enemy, one of the most die-hard of the republican leaders, Marcus Claudius Marcellus, and Cicero made a speech of thanks. *Pro Marcello* ('For Marcellus') praises Caesar's clemency and urges him to proceed with his work of reform; it also sets out Cicero's case to be accepted as a mediator between Caesar and the former Pompeians. *Pro Ligario* ('For Ligarius', 46) and *Pro rege Deiotaro* ('For King Deiotarus', 45) are other speeches of this period in which Cicero begs Caesar to spare Pompeian enemies. In their circumstances of delivery and in their tone they are a far cry from the speeches in which Cicero addresses a jury and is free to say what he wishes. Here he is addressing a monarch in his palace.

Caesar's autocracy led of course to his assassination in the senate on the Ides (15th) of March 44, just a few weeks after he had had himself made *dictator perpetuo* ('dictator for life'). Cicero had offered discreet encouragement to the assassins, or 'liberators' as he calls them, but had not been let into the plot. He was actually present at the murder: Brutus raised his dagger and congratulated him on the recovery of their freedom. As the last of the senior republicans still surviving, Cicero had a symbolic value: he had become a token of the republic. And this time we do have evidence for his joy at the death of his enemy (if *Fam.* 6.15 does indeed refer to it).

After the assassination, political life began again. The surviving consul, Mark Antony (in Latin, Marcus Antonius), arranged a settlement under which Caesar's assassins would not be prosecuted, but his laws and appointments would remain in force. In April, however, the situation changed with the arrival in Italy of Caesar's principal heir, his 18-year-old great-nephew Gaius Octavius (who from his posthumous adoption as Caesar's son is known as Octavian, and from 27 is known as the first emperor, Augustus): calling himself Gaius Julius Caesar, he showed himself to Caesar's veterans, held games in Caesar's honour, and began paying Caesar's legacies to the Roman people. In September, Cicero made an enemy of Antony, for a relatively trivial reason: Antony had denounced him for his failure to attend a meeting of the senate at which posthumous honours for Caesar were to be voted. Cicero replied the next day with the *First Philippic*; Antony then delivered a bitter invective against him in the senate in his absence; and Cicero wrote (but did not deliver) a savage reply, the *Second Philippic*. This speech attacks and ridicules Antony's entire career, but particularly his behaviour under Caesar and his appropriation of state funds in the months since Caesar's death; it closes with a warning of assassination. It was Cicero's view that Antony ought to have been murdered at the same time as Caesar: if Cicero had been invited to the feast (i.e. let into the plot), there would have been no leftovers (*Fam.* 10.28.1, 12.4.1).

In November Antony left Rome for Gaul, which he had taken as his province; and Cicero assumed unofficial leadership of the senate. In the *Third Philippic*, he persuaded the senate to approve the refusal of Decimus Brutus, the governor of Cisalpine Gaul and one of Caesar's assassins, to hand over his legions to Antony; and in the *Fourth Philippic*, delivered before the people on the same day, he argued that Antony was in effect a public enemy. At the same time, he urged both senate and people to give their support to Octavian. In thinking that the young man could be praised, honoured, and then disposed of (to his embarrassment, his words (*Fam.* 11.20.1) were reported to Octavian), Cicero made a serious misjudgement. It was also unrealistic of him to suppose that Octavian would stay for long on the same side as Caesar's assassins. But Antony's destruction seemed to Cicero the immediate priority, and an alliance with Octavian was the only way to bring it about.

From this point, Cicero controlled events at Rome: nineteen years after his consulship, he was once again leading the republic at a moment of supreme national crisis. In a further ten *Philippics* (January to April 43), he directed the senate in its actions against Antony, urging it not to compromise, and presented his view of events to the people. It was his 'finest hour'. In April 43 Antony was defeated near Mutina and declared a public enemy. Cicero, it seemed, had saved his country a second time. But events then took an unwelcome turn. Antony escaped and succeeded in acquiring further legions from Marcus Aemilius Lepidus, the governor of Narbonese Gaul and Nearer Spain; and Decimus Brutus was deserted by his troops and killed on Antony's orders. Octavian, though only 19, demanded the consulship (both consuls had been killed in battle); he may have considered having Cicero as his colleague, but the evidence for this is doubtful. When his demand was refused by the senate, he marched on Rome and, in August, held an irregular election and took the consulship, with his uncle as his colleague. With nothing more to be got from Cicero and the senate, he then changed sides, holding a meeting with Antony and Lepidus near Bononia. The 'second triumvirate' was formed, and the three men gave themselves supreme power for five years, and divided out the empire between them. To rid themselves of their enemies and raise funds for their veterans they initiated a proscription, as Sulla had done in 82. So once again the lists of those to be killed were posted in the forum. Cicero met his end, on 7 December, with great courage. He was 63. His head and hands were cut off and displayed on the rostra in the forum— the scene of so many of his successes.

Octavian defeated Antony at Actium in 31, and in 30 he chose Cicero's son as his colleague in the consulship. Many years later, as the emperor Augustus, he happened to catch his grandson reading one of Cicero's books. He took the book, looked through it, and handed it back saying, 'He was a master of words, child, a master of words and a patriot' (Plut. *Cic.* 49.3).

# NOTE ON THE TRANSLATION

CICERO'S orations are not written in the language of ordinary speech: instead, they are composed in a highly artificial style which must have impressed, astonished, and mesmerized those who listened to it. Sentences are long, sometimes as long as a third of a page of a modern printed text, and occasionally longer. The style is 'periodic'; that is, once the sentence or 'period' has begun, the listener has to wait some time before the various subordinate clauses have been delivered and the sense is complete. While the period is evolving, the listener has certain expectations about how it is going to continue and end (grammatically, and in sense), and when it is finally completed these expectations are either fulfilled (giving the listener a sense of satisfaction) or, more rarely, cheated (startling the listener). The clauses which make up the period can sometimes be mere padding, but this is unusual; often they make the argument more impressive or powerful, and in addition they serve to delay the completion of the period, providing a greater feeling of satisfaction when the grammar and sense are finally completed. The clauses themselves and the words or groups of words within them are often arranged in carefully balanced pairs, sometimes so as to form a contrast, or sometimes in a symmetrical pattern; or they can be arranged in threes, with increasing weight placed on each item, or greater weight placed on the final or second and final item. Formal English style also uses these techniques; thus I have written 'impressed, astonished, and mesmerized' above, providing more terms than is strictly necessary for the sense ('mesmerized', the strongest term and therefore placed last, would have sufficed). In periodic style, the most important part of the period is the end (the beginning is the next most important), because it is here that the sense of completion is delivered. In accordance with the techniques of Hellenistic Greek oratory, Cicero always makes sure that the ends of his periods, and even of the more important clauses ('cola'), sound right: certain rhythmical patterns ('clausulae') are favoured and others (mainly those which resemble verse) avoided. This 'prose rhythm' is one of the most prominent features of his style. Scholars have tried to analyse it, with varying results. It must have taken a great deal of training to be able to achieve the appropriate rhythms automatically, without thinking about it, in the way that Cicero could (*Orat.* 200). Roman audiences were discriminating, and appreciated the skilful use of prose rhythm: there is an anecdote about a group of listeners bursting into applause when an orator produced some striking cadences (*Orat.* 213–14; cf. 168). Besides rhythm, there are many other techniques used by Cicero to enliven or adorn his prose, such as rhetorical questions (questions that do not expect an answer), anaphora (repetition of a word or phrase in successive clauses), asyndeton (omission of connectives), apostrophe (turning away to address an absent person or thing), exclamation, alliteration and assonance, wordplay, and metaphor.

In this translation I have followed the same policy as I adopted in *Defence Speeches*: to preserve as much of Cicero's style and artistry as possible, and to make the translation strike the reader in as near as possible the same way as I think the Latin text would have struck its original readership. I have rendered long Latin sentences by long English ones, and for the most part have chopped up the Latin sentences only where the length was longer than a modern reader would tolerate. Similarly, I have retained the periodicity of the Latin as far as possible: I have tried to keep the clauses, phrases, and sometimes even the actual words in the same order as they occur in the original. Each word contains an idea, and in the original these ideas are conveyed to the reader in a particular order; so I have felt it desirable to refrain as far as possible from doing violence to that order. If a significant idea is withheld until the end of a sentence (as commonly happens in periodic style), then I have also withheld it until the end. This policy has allowed me, I hope, to preserve the movement of the original.

A good example of the desirability of keeping the words in the order in which Cicero presents them is provided by *Marc.* 1. One day in the senate in 46 BC, in the presence of the dictator Caesar, Cicero rose to speak. The greatest orator Rome had ever known, he had not spoken in public for almost six years. During those six years, a civil war had been fought, the republic had fallen, and a dictatorship had been established. As he stood up, the senate must have been astonished: could Cicero's self-imposed silence really be about to be broken? He began to speak: 'Diuturni silenti, patres conscripti . . .'. The other translators of this speech into English begin their versions as follows: 'This day, O conscript fathers . . .', 'This day, senators . . .', 'To-day, Conscript Fathers . . .', 'During this recent period, senators . . .'. The effect of Cicero's opening words must have been electrifying—and that effect can only be conveyed by beginning with the same words as the orator himself did: 'The long silence, conscript fathers . . .'.

If we turn now from periodicity to prose rhythm, we find that unfortunately there is little that a translator can do, since prose rhythm is a feature of the original that cannot normally be reproduced: crowds do not burst into applause when English speakers produce striking cadences. Good English does, however, avoid certain rhythms—to a greater extent, perhaps, than is commonly realized: without conscious thought, speakers and writers will produce sentences that sound elegant. In writing English translation, then, the translator can at least take care that the English he is writing does not strike the ear harshly.

As for rhetorical devices, I have retained these as far as possible. Questions have been translated as questions, exclamations as exclamations, direct speech as direct speech, and indirect speech as indirect speech. I have also tried to reproduce the many examples of alliteration, assonance, wordplay, and metaphor that feature in Cicero's writing. It has very often been impossible to provide an alliterative effect using the same letter as Cicero, and in such cases I have introduced alliteration of some other letter (when an ancient author uses alliteration, my feeling is that it is generally the alliteration that is significant, not the letter). I have followed the same policy with regard to assonance.

I have been careful not to introduce material that has no basis in the Latin, and not to omit any of the original—and here I have been presented with a dilemma. Cicero is exceedingly fond of doublets, particularly in the first three of the speeches in this collection, but in good English doublets ('aims and objectives', 'terms and conditions') are used only sparingly, if at all. When Cicero uses a doublet with two words of identical meaning, as he quite frequently does, should the translator preserve the doublet and write intolerably verbose English or solve the problem by omitting one half of the doublet? It would not be acceptable, in my view, to omit a word that Cicero has included, and especially to omit a stylistic feature, a doublet, when Cicero has wished it to be there; but equally I feel it would not be acceptable to write bad English. My solution in such cases has therefore been to keep the doublet, but choose two English words which are similar in meaning, but not quite synonymous.

One phrase of Cicero's that translators are often inclined to omit is *populus Romanus*, 'the Roman people': Cicero's speeches (especially, in this collection, *In Verrem* I and II.5) are full of references to 'the Roman people'. I have always included such references in full, and not abbreviated them to 'the people' (which in British English sounds ideological and rather leaden). The result is that these speeches retain their popular feel, and serve as useful reminders of the prominence of the democratic element in Roman politics. Similarly, *equites Romani* is translated as 'the Roman equestrians', and not 'the equestrians'; the *equites* were, I think, particular about such niceties.

The translator needs to decide how he is going to render the Roman names that are mentioned in the text: prominent Romans generally had at least three names (*praenomen*, *nomen*, and *cognomen*), but normally only one or two are used when the person is referred to. My own practice has been to translate the names exactly as Cicero gives them, adding (where necessary) an explanatory note at the end of the book giving the full form of the name together with any other relevant information. This allows the translation to present an accurate reflection of the Romans' customs of naming. Some prominent Romans have a traditional English version of their name which will be more familiar to readers than their Latin name. I have therefore written 'Gnaeus Pompeius', 'Lucius Catilina', and 'Marcus Antonius' in the text, but 'Pompey', 'Catiline', and '(Mark) Antony' in the introductions and notes. Where Cicero refers to Catiline without *praenomen*, however, as he almost invariably does (in order to abuse him), I have written 'Catiline', not 'Catilina'.

Finally, I should mention the paragraphing—the first matter to which a translator turns his attention. The medieval manuscripts of Cicero's speeches do not preserve Cicero's original paragraphing (if there ever was any, which is unlikely), and since the text of Cicero is very difficult to divide up, modern editions tend to insert new paragraphs only every several pages. The decision as to where to start a new paragraph requires one to think very hard about the structure of the argument, and I have found this almost the most difficult aspect of my task. I have reparagraphed the entire text, and I hope that the new paragraphing will substantially aid the understanding of these speeches.

Some authors, particularly poets, are simply untranslatable: a translation cannot provide an experience which is close enough to that of reading the original to be satisfactory. Cicero is not one of these authors; and it is my hope that these translations will indeed convey some impression of his extraordinary mastery of language, his intelligence, his persuasive power, his lively sense of humour, and the fluency, vividness, and beauty of his writing. But reading the original, of course, is an experience of a different order from that of reading a translation. Many people who are reading this book will be doing so at a point in their lives when they have an opportunity to learn some Latin. If you are one of them, I hope that this book will encourage you to seize that opportunity.

# NOTE ON THE LATIN TEXT

FOR each speech I have translated the most satisfactory existing edition of the Latin text, with occasional departures from it. These editions, and my departures from them, are listed below. The numerous differences of paragraphing and punctuation are not recorded (such features have no ancient authority, but are added by editors according to their understanding of the sense).

## In Verrem I

Text: A. Klotz, Teubner (Leipzig, 1923).

1     *apud populum Romanum sed etiam*: I translate *apud nos sed*.

4     *praetori*: I translate *praetori populo Romano*.

39    *quod in C. Herennio . . . factum sit . . . inventi sint . . . inventus sit*: I translate *<quid?> quod in C. Herennio . . . factum est . . . inventi sunt . . . inventus est*.

48    *hominum*: I omit.

55    *ut crimen totum*: I translate *ut <primum unumquodque> crimen totum*.

## In Verrem II.5

Text: A. Klotz, Teubner (Leipzig, 1949).

31    *parique*: I translate *talarique*.

55    *iste dedit ut*: I translate *isti dedit ut*.

83    *ubi ternis denariis . . . permissa et data*: I omit.

133   *[hoc Hennenses]*: I retain.

143   *quae lautumiae vocantur*: I omit.

181   *Caelium*: I translate *Coelium*.

## De imperio Cn. Pompei

Text: A. C. Clark, Oxford Classical Text (Oxford, 1905).

7   *omnis*: I omit.
21  *inflammata*: I translate *inflata*.
24  *se et suam manum iam confirmarat eorum opera qui ad eum ex ipsius regno concesserant*: I translate *et suam manum iam confirmarat*.
56  *et ea*: I translate *ea*.
58  *Caelius*: I translate *Coelius*.
62  *alium*: I translate *curulem*.

## In Catilinam I–IV

Text: T. Maslowski, Teubner (Munich and Leipzig, 2003).

1.22  *tua ista*: I translate *ista*.
2.3   *non putarent*: I translate <*coniurationem factam*> *non putarent*.
2.10  *fortunatum*: I translate *fortunatam*.
3.4   *eodemque itinere cum litteris mandatisque*: I translate *cum litteris mandatisque eodemque itinere*.
3.24  *eiecit ex urbe*: I omit.
4.11  *a crudelitatis vituperatione prohibebo*: I translate *crudelitatis vituperatione populus Romanus exsolvet*.
4.13  <*iure*>: I omit.

## Pro Marcello

Text: A. C. Clark, Oxford Classical Text (Oxford, 1918$^2$).

26  *civis*: I omit.

## Philippic II

Text: J. T. Ramsey, Cambridge Greek and Latin Classics (Cambridge, 2003).

21   *opportebat*: I translate *oportebat*.

58   *comites nequissimi*: I omit.

91   *propter proximum dictatorem*: I omit.

103   *quo ore*: I translate *quo more*.

# SELECT BIBLIOGRAPHY

Articles (but not books) in foreign languages are excluded.

### General

Albrecht, M. von, *Cicero's Style: A Synopsis* (*Mnemosyne*, Suppl. 245; Leiden and Boston, 2003) (*Ver.* II.5, *Marc.*).

Alexander, M. C., *Trials in the Late Roman Republic, 149 BC to 50 BC* (*Phoenix*, Suppl. 26; Toronto etc., 1990).

—— *The Case for the Prosecution in the Ciceronian Era* (Ann Arbor, 2002) (*Ver.*).

Atkinson, J. M., *Our Masters' Voices: The Language and Body Language of Politics* (London and New York, 1984).

Berry, D. H., '*Equester Ordo Tuus Est*: Did Cicero Win his Cases because of his Support for the *Equites*?', *CQ*, NS 53 (2003), 222–34.

—— 'Oratory', in S. J. Harrison (ed.), *A Companion to Latin Literature* (Oxford, 2005), 257–69.

—— and Heath, M., 'Oratory and Declamation', in S. E. Porter (ed.), *Handbook of Classical Rhetoric in the Hellenistic Period 330 BC–AD 400* (Leiden, 1997), 393–420.

Broughton, T. R. S., *The Magistrates of the Roman Republic*, i (New York, 1951), ii (New York, 1952), iii (Atlanta, 1986).

Butler, S., *The Hand of Cicero* (London and New York, 2002) (*Ver., Cat.* 3, *Phil.* 2).

Clarke, M. L., rev. D. H. Berry, *Rhetoric at Rome: A Historical Survey*[3] (London, 1996).

Classen, C. J., *Recht-Rhetorik-Politik: Untersuchungen zu Ciceros rhetorischer Strategie* (Darmstadt, 1985) (*Imp.*).

Corbeill, A., *Controlling Laughter: Political Humor in the Late Roman Republic* (Princeton, 1996).

Craig, C. P., *Form as Argument in Cicero's Speeches: A Study of Dilemma* (APA American Classical Studies, 31; Atlanta, 1993) (*Phil.* 2).

Crook, J. A., Lintott, A. W., and Rawson, E. D., *The Cambridge Ancient History*[2], ix: *The Last Age of the Roman Republic, 146–43 BC* (Cambridge, 1994).

Dorey, T. A. (ed.), *Cicero* (London, 1964), esp. ch. 3 by R. G. M. Nisbet (*Ver., Cat., Marc., Phil.*).

Douglas, A. E., *Cicero*[2] (Oxford, 1979).

Fuhrmann, M., *Cicero and the Roman Republic*, trans. W. E. Yuill (Oxford, 1992).

Greenidge, A. H. J., *The Legal Procedure of Cicero's Time* (Oxford, 1901).

Gruen, E. S., *Roman Politics and the Criminal Courts, 149–78 BC* (Cambridge, Mass., 1968).

—— *The Last Generation of the Roman Republic* (London, 1974).

Habicht, C., *Cicero the Politician* (Baltimore and London, 1990).

Jones, A. H. M., *The Criminal Courts of the Roman Republic and Principate* (Oxford, 1972).

Kennedy, G. A., 'The Rhetoric of Advocacy in Greece and Rome', *AJP* 89 (1968), 419–36.

—— *The Art of Rhetoric in the Roman World, 300 BC–AD 300* (Princeton, 1972).

Laurand, L., *Études sur le style des discours de Cicéron*[4], 3 vols. (Paris, 1936–8).

Ludwig, W., and Stroh, W. (eds.), *Éloquence et rhétorique chez Cicéron* (Entretiens sur l'antiquité classique, 28; Geneva, 1982) (W. Stroh: *Phil.*).

MacKendrick, P., *The Speeches of Cicero: Context, Law, Rhetoric* (London, 1995) (*Imp., Cat., Marc.*).

May, J. M., *Trials of Character: The Eloquence of Ciceronian Ethos* (Chapel Hill, NC, and London, 1988) (*Ver.* I, *Cat.* 2).

—— (ed.), *Brill's Companion to Cicero: Oratory and Rhetoric* (Leiden etc., 2002).

Millar, F., *The Crowd in Rome in the Late Republic* (Ann Arbor, 1998).

Mitchell, T. N., *Cicero: The Ascending Years* (New Haven and London, 1979).

—— *Cicero: The Senior Statesman* (New Haven and London, 1991).

Morstein-Marx, R., *Mass Oratory and Political Power in the Late Roman Republic* (Cambridge, 2004).

Neumeister, C., *Grundsätze der forensischen Rhetorik gezeigt an Gerichtsreden Ciceros* (Munich, 1964).

Powell, J. G. F., and Paterson, J. J. (eds.), *Cicero the Advocate* (Oxford, 2004).

Rawson, E. D., *Cicero: A Portrait* (London, 1975).

Riggsby, A. M., *Crime and Community in Ciceronian Rome* (Austin, 1999), ch. 5 (*Ver.*).

Shackleton Bailey, D. R., *Onomasticon to Cicero's Speeches*[2] (Stuttgart and Leipzig, 1992).

Steel, C. E. W., *Cicero, Rhetoric, and Empire* (Oxford, 2001) (*Ver., Imp.*).

—— *Reading Cicero: Genre and Performance in Late Republican Rome* (London, 2005).

Stockton, D. L., *Cicero: A Political Biography* (Oxford, 1971).

Stroh, W., *Taxis und Taktik: Die advokatische Dispositionskunst in Ciceros Gerichtsreden* (Stuttgart, 1975).

Vasaly, A., *Representations: Images of the World in Ciceronian Oratory* (Berkeley etc., 1993) (*Ver.*, *Cat.* 1, 3).

Wiedemann, T. E. J., *Cicero and the End of the Roman Republic* (London, 1994).

Winterbottom, M., 'Schoolroom and Courtroom', in B. Vickers (ed.), *Rhetoric Revalued* (Medieval & Renaissance Texts & Studies, 19; New York, 1982), 59–70.

## In Verrem I, II.5

Alexander, M. C., 'Hortensius' Speech in Defense of Verres', *Phoenix*, 30 (1976), 46–53.

Brunt, P. A., 'Patronage and Politics in the *Verrines*', *Chiron*, 10 (1980), 273–89.

Canter, H. V., 'The Impeachments of Verres and Hastings: Cicero and Burke', *CJ* 9 (1914), 199–211.

Dilke, O. A. W., 'Divided Loyalties in Eastern Sicily under Verres', *Ciceroniana*, 4 (1980), 43–51.

Frazel, T. D., 'The Composition and Circulation of Cicero's *In Verrem*', *CQ*, NS 54 (2004), 128–42.

Levens, R. G. C., *Cicero:* Verrine 5 (London, 1946).

McDermott, W. C., 'The Verrine Jury', *Rheinisches Museum*, 120 (1977), 64–75.

Mitchell, T. N., *Cicero:* Verrines II.1 (Warminster, 1986).

Nisbet, R. G. M., 'The Orator and the Reader: Manipulation and Response in Cicero's *Fifth Verrine*', in A. J. Woodman and J. G. F. Powell (eds.), *Author and Audience in Latin Literature* (Cambridge, 1992), 1–17.

Pritchard, R. T., 'Gaius Verres and the Sicilian Farmers', *Historia*, 20 (1971), 224–38.

## De imperio Cn. Pompei

Jonkers, E. J., *Social and Economic Commentary on Cicero's* De imperio Cn. Pompei (Leiden, 1959).

Keaveney, A., *Lucullus: A Life* (London, 1992).

King, J. R., *Cicero:* Pro lege Manilia (Oxford, 1917).

Macdonald, C., *Cicero:* De imperio Cn. Pompei (London, 1966).

McGing, B. C., *The Foreign Policy of Mithridates VI Eupator King of Pontus* (*Mnemosyne*, Suppl. 89; Leiden, 1986).

Magie, D., *Roman Rule in Asia Minor to the End of the Third Century after Christ*, 2 vols. (Princeton, 1950).

Select Bibliography xxxvii

Nicol, J. C., *Cicero:* De imperio Cn. Pompei (Cambridge, 1899).
Rose, P., 'Cicero and the Rhetoric of Imperialism: Putting the Politics Back into Political Rhetoric', *Rhetorica*, 13 (1995), 359–99.
Seager, R. J., *Pompey the Great: A Political Biography*[2] (Oxford, 2002).
Sherwin-White, A. N., *Roman Foreign Policy in the East, 168 BC–AD 1* (London, 1984).
Wilkins, A. S. (after K. Halm), *Cicero:* De imperio Cn. Pompei (London, 1879).

## In Catilinam I–IV

Batstone, W. W., 'Cicero's Construction of Consular *Ethos* in the *First Catilinarian*', *TAPA* 124 (1994), 211–66.
Cape, R. W., 'The Rhetoric of Politics in Cicero's *Fourth Catilinarian*', *AJP* 116 (1995), 255–77.
Drummond, A., *Law, Politics and Power: Sallust and the Execution of the Catilinarian Conspirators* (*Historia* Einzelschriften 93; Stuttgart, 1995).
Dyck, A. R., *Cicero:* Catilinarian Speeches (Cambridge, forthcoming).
Hardy, E. G., *The Catilinarian Conspiracy: A Re-Study of the Evidence* (Oxford, 1924; = *JRS* 7 (1917), 153–228).
Lintott, A. W., *Violence in Republican Rome*[2] (Oxford, 1999), ch. 11.
March, D. A., 'Cicero and the "Gang of Five"', *Classical World*, 82 (1988–9), 225–34.
Phillips, E. J., 'Catiline's Conspiracy', *Historia*, 25 (1976), 441–8.
Price, J. J., 'The Failure of Cicero's *First Catilinarian*', in C. Deroux (ed.), *Studies in Latin Literature and Roman History*, 9 (Brussels, 1998), 106–28.
Seager, R. J., '*Iusta Catilinae*', *Historia*, 22 (1973), 240–8.
Stewart, R., 'Catiline and the Crisis of 63–60 BC: The Italian Perspective', *Latomus*, 54 (1995), 62–78.
Waters, K. H., 'Cicero, Sallust and Catiline', *Historia*, 19 (1970), 195–215.
Wilkins, A. S. (after K. Halm), *The Orations of Cicero against Catilina*[2] (London, 1894).
Yavetz, Z., 'The Failure of Catiline's Conspiracy', *Historia*, 12 (1963), 485–99.

## Pro Marcello

Dyer, R. R., 'Rhetoric and Intention in Cicero's *Pro Marcello*', *JRS* 80 (1990), 17–30.
Fausset, W. Y., *Cicero:* Orationes Caesarianae[2] (Oxford, 1906).
Gotoff, H. C., *Cicero's Caesarian Speeches: A Stylistic Commentary* (Chapel Hill, NC, and London, 1993).

Levene, D. S., 'God and Man in the Classical Latin Panegyric', *Proceedings of the Cambridge Philological Society*, 43 (1997), 66–103.

Ruch, M., *Cicero:* Pro Marcello (Paris, 1965).

Winterbottom, M., 'Believing the *Pro Marcello*', in J. F. Miller *et al.* (eds.), Vertis in Usum: *Studies in Honor of Edward Courtney* (Munich, 2002), 24–38.

## Philippic II

Denniston, J. D., *Cicero:* Philippics *I–II* (Oxford, 1926).

Frisch, H., *Cicero's Fight for the Republic: The Historical Background of Cicero's* Philippics (Copenhagen, 1946).

Johnson, W. R., *Luxuriance and Economy: Cicero and the Alien Style* (Berkeley, 1971).

Lacey, W. K., *Cicero:* Second Philippic Oration (Warminster, 1986).

Ramsey, J. T., *Cicero:* Philippics *I–II* (Cambridge, 2003).

Shackleton Bailey, D. R., *Cicero:* Philippics (Chapel Hill, NC, and London, 1986).

Wooten, C. W., *Cicero's* Philippics *and their Demosthenic Model: The Rhetoric of Crisis* (Chapel Hill, NC, and London, 1983).

## Further Reading in Oxford World's Classics

Caesar, *The Civil War*, trans. and ed. John Carter.

—— *The Gallic War*, trans. and ed. Carolyn Hammond.

Catullus, *The Poems of Catullus*, trans. and ed. Guy Lee.

Cicero, *Defence Speeches*, trans. and ed. D. H. Berry.

—— *The Nature of the Gods*, trans. and ed. P. G. Walsh.

—— *On Obligations*, trans. and ed. P. G. Walsh.

—— *The Republic* and *The Laws*, trans. Niall Rudd, ed. Jonathan Powell.

Plutarch, *Roman Lives: A Selection of Eight Roman Lives*, trans. Robin Waterfield, ed. Philip A. Stadter.

# CHRONOLOGY

The dates are BC.

106    Cicero born (3 January).

104–100 Second Sicilian Slave War.

91–87  Social War; Cicero serves under Gnaeus Pompeius Strabo (89) and Sulla (88); Italians win Roman citizenship (90, 89).

88     Sulla occupies Rome.

88–85  First Mithridatic War.

87     Marius and Cinna occupy Rome; domination of Cinna (87–84).

86     Marius dies.

83–81  Second Mithridatic War.

82     Sulla occupies Rome and is made dictator (82–81); proscriptions (82 to 1 June 81).

81     Sulla's reforms, including establishment of seven permanent criminal courts with senatorial juries; *Pro Quinctio*.

80     *Pro Roscio Amerino*; Cicero defends the freedom of a woman from Arretium (80 or 79).

79–77  Travels abroad; visits Molon of Rhodes.

78     Sulla dies.

75     Cicero quaestor in western Sicily; henceforward a senator.

73–71  Spartacus' slave revolt; Verres governor of Sicily.

73–63  Third Mithridatic War.

70     Pompey and Crassus consuls; *In Verrem*; *lex Aurelia* makes juries two-thirds equestrian.

69     Cicero plebeian aedile; *Pro Fonteio*.

67     Lucullus relieved of Mithridatic command; *lex Gabinia* gives Pompey command against pirates.

66     Cicero praetor in charge of extortion court; *De imperio Cn. Pompei*; *lex Manilia* gives Pompey Mithridatic command; *Pro Cluentio*.

63     Cicero consul; *De lege agraria*; *Pro Rabirio perduellionis reo*; Catilinarian conspiracy; *Pro Murena*; execution of the conspirators (5 December).

62     Catiline defeated and killed; *Pro Sulla*; *Pro Archia*; Bona Dea scandal; Pompey returns to Italy.

61     Clodius acquitted of sacrilege.

60     Publication of *In Catilinam*; formation of 'first triumvirate'.

59     Caesar consul; Clodius adopted into a plebeian family; *Pro Flacco*.

58     Clodius tribune; Cicero exiled; Caesar conquers Gaul (58–50).

57   Cicero recalled; returns to Rome (4 September); *Post reditum in senatu*; *Post reditum ad quirites*; *De domo sua*.

56   *Pro Sestio*; *In Vatinium*; *Pro Caelio*; 'first triumvirate' reaffirmed; *De haruspicum responsis*; *De provinciis consularibus*; *Pro Balbo*.

55   Pompey and Crassus consuls; *In Pisonem*; Cicero begins philosophical and rhetorical works.

54   Defends Vatinius; *Pro Plancio*; *Pro Scauro*; defends Gabinius (54 or 53).

53   Crassus killed at Carrhae; Cicero is made augur (53 or 52); *Pro Rabirio Postumo* (53–52).

52   Clodius killed by Milo (18 January); Pompey appointed sole consul; Cicero defends Milo (7 April); publication of *Pro Milone* (52 or 51).

51–50  Cicero governor of Cilicia.

50   Hortensius dies.

49   Caesar dictator; Civil War begins; Pompey crosses to Greece (17 March); Caesar visits Cicero (28 March); Cicero crosses to Greece (7 June).

48   Pompey defeated at Pharsalus (9 August) and murdered in Egypt (28 September); Cicero returns to Brundisium.

47   Cicero pardoned and allowed to move on to Rome.

46   Pompeians defeated at Thapsus (6 February); Cato commits suicide; Cicero resumes philosophical and rhetorical works; *Pro Marcello*; *Pro Ligario*.

45   Pompeians defeated at Munda (17 March); *Pro rege Deiotaro*.

44   Caesar and Antony consuls; Caesar *dictator perpetuo*; Caesar assassinated (15 March); Octavian named as his heir; Cicero falls out with Antony (September); *Philippics* I–IV.

43   Civil War; *Philippics* V–XIV; Antony declared public enemy (April); Octavian occupies Rome and is elected consul (August); formation of 'second triumvirate'; proscriptions; Cicero murdered (7 December).

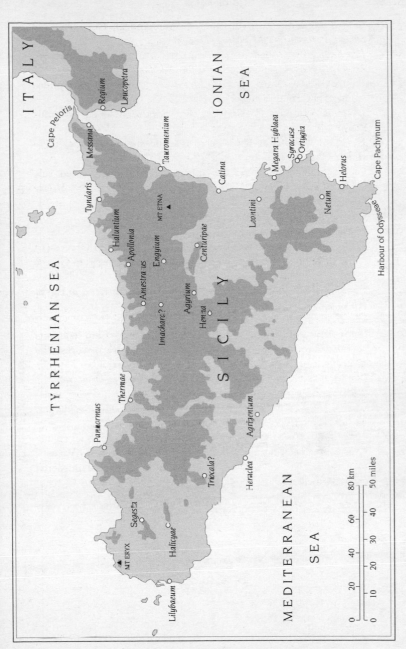

MAP 1 Sicily in the time of Verres (73–71 BC)

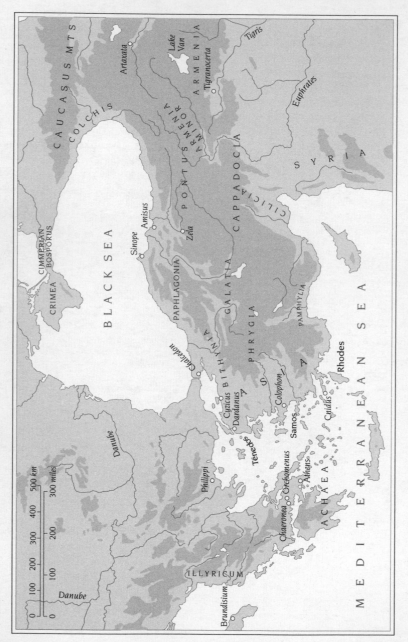

MAP 2  Asia Minor in the time of Mithridates VI (120–63 BC)

# POLITICAL SPEECHES

# IN VERREM
## ('AGAINST VERRES')

DATE: 70 BC (first hearing held on 5–13 August)
DEFENDANT: Gaius Verres
LAW: *lex Cornelia de repetundis* (Cornelian law concerning extortion)
CHARGE: misconduct as governor of Sicily, 73–71 BC
PROSECUTOR: Marcus Tullius Cicero
DEFENCE ADVOCATES: Quintus Caecilius Metellus Pius Scipio Nasica,
    Lucius Cornelius Sisenna, Quintus Hortensius Hortalus
PRESIDING MAGISTRATE (PRAETOR): Manius Acilius Glabrio
VERDICT: conviction (upon defendant's failure to appear at second
    hearing)

Cicero's speeches *In Verrem* ('Against Verres', a corrupt Roman governor of Sicily) are the only forensic (judicial) speeches in this volume, and in fact have more in common with the speeches previously translated in *Defence Speeches* than with the other speeches included here. Nevertheless, the *Verrines* (as they are traditionally known) are political in context and tone: they are concerned with (and are some of our best evidence for) Roman provincial government; and they date from the moment when Sulla's controversial reforms of eleven years earlier were suddenly swept away. Verres' trial for extortion (i.e. misconduct while holding a magistracy in the provinces) took place in one of Sulla's courts, before a jury that consisted exclusively of senators. While the trial was under way, moves were being made to replace the senatorial juries with juries drawn from elsewhere (it was not yet clear from where). In these speeches, Cicero is able to exploit the uncertainty, warning the senators that if they wish to remain in control of the courts, they had better do the right thing by rejecting Verres' bribes and voting for his conviction.

There are seven *Verrines* in all (referred to as a set by Cicero at *Orator* 103, although called the *Accusatio*, 'Prosecution', not the *Verrines*); they occupy 464 pages of Latin in the Oxford edition. First there is *Divinatio in Caecilium* ('Preliminary hearing against Caecilius'), a speech against a rival prosecutor; then *In Verrem* I, the speech which Cicero gave at the first hearing; and finally *In Verrem* II.1–5, the five long speeches which Cicero intended to give at the second hearing, but was unable to because Verres had already fled into exile. In this selection I have chosen to offer the reader the two most famous speeches, I and II.5. *In Verrem* I is the most political of the speeches, the one in which Cicero focuses the jurors' attention on the political implications of the trial and the possibility that the outcome will influence imminent legislation on the composition of juries. II.5, which is familiarly, though somewhat inaccurately, known as the 'fifth *Verrine*' (it is actually the seventh), is perhaps the most entertaining, and certainly the most powerful, of the speeches: it consists of an account of Verres' scandalous neglect of his military responsibilities as governor, and of his tyrannical cruelty towards Sicilians and Roman citizens in his province.

Gaius Verres was the son of a senator, but did not belong to one of the great Roman aristocratic families. His public career began in 84, during the domination of Cinna: Marius was dead, but Sulla had not yet returned to Italy and taken control of Rome. Verres held the quaestorship, serving under the consul Gnaeus Papirius Carbo, the successor of Cinna (who was killed at the beginning of the year), in Picenum. In the following year he continued under Carbo in Cisalpine Gaul; but then, seeing which way the wind was blowing, he deserted to Sulla, taking Carbo's military treasury with him. In 82 Sulla captured Rome, had himself appointed dictator, and instituted the proscriptions, rewarding Verres with property taken from proscribed landowners at Beneventum. In 81 he then carried his reforms, a programme designed to restore to the senate the authority and powers it had possessed in the years before the Gracchan reforms nearly half a century earlier. He began by creating 300 new senators, most of whom (like Publius Sulpicius, *Ver.* 30) would have entered the senate, unusually, without first having held the quaestorship. He removed the tribunes' power to initiate legislation and to exercise limited jurisdiction, curtailed their right of veto, and disqualified them from holding further public office. He also established seven permanent criminal courts, staffed by exclusively senatorial juries, to try the major crimes. It was in one of these new senatorial courts, the one for murder, that the 26-year-old Cicero gave his first speech in a criminal case the following year. This was his sensational *Pro Roscio Amerino* (translated in *Defence Speeches*), the speech which brought him to public notice.

In 80–79 Verres served as a legate under Gnaeus Cornelius Dolabella, and joined him in plundering Cilicia and Asia, a crime for which Dolabella was convicted in 78, after his return to Rome; Verres escaped punishment himself by testifying against his superior. Sulla died in 78, and in 75 the first step was taken in abolishing his reforms: the bar on tribunes holding further public office was removed. In this year Cicero served his quaestorship under Sextus Peducaeus in western Sicily, where by his own account he endeared himself to the provincials by his just management of their affairs; and on his return he became, like all ex-quaestors, a member of the senate. The next year, 74, Verres held the important office of city praetor, and according to Cicero abused his judicial powers in order to enrich himself, sometimes at the prompting of his mistress Chelido. Finally, in 73–71 he served as governor of Sicily (the normal one-year term was extended because his intended successor, Quintus Arrius, was needed for the war against Spartacus). During these three years, according to Cicero, Verres stripped the province of everything of value, particularly works of art, ran down the military forces which it was his duty to maintain, and illegally executed Roman citizens. We need not believe everything Cicero says regarding his crimes, and in fact the accusation that he ran down the military forces is contradicted by the historian Sallust, who says that he actually strengthened the maritime defence of eastern Sicily (*Histories* 4 fr. 32 Maurenbrecher; contrast *Ver.* 2.5.5). Even so, Verres has ever since been universally regarded as the most wicked and exploitative governor in history. He was succeeded in the governorship of Sicily, in 70, by Lucius Caecilius Metellus, who set about putting right some of the damage that his predecessor had caused.

Throughout Verres' governorship, prominent Sicilians had been complaining to Rome about him; the consuls of 72 had tried to check his behaviour with a senatorial decree, and the tribunes of 71 had carried a resolution protecting one of his victims. As soon as he was no longer in post, all the Sicilian states except Syracuse and Messana (where there were people who had colluded with him or benefited from his actions) joined in asking Cicero to prosecute him. Cicero had been a friend of the Sicilians since his quaestorship in 75, and was now one of the leading advocates in Rome, although he had never undertaken a prosecution. Prosecution of a senior senator was the traditional means by which an aspiring politician, particularly one who was not of noble family (or even, in Cicero's case, of senatorial family), could attract public notice and win friends and clients; and there was the particular advantage that a successful prosecutor, if a senator, acceded to his victim's rank of seniority in the senate. Thus, if he were successful against Verres, Cicero would be called on in the senate to speak with those of praetorian rank; this would give him much greater prominence and status. Of course, undertaking a prosecution was also a means of acquiring enemies. But in Verres Cicero was lucky enough to have an opponent who was of relatively undistinguished birth (many of the nobles would have disapproved of him) and whose crimes were genuinely shocking. There was one complication in that Cicero would have to prepare his prosecution at the same time as he was standing for election to a plebeian aedileship for the following year; but he thought at this stage that the trial would be over well before the elections. Indeed, the prosecution would probably assist his campaign. It had become clear that the consuls of 70, Pompey and Crassus, intended to sweep away much of Sulla's remaining legislation. In the first half of the year, they restored the powers of the tribunes in full (this is referred to as having already taken place at *Ver.* 46). But it was unclear what was going to be done about the senatorial juries, which were unpopular and were believed to have been responsible for a number of miscarriages of justice. Cicero planned to use his prosecution to speak about the issue, and to threaten the jury with the possibility that a miscarriage of justice in this case would result in senatorial juries being abolished—replaced, very likely, by equestrian ones. Such a line would certainly give Cicero a political prominence, and the popular tone of his remarks would stand him in good stead with the plebeian assembly (which elected the plebeian aediles). For all these reasons, therefore, he accepted the invitation of the Sicilians, and in January of 70 he formally applied to Manius Acilius Glabrio, the praetor in charge of the extortion court, for permission to prosecute Verres for misconduct as governor of Sicily.

At this point we must pause to consider the history and procedure of the extortion court at Rome. The first permanent extortion court (and Rome's first permanent court) was set up by the *lex Calpurnia* in 149 BC. Its procedure was civil; the jurors were senators, and the penalty on conviction was simple restitution of the property stolen. Later, in 122 (or 123), the *lex Acilia* was carried by an associate of Gaius Gracchus, Manius Acilius Glabrio, the father of the praetor who presided over Verres' trial. This law, the text of which survives on a fragmentary bronze inscription known as the *Tabula Bembina*, established a new permanent extortion court with criminal procedures that were to serve as a model for the criminal courts that were established later. The jurors were *equites* (who would be much less likely to be lenient towards the senatorial defendants than their senatorial predecessors); the penalty was double restitution of the property stolen. In the years which followed, the extortion court became a political battleground between the senators and the *equites*. In 106 the *lex Servilia Caepionis* changed the juries in the extortion court to a mix of senators and *equites*; but exclusively equestrian juries were restored in *c.*104 by the *lex Servilia Glauciae*, which also established a new feature of procedure, a compulsory adjournment of at least one day (*comperendinatio*) during the course of the trial. This meant that the trial would be split into two separate hearings; in effect, the whole case would be gone over twice. In 81 Sulla, as we have seen, carried a *lex Cornelia* which enacted a complete reform of the criminal courts and prescribed exclusively senatorial juries for all of them. For the extortion court, the method of selection and the size of the jury were also changed, and an official penalty of death appears to have been added to the financial penalty. As in the other courts, however, a death penalty for criminals of

high social status meant in practice merely self-imposed or 'voluntary'
exile in a federate (thus technically non-Roman) state, followed by inter-
diction (debarment from fire and water, in other words outlawry). As long
a criminal did not return to Italy, he would be safe.

The procedure in the Sullan extortion court (in which Verres was tried)
was as follows. Each year a jury list (*album*) was compiled from the 600 or
so members of the senate, and the names on the list were divided into
numbered panels (*decuriae*). When the praetor in charge of the court
accepted a case for trial, a panel was assigned to it, and jurors were
selected from that panel by lot (*sortitio*). Each side could reject a set
number of these jurors (*reiectio*), and the jurors who remained would be
those who would sit on the case. The final number of jurors is unknown,
and may have been as small as twelve or fifteen—a very low number by
Roman standards, and one which may have contributed to the problem of
judicial corruption during the 70s. The actual trial was divided into two
hearings, as prescribed by the *lex Servilia Glauciae*. In the first, prosecution and then defence each made full-scale speeches (*orationes perpetuae*),
after which the evidence was taken and witnesses cross-examined; then in
the second hearing prosecution and then defence each made further full-
scale speeches. So the speeches in the first hearing would refer forward to
evidence that had not yet been revealed and would only be known to one
side or the other (the usual custom in other criminal courts, where there
was as far as we know only a single hearing), whereas those in the second
would refer back to evidence which had already been heard and examined.
At the end of the second hearing, the jurors (but not the praetor) voted by
secret ballot to acquit, convict, or abstain, and the verdict was reached by
majority (if the votes were equal the defendant was acquitted). If the
defendant was found guilty, he would retire into exile within a few days
(he was not required to vanish instantly). A separate session would then be
held at a later date to assess the damages to be paid from his estate to the
injured party (*litis aestimatio*).

In January of 70, then, Glabrio received Cicero's application to prosecute Verres. But he also received a second application to undertake the
same prosecution, submitted by Quintus Caecilius Niger, who had been
Verres' quaestor in Sicily in 72 (probably, like Cicero, in western Sicily).
It is not clear whether Caecilius genuinely wished to see Verres convicted
(as Cicero maintains at *Ver.* 2.1.15) or whether he was in collusion with
him (as he maintains at *Div. Caec.* 12–13, 23, 29, and 58); at all events, the
Sicilians had approached Cicero, and Verres must have wanted Caecilius,
who was the lesser orator. A preliminary hearing (*divinatio*) was held to
decide which man should be given the case. Cicero delivered *Divinatio in
Caecilium*, and was judged the more suitable prosecutor; Caecilius was

even denied the right to join him as assistant prosecutor (which suggests that collusion was suspected). Cicero then formally brought the charge, requesting 110 days to go to Sicily to collect evidence. Given the difficulty of travelling, this was a very short period, but he wished to have the trial out of the way as early as possible so that he could turn his attention to his campaign for the aedileship. The trial must have been scheduled to begin around the beginning of May.

Verres, meanwhile, had assembled powerful advocates for his defence. Chief among these was Quintus Hortensius Hortalus, Rome's most famous orator and the leading advocate of the day. Hc had been praetor in charge of the extortion court himself in 72, and now he was standing for the consulship of 69. His politics were aristocratic and conservative; he was a formidable adversary. He and Cicero had actually faced each other in court once before, in a civil action undertaken by Publius Quinctius in 81; this was Cicero's first case (he was 25), and it is likely that he lost (despite this, he published his *Pro Quinctio*, 'For Quinctius', which survives). Hortensius was encouraged to undertake Verres' defence by the gift of a valuable bronze sphinx (Quint. *Inst.* 6.3.98; cf. Plin. *Nat.* 34.48; Plut. *Cic.* 7.6), and no doubt also a substantial pecuniary payment (*Ver.* 40).

But just as importantly, Verres had the support of the Metelli, the most powerful family in Rome at the end of the second century and still enjoying tremendous prestige and influence. There were three brothers who, though they were not advocates in the case, nevertheless helped in various ways. One, as we have seen, was Verres' successor in Sicily, Lucius Caecilius Metellus, later consul of 68; the other two were Quintus Caecilius Metellus, who, like Hortensius, was standing for the consulship for 69, and Marcus Caecilius Metellus, who was standing for the praetorship for 69. Hortensius was supported in the defence by two advocates: Quintus Caecilius Metellus Pius Scipio Nasica, a cousin of the three Metelli brothers and the future consul of 52, and Lucius Cornelius Sisenna, who had perhaps been governor of Sicily himself in 77. Sisenna was a friend of Hortensius and was incidentally the most important historian that Rome had so far produced; Cicero thought him better as a historian than as an orator (*Brut.* 228; *De legibus* 1.7). The reason that the Metelli were so solidly behind Verres was partly because there was some link between their families, but also, and no doubt more importantly, because Verres (at least according to Cicero) had taken care of the bribery at their various elections.

The defence's strategy throughout was to try to have the trial put off for as long as possible. Accordingly, they arranged for someone (perhaps Quintus Caecilius Metellus Nepos, the future consul of 57) to prosecute a former governor of Achaea in the extortion court and to ask for 108 days to collect evidence. This would mean that their prosecution would start just before Cicero's, which as a result would be severely delayed. If, on the other hand, Cicero failed to return from Sicily within the 110 days that had been granted to him, all they had to do was to drop their prosecution, and Cicero's one would be called—and lost by default. So the defence's tactic was an adroit move which had the effect of delaying Cicero without giving him extra time to collect evidence in Sicily.

Cicero spent fifty days in Sicily. He later claimed, rather colourfully, that he had called on the ploughmen at their homes, and the men had spoken to him from their plough-handles (*Scaur.* 25). Certainly he worked with extraordinary thoroughness and indeed courage. At Syracuse, he became involved in physical violence with a friend of Verres and had to engage in arguments with the governor Lucius Metellus, who would not allow him a copy of the Syracusans' decree. Metellus obstructed him at every turn, rebuked him for addressing the Syracusans in Greek (their native tongue), and wrote to the consuls in Verres' support.

But Cicero overcame all these obstacles and returned to Rome within the 110 days around the beginning of May. Since he had returned on time, the other trial did go ahead, and he had to wait three months until the court was free once more (the outcome of the other trial is unknown; it may have been dropped before the verdict). During these three months, May to July, it is natural to assume that he wrote up the six remaining *Verrines*, while at the same time campaigning for his aedileship.

In mid-July, the selection and rejection of the jurors for Verres' trial finally took place. The result was largely favourable to Cicero, although Sextus Peducaeus, the governor of Sicily under whom Cicero had served, was rejected by Verres. Marcus Metellus, on the other hand, was rather surprisingly retained by Cicero (he could only reject a certain number, and there must have been other jurors whom he considered more hostile). Soon afterwards the elections for 69 were held. Hortensius and Quintus Metellus were both elected consul, and Marcus Metellus was elected praetor and appointed president of the extortion court, in succession to Glabrio (he would therefore cease to be a juror on taking up office). Cicero, on the other hand, was successful in obtaining his aedileship, despite an attempt by Verres to prevent this by bribery. The defence felt greatly encouraged by their electoral successes, and Hortensius and Quintus Metellus lost no time in attempting to use their new authority as consuls-elect to intimidate the Sicilian witnesses.

At Rome, courts (except for the violence court) did not sit on public holidays, and on 16 August a long sequence of games was due to begin. With the exception of odd days, the whole of the period 16 August to 18 September and then 27 October to 17 November would consist of public holidays. So the defence now felt that they had an excellent chance of prolonging the trial into 69, when they would be in a good position to determine the outcome. Cicero, they calculated, would take until 15 August to present his case. Hortensius therefore would not have to reply until after 18 September, by which time the jury would have forgotten much of what Cicero had said. Hortensius would spin out his reply for as long as possible, and then the evidence would be taken. After that there would be the compulsory adjournment and later the whole of the second hearing; and that, combined with the second set of public holidays in October and November, would in all likelihood result in the trial running out of time at the end of the year. When it resumed in January, Hortensius and Quintus Metellus would be the consuls, Marcus Metellus would be the president of the court, and some of the jurors would have gone to other duties and been replaced by more sympathetic ones (Marcus Metellus as president would be able to see to this). It would then be a relatively simple matter, the defence concluded, to secure Verres' acquittal.

At 4 p.m. on 5 August the trial began. Cicero calculated that, in order to avert the possibility of its continuing into 69, he must ensure that the whole of the first hearing was completed before the start of the first set of holidays on 16 August. He therefore decided to forgo the full-scale speech to which he was entitled, and gave instead just a short introduction to the case, *In Verrem* I. In contrast to a normal prosecution speech, this did not detail the charges at all; instead, it revealed the defence's plans for delay, exposed their bribery and intimidation, and discussed the political implications of the trial. In particular, Cicero warned the jurors that if they did not act honestly and convict so obvious a criminal as Verres, then the courts would very likely be taken out of their hands and returned to the *equites*. The defence must have been greatly surprised by the brevity and content of the speech, and by the omission of detailed charges. At the end, Cicero explained that he would proceed directly (after Hortensius' reply, that is—though he does not say so) to his witnesses and documents, introducing and presenting each one in turn, and offering Hortensius the opportunity to cross-examine the witnesses in the usual way.

This speech did not save time merely by being brief: it also did so by giving Hortensius, whose aim had been to try to spin the trial out, very little to reply to. Hortensius did not yet know the charges, and naturally would not want to spend time speculating as to what they might be and then attempting to explain them away. Cicero had also wrong-footed him in that he had not been expecting to have to say anything until after 18 September; he must have been caught completely unawares. No doubt the speech he gave was brief, and largely devoted to complaint against the unfairness of Cicero's tactics. (Scholars have disputed whether Hortensius in fact spoke at all, since the evidence is ambiguous; but it is surely inconceivable that he failed to say something in his client's defence.)

When Hortensius had said what he could, the evidence was taken. It was utterly damning. After two days, Verres stayed at home, pretending to be ill. Hortensius for the most part declined to cross-examine: cross-examination would merely have given the witnesses an opportunity to repeat and emphasize their allegations. At one point during the process he became confused and said to Cicero, 'I don't understand these riddles.' Immediately Cicero answered with an allusion to the gift that Hortensius had received from Verres: 'Well, you ought to—after all, you've got a sphinx in your house!' On 13 August the end of the first hearing was reached, as Cicero had planned, and the case was adjourned until after 18 September. There was now no possibility of the trial being prolonged into January.

Verres did not give up immediately. During the games which followed, he went round to the house of his advocate Sisenna, and was observed inspecting Sisenna's silver (*Ver.* 2.4.33–4; Cicero adds that Sisenna's slaves would no doubt have kept a close eye on him, having heard of the evidence against him). But in September when the second hearing was due to begin, he failed to appear. He had abandoned his defence and departed for exile at Massilia (Marseilles), taking with him most of his Sicilian plunder, together with the paintings and statues stolen during his time in Asia. He was therefore convicted in absence. At the later session that was held to assess the damages, Cicero agreed to a low assessment, three million sesterces. It was probably all that remained from the forty million that Verres had stolen. Nevertheless, the Sicilians were pleased (Plut. *Cic.* 8.1), and remained Cicero's clients for the rest of his life (*Att.* 14.12.1).

Meanwhile, towards the end of the year a new law, the *lex Aurelia*, was carried, abolishing senatorial juries. The *equites* were not given exclusive control of the courts, however. Instead, juries would henceforward consist of one-third senators, one-third *equites*, and one-third *tribuni aerarii* ('treasury tribunes'). In effect, this made the juries two-thirds equestrian, since the difference between the *equites* and the *tribuni aerarii* was probably purely technical (in his speeches Cicero treats the *tribuni aerarii* as *equites*). The compromise imposed by the *lex Aurelia* proved to be a successful one, and ended the bitter controversy over whether juries ought to be composed of senators or of *equites*. Although the bill had not yet been published when Verres' trial took place (*Ver.* 2.5.178), most scholars think it must have been at an advanced stage of drafting, in which case it would be unlikely that the trial had any effect on its provisions. Had Verres been acquitted, however, it is not impossible that the scandal would have resulted in the *equites* being given exclusive control of the courts after all. Cicero's remarks about the trial's political significance should not, therefore, be dismissed as unjustified and absurd. But the trial might well have been of greater significance if it had taken place in May, as was originally envisaged.

After the trial Cicero published his seven *Verrines*, the two that he had delivered and the five that he would have gone on to deliver at the second hearing. These last five provide the discussion of the charges that Hortensius and Verres were prevented from hearing by Cicero's decision to forgo a full-scale speech in the first hearing. *In Verrem* II.1 covers Verres' career before becoming governor; II.2 his corruption of justice in Sicily; II.3 his abuse of the Sicilian tax system; II.4 his theft of works of art; and II.5 his ruination of the Sicilian navy and his illegal executions of Roman citizens (a matter not strictly relevant to the charge of extortion, but nevertheless constituting an effective and damning finale). For Cicero the result of the trial, capped by his triumphant publication of the complete Verrine corpus, was that he completely eclipsed Hortensius and was henceforward regarded as Rome's foremost advocate. The trial also marked him out as a politician destined for higher things. Having defeated Verres, he presumably rose to praetorian status in the senate. Then when he actually became praetor in 66, he was made president of the extortion court. His published *Verrines* were regarded as a model prosecution and would have been carefully studied by every prosecutor, and by every speaker in an extortion trial. Having achieved this great success, however, he was careful to avoid prosecuting thereafter: we know of only one other prosecution which he undertook, that of a personal enemy, Titus Munatius Plancus Bursa, for violence, in 51 (Plancus was also driven into exile).

Verres spent the rest of his life at Massilia. In 43, he was proscribed by Mark Antony, allegedly because he had refused to part with his bronze statues, which Antony coveted. His one consolation was that Cicero had recently died in the same proscription, and that he had been murdered as a consequence of his devastating oratory.

# IN VERREM I

[1] The very thing that was most to be desired, members of the jury, the one thing that will have most effect in reducing the hatred felt towards your order* and restoring the tarnished reputation of the courts, this it is which, in the current political crisis, has been granted and presented to you; and this opportunity has come about not, it would appear, by human planning, but virtually by the gift of the gods. For a belief, disastrous for the state and dangerous for you, has become widespread, and has been increasingly talked about not only among ourselves but among foreign peoples as well—the belief that, in these courts as they are currently constituted, it is impossible for a man with money, no matter how guilty he may be, to be convicted. [2] Now, at this moment of reckoning for your order and your courts, when people are ready to use public meetings and legislation to stoke up this hatred of the senate, a defendant has been put on trial—Gaius Verres,* a man already convicted, according to universal public opinion, by his character and actions, but already acquitted, according to his own hopes and assertions, by his immense wealth.

I have taken on this prosecution, gentlemen, with the complete support and confidence of the Roman people, not because I want to increase the hatred felt towards your order, but in order to mend the tarnished reputation which we both share.* The man I have brought before you is a man through whom you will be able to retrieve the good reputation of the courts, restore your popularity with the Roman people, and gratify foreign nations—being as he is an embezzler of the treasury, a plunderer of Asia and Pamphylia, a cheater of city jurisdiction,* and the disgrace and ruination of the province of Sicily. [3] If you pronounce a fair and scrupulous verdict against this man, you will hold on to the influence which ought by rights to be yours. But if on the other hand his colossal wealth succeeds in destroying the scrupulousness and fairness of the courts, then I shall achieve at least one thing—a recognition that the country had the wrong jurors, and not that the jurors had the wrong defendant, or the defendant the wrong prosecutor.

Let me make a personal admission, gentlemen. Gaius Verres set many traps for me by land and sea, some of which I was able to avoid by keeping a careful lookout, and others that I managed to resist through the loyalty and determination of my friends. Even so, I never considered myself in such great danger, or was so totally afraid, as I am now here in this court. [4] It is not so much the expectations aroused by my prosecution or the enormous crowds of people attending this trial that disturb me—although they do in fact make me feel deeply anxious—as the criminal plots that the defendant is attempting to launch simultaneously against me, your-selves, our praetor Manius Glabrio,* the Roman people, our allies, foreign nations, and finally the senatorial order and the very name of 'senator'. He keeps repeating that people have good reason to be afraid if they have stolen only enough to satisfy their own needs, whereas he himself has plundered enough to keep many people happy; and he adds that there is nothing so sacred that money can-not corrupt it, and nothing so well defended that money cannot overthrow it.

[5] But if he had been as discreet in carrying out his crimes as he was reckless in attempting them in the first place, he might perhaps at some time, in some respect or other, have escaped my notice. But as luck would have it, his unbelievable recklessness has so far been accompanied by singular stupidity. For just as he has been quite public in his theft of money, so in his aim of corrupting the court he has made his plans and ambitions clear to everyone. He tells people that he was really afraid only once in his life, when I formally indicted him. And this was not simply because he had returned from his province to a blaze of hatred and discredit (his return may have been recent, but his unpopularity was well established and of long standing); no, the problem was that it was, as it happened, a bad time to attempt to corrupt the court. [6] This explains why, when I had applied for a very short period of time for going to Sicily to collect evidence, he found someone to ask for a period of two days less for going to Achaea.* The idea was not that this man should by his application and industry achieve what I accomplished by my own hard work and long hours; in fact that Achaean investigator did not even get as far as Brundisium!* I, on the other hand, covered the whole of Sicily in fifty days and so managed to discover, and collect evidence for, all the wrongs done to individuals and communities. Anyone could see, therefore, that the defendant had sought out this investigator not for the purpose of bringing a prosecution of his own,

but to use up the time that would otherwise be devoted to the one that I was bringing.

[7] But now this reckless, insane individual is thinking along these lines. He fully realizes that I have come to court ready and prepared to impress his thefts and crimes not only on your ears, but on everyone's eyes as well. He sees the many senators that have come to testify to his criminality, he sees the many Roman equestrians, and many citizens and allies to whom he has done terrible wrongs, and he sees how many important delegations have assembled here, sent with certified public documents by states that are our friends. [8] But despite all this, he nevertheless holds such a poor opinion of respectable people, and thinks that the senatorial juries are so venal and corrupt that he keeps openly repeating that he has had good reason to be greedy, since in his experience money is such a strong protection. And he boasts of how he successfully managed the most difficult thing of all, the purchase of the ideal date for his trial; and this would make it easier for him to purchase everything else afterwards and ensure that, since it was not possible for him to escape the force of the charges altogether, he could at least avoid the worst of the storm. [9] But if he had had the slightest confidence not just in his case, but in any honourable means of defence or in anyone's eloquence or influence, he would surely not have had to scrape together and go chasing after such expedients as these. And he would not have scorned and despised the senatorial order to the extent that he arbitrarily selected from it someone he could prosecute, someone who would have to make his defence before him, leaving him free then to make his own preparations.

[10] What his hopes and intentions are in all of this, I can see very clearly. But how he imagines he can get what he wants with this praetor and this court, I fail to understand. But one thing I do understand, and the Roman people came to the same conclusion when the rejection of jurors* was being held—that his hopes were so desperate that money was his only means of escape, and that if that protection were taken from him, he believed that nothing else could save him.

Indeed, what talent could be large enough, what eloquence or fluency great enough* to make any kind of a defence of this man's career, guilty as he is of so many vices and crimes, and long since condemned according to the wishes and judgement of the whole world? [11] I may as well pass over the shame and disgrace of his early life. But as for his quaestorship, the first stage in an official career, what did it consist of except public money stolen from Gnaeus Carbo by his own quaestor,* a consul stripped and betrayed, an army deserted, a province abandoned, and the sacred personal tie imposed on him by the lot violated? His period of service as a legate spelled disaster for the whole of Asia and Pamphylia, provinces in which he stole from many private houses, a great many cities, and all the shrines. Moreover, he resumed and repeated against Gnaeus Dolabella that previous crime of his that he had committed during his quaestorship: as a result of misdeeds that were entirely his own, he brought disgrace on a man whose legate and proquaestor he had been, and in his superior's hour of danger he did not merely desert him but actually attacked and betrayed him. [12] His city praetorship consisted of a general ransacking of sacred temples and public buildings and, in his judicial rulings, of the assignment and bestowal of goods and property in a manner which violated every precedent.

But the greatest and most numerous monuments and testaments to all his vices are those which he has now set up in Sicily—the province which he oppressed and ruined so effectively over a three-year period that it is now impossible for it to be restored to its previous state. Indeed, it is doubtful whether a succession of good governors over many years could bring about even a partial recovery. [13] While he was governor, the Sicilians were not allowed the use of their own laws, or the decrees of our senate, or the common laws of mankind. All the property that anyone owns in Sicily today is that which has either escaped the notice of this monster of avarice, or has been left over after his greed was satisfied. Over those three years, no lawsuit was decided except by his say-so, and no man's inheritance from his father and grandfather was so secure that it could not be confiscated at Verres' order. By a new and corrupt ruling, arable farmers were forced to hand over vast sums of money from their capital; our staunchest allies were classed as enemies; Roman citizens were tortured and executed like slaves; criminals were acquitted through bribery; innocent and respectable men were prosecuted in their absence and convicted and exiled without a defence; the most strongly fortified harbours and the biggest and best-protected cities were left vulnerable to pirates and brigands; Sicilian soldiers and sailors—our friends and allies—were starved to death; and the finest

and best-equipped fleets were, to the great disgrace of the Roman
people, lost and destroyed. [14] Ancient monuments, some the gift
of wealthy kings who intended them to adorn their cities, others set
up by our own victorious generals* who either donated or restored
them to the cities of Sicily—all these this same praetor plundered
and stripped bare. And he did not do this only to the public statues
and works of art: he also stole from all the temples, places sanctified
by holy veneration, and he did not leave the Sicilians with a single
god that seemed to him to have been made with above average artistic skill or with ancient craftsmanship. As for his sexual crimes and
immorality, considerations of decency prevent me from relating his
outrageous behaviour; and at the same time I am reluctant thereby to
add to the grief of those whose wives and children could not be
protected from his violent assaults. [15] 'But he did all this dis-
creetly, so that it would not become public knowledge.' On the contrary, I do not think there is anyone who has heard the name of
Verres who could not also enumerate the terrible crimes he has
committed. I am therefore much more frightened of being thought
to have missed out many of his crimes than to have made any up.
Indeed, I do not think that this great crowd which has come to listen
today is wanting to find out from me what Verres is accused of so
much as to go over with me what it already knows.

Since that is how things stand, this depraved lunatic has chosen
another means of fighting me. He is not, in truth, setting out to use
somebody's eloquence against me, nor is he relying on anyone's
influence, authority, or power. He pretends that these are the things
he is relying on, but I can see what he is up to. Indeed, he makes no
great secret of it. He confronts me with the empty names of nobility,
in other words of arrogant aristocrats, who do not so much damage
my case by their nobility as help it by their notoriety. He makes out
that he is relying on their protection, while all the time he has been
engineering something different. [16] I will go on to tell you briefly,
gentlemen, what hopes he has in his heart and what he is planning;
but first please let me explain to you how he has dealt with the
situation from the outset.

As soon as he returned from his province, a contract was undertaken, at great cost, for buying up this court. The contract remained
on its original terms and conditions up to the point when the rejection of jurors was held. Once this had taken place—since the good

fortune of the Roman people had shattered Verres' hopes when the lots were cast,* and my own carefulness had triumphed over the opposition's shamelessness when the rejection of jurors was held— the entire agreement was repudiated. [17] For me, then, everything was going splendidly. Everyone had a copy of the list of your names as members of this court; it seemed impossible that any mark, colour, or smudge could be put on the voting-tablets.* Verres, having formerly been confident and optimistic, suddenly appeared so downcast and crushed that he gave the impression, not just to the Roman people but even to himself, of a condemned man. But suddenly in the past few days, since the consular elections,* lo and behold, the same old intrigues of his are being revived, but with even more money than before, and the same attacks are being organized, through the same people—attacks on your reputation and on everyone's fortunes.

This information was first revealed to me, members of the jury, by a tiny piece of suggestive evidence. But once the door of suspicion had been opened, a direct route led me to all the secret plans of Verres and his supporters. [18] An enormous crowd was escorting Quintus Hortensius home from the Campus Martius as consul-elect, and Gaius Curio* happened to get caught up in it. Now my reference to this gentleman should not be taken as derogatory, but as a mark of respect. Indeed, if he did not wish the remark which I am about to quote to be repeated, he would not have made it so openly and publicly, and in the presence of such a large crowd of people. Even so, I will repeat it with some hesitation and diffidence, so that it will be clear that I am paying due consideration both to the friendship between us and to his high rank. [19] Curio, then, was at the Arch of Fabius,* and among the crowd he caught sight of Verres. He called out to him, and loudly shouted his congratulations. To Hortensius who had just been elected consul, and to his friends and relations who were with him, he said not a word. Instead, it was Verres he went to talk to, Verres he embraced, Verres he told not to worry. 'I formally declare* to you,' he said, 'that at today's elections you have been acquitted!'

A large number of people of the greatest respectability witnessed this remark, and so I was immediately informed of it; or rather, whenever I met anyone it was the first thing they said to me. To some it appeared scandalous, to others absurd—absurd to those who thought that the trial depended on the reliability of the witnesses, the handling of the charges, and the power of the jurors, rather than the outcome of a consular election; and scandalous to those who looked deeper and realized that these congratulations pointed to the corruption of the court. [20] For this is what they concluded, this is what those respectable individuals said to each other and to me: that it was now clear and obvious that the courts did not exist. How can a defendant one day consider himself convicted, and then the next day, when his advocate is elected consul, be acquitted? How can this be? What about the fact that the whole of Sicily, all its inhabitants, all its business community, all its public and private records are here in Rome—does this count for nothing? Nothing, if the consul-elect so decides. Really? Will the jury take no account of the charges, or the witnesses, or the opinion of the Roman people? No: everything will be subject to the power and influence of one man.

I will speak frankly, gentlemen. This made me deeply concerned. All the best people were saying: 'Verres will escape your clutches— but we will no longer be in charge of the courts. For once Verres has been acquitted, who will be able to stop the transfer of the courts?'* [21] Everyone was dismayed; and it was not the sudden joy of this criminal that upset them so much as the unheard-of congratulations uttered by so distinguished a personage. I wanted to hide the fact that I too was dismayed; I wanted to conceal my anguish by looking unconcerned and cover it up by saying nothing.

Then a few days later, when the praetors-elect were drawing lots* and Marcus Metellus* obtained the presidency of the extortion court, I was suddenly informed that Verres had been warmly congratulated on this and had actually sent some slaves back to his house to tell his wife the good news. [22] Naturally, I was not very pleased at this; but I did not think that Metellus' gaining the extortion court was anything for me to worry about particularly. But one thing I did discover, from certain individuals who kept me informed of everything, was that a number of chests filled with money from Sicily had been conveyed by a certain senator to a Roman equestrian;* that out of the original number, about ten chests had been kept back at the senator's house and earmarked for use at my election;* and that bribery-agents for all the tribes had been summoned to Verres' house at night. [23] One of these agents, a man who considered himself duty-bound to help me in any way he could, came to see me that very night and

told me what Verres had said to them. He had reminded them how
generously he had treated them in the past, both when he had been
standing for the praetorship* and at the recent consular and praetorian elections; then he had immediately promised them as much
money as they wanted in return for blocking my election to the
aedileship. At this some replied that they dared not try it, others
that they did not think it could be done. However, they managed to
find a trusty friend of his from the same clan, Quintus Verres of the
Romilian tribe,* a bribery-agent of the old school, a pupil and friend
of Verres' father, who promised that he would see the job done for
half a million sesterces down; and some of the others then said that
they would join him. In view of this, my friend kindly advised me to
take every possible precaution.

[24] So I had to face a number of extremely worrying problems all
within a narrow space of time. My election was imminent, and here
I had an enormous sum of money fighting against me. The trial was
also coming up, and in this matter too those chests from Sicily were
threatening me. Fear about the election prevented me from making
the necessary preparations for the trial; and because of the trial it was
impossible for me to concentrate on my candidature. Furthermore,
there was no point in my threatening the bribery-agents, because
I could see that they were well aware that I would be completely
preoccupied and tied down by the present trial.* [25] It was at this
moment that I heard for the first time how Hortensius had summoned the Sicilians to attend at his home; and how they, realizing
why they had been sent for, showed themselves to be free agents and
stayed away. The election, meanwhile, began to take place. Verres
thought that he was lord and master of it, as of all the other elections
this year. Accompanied by his suave and ingratiating son, this great
potentate rushed from tribe to tribe, canvassing and meeting with all
his family friends—that is, with the bribery-agents. But the Roman
people, once they had noticed and understood what was going on,
ensured most wholeheartedly* that the man whose riches had not
succeeded in diverting me from my duty was similarly unsuccessful
in using money to dislodge me from my office.

[26] Released from my considerable anxiety about the election, I
began, my mind now much more free and at ease, to devote all my
thoughts and actions exclusively to the trial. And I discovered,
members of the jury, that the plan which my opponents had formed

and set in motion was this: to spin out the proceedings by whatever
means necessary so that the case might then be heard before Marcus
Metellus as praetor. There were several advantages to this. First,
Marcus Metellus himself would be on their side. Secondly, not only
would Hortensius be consul, but Quintus Metellus* too, and I ask you
to take note of how good a friend he is to Verres: for he has given him
such a preliminary vote of confidence that he seems already to have
repaid Verres for delivering to him the preliminary votes at his
election.*

[27] So did you expect me to say nothing about such important
matters? At such a critical moment for the country and for my own
reputation, did you suppose I would have a thought for anything
except my duty and my own position? The second consul-elect*
summoned the Sicilians; some of them came, mindful of the fact that
Lucius Metellus* was governor of Sicily. He then spoke to them as
follows: 'I am consul. One of my brothers is governor of Sicily; the
other is about to become president of the extortion court. We have
gone to great lengths to make sure that Verres comes to no harm.'*
[28] I ask you, Metellus: intimidating witnesses, particularly ruined
and fearful Sicilians, and not just with your own authority but with
the fear inspired by the position of consul and the power of two prae
tors*—if this is not judicial corruption, then could you please tell me
what is? What would you not do for someone who was innocent and
a relative of yours, seeing that you abandon your duty and the dignity of your position for a criminal who is unrelated to you, and lead
those who do not know you to conclude that what he keeps saying
about you is true? [29] For I am told that Verres says that you were
made consul not by fate,* like the other members of your family, but
by his own efforts.

So he will have two consuls and the president of the court on his
side.* 'And,' he says, 'we won't merely escape a president of the court
who is too conscientious by far, and far too protective of his good
reputation—Manius Glabrio.* No, we will have this other advantage
too: Marcus Caesonius is currently a member of the jury, the colleague of our prosecutor,* a man who has already been tried and
tested as a juror, and someone we certainly don't want in a court that
we are in any way trying to corrupt. Before, when he was a juror in
Junius' court,* he didn't just disapprove of the terrible corruption
that took place, he actually exposed it. So after 1 January, we won't

have him in the jury. [30] And as for Quintus Manlius and Quintus Cornificius,* two strict and incorruptible jurors, they will both be tribunes of the plebs, and so we won't have them on the jury either. Publius Sulpicius,* another severe and incorruptible juror, will have to take up his post on 5 December. Marcus Crepereius, who comes from a strict and traditional equestrian family, Lucius Cassius, whose family is rigorous in everything and particularly in jury service, and Gnaeus Tremellius,* who is extremely conscientious and scrupulous—these three men of the old school have all been elected military tribunes, and so from 1 January will not be on the jury. And we shall also be having a supplementary ballot to fill Marcus Metellus' place,* since he is becoming president of this court. After 1 January, then, both the presiding magistrate and virtually the entire jury will have changed.* This will allow us to escape the serious threats of the prosecutor and the great expectations that there are regarding the outcome, and to arrange things exactly as we choose.'

[31] Today is 5 August, and you did not convene until 4 p.m.: they think that today does not even count. There are ten days to go before Gnaeus Pompeius holds the Votive Games;* these will take up fifteen days. The Roman Games then follow immediately. This means that there will be an interval of nearly forty days before they reckon they need to reply to what I am going to say. Then they think that by making speeches and obtaining adjournments they can easily spin the trial out until the Games of Victory, after which the Plebeian Games immediately follow; and after that there will be either no or very few days on which legal business can take place. By this time the prosecution will have gone off the boil and run out of steam, and the whole case will then come up before the new president of the court, Marcus Metellus. As regards this gentleman, if I had had any doubts about his honesty, I would have included him among the jurors I rejected.* [32] Now, however, my feeling is that I would rather see the trial out with him as a juror than as president of the court, and I would rather trust him on oath and with his own voting-tablet than not on oath and with the voting-tablets of the others.

Now, gentlemen, I should like to ask you what you think I should do. But I am sure that without even speaking you will advise me to take the course I realize I must follow. If I devote the time to which I am entitled to making a speech, I will certainly reap the fruits of my effort, industry, and conscientiousness, and through my prosecution

I will ensure that no one in the whole of history ever came to court more ready, more vigilant, or better prepared. But amidst all the praise I will receive for my hard work, there is a real danger that the defendant will slip away. So what can be done? The answer is not, I think, obscure or hard to find. [33] The fruits of glory that could be reaped from a full-scale speech, these I must keep back for some other time; for the present I must prosecute the defendant instead with account books, witnesses, and public and private certified documents and evidence.

The whole business, Hortensius, will be between you and me. Let me speak frankly. If I thought that you were genuinely competing with me in speaking and in explaining away the charges in this trial, I would accordingly devote my efforts to making a prosecution speech and detailing the charges. But since you have begun to fight against me in a way that is determined not by your own character but by Verres' desperate situation, it is necessary for me to find some means of countering the sort of tactics you have adopted. [34] Your plan is to begin your answer to me only after the first two sets of games; mine is to reach the adjournment before the first set of games begins. The result will be that your strategy will be admired as a clever tactic, whereas mine will be thought of simply as the necessary response to it.

But as to what I had begun to say, that the business would be between you and me, what I meant was this. When I took on this case at the request of the Sicilians, I thought it a considerable credit to myself that the people who had previously put my innocence and self-restraint to the test* should now wish to put my integrity and conscientiousness to the test also. Yet once I had taken the case on, I decided to adopt a more ambitious aim, one which would allow the Roman people to witness my devotion to our country [35] To prosecute a man already convicted by universal public opinion hardly seemed to me a task worth all the effort I would have to spend on it—were it not for the fact that that intolerable arrogance of yours and the greed that you have displayed in various trials of recent years are now being brought into play once again in defence of such an utterly worthless person. So now, since you take so much pleasure in your tyrannical domination of the courts, and since there exist men who are neither ashamed nor tired of their own selfish and scandalous behaviour, who seem almost deliberately to incur the hatred and detestation of the Roman people, I therefore declare that I have taken on a task which, though it may be a difficult and dangerous one for me personally, is nevertheless one which is fully worthy of my devoting to it all my youthful energy* and effort.

[36] Since our entire order* is being oppressed by the wickedness and criminality of a few individuals and is tainted by the bad reputation of the courts, I declare to men of this type that I intend to be their hated prosecutor and their hateful, unrelenting, and bitter adversary. I am going to take on this role, indeed I claim this role, which I shall fulfil in my magistracy, which I shall fulfil in that place* from which the Roman people have asked me, from 1 January, to collaborate with them over our national affairs and over the criminal elements. I promise the Roman people that this will be the grandest and the most impressive spectacle of my aedileship.* Let me advise, warn, and give notice:* those who deposit bribes or accept them or guarantee them or promise them or act as intermediaries or as agents for corrupting a court, and those who have volunteered their power or their effrontery for this purpose, all such persons must, in the present trial, keep their hands and their minds free from this heinous crime. [37] Hortensius will then be consul, with a consul's power and authority, whereas I will be aedile—that is to say, little more than an ordinary citizen. Yet the action which I am promising to take is so welcome and so agreeable to the Roman people that, on this issue, the consul himself will appear, compared to me, less even (if such a thing were possible) than an ordinary citizen.

I am not only going to touch upon, but (after revealing certain information) will actually discuss in detail all the wicked and disgraceful crimes which have been committed in connection with the courts over the ten years* since they were transferred to the senate. [38] I will tell the Roman people how it is that, when juries consisted of equestrians, there was for nearly fifty years* not even the least suspicion of a juror ever having accepted a bribe in return for giving a particular verdict; how it is that, once the courts had been transferred to the senatorial order and the Roman people's control over each one of you had been removed, it was possible for Quintus Calidius* to declare on his conviction that no ex-praetor could be convicted honourably for less than three million sesterces; and how it is that, when the senator Publius Septimius* was convicted, at the time when Quintus Hortensius was the praetor in charge of the extortion court, the damages that were assessed explicitly took account of the fact that Septimius had accepted a bribe in a previous case. [39] Again, at the trials of Gaius Herennius and Gaius Popillius,* two senators who were convicted of embezzlement, and at that of Marcus Atilius* who was convicted of treason, it was established that they had all accepted bribes in previous cases; when Gaius Verres was drawing lots as city praetor,* senators were produced who, chosen by the lot, convicted a defendant without holding a proper trial; and a senator was found* who, while serving as a juror in one and the same court, both took money from a defendant to distribute among the other jurors and at the same time took money from the prosecutor to find the defendant guilty. [40] And now, what words can I use to deplore that shame, disgrace, and catastrophe for the whole senatorial order, the fact that in this country of ours, while senators supplied the juries, the voting-tablets of jurors under oath were marked with symbols of different colours?* I give you my promise that I will go over all these crimes rigorously and in detail.

Now tell me, what view do you think I am going to take if I find out that in this trial too a similar violation has been committed? Especially when I have numerous witnesses to prove that Gaius Verres, when he was in Sicily, repeatedly said in many people's hearing that he had a powerful friend* he could rely on while plundering the province; and that he was not taking money for himself alone, but had his three-year governorship of Sicily parcelled out in such a way that, he said, he would be doing very nicely if he kept his gains from the first year for his own use, handed over those of the second to his advocates* and supporters, and reserved those of the third year—the richest and most lucrative of the three—entirely for his jurors.

[41] This prompts me to tell you of a remark which I recently made before Manius Glabrio when the rejection of jurors was being held,* and which I noticed made a profound impression on the people of Rome. I said that I thought that there would come a time when foreign peoples would send delegations to Rome to request that the extortion law and this court be abolished. For if there were no courts, they believe that each governor would only carry off enough for himself and his children. With the courts as they are now, on the other hand, they reckon that each governor carries away enough for himself, his advocates, his supporters, the president of the court, and

the jurors—in other words, an infinite amount. Their conclusion is
that they are capable of satisfying the avarice of one greedy individual, but incapable of subsidizing a guilty man's acquittal.
[42] How remarkable are our courts and how glorious the reputation
of our order, when the allies of the Roman people hope for the
abolition of the extortion court, which our ancestors established for
their benefit! Would Verres ever have been so optimistic about his
own chances if he had not absorbed the same bad opinion of yourselves? This ought to make your own hatred of him even greater
than the Roman people's, if such a thing were possible, seeing that he
imagines that you are his equals in avarice, criminality, and perjury.

[43] By the immortal gods, gentlemen, I beg you to consider this
situation and take the necessary action! I advise and warn you of
what I myself have realized, that this is a golden opportunity which
the gods have given you to rid our whole order of hatred, unpopularity, scandal, and disgrace. It is widely believed that there is no strictness in the courts, no honesty—and that there are now in fact no
courts worthy of the name. As a result, we are scorned and despised
by the Roman people, and we now burn with an extreme and long-
lasting infamy.

[44] It was for this reason and no other that the Roman people
were so determined to see the restoration of the tribunes' powers.*
When they were demanding that, that was what they seemed on the
surface to be demanding, but in reality they were demanding courts.
And this fact did not escape the distinguished and wise Quintus
Catulus.* When the valiant and illustrious* Gnaeus Pompeius raised
the question of the tribunes' powers before the senate, Catulus, on
being asked for his opinion, replied with the greatest authority, saying straightaway that the conscript fathers were managing the courts
in a wicked and scandalous fashion, and that if, while acting as
jurors, they had paid heed to what the Roman people thought, then
the tribunes' loss of their powers would not have been so keenly
regretted. [45] Furthermore, when Gnaeus Pompeius himself as
consul-elect first held a public meeting outside the city* and revealed
that he was intending to restore the tribunes' powers (the thing
which it was supposed people were most waiting for), there was a
hum of approval and a murmur of appreciation among the audience.
But when later in the same speech he pointed out that the provinces
had been plundered and devastated, that the courts were behaving

scandalously and disgracefully, and that he wanted to consider this problem and take action, at that moment not with a mere murmur but with a deafening shout the Roman people signified that this was their own wish too.

[46] So now people are on the lookout, watching to see how each one of us conducts himself, whether he stays honest and abides by the laws. They note that since the law about the tribunes* was passed, only a single senator has been convicted, and he a man of slender means.* They do not actually criticize this, but they do not find much in it to praise either. After all, there is no great glory in being honest when there is nobody who is able, or attempts, to corrupt you.

[47] This is a trial in which you will be passing verdict on the defendant, but the Roman people will also be passing verdict on you. This case will determine whether it is possible, when a jury consists of senators, for a very guilty but very rich man to be convicted. Moreover, this is a defendant who has only two characteristics, extreme guilt and immense wealth; so if he is acquitted, no other conclusion could possibly be drawn except the least favourable one. Neither popularity, nor family tie, nor any good deed done in the past, nor even any fault of a venial kind will be thought to have compensated for his numerous and abominable crimes. [48] Lastly, I will put the case before you so clearly, gentlemen, and I will present you with facts so familiar, so well attested, so damning, and so conclusive that no one will dream of asking you to acquit this man as a personal favour. I have a definite and properly thought-out strategy which I will use to track down and pursue all the opposition's schemes; and I will conduct my prosecution in such a way that their intrigues will all appear manifest not only to the ears of the Roman people, but to their eyes as well.

[49] You have the power to wipe out and destroy the disgrace and scandal by which this order has for some years now been affected. It is universally agreed that since the courts were constituted in their present form, no panel has been so eminent and admired as this one. So if anything should go wrong in this trial, everyone will conclude not that more suitable jurors should be selected from the same order—since no such men exist—but that a different order altogether* should be found to judge cases.

[50] Therefore, members of the jury, I first ask the immortal gods to grant what I think I have grounds for believing will be the case,

that no one in this trial will prove to be dishonest, barring only him*
who has long ago been found to be so. Secondly, if there are some
who are found to be dishonest, then I promise to you, gentlemen, and
to the Roman people that only death—by Hercules!—will prevent
me from opposing their corruption with vigour and perseverance.

[51] My promise, then, is that, at the cost of toil, danger, and
hostility to myself, I will strongly oppose this shameful conduct once
it has been committed. Your task, Manius Glabrio, is on the other
hand to use your authority, wisdom, and diligence to prevent it happening in the first place. Take up the cause of the courts, take up the
cause of justice, honesty, principle, and conscience—and take up the
cause of the senate, so that it may pass the test of this particular trial
and win the respect and gratitude of the Roman people! Reflect on
who you are, on where you are, on what you owe to the Roman
people, and on what you should repay to your ancestors! Remember
your own father's Acilian law,* which gave the Roman people, in
extortion cases, the best courts and the strictest jurors! [52] You have
the greatest precedents surrounding you: they do not allow you to
forget the glory your family has won, and they remind you day and
night of your valiant father, your wise grandfather, and your distinguished father-in-law. So if you have indeed acquired the vigour
and energy of your father Glabrio in standing up to the criminal
elements, if you have acquired the foresight of your grandfather
Scaevola* in looking out for the traps which are being prepared to
damage your reputation and that of these jurors, and if you have
acquired the steadfastness of your father-in-law Scaurus* in never
being deflected from a fixed and true judgement, the Roman people
will then surely realize this—that with an upright and honourable
praetor and a carefully chosen jury, immense wealth is far more
likely to increase the suspicion of a criminal's guilt than to provide
him with a means of acquittal.

[53] I am determined not to do anything that will result in the
praetor in this case or the court being changed. I will not allow the
trial to be spun out until a time when people who collectively refused
to obey a summons—one wholly without precedent—from the
slaves of consuls-elect are then forced to obey a similar summons,
from the lictors of consuls.* Nor will I allow it to be spun out until a
time when wretched individuals, formerly the friends and allies of
the Roman people but now our slaves and suppliants, will not only

lose their rights and fortunes through the power of those consuls, but will even be denied the opportunity to protest against their loss. [54] I will certainly not permit a speech delivered by me to be replied to only after forty days have gone by,* when my allegations have been forgotten owing to the passage to time. I will not do anything that will result in a verdict being given only when these crowds from all over Italy have left Rome—people who have come from everywhere all at the same moment to attend the elections, the games, and the census.* In this trial, both the reward of glory and the risk of unpopularity ought, I think, to belong to you; the anxiety and hard work should belong to me; but the knowledge of what is done here and the memory of what was said by both parties should belong to the whole of the general public.

[55] The procedure I am going to follow is not unprecedented: it has been adopted in the past by men who today are leaders of our country.* I am going to call my witnesses immediately. What you will find unusual, gentlemen, is the way I deploy these witnesses. First of all I shall explain a particular charge in detail, and then, when I have established it with arguments and a speech, I will bring on the witnesses relevant to that charge. There will be no difference between this method of prosecution and the normal one, except that, in a normal prosecution, witnesses are produced only once all the speeches have been made, whereas in this one they will be produced to back up each separate charge. The defence will of course have the opportunity to cross-examine the witnesses, to argue their points, and to make speeches. If anyone feels sorry at missing a full-scale prosecution speech, they will have that in the second hearing. I am sure they will appreciate that what I am doing is absolutely necessary: I have to have a means of countering the trickery of my opponents.

[56] In the first hearing, my case will be as follows. I accuse Gaius Verres of having committed many arbitrary and cruel actions against both Roman citizens and allies, and many acts of wickedness against both gods and men, and in particular of having illegally taken forty million sesterces out of Sicily. I will prove this to you so conclusively, by means of witnesses, private account books, and certified public documents, that you will realize this: that even if I had had all the time in the world for speaking just as I chose, there would still have been no need at all for a lengthy oration. I have finished.

[1] Members of the jury, I see that none of you is in any doubt that Gaius Verres has openly plundered everything in Sicily that is sacred or profane, public or private,* and that he has engaged in every type of theft and robbery not merely without any compunction, but without even the slightest attempt at concealment. But a brilliant and impressive defence of the man is nevertheless being mounted; and I must work out well in advance, gentlemen, how I am to counter it. The case that is being drawn up is this: that Verres by his bravery and by his exemplary vigilance during a time of terrifying danger kept the province of Sicily safe from runaway slaves and from the threat of war.* [2] What am I to do, gentlemen? Where am I to direct the thrust of my prosecution? Where am I to turn? Against all my attacks the description 'a good general' blocks my way like a wall. I know the ground. I see where Hortensius will disport himself. He will enlarge upon the dangers of war, the national emergency, and the shortage of generals; then he will beg of you, then he will insist as of right that you refuse to allow the Roman people to be deprived of such a fine general by the evidence of Sicilians, or to allow a general's glory to be tarnished by charges of greed.

[3] Gentlemen, I cannot hide my feelings from you. I am afraid that Gaius Verres, because of his outstanding military genius, may get away with everything that he has done. I am reminded of the trial of Manius Aquillius* and how impressive and how decisive the speech of Marcus Antonius* was considered to have been. Just before the end of his speech, Antonius, like the intelligent and indeed courageous speaker that he was, grabbed hold of Aquillius, placed him where everyone could see him, and tore the tunic from his chest, thus allowing the Roman people and the jurors to see the battle scars which he had on the front of his body. While he was doing this he spoke at length about the wound which Aquillius had received in the head from the enemy commander; and he made the jurors who were about to deliver their verdict seriously afraid that the man whom fortune had snatched from the weapons of the enemy, when he had had no thought of saving himself, should now appear to have been kept back not in order to receive the congratulations of the Roman

people, but to satisfy the cruelty of a jury. [4] That is the line of
defence which my opponents are now attempting—and that is the
result they are aiming for. Yes, he is a thief; yes, he is a sinner against
the gods; yes, he is more guilty than anyone of every conceivable crime
and vice—but he is a good general, one with luck on his side, and well
worth keeping in reserve in case of a dangerous national emergency.

Now I am not going to deal with you in the way I am fully entitled
to. I am not going to insist on the point which should perhaps be
allowed to me—that since this court is constituted under a specific
law,* what you ought to be demonstrating is not what great exploits
you achieved as a general, but how you kept your hands off other
people's property. I am not, I repeat, going to deal with you in that
way. Instead, I am going to ask, as I understand you wish me to, what
were your achievements in war, and how significant were they.

[5] So what are you claiming? That in the war against the slaves* it
was your military skill that saved Sicily? A praiseworthy achievement, and an honourable line of argument. But which war are we
talking about? I have always understood that since the war which
Manius Aquillius brought to an end, there has been no slave war in
Sicily. 'No, it was in Italy.' Certainly, and a very serious and terrible
war it was too. But surely you are not trying to claim part of the
credit arising from that war? Surely you do not imagine that you
have a share in the glory of that victory together with Marcus
Crassus or with Gnaeus Pompeius? Although I suppose it would not
be beyond the scope of your shamelessness to dare to assert a claim
of that kind. I suppose you prevented the slaves' army from crossing
over from Italy to Sicily.* Where? When? From which place? Did
they try to cross on rafts, or was it on ships? I for one certainly never
heard about it—although I did hear that, as a result of the courage
and foresight of the valiant Marcus Crassus, the runaway slaves
were prevented from lashing rafts together and crossing the strait to
Messana; though that would not have needed much preventing if the
slaves had actually had reason to believe that there were any forces in
Sicily waiting to attack them on their arrival.

[6] 'But when war was going on in Italy so near to Sicily, do you
really imagine that Sicily was unaffected?' And what is so surprising
about that? After all, when there was war in Sicily, Italy was entirely
unaffected—and Sicily is exactly the same distance from Italy as
Italy is from Sicily. In any case, what are you attempting to prove

here when you talk about the proximity of the two places? That it
was easy for the enemy to cross over, or that there was a likelihood of
Sicily being infected by a similar outbreak? For men who had no
means of obtaining ships, the way to Sicily was not merely
obstructed by water, it was completely impassable: those who you
claim were close to Sicily would have found it easier to make their
way to the Atlantic than to reach Cape Peloris. [7] And as for being
infected by a slave war, why should that relate to you any more than
to all the other provincial governors? Is it because there have been
slave wars in Sicily in the past?* But that is precisely why in that
province the danger was, and is, minimal. Ever since Manius Aquillius completed his term, each governor's regulations and edicts have
stipulated that no slave is allowed to possess a weapon. I will tell you
an old story, which, since it is a striking instance of severity, you have
probably all heard before. When Lucius Domitius* was governor of
Sicily, a gigantic boar was brought to him. He was very impressed,
and asked who had killed it. On being told that it was somebody's
shepherd, he ordered the man to be sent for. The shepherd came as
fast as he could, in all eagerness, expecting to be praised and
rewarded. Domitius asked him how he had managed to kill so large
an animal. The man replied that he had killed it with a hunting
spear—and was immediately crucified on the governor's order. Now
that may perhaps seem rather harsh. I make no judgement; I merely
observe that Domitius preferred to appear cruel in inflicting
punishment rather than lax in sparing it.

[8] These regulations, then, were introduced for Sicily, and the
result was that, even at the time when the whole of Italy was con-
sumed by the Social War, the not very energetic or valiant Gaius
Norbanus* was able to relax. Sicily could perfectly easily protect itself
against any internal outbreak. The Roman businessmen there have
the closest links imaginable with the Sicilians, sharing the same way
of life, interests, concerns, and feelings. The Sicilians themselves
have the sort of lives which depend on there being a state of peace,
and they are so devoted to the empire of the Roman people that they
do not in the least wish to see it made smaller or changed. Moreover,
the danger of a slave war has been guarded against by the governors'
regulations and also by the strictness of individual slave-owners. So
for all these reasons, there is no home-grown trouble which can
possibly come from within the province itself.

[9] Well then, are no slave risings, no conspiracies said to have taken place in Sicily during Verres' governorship? Certainly nothing that came to the notice of the senate and people of Rome, nothing that Verres sent an official letter to Rome about. And yet I have a suspicion that in some places in Sicily the slaves did indeed begin to revolt. I know this not so much from direct evidence as from what Verres himself did, and from his decrees. And please note the lack of malice in what I am about to say: I am actually going to bring forward and narrate matters which he himself would like to be aired,* and of which you have not so far been informed.

[10] In the district of Triocala, a place which at an earlier date* was held by runaway slaves, the slaves of a Sicilian called Leonidas were suspected of plotting a rising. This was reported to Verres. On his order the men who had been named were immediately and quite properly arrested and taken to Lilybaeum. Their owner was summoned to appear in court, and they were tried and convicted. So what happened next? What do you suppose? You will be expecting to hear, perhaps, of some act of theft or looting.* Don't expect the story to be the same every time. When there is a threat of war, how can there be any opportunity for stealing? Even if the situation had offered any prospect of this, the chance had been missed. Verres could have taken some money from Leonidas when he summoned him to appear.* There was some room for bargaining (no novelty in that) to prevent the case coming to court; or if it had already gone to court, he could have arranged their acquittal. But seeing the slaves had actually been convicted, how could there possibly be any profit? They would have to be led off for punishment: that was unavoidable. Their conviction had been witnessed by the members of the council, it had been witnessed by the public records, it had been witnessed by the fine citizens of Lilybaeum, it had been witnessed by the very large and highly respected community of Roman citizens there. There was nothing for it; they must be led off. Accordingly they were led off and tied to the post.* [11] Even now, gentlemen, you seem to be looking to me to find out what happened, as you are well aware that Verres never did anything without some gain to himself, some plunder. But what could be done in this type of situation? Choose whatever heinous crime you fancy; I shall still surprise each one of you. These men, who had been convicted of the crime of conspiracy, who had been handed over for execution, who had been

tied to the post, suddenly, in front of many thousands of onlookers, were set free and returned to their owner from Triocala.

What can you say in answer to this, you lunatic, except to answer a question which I am not going to put to you (a question which, in so scandalous a situation, it would not be proper to ask if there were any doubt—and in this case there is none): what you got out of this, how much it was, and how you obtained it? But I will save you from having to explain all this and free you from your anxiety about this. After all, I hardly need be afraid of the possibility of anyone accepting that you undertook for no payment the sort of crime which no one except yourself could ever be induced to undertake for any payment! I say not a word about your methods of thieving and plundering: the topic I am now covering is this great reputation you enjoy as a general.

[12] So what do you say, you fine guardian and defender of the province? You discovered that those slaves wanted to take up arms and start a war in Sicily, and you passed judgement in accordance with the verdict of your council. Then, when they had been handed over for punishment in the traditional fashion, did you dare to pluck them from the jaws of death and set them free—intending, no doubt, that the cross you had had set up for convicted slaves should be reserved instead for unconvicted Roman citizens? States that are on the brink of annihilation, with everything already lost, generally adopt the lethal expedient of pardoning their convicts, releasing their prisoners, recalling their exiles, and reversing their judicial decisions. When these things happen, everyone realizes that the country is heading for destruction; when such things take place, everyone concludes that there is no hope left. [13] Wherever this has happened, the effect has been to release people of the popular or the aristocratic faction* from execution or exile. But the release was never granted by the same people who passed sentence; nor did it follow on immediately after the passing of the sentence; nor did it apply in the case of people convicted of attacking the lives and property of the entire community. This action, on the other hand, is unprecedented, the sort of action which will be believed more from the character of the man who perpetrated it than from the action itself. The men set free were slaves; they were released by the same man who had passed sentence on them; he released them immediately, when their punishment was already under way; and the slaves were convicted of a crime which threatened the life-blood of all free people.

[14] What a brilliant general, to be compared no longer with the valiant Manius Aquillius, but with Paullus, Scipio, and Marius!* What foresight he displayed in his province's hour of fear and danger! When he saw that the slaves in Sicily were restless because of the slave war in Italy, what fear he inspired in them to deter them from rising themselves! He ordered their arrest. Who would not be afraid at that? He summoned their owner to court. What could be more terrifying to a slave? He made a pronouncement of 'guilty'—and thus, through the pain and death of a few individuals, extinguished, or so it appeared, the flame that had arisen. And then what happened? The lash, the burning torches, and those ultimate measures which serve to punish those convicted and deter the rest—torture and the cross. From all such punishments the men were set free. Who can doubt that he must have crushed the slaves' minds with the greatest imaginable terror, when they saw the governor so obliging as to spare the lives of slaves who had been convicted of the crime of conspiracy, with the executioner himself brokering the deal?

[15] And did you not do precisely the same in the case of Aristodamus of Apollonia? And in the case of Leo of Imachara? And that rising of the slaves and sudden fear of a war, did it prompt you to a belated diligence in protecting your province, or to a new means of making dishonest profit? Eumenidas of Halicyae, a man of rank and reputation, had an agent—a slave worth a great deal of money—who at your instigation was accused of conspiracy. But you took sixty thousand sesterces from his owner, a transaction which has just been explained in the sworn evidence of Eumenidas himself. From the Roman equestrian Gaius Matrinius,* while he was away at Rome, you took six hundred thousand sesterces, because you said you had grounds for suspecting his agents and shepherds. This has been stated by Matrinius' representative Lucius Flavius,* who paid the money over to you; it has been stated by Matrinius himself; and the same statement is made by the illustrious Gnaeus Lentulus,* the censor. He it was who, being concerned for Matrinius, sent you a letter at the beginning of the affair, and arranged for others to write as well.

[16] And can I pass over Apollonius Geminus of Panhormus, the son of Diocles? Can anything be cited that is more notorious throughout Sicily, anything more shocking, anything more blatant?

When Verres arrived at Panhormus, he ordered Apollonius to be sent for and a legal summons to be issued against him; there was a large crowd of people present, including a substantial number of the Roman citizens who were resident there. People immediately started saying, 'I was surprised that a man as wealthy as Apollonius remained unharmed by our governor for so long. Verres has thought up some scheme or other and has put it into action. Certainly a rich man would never be summoned by him like this unless he had some motive.' Everyone was waiting eagerly to discover what was going on, when Apollonius suddenly came running in, out of breath and accompanied by his young son. (Apollonius' aged father had been bedridden for some time.)* [17] Verres then gave the name of a slave who he said was in charge of Apollonius' sheep, and said that he had formed a conspiracy and had incited the slaves on other estates to revolt. There was in fact no such slave on Apollonius' estate. Nevertheless, Verres gave orders that he be produced instantly. Apollonius declared that he did not own any slave whatsoever with that name. Then Verres ordered that Apollonius be dragged from the court and thrown into prison. As he was being led away, he protested that he, poor man, had done nothing wrong, that he had committed no crime, that all his money was invested, and that he currently had no ready cash. It was while he was actually making this declaration, in front of a large crowd of witnesses, so that anyone could appreciate that he was being treated with such terrible injustice precisely because he had not paid up—it was, I repeat, exactly at that moment, while he was shouting about his money, that he was cast into chains.

[18] Please observe the consistency of this governor—a governor who, on this subject, is not merely being defended as a governor of average abilities, but is being lauded as a brilliant general. At a time when people were worried about the possibility of a slave war, he inflicted on slave-owners who had not been convicted the very punishment from which he exempted slaves who had been convicted. Apollonius was an extremely rich man, who stood to lose his substantial wealth if the slaves were to start a war in Sicily, yet on the pretext of a slave war Verres put him in chains without a trial. The slaves, on the other hand, he had, on the advice of his council, found guilty of conspiring to start a war, yet without the support of his council and on his own initiative he had exempted them from all their punishments.

[19] Now, suppose Apollonius did indeed commit some crime which warranted his punishment. Am I then going to treat this matter as if Verres were committing a crime, or doing something of which we would disapprove, if he handed down a verdict that was a little too harsh? I will not be so critical as that; I will not make use of the normal practice of prosecutors whereby if someone has shown clemency, he is accused of being remiss, but if he has punished with severity, it is treated as evidence of his cruelty. I will not argue on those lines. I will accept the verdicts you have passed; I will support your decisions to any extent that you want me to. But as soon as you yourself start overturning the verdicts you have made, stop criticizing me. For I contend, as I have every right to, that a man who has pronounced himself guilty ought also to be pronounced guilty by the votes of sworn jurors.

[20] I am not going to defend Apollonius, though he is a friend of mine and someone whose hospitality I have enjoyed: I do not want to seem to be overturning your verdict. I will say nothing about his sober habits, his excellent qualities, his capacity for hard work. I will pass over the point I have already made, that his wealth was tied up in slaves, livestock, farms, and investments, and that any rising or war in Sicily would therefore have been as disastrous to him as to anyone. I will not even make the point that, supposing Apollonius were wholly guilty, as the most honourable man in a most honourable city he ought not to have been so severely punished without a trial. [21] Nor will I stir up hatred against you, not even by referring to how, when such an admirable man was lying in prison, in darkness, in squalor, and in rags, your tyrannical orders forbade his aged father and his young son from ever visiting him in his wretchedness. I will also pass over the fact that, each time you came to Panhormus during those eighteen months (for Apollonius was in prison as long as that), the senate of Panhormus, together with the magistrates and priests of the city, came to you in supplication, begging and beseeching that that poor, innocent man be finally set free from the disaster which had overtaken him. All these points I will forgo. But if I wished to pursue them, I could easily demonstrate that, by your cruelty towards others, you have long ago debarred yourself from the clemency that the jurors might otherwise show to you.

[22] All such arguments I will concede to you and refrain from using. For I can see what Hortensius' defence will be. He will admit

that neither the age of the father, nor the youth of the son, nor the tears of either of them carried more weight with Verres than the welfare and safety of his province. He will say that the state cannot be governed without strictness and intimidation. He will ask why rods of office* are carried before the governors, why axes are granted to them, why a prison has been constructed, and why so many punishments have traditionally been prescribed for criminals. When he has said all of this, so sternly and impressively, I shall then ask why Verres, after no new facts had come to light and no defence had been made, suddenly, for no apparent reason, ordered that this same Apollonius should be released from prison. And I shall venture to suggest that the grounds for suspicion on this charge are so strong that I may now leave it to the jurors themselves, without any argument on my part, to draw their own conclusions as to what type of robbery this would appear to be, how wicked, how scandalous, and how immense and boundless in its scope for gain.

[23] Now first please briefly consider the number and extent of the sufferings which Verres inflicted upon Apollonius—then weigh them up and reckon how much they are worth in terms of money. What you will find is that they were all directed at this one wealthy individual with the aim of making other people afraid of what could happen to them, and giving them examples of the dangers that they too could face. To begin with, there was the sudden allegation of a capital and hateful crime. Decide how much you think that is worth, and how many people must have paid up to avoid it. Next there was the charge made without a prosecutor, the verdict given without a court, the conviction handed down without a defence. Calculate the price of each of these injustices, and reflect that it was only Apollonius who fell victim to them—which means that there must have been an awful lot of people who escaped by paying up. Finally, there was the darkness, the chains, the prison, the punishment of being locked up, and being locked away from the sight of one's parents and children, and from the open air and the light of day— the things which all other people freely enjoy. These are punishments which people may justifiably give their lives to escape; I do not myself think they can be reckoned up in terms of money.

[24] In the end Apollonius did indeed escape them—but by then he was a broken man. Nevertheless, his example served to teach everyone else that they must strike a deal with this avaricious criminal

before they too suffered the same fate. For you cannot seriously
believe that so wealthy a man was selected to face so implausible
a charge for any reason other than financial gain, or that he was
suddenly released from prison for any different reason, or that
Verres tried and applied this method of robbery only in the case of
Apollonius, and that he did not use that man's punishment as a
means of striking fear into all the rich men in Sicily.

[25] I hope, members of the jury, that Verres will remind me,
while I am on the subject of his military glory, of any point that I
should happen to leave out. I think I have now managed to cover all
of his achievements that relate to the possibility of a slave war; at
least I am certain that I have not consciously omitted anything. You
have all the facts to do with his planning, his diligence, his watchfulness, and his defence and guardianship of his province. There is, it
is true, more than one type of general, and my main purpose is that
you should understand to which type he belongs. These days, there
is a general lack of fine soldiers,* and so it is important that no one
should continue to be unaware of the sort of commander we have in
Verres. His is not the wisdom of Quintus Maximus, nor the speed in
action of the elder Africanus, nor the exceptional intelligence of
the younger one, nor the systematic discipline of Paullus, nor indeed
the vigour and valour of Gaius Marius.* No, as I will explain to you,
Verres was a different sort of general altogether—one we should be
sure to retain and cherish!

[26] First, regarding the laborious task of travelling—quite the
most important aspect of soldiering, gentlemen, and in Sicily the
most essential task of all—allow me to tell you how straightforward
and indeed agreeable Verres, by his intelligent planning, made this
for himself. To begin with, to counteract the extreme cold in winter
and the violence of the storms and swollen rivers, he devised for
himself the perfect expedient. He chose the city of Syracuse, whose
situation, topography, and climate are said to be such that even
during the most wild and stormy weather there has never been a day
when the sun has not been visible at least part of the time. Here this
fine general lived during the winter months, and he was so much at
home there that it was not often that anyone saw him out of doors, or
even standing up. The short days were taken up with eating, and the
long nights with unspeakable sexual acts.

[27] But when spring came round—whose arrival he discerned

not from the west wind, nor from the stars, but when he saw the first roses:* that was for him the first sign of spring—then at that point he turned to the laborious business of travelling. And in this he proved himself so tough and energetic that no one ever saw him riding on a horse. Instead, as the Bithynian kings used to do, he had himself conveyed by eight bearers in a litter, one which boasted a diaphanous divan of Maltese wool, stuffed with rose petals. He wore one garland on his head, another round his neck, and to his nostrils he clasped a delicate, fine-meshed linen sachet, again filled with rose petals. Whenever he arrived at some town, after completing his march in the manner described, he had himself carried in this same litter straight into the bedroom. There the Sicilian magistrates would come to visit him, there the Roman equestrians would come, as you have heard from numerous sworn witnesses. Legal disputes were submitted to him there in secret, and shortly afterwards his decisions were carried forth. Then when a short time later he had finished making legal rulings in his bedroom—on considerations of money, not justice—he concluded that he owed the rest of his time to Venus and to Bacchus.

[28] While we are on this subject I think I should not pass over our glorious general's outstanding, unique diligence. For I have to tell you that, in all the towns in Sicily where governors stay and hold assizes, there is none in which a woman from a respectable family was not specially selected to satisfy his lusts. Some of these were openly brought to his table, while any who were more modest in their behaviour came later at a prearranged time, avoiding the light and the crowd of people. His dinner parties were not the quiet affairs one expects with governors and generals, nor the decorous occasions that magistrates put on, but were noisy and bad-mannered events; sometimes they even descended into hand-to-hand fighting. For this strict, diligent governor, although he never obeyed the laws of the Roman people, carefully observed all the drinking rules that are prescribed at parties. And his entertainments generally ended up with someone being carried from the feast as if from the battlefield, someone else being left for dead, and the majority sprawling, with no awareness of who or where they were—so that anyone who saw them would believe that they were looking not at a governor's official dinner, but at an outrage reminiscent of Cannae.*

[29] As soon as midsummer arrived, the period which all previous

governors of Sicily have always spent travelling, believing that to be
the best time for inspecting the province, when the grain is on the
threshing-floor—because that is when the slaves are all brought into
one place and can see how many of them there are, and that is when
their work is particularly onerous, and the sheer volume of the grain
makes an impression on them, and the time of year does not stand in
their way*—at this time, I tell you, when the other governors have
always kept on the move, this general of an entirely new type built
himself a fixed camp in the loveliest part of Syracuse.

[30] At the mouth of the harbour, where the gulf from the open
sea begins to turn inwards from the coast towards the city,* he sited a
series of marquees made out of linen sheeting. Moving out of the
governor's residence, which was the former palace of King Hiero,* he
took up residence here instead, and during that whole period no one
ever saw him in any other place. The only people who were allowed
access to it were those who could share in, or satisfy, his lust. Here
flocked all the women with whom he had been passing his time
(and it is remarkable what a large number of them there were in
Syracuse);* here came the men, too, who were worthy to be his
friends—worthy, that is, to share in his style of life and his revelries.
It was among men and women of this sort that his teenage son
socialized, so that even if his nature made him less like his father, his
nurture and habits made him his father's son.

[31] The arrival here of the woman Tertia, separated from her
Rhodian piper by violence and trickery,* is said to have caused great
disruption in Verres' camp. The aristocratic wife of Cleomenes of
Syracuse and the wife of Aeschrio,* a woman of good family, took
exception to the inclusion of the daughter of Isidorus the pantomime
actor within their social circle. But this Hannibal here thought that
in his camp promotion should be by merit and not by birth,* and
indeed he thought so highly of this woman Tertia that he actually
took her away with him when he returned home from his province.

Throughout this period while, dressed in a purple Greek cloak
and a tunic down to the ankles, he was enjoying himself with his
women, nobody minded or took it amiss that the governor was
absent from the forum, legal disputes were not being heard, and the
courts were not in session. That place by the shore might re-echo all
around with women's voices and the sound of music, and in the
forum the silence of the courts and the law might be complete—but

nobody minded. For it seemed to them as if what was absent from the forum was not legal business, but violence, brutality, and the cruel and shocking plundering of their property.

[32] So you are basing your defence on his ability as a general, Hortensius? Are you trying to hide his thefts, his robberies, his greed, his cruelty, his arrogance, his criminality, and his wickedness behind his great achievements and his glory as a general? I suppose I should be afraid that at the end of your speech you will have recourse to that old oratorical trick which Antonius was the first to use,* that you will bring Verres forward, bare his chest, and let the Roman people gaze on his scars—women's love-bites, the evidence of his wickedness and sexual excess! [33] I beg the gods that you actually will have the gall to bring up his military service, his service in war! Then the whole of his military career will be exposed, and you will find out not only how he conducted himself when he was in command, but how he behaved in the ranks. His early 'service' will be gone over again, the period when he used to be pulled out of the forum rather than, as he himself maintains, pulled in it.* The camp of the gambler from Placentia* will be mentioned, a place where he was on duty so regularly that his pay was stopped. Indeed, his many financial losses from his time in the ranks will be referred to—debts which were paid off and discharged from the proceeds of his youth.

[34] Eventually he became hardened by his submission to this sort of disgrace, by which time others—though not himself—had tired of it. Do you really need me to tell you what kind of a man he was by that stage, and how many well-guarded strongholds of modesty and chastity he captured by force and recklessness? And do you really want me to tell you of scandals which dishonoured other people too? I will not do this, gentlemen; I will pass over all these things that took place some time ago. Two scandals only I will put before you, recent ones which do not reflect badly on anyone else; and from them you will be able to come to your own conclusions about everything that I leave out. The first is so famous and universally well known that no peasant coming to Rome from his home town on legal business during the consulship of Lucius Lucullus and Marcus Cotta* would have been unaware of it—that all the judgements of the city praetor were decided on the say-so of the tart Chelido. The other is that when Verres had already left the city in his general's cloak, and had already pronounced the solemn vows for his tenure of

office and the general welfare of the country, he used to have himself carried back inside the city* in a litter at night, in order to commit adultery with a woman who was married to one man but available to everyone. This practice was against morality, against the auspices, and against every religious principle human and divine.

[35] Immortal gods, how people differ from one another in their minds and ways of thinking! In my own case, when I took on those public offices which the Roman people have so far entrusted me with, I considered myself bound by obligations of the most solemn kind—and may I forfeit your backing, and that of the Roman people, for my intentions and aspirations during the rest of my life if this is not the case! When I was elected to the quaestorship,* I considered that that office had not merely been granted me, but had been entrusted to me and invested in me. While I was carrying out my duties as quaestor in the province of Sicily I supposed that everyone's eyes were looking at me alone. I felt that I and my quaestorship were being presented before the whole world as if on a theatre stage. And I consistently denied myself everything that is regarded as pleasurable—not merely the immoderate desires of the present day, but even such comforts as are natural and necessary.

[36] I am now aedile-elect, and fully conscious of the responsibility which the Roman people have placed on me. I must put on, with the greatest reverence and care, the holy games for Ceres, Liber, and Libera; I must win the favour of our mother Flora for the Roman people and plebs by providing well-attended games; I must put on, with the greatest dignity and solemnity, the ancient games for Jupiter, Juno, and Minerva, games which were the earliest ones to be described as 'Roman';* and I must look after the sacred temples and protect the whole of the city. In return for the effort and anxiety which these duties entail, I have been given certain benefits: precedence in being called for my opinion in the senate, the purple-bordered toga, the curule chair, and the right to hand down a portrait mask of myself to posterity.* [37] But although I hope that all the gods will be well disposed towards me, and although the office granted to me by the Roman people is in itself something which gives me great pleasure, nevertheless all these benefits, gentlemen, give me more anxiety and worry than enjoyment. For I am anxious that this aedileship itself should not appear to have been given to me simply because it had to be given to one or other of the candidates

who stood for it, but should seem instead to have been rightly
assigned and bestowed in the proper quarter by the considered
judgement of the people.

[38] But you, when your election as praetor* was announced, however that was achieved (I will pass over that and say nothing about
what actually went on)—when, as I say, your election was announced,
were you not stirred by the voice of the crier? When time after time
he proclaimed that the centuries of seniors and juniors had endowed
you with that office,* did it not make you reflect that a certain part of
the state had been entrusted to you, and that for that one year you
would have to keep away from the house of a prostitute? And when
you were then allotted the job of city praetor,* did you never think
how much work, how much responsibility this would involve? Did
you never consider—if you could ever rouse yourself sufficiently to
consider anything—that this job, which it would be difficult enough
for a man of exceptional wisdom and integrity to do, had been given
to someone of supreme stupidity and wickedness? No, you did not.
And so far from banishing Chelido from your house during your
praetorship, you in fact spent the whole of that year in hers.

[39] Next came your provincial governorship. As governor, it
never occurred to you that those rods and axes,* the absolute power of
your office, and all those symbols of rank and prestige had not been
given to you simply to allow you to break down every barrier of duty
and restraint, to view everybody's property as plunder for yourself,
and to make it impossible for anyone's possessions to be safe, anyone's home secure, anyone's life protected, or anyone's chastity
guarded against your greed and wickedness. As governor, you
behaved in such a way that now, when you are caught out, you are
forced to take refuge in a war against fugitives.* But by now you will
have realized that, far from being a defence, this is an important
source of charges against you—unless of course you intend to talk
about the remnants of the slave war in Italy and the setback at
Tempsa,* something which would have been a golden opportunity for
you if you had possessed any courage or energy, instead of which you
proved yourself to be just as you had always been.

[40] The people of Vibo Valentia came to see you, and their
spokesman, the eloquent and high-ranking Marcus Marius, begged
you to take the situation in hand. Since you had the title of praetor
and a praetor's powers, he wanted you to act as their chief and leader

in suppressing the small gang of rebels. However, not only did you shrink from the task, but all the time that you were there on the coast, that woman Tertia, whom you were carrying back to Rome with you, could be seen by everyone. And not only that: when you were giving your official reply, on a matter of such importance, to the citizens of such a well-known, respectable town as Vibo Valentia, you wore a workman's smock and a Greek cloak.*

What do you think of his behaviour when he was leaving for his province,* what do you think of his behaviour in the province itself, when you see him, returning from that province not to hold a triumph but to face trial, and not even bothering to avoid disgrace for the sake of something* which can scarcely have given him any particular pleasure? [41] How divinely inspired were those murmurs of disapproval at the crowded meeting of the senate in the temple of Bellona!* You will remember, gentlemen, how it was drawing towards evening, and the bad news had just been brought in about Tempsa. We did not have anyone with military authority who could be sent there, and then someone said that Verres was not far from there: remember how strongly everyone murmured their disapproval, and how openly the leading senators opposed the suggestion! So does the man who has now been proved guilty by so many charges and so much evidence place any hope at all in the secret votes of all those jurors who, even before they had heard this evidence, openly voiced their condemnation?

[42] So there it is. He has gained no credit from the war against the runaway slaves, or from the threat of that war, because in Sicily there was no such war, or any danger of a war, nor did he take any steps to prevent one happening. 'But he did keep the fleet properly equipped for a war against the pirates, and he devoted exceptional care to this matter, so the province was indeed brilliantly defended by the defendant during his governorship.' I will tell you about the war against the pirates, members of the jury, and about the Sicilian fleet. But I wish first to state that under this single heading are numbered all his worst crimes of greed, treason, insanity, lust, and brutality. Please be so kind as to pay me close attention, as you have done up to this point, while I briefly set out these matters for you.

[43] I wish to state, first, that the naval defence of Sicily was run not with the intention of defending the province, but as a means of using the fleet to make money. Earlier governors used to require the

various states to provide ships and a stated number of soldiers and sailors—yet from the extremely important and wealthy state of Messana you required none of these things. How much money the people of Messana secretly gave you in return we shall find out later, if that seems a sensible plan, from their own witnesses and accounts.

[44] I can further reveal that an enormous vessel, as big as a trireme, a very beautiful, well-equipped merchant ship was quite openly built at public expense to your order, that the whole of Sicily knew about it, and that it was presented and handed over to you free of charge by the chief magistrate and senate of Messana. While Verres was on his way home, this ship, loaded with his loot from Sicily—and indeed itself part of that loot—put in at Velia* with its substantial cargo, including those items which he did not want to send on in advance to Rome with his other thefts because they were of particularly high value and especially treasured by himself. I saw this ship myself at Velia not long ago, and many others have seen it too, a beautiful, well-equipped vessel, gentlemen—one which appeared to everyone who set eyes on it to be already looking forward to its master's exile, and getting ready for his escape.

[45] What answer do you have for me on this point? Except possibly the one which, although it does not excuse you at all, a man on trial for extortion would have to give—that the ship was built at your own expense. Go on, say this: you have no alternative. Do not worry, Hortensius, that I am going to ask what right a senator had to build a ship. The laws which forbid this* are old—'dead letters', as you are fond of saying. It is a long time since our country was like that; it is a long time since our courts were so strict that prosecutors considered that charge one of the more serious ones. In the first place, then, what did you want a ship for? If you are going somewhere on public service, ships are provided at public expense for you to travel in in safety. And unless you are on public service, you are not permitted to travel anywhere at all,* nor to transport goods over the sea from places where you are not allowed to own them. [46] Secondly, why did you acquire something when it was against the law? This charge would have counted strongly against you in the days when strict moral standards prevailed in our country. But now not only do I decline to make this a charge against you, I do not even make a general criticism of you, as well I might, on lines such as these. Did you consider that there would be nothing shameful, nothing

blameworthy, nothing offensive in having a cargo ship built for yourself openly in a centre of population in a province of which you were
the governor? What did you suppose those who saw it would say,
those who heard about it think? That you were going to sail that ship
to Italy empty? That you were going to set up a shipping concern
when you arrived back in Rome? Nor could anyone suppose that you
had an estate on the coast of Italy, and were acquiring a ship of such
great capacity merely to take your produce to market. No, you were
perfectly happy to have everyone talking about you, saying openly
that you were acquiring that vessel in order to ship your loot out of
Sicily, and then to keep coming back again to collect the thefts you
had left behind.

[47] All these points, however, I am willing to withdraw and forgo,
if you can prove that the ship was built at your own expense. But,
lunatic that you are, do you fail to understand that this line of
defence was ruled out in the first hearing by those who spoke in
praise of you, the people of Messana themselves? For Heius, the
leader of the deputation sent here to speak in your favour, said that
the ship had been made for you by state-employed workmen at
Messana, and that a member of the senate of Messana had been
officially put in charge of the work. There remains the timber. This,
because Messana has no timber, you officially ordered from Regium,
as the people of that city themselves testify (you cannot deny it). If
both the material for building the ship and the people who built it
were procured on your authority as governor and not by payment,
where are we to find whatever it was that you claim was paid for with
your own money?

[48] 'But there is nothing in the account books of Messana.' First,
it may have been the case that the ship was built at public expense
without money actually having to be taken out of the city treasury.
Even the temple on the Capitol* could have been built and completed
as a public work by compulsorily enlisted masons and conscripted
workmen without payment—and this was how it was done originally,
in our ancestors' time. Secondly, I notice—and I will call on the
appropriate witnesses and prove it from their own accounts—that
substantial sums of money paid over to Verres were entered as applying to building contracts that were fictitious and non-existent. It is of
course no cause for surprise that the people of Messana should have
left out of their accounts anything that might lead to the conviction

of a man who had done them a considerable favour and who had shown himself to be more of a friend to them than he was to the Roman people. But if we accept that the absence of a record of a payment to you in the accounts of Messana proves that no payment was made, then we must also accept that your inability to produce any record of any purchase made or contract placed proves that you were given the ship free of charge.

[49] But, you answer, the reason you did not require Messana to provide a ship was that it was a federate state. The gods be praised! Here we have a man brought up at the hands of the fetials,* a man excelling all others in his reverent conscientiousness towards the state's treaty obligations! Let all those who were governor before you be handed over to the people of Messana for punishment because they required them to provide a ship in violation of the terms of the treaty! But tell me, reverend and holy sir, why did you require Tauromenium to provide a ship, given that that too is a federate state? Or will you succeed in demonstrating that the rights and positions of two states on the same footing were interpreted in such different and unequal ways without a bribe being paid? [50] But in fact, gentlemen, I will show that the two treaties of the two states were as follows: the treaty with Tauromenium expressly stipulated that the city was exempt from the obligation to provide a ship, whereas the one with Messana laid down and prescribed that a ship must be provided. So given that Verres violated each of the two treaties in both requiring Tauromenium to provide a ship and exempting Messana from providing one, can anyone doubt that, when Verres was governor, that merchant ship did the people of Messana more good than their treaty did the people of Tauromenium? Please now read out both treaties to the court.

(*The treaties are read to the court.*)

So by this exemption of yours, which you yourself call an act of generosity, but which the facts show to be bribery and corruption, you have impaired the high standing of the Roman people, impaired the defences of the state,* impaired the forces which were provided by the valour and wisdom of our ancestors, and have destroyed the rights of our empire, the obligations of our allies, and the memory of our treaty. By the terms of that treaty the people of Messana were obliged to send a ship, if we ordered them to, even as far as the Atlantic, fully armed and equipped, and at their own expense and risk. Yet for a bribe you sold them exemption from the terms of the treaty and from their obligations towards us, so that they should not even have to patrol the strait* in front of their houses and homes, or defend their own walls and harbours.

[51] When this treaty was originally drafted, what effort, trouble, and money do you think the people of Messana would not have been happy to expend in order to avoid the insertion of this clause about the bireme, if there had been any possibility at all of obtaining this from our ancestors? For the imposition of so onerous an obligation on the city somehow brought to that treaty of alliance a suggestion, one might say, of servitude. Even though they had recently done us good service,* and the matter was still open, and the Roman people were not in trouble, nevertheless the people of Messana failed to induce our ancestors to remove the clause from the treaty. But now, when they have done us no further services, and we are many years further on, with our demand of them under the treaty having been made and upheld every year, and at a time when the Roman people are very much in trouble regarding ships, the people of Messana finally obtain this concession from Gaius Verres—for a bribe. And not only do they obtain the concession not to provide a ship: during the three years of your governorship, did Messana provide a single soldier, a single sailor to serve either in the fleet, or in the garrison?

[52] Finally, although a senatorial decree and the Terentian-Cassian law* required grain to be purchased equally from all the Sicilian states, you exempted Messana from this too—even though the requirement was not burdensome and fell equally on all. You will answer that Messana was not obliged to supply us with grain. To supply in what sense? Do you mean not obliged to sell it to us? For we are not talking about grain required as tribute, but grain we would pay for. All right, then; on your interpretation of the treaty, Messana had no obligation to assist the Roman people even by trading with them and selling them supplies. [53] What state, then, did have an obligation to do this? There is no uncertainty as to what the farmers of public land were obliged to supply as it is stipulated in the censors' law;* why, then, did you require them to supply a further amount on a different basis? As for those farmers who were liable to pay the tithe stipulated by the law of Hiero,* surely they were not obliged to provide anything over and above the basic tithe? In that

case, why did you fix an additional amount of grain that they had to sell to us? And then what of the states that were exempt? They at least did not have to supply anything. But not only did you make them sell us grain, you made them supply more than they were capable of, by making them produce the annual 60,000 measures which you had exempted Messana from providing. Now I am not saying that Verres was wrong to require all these states to sell us grain. What I am saying is that Messana was in the same position as the others; that all previous governors had required it to sell us grain just like the other states, and had paid for it in accordance with the senatorial decree and the law;* and that Verres was wrong to give Messana an exemption.

Verres wanted to hammer into place his so-called benefaction, and so he brought Messana's case before his council, and then announced that, on the advice of the council, he would not require Messana to sell us grain. [54] Please listen to the decree of this mercenary governor, taken from his own notebook,* and note how sober the language is, and how impressive his settling of this point of law. Please read it out.

(*The decree is read to the court from the notebook.*)

He says that he freely grants the concession on the advice of his council; that is how he records it. But what if you had not used the word 'freely'? I suppose we would conclude that you took the bribe grudgingly! And 'on the advice of his council'? Gentlemen, you heard the membership of this eminent body being read out. As you listened, did you think it was a governor's council whose names you were hearing, or the partners and associates of an outrageous thief? [55] Here are our interpreters of treaties, our devisers of alliances, our authorities in religion!* Every time there has ever been an official purchase of grain in Sicily, Messana has been required to provide its share—until this select and distinguished council gave Verres permission to take money from that city and behave in his customary fashion. His decree remained in force for no longer than it deserved to, given that it had been issued by someone who had sold his decision to people from whom he should, by contrast, have been buying grain. For as soon as Lucius Metellus succeeded him as governor, he reverted to the written precedent of Gaius Sacerdos and Sextus Peducaeus,* and required Messana to sell us grain. [56] At that point the people of Messana realized that they could no longer keep the concession they had bought from a man who had had no right to sell it to them in the first place.

Well now, you who wanted to be thought so conscientious an interpreter of treaties, answer me this: why did you require Tauromenium to sell us grain, and why did you require Netum to do so? They are both federate states. Indeed, the people of Netum stood up for their rights. As soon as you announced that you were freely exempting Messana, they came to see you and pointed out that their case under the treaty was the same as its. You could hardly make a different ruling when their case was exactly the same, and so you announced that Netum did not have to supply grain—but then forced them to supply it anyway. Let us hear the governor's documents relating to the decrees he made and the grain he required to be sold.

(*The documents relating to the decrees are read to the court.*)

In view of this glaring, shocking inconsistency, gentlemen, how can we avoid the inescapable conclusion? Either he asked Netum for money and they refused to pay, or else he intended to make the people of Messana realize how wise they had been to invest so many gifts and bribes in him, when others in the same position were not able to obtain the concession that they had obtained.

[57] At this point he will no doubt have the temerity to point out that the people of Messana have submitted a testimonial in his favour. But I am sure that none of you, gentlemen, will fail to appreciate the degree to which a testimonial of this kind will damage his case. In the first place, when a defendant cannot produce ten people to give testimonials for him, it is better that he should produce none at all than fail to produce the requisite number prescribed by custom. Sicily has a great many cities, and you were their governor for three whole years; yet most of those cities give evidence against you, a few minor ones are intimidated and say nothing, and one, only, praises you. What are we to conclude from this except that you understand the advantage of a genuine testimonial, but that the character of your administration of the province was of a kind which must inevitably deprive you of this advantage? [58] In the second place, as I said in one of the earlier speeches, what does it say about a testimonial when the delegates sent to deliver it, including their leaders, have stated that, collectively, they built you a ship, and individually they were robbed and plundered by you? Finally, when the people of Messana are the only ones in the whole of Sicily to speak in

your favour, what else are they actually doing other than testifying to us that it was they to whom you passed on everything that you had stolen from our country? In Italy, what settlement of citizens is there so privileged, what town with citizen rights is there so free of responsibilities as to have enjoyed, during those years, such a profitable exemption from all burdens as Messana has enjoyed? For those three years, they were the only people who did not provide what they were obliged by their treaty to do, they were the only people under Verres who were exempt from all burdens, they were the only ones under his governorship who lived under this principle—that they need not give the Roman people anything, so long as they denied Verres nothing.

[59] But let me return to the fleet, the subject from which I digressed. You accepted one ship from Messana against the laws, and you exempted another one against the treaties. Thus in the case of this single city you have twice revealed yourself to be a criminal, in both exempting what you ought not to have exempted and accepting what you should not have accepted. You ought to have demanded a ship to sail against looters, not one to sail away with loot, a ship to prevent the province being despoiled, not to carry away the province's spoils. The people of Messana provided you with a city in which to collect together your various thefts from far and wide, and a ship in which to transport them to their destination. That town was a holding area for your plunder; those people were the witnesses and custodians of your thefts; those people provided you with a place to store your plunder, and a vessel in which to remove it. The result of this was that, even when you had lost the fleet through your wickedness and greed, you still did not go so far as to make Messana supply a ship. At a time when the shortage of ships was so severe, and when Sicily was in such danger, they would surely have given you a ship, even if you had had to ask them as a favour. But your power to command and even your freedom to make a request were taken away by that famous vessel—not a bireme contributed to the Roman people, but a merchant ship presented to the governor. That was the price of our sovereignty, of the aid they were required to supply, and of their exemption from their legal obligation, from precedent, and from their treaty.

[60] You have now heard how the valuable aid of one particular state was lost and sold for a bribe. Now let me inform you of a

completely new method of plundering first devised by the defendant. It always used to be the case that each state gave all the money to
be spent on the fleet—for pay, subsistence, and so on—directly to
their captain. He would never dare risk being accused of wrongdoing
by the men under his command, and he also had to submit accounts
to his fellow-citizens; so his job involved not only work, but personal
risk. This, as I say, was the universal practice not only in Sicily, but
in all the provinces, as well as being the practice with the pay and
expenses of the Italian allies and Latins, in the days when they
provided us with auxiliary troops.* Verres was the first person since
our empire was founded to rule that all the money from the states
should be paid over to himself, and that it should be a man of his own
appointment who handled the money. [61] Who can be in any doubt
as to why you were the first to change such a universal and long-
standing practice, why you disregarded the considerable advantage
of having others take responsibility for the money, and why you took
on such a difficult and troublesome task which would result in your
being suspected and accused of wrongdoing?

Next, other schemes for making money were set in motion—and
notice how many of them come under this heading of the fleet. He
accepted bribes from states which wanted to escape their obligation
to supply sailors; he exempted individual sailors from service for a
fixed sum; he pocketed all the pay of those he had exempted; and he
withheld the pay that was owed to the rest. Listen to the proof of all
these charges from the evidence of the states themselves. Please read
it out.

(*The evidence of the states is read to the court.*)

[62] Look at this man, members of the jury, look at his effrontery,
look at his audacity! That he should draw up a list of the sums of
money that each state should pay him, according to how many sailors
were to be exempted! And that he should fix on the specific sum of
six hundred sesterces as the price for exempting an individual sailor!
The man who handed over that amount secured exemption from
service for the entire summer, whereas Verres pocketed the amount
which he had taken for that sailor's pay and subsistence. In this way
he profited twice over from each exemption. The province was suffering from pirate attacks and was in considerable danger, but this
lunatic conducted this business so openly that even the pirates themselves were aware of it, and the whole province was a witness to it.

[63] As a result of this greed of Verres', the Sicilian fleet was a fleet in name only: in reality it consisted of empty vessels more suited to bringing loot to the governor than terror to the pirates. Even so, while Publius Caesetius and Publius Tadius* were sailing around in their ten half-manned craft, they did come across one particular pirate ship, loaded with plunder—a ship they did not so much overwhelm as tow away, since it was already overwhelmed and indeed half-sunk by the load it was carrying. It was full of very good looking young men,* full of silverware and silver coin, and it also contained a large quantity of textiles. This ship, all on its own, was not actually captured by our fleet, but merely discovered off Megaris,* a place not far from Syracuse. When the news was brought to Verres, he was lying on the beach with some girls, drunk. All the same, he managed to lift himself up, and immediately sent several of his guards to his quaestor and his legate with instructions that everything be brought to him intact as soon as possible for him to inspect.

[64] So the ship was taken to Syracuse, and everyone was expecting to see due punishment carried out. But Verres behaved as if plunder had been brought before him, not as if pirates had been captured. Any of the pirates and their captives that were old and ugly, he treated as enemies; but any who possessed any youth, beauty, or technical skill he took away and distributed among his secretaries, his staff, and his son, while six musicians he sent as a present to a friend of his in Rome. The whole night was spent unloading the ship. Nobody saw the captain of the pirates, who ought to have been executed. Today everyone believes—and I will let you judge for yourselves whether they are right or not—that Verres was secretly bribed by the pirates to spare their captain.

[65] 'But that is just a guess.' No one can be a competent juror if he does not pay heed to plausible suspicions. You know that man. And you also know the universal practice whereby someone who has captured a pirate or enemy leader will be only too delighted to display him publicly in front of everyone. Gentlemen, out of all of the considerable number of Roman citizens at Syracuse I did not meet a single one who claimed to have seen the captured pirate captain, despite the fact that everyone, as is the custom, and as always happens, had come together in a crowd and asked where he was and demanded to see him. What happened to cause that man to be hidden away so completely, so that no one was able to catch even the slightest

glimpse of him? The people who lived on the coast at Syracuse had often heard that pirate's name and shuddered at the very mention of it. They wanted to feast their eyes and glut their souls on his torture and execution. But no one was even permitted to set eyes on him.

[66] Publius Servilius* alone captured more pirate captains alive than all governors before him put together—and was anyone ever deprived of the enjoyment of viewing a captured pirate? On the contrary, wherever he journeyed he presented everyone with the gratifying spectacle of captured enemies in chains. The result was that crowds flocked from all over to witness the sight, coming not just from the towns on the route, but from neighbouring ones as well. And why do you think his triumph was the most popular and welcome one that the Roman people have ever experienced? Because there is nothing sweeter than victory, and there is no more definite proof of victory than seeing the people you have many times been afraid of being led in chains to their execution.

[67] Why, then, did you not do this? Why was that pirate kept out of sight as if it would have been sacrilege to let him be seen? Why did you not execute him? For what purpose did you let him live? Do you know of any pirate captain who has ever been captured in Sicily in the past and not been beheaded? Go on, cite me one precedent for what you have done, give me one example. You kept the pirate captain alive—why? To have him led before your chariot, I suppose, at your triumph—for after the magnificent fleet of the Roman people had been lost and the province plundered, there would of course have been nothing for it but for the senate to grant you a naval triumph!

[68] All right, then, he preferred this novel procedure of keeping the pirate captain a prisoner rather than follow the normal practice and have him beheaded. So to what sort of imprisonment was the man subjected? With whom was he kept and in what conditions? You have all heard of the quarries at Syracuse,* and most of you have seen them. They are a colossal, stupendous piece of work, the creation of kings and tyrants. They consist of an astonishingly deep excavation into the rock, cut by a vast force of workers. Nowhere so shut in, nowhere so completely enclosed, nowhere so secure for keeping men under guard could possibly be created or imagined. All who are officially to be kept in custody, even people from the other Sicilian states, are ordered to be taken down into those quarries.

[69] Now Verres had imprisoned a number of Roman citizens in this place, and he had also ordered the rest of the pirates to be held there. He therefore realized that, if he were also to imprison there this man who was only masquerading as the pirate captain,* many of those in the quarries would start asking questions about where the real pirate captain was. He did not dare, therefore, to send his fake pirate to this best and most secure of prisons. Indeed, he felt nervous about imprisoning him anywhere in Syracuse. So he sent him to—where? Lilybaeum perhaps? Ah, I see; Verres did not feel nervous about all coastal communities, only Syracuse. No, it was not Lilybaeum, gentlemen. Panhormus, then? So I hear; although since the pirate was captured off Syracuse, Syracuse was the proper place for his imprisonment—if not for his execution. But no, it was not Panhormus even. [70] So where was it? Where do you imagine? The fake pirate was sent to a place where the inhabitants have no reason to fear and be anxious about pirates, to people who have nothing to do with shipping and maritime matters—to Centuripae.* The Centuripans are an entirely inland people, predominantly farmers, who have never had any cause to worry about seagoing pirates. In fact, the only pirate captain they were afraid of during your governorship was one who confined his piratical activities to dry land—Apronius!* Anyway, to allow the fake pirate to pass himself off without any trouble or difficulty as the real one, Verres ordered the Centuripans to supply him with food and everything else he needed on the most generous and lavish scale—thus giving the game away entirely and letting everyone see what it was that he had done.

[71] The Syracusans, however, being educated and canny people, were able not merely to see what was obvious, but to make inferences about what was being hidden from them. So each day they counted up the number of pirates who were executed. They calculated the total that there should have been from the size of the ship that had been captured and the number of its oars. Verres, having removed and spirited away all those who had any technical skill or were at all good looking, reckoned that there would be a general outcry if he followed the normal practice and tied all the remaining pirates to the post* at the same time, given that far more had been taken away than not. He had therefore decided to bring them out at different times in dribs and drabs. Nevertheless, there was no one in the entire city who did not keep a note of the running total, and not merely notice

the ones that were missing, but actively ask for them and demand that they be produced.

[72] Since there were a great many pirates missing, this wicked defendant therefore began to put others in the place of the pirates he had taken away to his own house, substituting Roman citizens that he had previously cast into prison. Some of these, he claimed, were soldiers from the army of Sertorius* who had fled from Spain and put in at Sicily. Others were people who had been trading or were at sea for some other reason, and had themselves been captured by the pirates: Verres made out that they were with the pirates of their own volition. Of these Roman citizens, some were dragged out of prison to meet their deaths at the post with their heads covered up, to prevent their being recognized; others were recognized by numerous Roman citizens who all spoke out in their defence—but the men were nevertheless beheaded. I will talk about their terrible torture and cruel deaths when I come to that topic; and I shall speak so powerfully that if in protesting against the defendant's savagery and the shameful deaths of those Roman citizens my strength or even my life should fail me, I would still consider it a glorious and worthwhile thing to have spoken out in this manner.

[73] This, then, is Verres' achievement, this his glorious victory: a pirate galley captured, its captain freed, musicians sent to Rome, good looking young men and those with particular skills sent to the governor's house, their places taken by an equal number of Roman citizens who are tortured and executed as if they were enemies, all the textiles removed, and all the gold and silver taken away and appropriated.

But how he incriminated himself in the first hearing! For many days he said nothing at all. Then when the worthy Marcus Annius* testified in the course of his evidence that a Roman citizen had been beheaded but that the pirate captain had not, Verres suddenly sprang up, roused by his knowledge of the crime he had committed and also by the madness that his misdeeds had inspired in him, and declared that he had been well aware that he would be accused of having taken a bribe not to execute the real pirate captain, and that was why he had not executed him—and he added that there were, at his house, *two* pirate captains!* [74] What mercy the Roman people showed you—or rather, what astonishing and unparalleled forbearance! A Roman equestrian, Marcus Annius, declares that you beheaded a

Roman citizen: you do not deny it. He says that you failed to execute
a pirate captain: you admit it. Gasps and shouting can be heard from
everyone; but the Roman people then check themselves and refrain
from inflicting immediate punishment on you, leaving the necessary
measures for their own safety* to be taken instead by the strict jurors
of this court.

And you knew that you would be accused of committing a crime?
How did you know this? What reason did you have for thinking it?
You had no particular enemy—and if you did, your way of life was
surely not so bad as to make you afraid of being brought to justice.
Or perhaps, as is often the case, it was your awareness of your own
guilt that made you timid and suspicious? All right, when you were
governor, you were terrified of being accused and put on trial. But
if that is the case, can you really now seriously doubt, when so many
witnesses are demonstrating your guilt, that you are going to be
convicted?

[75] But if you were really afraid of being accused of not executing
the real pirate captain but executing a substitute instead, which possible course of action did you think would leave you with a stronger
line of defence—producing at your trial, on my compulsion and
insistence, in front of people who did not know him, and long after
the event, a man whom everyone had only your word for it that
he was a pirate captain at all, or executing the man at Syracuse,
immediately after the event, in front of people who recognized him,
and with virtually the whole of Sicily looking on? Notice how big a
difference it makes which of these courses of action was adopted.
With the latter, no one could criticize you; but the former leaves you
with no defence. That is why all previous governors have always
adopted the latter policy—and I would like to know who prior to
you, who apart from you has ever adopted the former.

You kept that pirate alive. For how long? For the remainder of
your period of office. For what purpose, according to what precedent, and for what reason did you keep him as long as that? Why, I
repeat, when those Roman citizens whom the pirates had captured
were beheaded at once, did you allow those same pirates to enjoy the
right to life for so long? [76] All right; let us concede that you could
do as you liked for as long as you were governor. But even as a private
citizen, even when on trial, even on the point of conviction did you
still venture to keep enemy commanders in your own private house?

For one month, for two months, in the end for almost a year after they were captured, those pirates stayed at your house. And there they would be still, if it had not been for me—if, that is, it had not been for Manius Glabrio,* who granted my request and ordered that the men should be given up and consigned to prison. What legal right, what custom, what precedent is there for such a course of action? Here we have a fierce and bitter enemy of the Roman people, the common enemy of all mankind. Shall any human being be entitled, when only a private citizen, to keep an enemy like that at his own house, and inside the walls of Rome?

[77] Now let us imagine that the day before I forced you to admit that you had beheaded Roman citizens and then let the pirate captain live and stay at your house—let us imagine, as I say, that on the day before I made you admit that, he managed to escape from your house and succeeded in raising an armed force against the state. If that had happened, what would you now be saying? 'He stayed at my house, he lived with me. I kept him alive and unharmed for my trial, to make it easier for me to refute the charges my enemies would bring against me.' Really? Will you put the whole country in danger, just to make it easier for you to escape your own private dangers? Will you give defeated enemies their proper punishment at a time to suit yourself, rather than to suit the country? Will the enemy of the Roman people be kept in private custody? Triumphing generals, it is true, keep enemy commanders alive for a time so that they can lead them in their triumphs and allow the Roman people to view the impressive spectacle and reap the fruits of victory. But even so, when they start to turn their chariots out of the forum and up to the Capitol, they give orders for the captives to be taken over to the prison, and one and the same day thus brings an end both to the command of the victor and to the life of the vanquished.

[78] You tell us that you were certain you were going to have to face trial. So I take it that no one could possibly doubt that you would ever have let the pirate captain escape execution, thus allowing him to live on and so present a serious danger to you—one you could see before your very eyes. For suppose the pirate had died (and you say that you were afraid of being prosecuted): who would then have believed your defence? It would be established that no one at Syracuse had actually seen the pirate captain, but that everyone was wondering where he was. No one would doubt that you had taken a

sum of money to set him free. It would have been rumoured that a substitute had been put in his place whom you were trying to pass off as the real pirate. You yourself would have admitted that you had long been afraid of being accused of doing exactly this. So if you suddenly announced that the man had died, who would have believed you? [79] Even as it is, when you produce this captive of yours, whoever he is, alive, you will be laughed out of court. And suppose he had escaped, suppose he had broken his chains like that king of pirates, Nico, whom Publius Servilius* miraculously captured and then no less miraculously recaptured: what would you now be saying? But the crux of the matter is this: if the real pirate had been beheaded, you would not have got your money; but if this fake one had died or escaped, it would not have been difficult for you to put another substitute in his place.

I have said more than I intended to about this pirate captain. Even so, I have passed over the strongest proofs of Verres' guilt on this particular charge. This is because I want to keep the whole charge separate: there is a separate place, a separate law, and a separate court* in which this matter will be dealt with.

[80] Acquiring so much loot and gaining so much wealth in the form of slaves, silver, and textiles did not make Verres any more conscientious in equipping the fleet or in calling up and provisioning the sailors—even though, in addition to making his province safer, that might have resulted in more plunder for himself.* The height of summer is the time when other governors normally travelled around the province from place to place or even, in view of the concern about the pirates and the danger they posed, put to sea themselves. But at this time of year Verres judged that his own royal residence* was not sufficient to satisfy his expensive and dissolute tastes. To spend the summer in the style to which he had become accustomed, he gave orders, as I have already said, that a series of marquees made out of linen sheeting should be sited along the shore—the shore, that is, of the Island at Syracuse,* beyond the spring of Arethusa, next to the mouth and entrance of the harbour, a delightful spot, and safe from prying eyes.

[81] It was here that the governor of the Roman people, the guardian and defender of the province, spent the summer giving parties for his women friends each and every day. No man ever sat down to dinner except for him and his young son—although since they were

the only ones, it would be more accurate to say that only women were present. But sometimes the freedman Timarchides* was also invited along. The women, on the other hand, were all married and well born, with one exception, the daughter of Isidorus the pantomime actor,* whom Verres had fallen in love with and taken away from her Rhodian piper. There was one Pipa, the wife of Aeschrio of Syracuse, a woman who is the subject of many poems, relating to Verres' passion for her, which are currently enjoying great popularity throughout Sicily. [82] Then there was Nice, the wife of Cleomenes of Syracuse, and said to be an exceptionally attractive woman. Her husband did indeed love her, but he had neither the power nor the courage to oppose Verres' sexual impulses, and at the same time he was inhibited by the numerous gifts and favours which the defendant had bestowed on him.

You are well aware how shameless Verres is. But despite this, he did not feel entirely free and easy in his mind keeping Nice with him on the beach day after day during this period, when her husband was also in Syracuse. He therefore devised an original way out of the problem. He handed over to Cleomenes the ships which his legate had previously been in charge of, and so ordained that a Syracusan, Cleomenes, should be in command of, and issue orders to, the fleet of the Roman people. His motive was not simply to keep him away from Syracuse during the time he would be at sea, but to make him quite happy about being kept away, since he had been given a position which involved considerable rewards and prestige. So with the husband sent away and got rid of, Verres kept the wife at his side not more easily than before—for who was ever able actually to stop him getting his way?—but with a slightly easier mind. It was as if he had disposed of not so much a husband as a rival.

[83] Cleomenes of Syracuse, then, took charge of the ships of our friends and allies. What aspect of this should I criticize or lament first? That the power, prestige, and authority of a legate, a quaestor, even a governor was handed over to a Sicilian? If your business with women and parties prevented you from undertaking this duty yourself, what about the quaestors, what about the legates,* and—if it comes to that—what about your own officers, what about your military tribunes? And if there was no Roman citizen fit to undertake the command, what of the states which have always been loyal friends of the Roman people? What about Segesta, what about Centuripae,

states which by their long-standing and loyal service to us, and also their kinship with us,* come near to the status of Roman citizens?

[84] Immortal gods! If a Syracusan, Cleomenes, has been put in command of the sailors, ships, and captains of states like these, has Verres not wiped out every mark of honour, fairness, and duty? Have we ever fought any war in Sicily when Centuripae was not on our side, and Syracuse with the enemy? I make this point simply as a matter of historical record: I do not mean to disparage that city. But that was the reason why that great general, the illustrious Marcus Marcellus,* by whose bravery Syracuse was captured and by whose clemency it was preserved, would not allow any Syracusan to live on the Island. Even today, let me tell you, no Syracusan is allowed to live in that part of the city, because it is a place that a tiny number of people could hold against attack. Because of this, Marcellus was not prepared to entrust it to any people whose loyalty was not entirely certain, and besides, it is here that ships coming in from the Mediterranean enter the city. That was why he judged that the keys to the place should not be entrusted to people who had on many occasions refused admittance to our armies.

[85] See what a difference there is between your wanton behaviour and the authority of our ancestors, between your lustfulness and madness and their prudence and foresight. They deprived the Syracusans of access to the shore: you gave them command of the sea. They would not allow any Syracusan to live in that part of the city where ships could approach: you placed a Syracusan in command of our fleet and our ships. They deprived the Syracusans of a part of their city: you granted them part of our empire. The Syracusans obey our orders because of the help we have been given by our allies: you made those allies obey the orders of a Syracusan.

[86] Cleomenes sailed out of the harbour in a quadrireme from Centuripae, followed by one ship each from Segesta, Tyndaris, Herbita,* Heraclea, Apollonia, and Haluntium—to all appearances a magnificent fleet, but weak and ineffective because of the exemptions given to sailors and oarsmen. This hard-working governor saw the fleet that was under his authority only for as long as it took to sail past the scene of his outrageous parties. He himself had not been seen for many days, but on this occasion he did at least show himself to his sailors briefly. He stood on the shore—a governor of the Roman people—dressed in sandals, a purple Greek cloak, and a

tunic down to the ankles, and leaning on a girl. Indeed, a great many Sicilians and Roman citizens had often seen him before in this get-up.

[87] The fleet sailed on its journey, and on the fifth day it finally completed the short distance to Pachynum.* By this time the sailors were driven by hunger to gather the roots of wild palms*—a plant common in that area, as in most of Sicily—and the poor wretches kept themselves alive on these. But Cleomenes, who considered himself another Verres not just in extravagance and wickedness but also in power, set up a tent on the shore and spent day after day drinking, in imitation of his governor.

So with Cleomenes drunk and everyone else starving, suddenly news arrives that there are pirate ships in the harbour of Odysseae (that is the name of the place—our fleet was in the harbour at Pachynum). Now there was a land garrison there, at least on paper, and so Cleomenes counted on being able to take enough soldiers from it to make up the full complement of sailors and oarsmen. But it transpired that this grasping governor had applied the same methods to the land garrisons as he had to the fleet, for there were hardly any soldiers at all, the vast majority having been exempted.

[88] Cleomenes, who was in front in the quadrireme from Centuripae, ordered the mast of his ship to be raised, the sails spread, and the anchor cables cut, and at the same time that the signal be given to tell the others to follow.* This ship from Centuripae was in fact an astonishingly fast vessel when under sail. During Verres' governorship, no one had had the opportunity to find out how fast each ship could go under oar—although in this quadrireme, because of Cleomenes' rank and influence, there was less of a shortage of oarsmen and sailors than in the other ships. The fleeing quadrireme had now flown almost out of sight, while the rest of the ships were all still struggling in their original position. [89] But their crew were men of courage:* although they were few in number, and in a desperate situation, they nevertheless shouted that they preferred to fight, and were ready to yield up to the sword whatever life and strength remained in their famished bodies. In fact, if Cleomenes had not raced so far ahead, they would have had at least some hope of resisting. His ship was the only one with a deck, and it was big enough to offer protection to the other ships; in a fight with the pirates, it would have looked like a city among the pirate galleys. But helpless

as they were, and abandoned by their leader, the admiral of the fleet, they had no alternative but to begin to follow in his wake.

[90] So they set off, like Cleomenes himself, in the direction of Helorus, not so much fleeing from the pirates who were about to attack them as following the man who was supposed to be commanding them. As each ship became the last in the line of flight, so it became the first to be attacked, as the pirates fell on the hindmost one in turn. Thus the first to be taken was the ship from Haluntium, commanded by a high-ranking man of that city, Phylarchus; he was later to be ransomed from the pirates at public expense by the people of Locri.* In the first hearing he told you under oath what happened and why. The second ship to be taken was the one from Apollonia; its captain Anthropinus was killed.

[91] While this was happening, Cleomenes meanwhile had already reached the coast at Helorus, and had thrown himself off the ship and onto dry land, leaving the quinquireme where it was. The captains of the other ships, finding that their admiral had gone ashore, were in no position either to offer resistance or to escape by sea; they therefore put in at Helorus and went off after Cleomenes. At this point the pirate captain, Heracleo, suddenly and unexpectedly found himself victorious—not because of any military ability of his own, but simply as a result of Verres' avarice and wickedness. He came across the magnificent fleet of the Roman people cast up and abandoned on the shore, and gave orders to his followers to wait until it began to get dark, and then to set the ships on fire and burn them. [92] What a miserable, sickening moment for the province of Sicily!* What a catastrophic, fatal disaster for so many innocent people! What exceptional disgrace and wickedness on Verres' part! On one and the same night the governor was burning with the flames of a scandalous passion, and the fleet of the Roman people with pirates' fire.

At the dead of night, the dreadful news of this disaster reached Syracuse. There was a rush in the direction of the governor's residence, to which only a short while beforehand women had escorted Verres home with music and song, after a splendid banquet. Although it was night, Cleomenes did not dare show his face in public. He shut himself away in his house; but his wife was not at home to comfort him in his misery. [93] As for our brilliant general, his domestic staff were so well drilled that, even when the situation was so serious and the news so dire, no one was admitted: no one

dared to wake him if he was asleep, or interrupt him if he was awake.
But once everyone else had found out what had happened, an enormous crowd gathered throughout the city. This time, it was not, as
had always been the case before, a fire from a beacon on some tower
or hill that gave notice of the imminent arrival of the pirates: no, it
was the flames from the actual burning of the fleet that announced
the catastrophe that had occurred and the danger still to come.

People tried to find out where the governor was; it became clear
that no one had told him the news. The crowd then made a full
onslaught on his residence,* shouting noisily. [94] That woke him
up—and he learned the full story from Timarchides. Then the governor put on his military cloak (it was nearly dawn by this time) and
came out into the open, heavy with wine, sleep, and sex. His appearance was greeted by shouting from the crowd, and its tone vividly
impressed on him the similarity with the danger he had faced at
Lampsacus.* But this time the danger seemed even greater, because,
although he had been equally hated by both mobs, this one was
exceptionally large. People started mentioning his beach parties, and
his scandalous banquets. The crowd called out the names of his
women, and asked him directly where he had been and what he had
been doing all that time, day after day, when no one had seen him.
They called for Cleomenes, the admiral he had himself appointed, to
be handed over to them; and the precedent that had been set at Utica
with Hadrianus* came within a hair's breadth of also being followed
at Syracuse, so as to result in the setting up of two tombs for two
wicked governors in two provinces. But then the crowd reflected on
the situation they were in, on the state of emergency, and on the high
standing and good reputation they shared—since the Roman citizens
of Syracuse are considered to be a credit not only to Sicily, but to
Rome as well. [95] As Verres stood there stupefied and half-awake,
they urged each other to action, took up arms, and occupied the
whole forum and the Island, which comprises a large part of the city.

The pirates waited for just that night at Helorus and then, leaving
our ships still smouldering, set off for Syracuse. I suppose they had
often heard that there was no sight more lovely than the walls and
harbour of Syracuse and decided that, if they did not go and see it
during Verres' governorship, they would never see it at all. [96] They
arrived first at the governor's summer quarters, at the very point on
the coast where Verres, during those summer days, had pitched his

tents and sited his camp of luxury. They found the place deserted. Realizing that the governor must have moved his camp to a different position, they immediately began, without any anxiety at all, to sail into the harbour itself. When I say the harbour, gentlemen (I must explain this carefully for the benefit of those who do not know the place), I mean that the pirates actually entered into the city, and into its very centre. The city, you see, is not bounded by its harbour, but the harbour is itself surrounded by and enclosed within the city. The sea, that is, does not lap against the outer side of the walls; rather, the harbour waters themselves flow into the heart of the city.

[97] Here it was that, while you were governor, the pirate Heracleo sailed around in his four little galleys, just as he pleased. Immortal gods! At a time when the empire of the Roman people was officially represented at Syracuse, a pirate galley has actually penetrated all the way to the forum of Syracuse and to every quay in the city. The proud fleets of Carthage, at the height of her naval power, never succeeded in approaching so near, despite repeated attempts in numerous wars; nor did the glorious navy of the Roman people, undefeated until you became governor, ever manage to penetrate the city, throughout a great many Punic and Sicilian wars.* The topography of the place is such that the Syracusans saw the enemy armed and victorious on their city walls, in their city, and in their forum before they saw a single enemy ship in the harbour.* [98] Here it was that, while you were governor, the pirates' small boats sailed to and fro where the Athenian fleet of 300 ships* once, by their strength and numbers, succeeded in forcing an entry—the only fleet in history ever to do so; and in that same harbour it was defeated and destroyed by the natural character of the land and the harbour. Here it was that the power of that great city was first shattered and brought low: in this harbour the nobility, empire, and glory of Athens are considered to have been wrecked. So did a pirate penetrate to a point in the city where he did not merely have the city on one side, but actually had a considerable part of it behind him? Indeed, he sailed past the whole of the Island. This is a city in its own right, and with its own walls, and a place where our ancestors, as I have already said, would not allow any Syracusan to live, because they understood that anyone who held that part of the city would also have control of the harbour.

[99] But look at how he sailed around the harbour! The pirates started waving the wild palm roots which they had discovered in our

ships, so that everyone should be aware of the wickedness of this defendant and the disaster that had befallen Sicily. Those Sicilian sailors were the sons of farmers. They were men whose fathers produced so much grain through their own hard work that they were capable of supplying the Roman people and the whole of Italy. And to think that those men, who were born on the island of Ceres* where corn is believed to have been first discovered, should have been reduced to consuming food of a type that their ancestors, by their discovery of corn, had saved other nations from having to eat! To think that, while you were governor, Sicilian sailors lived on palm stalks, and the pirates Sicilian grain! [100] What a miserable, sickening spectacle! To think that the glory of Syracuse, the name of the Roman people, and the vast population of the city, Roman and non-Roman alike, should be held up to mockery by that pirate galley! To think that that pirate should hold a triumph over the fleet of the Roman people in the harbour at Syracuse, while the oars of the pirate ships splashed seawater into the face of this utterly useless and wicked governor!

In due course the pirates left the harbour, not because they were frightened, but because they had had enough. People then began to ask what had been the cause of this appalling disaster. Everyone said, and argued openly, that with most of the oarsmen and sailors exempted, those who were left starved to death, and the governor spending all his days with girls in a drunken stupor, it was not in the least bit surprising that such a humiliating disaster had occurred. [101] These criticisms of Verres and the low esteem in which he was held were reinforced by the reports of the captains who had been appointed to the ships by their own communities. Those captains who had escaped to Syracuse after the loss of the fleet each gave an account of how many sailors they knew had been exempted from their own particular ship. It was clear what had happened; and Verres' criminal responsibility was proved not just by arguments but by reliable witnesses.

Verres was duly informed that in the forum and among the Roman citizen community no one had done anything all day but question the captains of the ships as to how the fleet had been lost; and that the captains had replied by explaining to one and all that the reason was the exemption of the oarsmen, the starvation of the rest, and the panic-stricken flight of Cleomenes. On learning this, Verres

began to think on these lines. As you heard him say himself during
the first hearing, he had already come to the conclusion before this
that he was going to be prosecuted; and he realized that if those
captains were to give evidence, it would quite simply be impossible
for him to answer so serious a charge.

The first plan that he devised was stupid, but it was at least
merciful. [102] He summoned the captains to appear before him;
they came. He reprimanded them for having spoken about him in the
way that they had, and asked them to stop talking like this, and
instead to say that each had had the full complement of sailors in his
ship, and that no sailors had been exempted. They naturally agreed
to do as he wanted. He did not delay for a moment. He immediately
called his friends and asked the captains one by one how many sailors
they had had; and each replied as he had been told to. Verres then
had their answers written down, and sealed with his friends' seals.
Far-sighted man that he was, his intention was to make use of these
supposed depositions to defend himself on the present charge,
should he ever have to do so. [103] His friends must surely have
laughed at the idiot and pointed out to him that these documents
would do him no good, since the governor's excessive precautions in
this matter would only make him look even more guilty. He had in
fact resorted to these stupid tactics many times before, ordering
deletions or additions to be made in the public records of Sicilian
communities, to suit his own purposes. But he now understands that
all this is doing him no good, now that his guilt has been proved by
reliable accounts, witnesses, and certified documents.

When he saw that the captains' statements, his own depositions,
and the other documents were not going to help him, he formed a
new plan—not the plan of a wicked governor, which would have
been just about bearable, but that of a brutal, crazed tyrant. He
decided that if he were to weaken the force of the charge (for he did
not imagine it could be eliminated entirely), then all the captains,
since they were witnesses to his guilt, would have to be put to death.

[104] But one thought ran through his mind. 'What should I do
about Cleomenes? Can I punish those I ordered to do as they were
commanded, and yet let off the man I put in command and authority
over them? Can I punish those who simply followed Cleomenes, and
yet pardon Cleomenes who ordered them to escape with him and
follow him? Can I show severity to those whose ships were not just

undermanned but without decks, and yet be lenient towards the one man who had a ship with decks and a less depleted crew? Cleomenes will have to die with them!' But what about loyalty, what about the vows of friendship, what about the handshakes and embraces, what about their comradeship in the service of love, on that delightful beach? It would be unthinkable not to spare Cleomenes!

[105] So he sent for him and told him that he had decided to punish all the captains; and that this was absolutely necessary to protect him from prosecution. 'I am going to spare you alone. I would rather take the blame myself for what has happened and be criticized for inconsistency than either show cruelty towards you or leave alive and intact so many very damaging witnesses.' Cleomenes thanked him, expressed his approval of the plan, and said that it had to be so. He added, however, that there was one point that had escaped his notice: he could not get away with punishing the captain from Centuripae, Phalacrus, because he had been in the Centuripan quadrireme with him. So what was Verres to do? Could he allow a highly respectable young man from so distinguished a city to survive and give evidence against him? 'For the time being, yes,' replied Cleomenes, 'since there is no alternative. But later on we will find some means of getting him out of our way.'

[106] Once all this had been settled and agreed, the defendant suddenly strode out of the governor's residence, inflamed with wickedness, rage, and cruelty. He entered the forum, and ordered the captains to be summoned. They feared nothing, and suspected nothing, and so came running at once. He then ordered the poor, innocent men to be cast into chains. They appealed to the governor and asked him why he was doing this to them. He replied that it was because they had betrayed the fleet to the pirates. This provoked an outcry. People were astonished that Verres could be so hypocritical and reckless as to blame others for the disaster which had been entirely the result of his own avarice, and to accuse others of betrayal when it was he himself who was believed to be in league with the pirates. And all this, they observed, was taking place a full two weeks after the fleet had been lost.

[107] People, meanwhile, were asking where Cleomenes was. It was not that anyone thought that he, for all his faults, should be punished for what had gone wrong, for what could he have done? I cannot accuse anyone falsely—so I say again, what on earth could

Cleomenes have done, when his ships, owing to Verres' greed, were empty? But then suddenly they noticed him sitting next to the governor and whispering familiarly into his ear, just as normal. And it struck every one of them that it was utterly disgraceful that highly respectable men, specially chosen by their own cities, should have been shackled and chained, whereas Cleomenes, because he had been the governor's partner in his disgraceful crimes, should now be his closest friend and confidant.

[108] Verres did at least hold a trial for the men, selecting as prosecutor a certain Naevius Turpio, a man who had been convicted of assault during the governorship of Gaius Sacerdos.* He was a man well placed to carry out Verres' criminal intentions, having been employed by him as his agent and go-between in the collection of tithes, in capital trials, and in every kind of false accusation.

The parents and relatives of the poor young men travelled to Syracuse, stunned by the sudden news of the disaster which they were facing. They saw their sons in chains, bearing on their necks and shoulders the price they were paying for Verres' cupidity. They came to court, spoke up for them, shouted in their defence, and appealed to your sense of fairness—something which did not exist and never had. One of the fathers was Dexo of Tyndaris, a highly respectable gentleman, and a man whose hospitality you had enjoyed. You had stayed in his house and addressed him as your host. When you saw this venerable man prostrate with grief, were his tears, his age, and the claims and entitlements of hospitality not enough to pull you back from crime to at least some sense of human decency? [109] But why do I mention the claims of hospitality in connection with this bestial monster? Sthenius of Thermae* was another of his hosts, and Verres, taking advantage of his position as his guest, emptied his house and stripped it bare, had him prosecuted in his absence, and condemned him to death without a defence. So shall we now appeal to such a man on the basis of the claims and duties of hospitality? And are we dealing with a cruel man or with a monstrous, savage beast? The tears of a father over the danger faced by his innocent son had no effect on you. Although you had a father of your own back in Rome, and had your own son with you in Sicily, did the presence of your son not make you think of how much parents love their children, and did your father's absence not remind you of the affection that fathers feel? [110] Dexo's son Aristeus, your host, was in chains. Why was that? 'He had betrayed the fleet.' For what reward? 'All right then, he was a deserter.' But was Cleomenes not a deserter? 'But Aristeus had shown himself a coward.' On the contrary, you had previously decorated him for bravery. 'But he exempted the sailors under his command.' No, in every case it was you who took bribes for the exemptions.

Another of the fathers, from a different part of Sicily, was Eubulida of Herbita, a distinguished and high-ranking man in his own town. Because he had criticized Cleomenes while defending his son, he had been left almost without a thing. What could anyone say in their defence? 'You are not allowed to mention Cleomenes.' But the case requires it. 'You will die if you say his name.' (Verres never used half measures when making threats.) But there were no oarsmen. 'Are you accusing the governor? Break his neck.' If it is not permitted to mention either the governor or the governor's rival in love, when the case depends entirely on these two men, then what is one supposed to do?

[111] Heraclius of Segesta, a high-ranking man of good family in his own town, was also among the men accused. Listen, members of the jury, as your humanity demands: you will hear of great harm and injury done to our allies. Heraclius' position was that he did not sail on that occasion because he had a serious eye infection, and had official permission to stay behind in Syracuse on sick leave. So there was no question of him betraying the fleet or running away in terror or deserting. If he had done this, he would have been punished at the point when the fleet left Syracuse. Nevertheless, he was treated exactly as if he had been caught committing a crime red-handed—even though no pretext could be found for bringing even a false charge against him.

[112] One of the captains was a man from Heraclea called Furius (yes, some of these people do have Latin names!).* He was someone whose distinction and high rank extended beyond his home town during his lifetime, and after his death were celebrated throughout the whole of Sicily. He was so brave that he did not just freely criticize Verres (since he saw that he was going to die anyway, he reckoned that nothing he did could put him in any worse danger): no, with death coming to him whatever happened, and with his weeping mother sitting beside him in the prison day and night, he wrote down his own defence. There is no one in Sicily today who

does not have a copy of that speech, who does not read it, and who is not constantly reminded by it of your wickedness and cruelty. In it he sets down how many sailors his town assigned him, how many he exempted and for how much each, and how many he ended up with; and he gives the same information for each of the other ships as well. When he went on to recite these figures in your presence, he was beaten in the face with rods. With death imminent, he could easily endure the physical pain. But he did shout out a remark that he has also left us in the written speech, that it was a shameful crime that the kisses of an adulterous woman should have had more success in persuading you to spare Cleomenes than the tears of a mother did in persuading you to spare his own life.

[113] I notice that, as he was about to die, he also said something relating to you, gentlemen—and which, assuming that the Roman people are correct in their opinion of you, he was not wrong in declaring. What he said was that it was impossible for Verres to blot out his crimes by killing witnesses; that wise jurors would regard him, Furius, as a more impressive witness if he testified from the dead than if he were produced alive in court; and that if he were alive, he would be a witness only to Verres' greed, but that, being dead, he can testify to his wickedness, criminality, and brutality. There are more fine words too: when your case came to trial, Verres, it would not only be crowds of witnesses that would appear in court, but the avenging spirits of the innocent and the Furies that punish crime would come up from the underworld. Also: he thought his own fate not so terrible because he had already grown used to the sight of the sharp edge of your axes, and the face and hands of Sextius your executioner, whenever Roman citizens, in the community of Roman citizens in that city, were beheaded on your orders. [114] I will not go on, gentlemen. But let me just point out that Furius made full use of the freedom which you have allowed our allies to have, while receiving the cruellest punishment that can be inflicted on the humblest slave.

Verres convicted all of them on the advice of his council. However, although the issue was such an important one and so many people were affected, he did not send for his quaestor Titus Vettius* to ask for his advice, nor did he consult his legate the excellent Publius Cervius* (in fact Cervius was the first person that Verres rejected as a juror, and he rejected him precisely because he had been his legate in

Sicily). So it was on the advice of his council that he condemned
them all—that is, on the advice of robbers.

[115] The Sicilians are our oldest and most loyal allies; our ancestors rewarded them with numerous privileges. When they heard the
verdict, they were deeply disturbed, and feared for their own lives
and property. They were outraged that the mildness and gentleness
of our rule had turned into such monstrous cruelty and inhumanity,
that so many people who had done nothing wrong should have been
convicted at the same time, and that a corrupt governor should seek
to justify his thefts by shamefully killing innocent men.

You could be forgiven, members of the jury, for supposing that, as
far as the defendant's corruption, madness, and savagery are concerned, that is all there is. That would be a reasonable enough
assumption. After all, if he were to compete in wickedness with
others, he would leave them all far behind. [116] But he also com-
petes with himself: he is constantly trying to outdo his worst crime
to date with some new criminal act. I said that Phalacrus of Centuripae was spared by Cleomenes, because Cleomenes had been sailing
in his quadrireme. The young man was extremely anxious, because
he saw that his own case was the same as that of the innocent men
who had been convicted. So Timarchides went to him and reassured
him that he was not in danger of being executed; but he advised him
to take care not to get flogged. I will spare you the details; you have
heard Phalacrus himself testify that this frightened him into paying
money to Timarchides,* [117] But in the case of Verres, these are
trivial charges. A ship's captain from a highly distinguished city paid
a bribe because he was afraid of being flogged: it is human nature.
Someone else pays a bribe to escape conviction: it happens. The
Roman people does not want Verres to be prosecuted on conventional charges. They demand new ones, they long for unprecedented
ones: in their eyes, this trial is not about a governor of Sicily, but
about an unspeakable tyrant.

The condemned men were shut up inside the prison.* Punishment
was prescribed for them, but it was also inflicted on the captains'
unhappy parents, who were forbidden access to their sons, and forbidden to bring their children food and clothes. [118] The fathers
who you see here in court lay in the doorway; the wretched mothers
spent the whole night at the prison entrance, denied the slightest
glimpse of their children, begging for nothing except to be allowed

to take up on their lips their sons' last breath. The prison warder stood by, the governor's executioner, the bringer of death and terror to allies and citizens alike—the lictor Sextius, to whom every shriek and cry of pain was worth a specific sum of money. 'To visit him, it will cost you so much; to bring food inside, so much.' Nobody refused. 'So what will you give me to kill your son with only one blow of my axe? Not to let him suffer too long, not to strike him too many times, not to let him feel the pain as his life is taken away?' Money was paid to the lictor even for this. [119] What great, intolerable suffering! What grievous, bitter bad luck! Parents were forced to pay not for their children's lives, but for the quickness of their deaths. And even the young men themselves talked to Sextius about the blow and that one single strike; and their final request to their parents was that they give the lictor what he wanted for minimizing the agony they were about to undergo.

Many terrible sufferings were inflicted on those parents and relatives, many—but the death of their sons is surely the last. No, it is not going to be. But how can cruelty go any further? A way will be found. For when the men have been beheaded and killed, their bodies will be thrown to the beasts. And if this distresses their parents, they can always pay for the privilege of burial. [120] You have heard Onasus of Segesta, a gentleman of the highest rank, testify that he paid Timarchides to be allowed to bury one of the captains, Heraclius. So you cannot say, 'fathers who have lost their sons are naturally going to come to court in a state of anger', because this is a leading man in his city and a man of exceptionally high rank, and he is not talking about his son. And can you name anyone at Syracuse at that time who has not heard or does not know that these deals with Timarchides for permission to bury the captains' bodies were actually struck with the men themselves before they were killed? Do you deny that they spoke openly to Timarchides about this, that they all called all their loved ones in, that they openly made formal arrangements for their funerals while they were still alive?

[121] When this business had all been settled and concluded, the men were led from the prison and tied to the post. Who on that occasion was so iron-hearted, who was so inhuman—except you alone—as not to be deeply moved by their youth, their noble birth, and their tragic situation? Who did not shed tears? Who did not think that the disaster which had befallen those men was not

something which affected them alone, but represented a danger that threatened everyone? They were beheaded. Amid everyone's cries of grief, you rejoiced and triumphed, overjoyed that the witnesses to your greed had been removed.

But you were wrong, Verres, very wrong to think that you could wash away the stains of your thefts and scandals with the blood of innocent allies. You must have been out of your mind to think that you could heal the wounds caused by your avarice by using cruelty as your medicine. For although those witnesses to your crimes are indeed dead, their nearest and dearest have not forgotten them—or you. And some of the captains are in fact still alive, and are here in court. Destiny, I believe, has kept them back to avenge their innocent comrades at this trial. [122] Phylarchus of Haluntium is here. He refused to flee with Cleomenes, and so was overcome by the pirates and taken prisoner. That disaster proved to be his salvation: had he not been taken by the pirates, he would have fallen to this brigand instead. He has testified to us about the exemption of the sailors, their lack of food, and how Cleomenes fled. Phalacrus of Centuripae is also present, a member of a distinguished family from a distinguished city. He tells the same story, and agrees with Phylarchus in every particular.

[123] Immortal gods! How do you feel after hearing all of this, members of the jury? How have you reacted to it? Am I being silly about it all, and being excessively affected by the terrible disaster and misery which has overwhelmed our allies? Or do you feel the same distress as I do at the dreadful agony of people who are innocent, and at the grief of their parents? For my part, when I tell you that a man from Herbita or a man from Heraclea has been beheaded, I see before my eyes the shameful injustice of what they suffered. They were citizens of those communities; they grew up in the fields from which, by their own effort and hard work, a vast quantity of grain is contributed every year to feed the Roman populace. Their parents brought them up and educated them to believe in our rule and our sense of justice. And now they have fallen victim to the monstrous barbarity of Gaius Verres and his deadly axe.

[124] Whenever that captain from Tyndaris, whenever the one from Segesta comes into my mind, I think both of the privileges that those cities have enjoyed in the past and the services that they have rendered us. These are cities that Publius Africanus* thought should

be adorned with spoils taken from the enemy; but now Gaius Verres has not only stripped them of those adornments, but has even, in an act of supreme wickedness, deprived them of their noblest sons. Listen to what the people of Tyndaris would freely declare: 'We are counted among the seventeen peoples of Sicily.* We consistently maintained our ties of friendship and loyalty with the Roman people throughout all the Punic and Sicilian Wars. We have always provided the Roman people with every requisite of war and every perquisite of peace.' But a fat lot of good their services did them while they were under the authority and power of Verres! [125] Once upon a time Scipio led your sailors* against Carthage; but now Cleomenes leads your ship—almost empty—against the pirates. Africanus shared with you the spoils of war and the rewards of victory; but now, because of Verres, you are despoiled, your ship is taken away by the pirates, and you are yourselves classed as enemies.

And what about Segesta's kinship with us*—something not merely recorded in books and recalled in speech, but validated and confirmed by that city's many services to us? I ask you, what benefits did this tie bring while Verres was governor? Clearly, gentlemen, the only privilege Segesta enjoyed was to have its noblest young citizen torn from the bosom of his country and handed over to Verres' executioner Sextius. Our ancestors gave this state extensive, fertile lands together with immunity from taxation. But with you its kinship with Rome, its loyalty, its antiquity, and its standing did not even secure for it the privilege of having its prayer answered when it appealed to prevent the bloody death of one honourable, innocent citizen.

[126] Where can our allies take refuge? To whom can they appeal? What hope can they have that their lives will be worth living, if you abandon them? Should they go to the senate? What for? To have Verres punished? But that would not be customary: that is not the senate's function. Should they take refuge with the Roman people? The people would have an answer ready: they would say that they have passed a law for the allies and that they have appointed you as its guardians and enforcers. So this is the only place where the allies can take refuge, this is their safe harbour, this is their citadel, and this is their sanctuary.

But they are not taking refuge here, as in the past, to secure restitution of their property. They are not asking for their silver, their gold, their textiles, and their slaves, nor for the works of art which have been removed from cities and temples. Ignorant as they are, they are afraid that the Roman people have come to condone such thefts and are happy to see them continue. For many years now we have put up with this and said nothing, despite seeing all the wealth of all the nations flow into the hands of a very few people. And the fact that none of those people hides what he has done or takes any trouble to conceal his greed only increases our apparent toleration and acceptance of what is going on. |127] In this beautiful city of ours, so well stocked with works of art, do you think there is a single statue, a single painting that was not taken from defeated enemies and brought here? On the other hand, the country houses of those men I am referring to are decorated and indeed stuffed with large quantities of beautiful treasures which have been looted from our most steadfast allies. Where do you imagine the wealth of all those foreign countries has gone, countries that are now so poor, when you observe that all Athens, Pergamum, Cyzicus, Miletus, Chios, Samos, and indeed all Asia, Achaea, Greece, and Sicily are now crammed inside a tiny number of country houses?

But, as I say, your allies are giving all this up and letting it go, gentlemen. By their services and loyalty towards us, they took steps to prevent their being officially plundered by the Roman people as a whole. When they found themselves unable to resist the private greed of only a small number of individuals, they were still able somehow to supply the loot required. But they have now reached the point where they have not only no means of resisting, but no means of satisfying the demand. So they let their property go. The name of this court is the court for the restitution of monies, but they do not ask for theirs to be returned: they give it up. Dressed in the clothes you now see them in, they take refuge before you. [128] Look, gentlemen, look at the filth and rags of our allies!*

Sthenius of Thermae* is with us today: look at his hair and clothing. His home has been completely ransacked, but he does not breathe a word about your thefts. Instead, he seeks restoration of his own self—nothing more. Through your criminal greed, you have forced him out of his own country, a country in which he, by his great merits and public-spirited actions, was the leading citizen. Dexo whom you see here is not asking for the return of the public property of Tyndaris or for his own private property which you stole, but in his wretchedness he asks for his only son, his excellent and entirely innocent son. He does not want to take home money from the damages that you, Verres, will have to pay, but to take instead some consolation from your ruin for his son's bones and ashes. The aged Eubulida here has not undertaken such a long and difficult journey at the very end of his life in order to recover some part of his property; no, he has come to watch your conviction with those same eyes with which he saw the blood spurting from his son's neck.

[129] And if Lucius Metellus had allowed it, gentlemen, the dead men's mothers and sisters would be here too. One of them came to meet me as I was approaching Heraclea one night. She was accompanied by all the married women of the city carrying torches; she addressed me as her saviour, and named you as her executioner. Calling out her son's name, the poor woman threw herself at my feet, as if I had the power to bring him back from the dead. In the other cities I visited the older women did exactly the same, as did the dead men's young children; and both of these alike, young and old, made appeals to my efforts and energy, and to your honour and pity.

[130] And so it is, gentlemen, that Sicily has come to me with this complaint, the one it feels most strongly about; and I took it up for them out of compassion, not through any hope of glory. My motive was simply to prevent false convictions, the prison, chains, whips, axes, the torture of the allies, the blood of the innocent, and even the pallid corpses of the dead and the grief of parents and loved ones becoming a source of financial gain to our magistrates. If, through your integrity and your sense of honour, gentlemen, I succeed in securing the defendant's conviction and so freeing Sicily from its fear of this happening again, I will conclude that I have done enough to satisfy my own sense of duty and the wishes of those who asked me to take on this case.

[131] So if, Verres, you find someone prepared to try to defend you on this charge about the fleet, he must do so without making use of the standard arguments which do not apply in this case. He must not say that I am blaming you for something that was simply a matter of bad luck, that I am misrepresenting a disaster as a criminal act, and that I am making you responsible for the loss of the fleet when there have in fact been many brave men in times past who, as a result of the uncertain hazards of war to which all are subject, have suffered reverses on both land and sea. The crimes I am accusing you of have nothing to do with luck; you have no justification for bringing

up reverses suffered by other people; you have no justification for citing instances of people's luck being wrecked. What I allege is that the ships were empty; that the sailors and oarsmen had been exempted; that those who remained were living on palm stalks; that a Sicilian was put in command of the fleet of the Roman people, and a Syracusan in command of our long-standing friends and allies; and that you spent all that time and all the days leading up to it getting drunk on the shore with girls. Moreover, I have witnesses to back up every one of these facts.

[132] So you cannot really complain, can you, that I am kicking you when you are down, preventing you taking refuge in the excuse of bad luck, and reproaching and accusing you for being a victim of the chances of war? As a matter of fact, the people who object to being blamed for their bad luck are generally those who have committed themselves to fortune in the first place, who have experienced its hazards and about-turns. In the disaster that you suffered, on the other hand, luck played no part. It is in battle, not at dinner, that men put the fortune of war to the test. In your own disaster, it is not Mars but Venus whose indiscriminate favours may be said to have determined the outcome.* But if it is unfair that bad luck should be made a charge against you, why did you not allow the excuse of bad luck in the case of those innocent men you executed?

[133] You should also forgo the argument that I am attacking you because you made use of the axe, and that I am using that to stir up prejudice against you: our ancestors, you will point out, also used the axe as a means of execution. My charge does not depend on your method of execution. I am not claiming that no one should ever be beheaded, nor am I arguing that fear should play no part in military discipline, or that commanders should not exercise severity, or that punishment should not be carried out when a crime has been committed. I fully admit that stern, harsh punishments have often been inflicted quite legitimately, and not just on the allies, but on our own citizens and soldiers too. So please do not take this line of argument.

The case I am making is that the blame lay fairly and squarely with you, not with the captains, and that you took money for exempting sailors and oarsmen. The captains who are still alive say that this is the case, as does the federate state of Netum in an official statement, as does Amestratus, as does Herbita, as do Henna, Agyrium, and Tyndaris, again in official statements, and as finally does your own witness, admiral, rival in love, and host Cleomenes, who states that he went ashore to pick up soldiers from the land garrison at Pachynum, to put them in the ships—something he would certainly not have done if his ships had had their full complement, since a fully manned and equipped ship does not have space for even one extra man, let alone a large number. [134] I further allege that such sailors as were on the ships were weak and almost dead from hunger and a complete lack of provisions. I allege either that none of the captains should be held responsible for this state of affairs; or that if blame is to be attributed to one of them, it should be attributed to the one who had the biggest and best ship, the most sailors, and the overall command; or that if they are all to be held responsible, Cleomenes should not have been made a spectator at their torture and execution. I also allege that at their actual execution, it was wrong to charge a fee for their weeping relatives, a fee for the wounds and blows they suffered, and a fee for their deaths and burial.

[135] If you wish, therefore, to make a reply to these charges, you will have to argue as follows: that the fleet had its full complement and was properly equipped; that none of the sailors was absent; that no oar was left dangling for lack of an oarsman; that there was a full supply of grain on board; that the captains are lying, that all these very important states are lying, and even that the whole of Sicily is lying; that Cleomenes was falsely incriminating you when he said that he had gone ashore to pick up soldiers at Pachynum; that the men were short of courage, not of supplies; that they had abandoned and deserted Cleomenes while he was fighting bravely; and that nobody took money for burials. If you do maintain all this, you will be proved wrong; but if you say anything different, it will be impossible for you to refute my allegations.

[136] So will you have the effrontery, at this stage in the proceedings, to say, 'This juror is a friend of mine, that one is a friend of my father's'? Surely, when charged with crimes like these, the more closely someone is connected with you, the more ashamed you ought to be in his presence? 'He is a friend of my father's.' If your father himself were a juror—perish the thought!—what could he do? He would have to say this to you: 'You, while governor of a province of the Roman people and in charge of a war at sea, exempted Messana for three years from providing the ship it was obliged to provide under its treaty. For you the people of Messana built, at their own

public expense, an enormous cargo ship for your private use. You used the fleet as a pretext for extorting money from the Sicilian states. You took bribes to exempt oarsmen. You spirited away the pirate captain from public view, when a pirate ship was captured by your quaestor and legate. You beheaded people who said they were Roman citizens and were widely known to be so. You had the temerity to remove pirates to your own house and produce a pirate captain from your house at this trial. [137] You, at a time of fear and danger to the most loyal allies and the most honourable Roman citizens of an exceptionally fine province, spent day after day lounging on the shore having parties. You throughout that time were never to be found at home or seen in the forum. You brought the wives of our friends and allies to those parties of yours. You encouraged your young son—my grandson—to mix among those women, so that at the most unstable and critical stage of his life his own father might provide him with models of immorality to imitate. You, a Roman governor, were seen in your province wearing a tunic and a purple Greek cloak. You, for reasons of passion and lust, took the naval command away from the legate of the Roman people and gave it to a Syracusan. Your sailors, in Sicily of all places, went without crops and grain. Your frivolity and greed caused the fleet of the Roman people to be captured by the pirates and burnt; [138] although in the whole history of Syracuse no enemy had ever penetrated the harbour, in your governorship the pirates for the first time did exactly that. Nor did you make the slightest attempt to conceal these many disgraceful actions, either by covering them up yourself or by encouraging others to stop talking about them and forget them. On the contrary, you snatched the ships' captains from the embrace of their parents—people whose guest you had been—and, without any good reason, tortured them to death. Those parents in their grief and tears appealed to you in my name, but you showed no trace of compassion: to you the blood of innocent men was not merely a source of pleasure, but a source of profit!' If your own father said that to you, would you be able to ask his pardon, would you be able to beg him to forgive you?

[139] I have now done enough to satisfy the people of Sicily, enough to discharge the obligations arising out of my friendship with them, enough to fulfil the promises and undertakings I made to them. The remaining part of my case, members of the jury, is not

something I have only just taken on, but something that has always existed deep inside me: it has not been brought to my attention, but instead has long been implanted in and engraved upon my heart and soul. My case is no longer to do with the well-being of our allies, but with the life and blood of Roman citizens—that is, of every one of us. Do not expect to hear arguments from me, gentlemen, that imply that there is an element of doubt about the matter: what I am going to tell you is so infamous that I could call on the whole of Sicily to witness its truth.

A type of insanity, closely linked to recklessness and criminality, overwhelmed the defendant's unbridled spirit and his brutal nature with such extreme madness that he never hesitated to inflict on Roman citizens, in full view of the Roman citizens of the province, punishments otherwise reserved exclusively for convicted slaves. [140] Need I remind you how many people he beat with rods? I will put it in a nutshell, gentlemen: while the defendant was governor, no distinction whatever was made between citizens and non-citizens; and in due course lictors routinely laid hands on Roman citizens without even waiting for the governor's say-so.

Surely you cannot deny, Verres, that amidst an extremely large gathering of Roman citizens in the forum at Lilybaeum, Gaius Servilius, a Roman citizen from Panhormus and a businessman of long standing, was beaten with rods and whips in front of the platform where you were sitting until he fell to the ground at your feet? Go on and deny this, if you can. Everyone at Lilybaeum saw it, and everyone in Sicily heard of its happening. I declare that a Roman citizen fell to the ground before your very eyes from the blows inflicted by your lictors. [141] And for what reason? Immortal gods! Even in asking such a question I am undermining the common interests and rights of all Roman citizens, as if there could be any legitimate reason for such a thing being done to a Roman citizen. Even so, I ask what the reason was in Servilius' case. Please forgive me, gentlemen, this once; in other cases I will not spend much time looking for the reasons.

Anyway, the reason was that Servilius expressed rather too free an opinion of the defendant's dishonesty and wickedness. As soon as this was reported to Verres, he ordered Servilius to give surety for his appearance at Lilybaeum to answer a charge brought by a slave of Venus.* Servilius did as he was told, and in due course presented himself at Lilybaeum. But no one turned up to bring any action against him, civil or criminal. At this point Verres started putting pressure on him to accept a challenge from one of his lictors to demonstrate that he, Servilius, 'was not making a profit by theft'. The sum was to be set at two thousand sesterces, and Verres said that he would supply arbitrators from among his own staff. Servilius refused to accept the challenge and complained that a capital court with biased jurors was being set up to try him, when no prosecutor had actually come forward to accuse him of anything. [142] While he was making this protest, Verres' six lictors surrounded him—big, strong men with an extensive record of attacking people and beating them up—and started hitting him violently with their rods. Then the head lictor Sextius, whom I have had occasion to mention several times already, began brutally striking the poor Servilius in the eyes with the butt-end of his rod. His eyes and face streaming with blood, Servilius fell to the ground, and as he lay there the lictors carried on hitting him in the ribs, until he eventually agreed to accept the challenge. Having been reduced to that state, he was then carried off as if dead, and shortly afterwards he did in fact die. Verres, being a devotee of Venus and himself a personage of grace and charm, took a silver Cupid from the dead man's property and deposited it in the temple of Venus. This, then, was how he misused the property of others, to fulfil the nocturnal vows which his lusts had prompted him to undertake.

[143] But why should I speak of all the other punishments inflicted on Roman citizens individually, rather than treat them collectively and comprehensively? Take the famous prison at Syracuse, constructed by the cruel tyrant Dionysius:* under Verres' governorship this became the permanent home of Roman citizens. Whenever Verres was irritated by the sight or thought of any one of them, that person was immediately cast into the quarries. I can see, gentlemen, that you all find this outrageous, and I noticed that you showed the same reaction when the witnesses were testifying to these facts in the first hearing. You believe, naturally, that it is not only here in Rome that people should retain their right to freedom, where there are tribunes of the plebs, where there are the other magistrates, where there is a forum filled with lawcourts, where the senate's authority is felt, and where the Roman people are present in large numbers to express their opinion. No, you believe that it makes no difference in

which country and among what people the rights of Roman citizens are violated: wherever this happens, it affects the freedom and standing of all citizens equally.

[144] Did you, Verres, have the temerity to incarcerate such a large number of Roman citizens in a place used for the imprisonment of foreign criminals and malefactors, and of pirates and enemies of Rome? Did you never give a thought to the court which would try you, to the public meetings which would denounce you, and to this great mass of people which now looks at you with absolute hostility and hatred? Did the dignity of the Roman people back in Rome, did the sight of this vast multitude here today never enter your mind or present itself before your eyes? Did you imagine you would never have to return to face these people, never have to re-enter the forum of the Roman people, never have to submit to the laws and the courts?

[145] But what lay at the root of that lust for cruelty, what was the motive for his committing so many crimes? Members of the jury, it was nothing but an unprecedented, unique programme of looting. Like those people we have read about in the poets,* who are said to have occupied bays on the coast or stationed themselves on promontories or precipitous cliffs in order to kill any sailors who were forced to put in there in their ships, so Verres lay in wait in every part of Sicily and threatened every sea. Whenever a ship arrived from Asia or Syria, from Tyre or Alexandria, it was immediately impounded by his guards and spies, men hand-picked for the purpose. The merchants were all cast into the quarries, and the goods and cargo were carted off to the governor's residence. After a long lapse of time Sicily had again become the haunt not of a second Dionysius or Phalaris*—for the island has in fact produced many cruel tyrants— but of an entirely new kind of monster, although one of the same bestiality as those who are said to have occupied the area in olden times. [146] In fact I do not think that either Charybdis or Scylla* was so dangerous to sailors in that strait as he was: he was the more dangerous because he had surrounded himself with dogs that were considerably more numerous and fierce than theirs. He was indeed a second Cyclops*—but much more horrific, because he controlled the whole of Sicily, whereas the Cyclops is only said to have dominated Mount Etna and the surrounding region.

But what, gentlemen, was the reason Verres himself put forward for his outrageous cruelty? The same reason that his defence team will offer shortly. Whenever anyone arrived in Sicily with a significant quantity of goods, he declared that they were soldiers in the service of Sertorius that had fled from Dianium.* These new arrivals then sought to avert the danger in which they found themselves by laying out their wares—Tyrian purple, incense, perfumes, linen, precious stones, pearls, Greek wines, slaves from Asia—so that people would see from these items where it was that they had come from. But the men did not foresee that the very goods which they supposed would demonstrate their innocence would actually be the cause of their destruction. For Verres announced that they had come by this property as a result of their friendship with the pirates, and he ordered the men to be cast into the quarries. He took particular care, however, to preserve their ships and cargoes.

[147] As a result of this practice, the prison was soon full of merchants; and then there followed what you have already heard the exceptionally distinguished Roman equestrian Lucius Suettius* testify to, and what you will hear others testify to also. In that prison, Roman citizens had their necks broken—an unspeakable crime. And in their case the traditional cry, 'I am a Roman citizen'—an appeal which has many times brought assistance and release to many people when among barbarians in the furthest corners of the earth—served only to bring forward these men's punishment, and to lead to a more agonizing death.

So, Verres, how are you planning to reply to this? Surely you cannot argue that I am lying, that I have made any of it up, that I am exaggerating what happened? Surely you will not dare to suggest to your advocates here that they argue on these lines? Go on, please at least let me have the copy of the records of Syracuse which he is hugging so tightly, which he supposes has been written to suit his purposes. Let me have the prison record which has been so carefully composed, and which shows the date on which each prisoner was taken into custody, and the date on which he died or was executed.

(*The records of Syracuse are read to the court.*)

[148] You see how Roman citizens were herded into the quarries in groups, you see how your own fellow-citizens were stacked up *en masse* in that degrading place. Now see if there is any shred of evidence that any of them ever left it. There is none. Did they all, then, die of natural causes? Even if that were a possible line of

defence,* it would strain the bounds of credibility too far. But in those very records there occurs a word which this blinkered barbarian was incapable of noticing, or of understanding had he noticed it. 'Edikaiōthēsan,' it says, an expression used in Sicily to mean 'punished by execution'.*

[149] If any king, if any foreign state, if any savage tribe had acted in this way towards Roman citizens, surely we would be taking official action to punish them, surely we would be declaring war on them? Could we really let such damage and such an insult to the honour of Rome go unpunished and unavenged? How many major wars do you think our ancestors undertook merely because word had reached them that Roman citizens had been hurt, ship-owners arrested, or merchants robbed? But I am not now complaining that these men were arrested; nor do I regard it as intolerable that they were robbed. My charge is that, after their ships, slaves, and goods had been taken from them, merchants were put in chains, and, while in chains, despite being Roman citizens, they were killed. [150] Now if I were discussing the dreadful executions of all those Roman citizens not in front of a large crowd of Roman citizens, nor before the country's most senior senators, nor in the forum of the Roman people, but in front of an audience of Scythians, the hearts even of barbarians such as those could not fail to be deeply moved. For this empire of ours is so glorious and the very name of 'Roman' carries such tremendous prestige among every nation on earth that it seems wrong that anyone at all should be allowed to treat our own people with that sort of cruelty.

How can I now think you have any means of escape, any place of refuge available to you, when I see you entwined by these strict jurors and completely netted* by this crowd of Roman citizens? [151] But if, by Hercules, you manage to free yourself from my snare and somehow extricate yourself by some strategem—something I do not consider remotely possible—then you will only stumble into an even larger net, and then I from a more commanding position* will inevitably dispatch you and cut you to pieces.

But suppose I were willing to allow him the plea he will make in his own defence. That plea, which is false, ought to be no less damaging to him than my accusation, which is true. So what is this plea he will make? It is this: that the people he intercepted and punished were fugitives from Spain.* So who gave you permission to punish them? By what right did you do so? Who else acted in the same way as you? What was the legal basis for your action? [152] We see the forum and the public halls full of that type of men,* and are not disturbed by the sight. For when our civil dissension or collective madness or bad luck or national calamity (whatever you choose to call it) comes to an end, we do not regard as intolerable an outcome in which those citizens who have survived are allowed to live on unharmed. But Verres (a man who in his earlier career himself betrayed a consul, changed sides when quaestor, and embezzled public money)* regarded himself as such an authority on matters of public policy that he would have inflicted a painful and cruel death on all such people—men whom the senate, the Roman people, and every magistrate had permitted to appear in the forum, to vote, to reside in Rome, and to take part in political life—if they had had the bad luck to end up in any part of Sicily.*

[153] After Perperna* had been killed, a large number of soldiers who had fought for Sertorius threw themselves on the mercy of the illustrious and valiant Gnaeus Pompeius. And of these, was there any that Pompeius did not do his very best to keep safe and unharmed? Was there any fellow-citizen who appealed for clemency to whom that undefeated right hand did not extend its protection and offer hope of being spared? Well? When he, a man whom they had fought against in battle, granted them a safe haven, did you, who by constrast had never done your country any important service, see fit to inflict on them torture and death instead? What a promising line of defence you have devised for yourself! By Hercules, I would prefer it if the case you were arguing were proved to the jury and the Roman people to be true, rather than the case I am alleging. I would prefer it, I tell you, if you were believed to be implacably hostile to that type of men* rather than to merchants and ship-owners. For my argument merely proves you to have been over-greedy; your own defence, on the other hand, convicts you of a type of monstrous frenzy, of unprecedented cruelty, and virtually of a new proscription.*

[154] But it is not open to me, gentlemen, to make use of this defence of Verres' for my own purposes; it is not open to me.* This is because the whole of Puteoli* is here in court. Merchants, wealthy and honourable men, have come to the court in large numbers to tell you that their business partners or their freedmen or their fellow freedmen were stripped of their property and cast into prison, and

that some of them were killed in prison and others taken out and beheaded. See now how fairly I am going to treat you. I am going to bring forward Publius Granius* as a witness. He will state that his freedmen were beheaded by you, and he will demand that you give him back his ship and his cargo. If you can refute his testimony, please do so. I declare that I will then abandon my witness, take your side, and give you my support. Prove that those men were with Sertorius, and that they fled from Dianium before putting in at Sicily. There is nothing that I would rather you proved—because no other crime that could be discovered or adduced would merit greater punishment.

[155] If you like, I will also bring back the Roman equestrian Lucius Flavius* to give evidence, since in the first hearing you did not cross-examine him or indeed any of the witnesses. (Your advocates keep saying what a wise innovation this was on your part. But everyone knows the real reason: you knew that you were guilty and that my witnesses were reliable.) Cross-examine Flavius, if you like. Ask him who Titus Herennius was—the man whom Flavius says was a banker at Lepcis,* and who, despite having more than a hundred Roman citizens of Syracuse who not only vouched for his being who he said he was but also wept and appealed to you on his behalf, was nevertheless beheaded in the presence of the city's entire population. I would like to see you refute this witness of mine, and demonstrate conclusively that Herennius was in reality a soldier from Sertorius' army.

[156] But what can we say about the many people who were led out for execution as if they were captured pirates, but had their heads covered up? Can you explain that unprecedented precaution, and your reason for devising it? Could it be that you were rattled by the outcry from Lucius Flavius and everyone else when Titus Herennius was executed? Or could it be that the considerable influence enjoyed by the highly respected and honourable Marcus Annius* had made you a little more cautious and circumspect? He was the one who recently stated in his evidence that it was no stranger from abroad that you had beheaded, but a Roman citizen who had been born in Syracuse, and who was personally known to all the other Roman citizens there. [157] After all these people's protests, when the executions had become widely known and widely objected to, Verres did not become more lenient in his punishments, but more

cautious: he started leading Roman citizens out to execution with their heads covered up. But he still wanted to kill them in public because, as I said earlier, the Roman citizens in Syracuse were keeping rather too careful a tally of the numbers of pirates accounted for.

So was this the deal for the Roman plebs while you were governor? Was this the end result of their trading that they were to look forward to? Was this the critical situation in which they lived their lives? Do merchants not have to undergo quite enough natural dangers already without having to worry about these extra risks at the hands of our magistrates in our own provinces? Sicily is our loyal neighbour, filled with steadfast allies and honourable citizens, and she has always been most happy to welcome any Roman citizen within her borders. So was it right that people who had sailed all the way from far-off Syria or Egypt, who had been treated with no little respect by barbarian peoples because they wore the toga, and who had escaped being ambushed by the pirates and wrecked by storms should have been beheaded on their arrival in Sicily—when they reckoned that at last they had come home?

[158] Now what am I to say, members of the jury, about Publius Gavius from the town of Consa?* What power of voice am I to use, what weighty words, what heart-rending emotion? I feel no lack of emotion on this subject; so my task will rather be to ensure that my voice and my words do justice to the affair, and to my feelings. The charge to which I now turn is so extraordinary that, when it was first brought to me, I did not think I would be able to make use of it. This was because, although I knew it to be completely true, I did not think anyone else would believe it. Yet I was impelled to take action by the tears of all the Roman citizens who do business in Sicily, and was urged on by the evidence presented to me by the honourable citizens of Vibo Valentia and all the people of Regium, as well as by numerous Roman equestrians who happened to be in Messana at the time. The result was that I used the minimum number of witnesses necessary in the first hearing to ensure that no one could be in any doubt as to what had happened.

[159] But what am I to do now? I have been speaking for hours on a single topic, Verres' appalling cruelty. I have nearly exhausted my entire stock of words appropriate to his crimes in saying what I have said so far, and I have done nothing to vary the nature of the charges and so keep you interested. How, then, am I to speak about such an

important affair? There is one way and one method only, I think: to put the facts out in the open. The matter is so serious that it does not require any eloquence of mine—or of anyone else, since I have none—to arouse your feelings of indignation.

[160] The man I am talking about, Gavius of Consa, was one of the Roman citizens whom Verres had cast into prison, and he had somehow managed to escape undetected from the quarries and make his way to Messana. At Messana, he was within sight of Italy, and could see the walls of Regium, a city of Roman citizens. He had escaped from his dark confinement and the fear of imminent death, and now, restored by the light of freedom and the fresh air of justice, he felt that he had returned to the land of the living. So he began to talk to people, and to complain that he, a Roman citizen, had been put in prison. He said that he was going straight to Rome, so as to be ready for Verres on his return there. The poor man did not realize that it made not the slightest bit of difference whether he said all this at Messana or in the governor's residence in front of Verres himself. For as I have already explained to you, Verres had specially chosen Messana to be his partner in crime, a holding area for his thefts, and an accomplice in all his wicked deeds. Gavius, therefore, was immediately brought before the chief magistrate of Messana, and as it happened Verres himself was visiting the city that very day. The case was put before him, that there was a Roman citizen who was complaining that he had been in the quarries at Syracuse; he had just been boarding ship, they said, uttering terrible threats against Verres, but they had hauled him back and kept him under guard, so that Verres could decide himself what he wanted to do with him.

[161] Verres thanked the men, and commended their diligence and loyalty towards himself. Then he strode into the forum, fired up with wickedness and rage. His eyes were ablaze, and cruelty shone out all over his face. Everyone was waiting to see what he would do, and how far he would go. Then, without warning, he ordered Gavius to be dragged out, stripped, and bound in the centre of the forum, and for the rods to be unleashed. Poor Gavius shouted out that he was a Roman citizen, and a citizen of Consa, and that he had served in the Roman army with the worthy Roman equestrian Lucius Raecius,* a businessman at Panhormus who could confirm to Verres everything that he was saying. But Verres replied that he had found out he was actually a spy sent to Sicily by the leaders of the

runaway slaves—although there was no informer who alleged this, nor any scrap of evidence to suggest this, nor the slightest suspicion in anyone's mind that this was the case. Then Verres gave the order for Gavius to be brutally flogged by several lictors at once.

[162] So a Roman citizen was beaten with rods, gentlemen, in the centre of the forum at Messana. And throughout his ordeal, amidst the excruciating crack of the rods on his body, no cry of pain, no sound was heard from the wretched Gavius, except these words: 'I am a Roman citizen.' He hoped, by asserting his citizenship in this way, to ward off the blows from his body and end his agony. However, he was not merely unsuccessful in averting the violence of his beating: as he repeated his appeals with increasing desperation and persisted in invoking his Roman citizenship, the cross—the cross, I tell you!—was made ready for that unlucky, miserable man, a man who had never even seen such an abomination in his life before.

[163] How sweet a thing is freedom! How superlative are our rights as citizens! How admirable the Porcian law and the Sempronian laws!* How keenly did the Roman plebs miss the tribunician power, now finally restored to them!* Have all these privileges now fallen so far into abeyance that a Roman citizen, in a province of the Roman people, and in a federate town, should be bound in the forum and beaten with rods by a magistrate who possessed his rods and axes only because the Roman people themselves had given them to him? And when fire, red-hot irons, and the other instruments of torture were then applied, if the man's heart rending appeals for mercy were not enough to make you desist, how could the tears and loud cries of the Roman citizens who were witnessing the scene fail to have an effect on you? And how could you have the temerity to crucify someone who told you that he was a Roman citizen?

I did not want to speak about this so passionately in the first hearing, gentlemen; I did not want to. The audience here were already quite stirred up enough against Verres, as you saw, by their feelings of indignation, hatred, and fear of the danger he represents. That was why I was careful not to go too far in what I said, and to make sure that my witness Gaius Numitorius,* an equestrian and gentleman of the first rank, did not do so either; and I was very happy that Glabrio acted as wisely as he did in abruptly adjourning the court before Numitorius had finished testifying. What Glabrio was afraid of was that the Roman people, worried that Verres might escape punishment by due legal process in your court, would take his punishment into their own hands and use violence against him. [164] But since it is now sufficiently clear to the Roman people just how weak your position actually is, and that you are going to be punished by this court whatever happens, I will argue my case as follows.

This Gavius, whom you say suddenly became a spy—I will prove that you cast him into the quarries at Syracuse. But I will not prove it only from the public records of Syracuse: if I did, you would claim that I had simply found someone with the name of Gavius in the records and then pretended that that was the same Gavius as the one who was executed. No, I will produce witnesses that you can choose from yourself: they will all say that the Gavius who was executed at Messana had been imprisoned by you in the quarries at Syracuse. I will also produce Gavius' friends and fellow-townsmen from Consa. They will now prove to you and to your jurors—to you too late, but to the jurors not too late—that the Publius Gavius you crucified was indeed a Roman citizen and a citizen of Consa, not a spy for the slaves.

[165] Once I have demonstrated all this—as I promise I shall do, fully, and to the satisfaction of even your closest supporters—I will then come to grips with the point that you yourself conceded to me; and I will declare myself content with that. When the other day you were seriously alarmed by the aggressive shouting of the Roman people and jumped to your feet, what was it, tell me, that you said? That the reason the man kept on shouting that he was a Roman citizen was that he was trying to get his punishment put off—but that he was in fact a spy. This proves that my witnesses are telling the truth. For is this not precisely what Gaius Numitorius is maintaining, and Marcus and Publius Cottius, high-ranking gentlemen from the district of Tauromenium, and Quintus Lucceius, a leading banker from Regium, and all the rest of them? For the witnesses that I have produced so far are not people who claimed that they knew who Gavius was, but people who claimed that they witnessed the crucifixion of a man who shouted that he was a Roman citizen. And this is exactly what you say yourself, Verres, when you admit that the man was shouting that he was a Roman citizen—but that not even the mention of citizenship was enough to make you hesitate for a moment, or induce you to grant a short delay to a brutal, horrifying punishment.

[166] This is the point I am holding on to. It is here, gentlemen, that I am making my stand. I am content just with this. I pass over and leave out all other points. His own admission will catch him out and dispatch him: there is no escaping it. You had no idea who he was, but thought he might be a spy. I do not ask what your reasons were for thinking that, but I accuse you from your very own words: he said he was a Roman citizen. If you, Verres, had been arrested in Persia or in remotest India, and were being led away to execution, what else would you be shouting except that you were a Roman citizen? Despite being a stranger among strangers, among barbarians, and among the most remote and far-off peoples, you would still have profited from your status as a Roman citizen, since that status is famous and respected the world over. Surely, then, that man— whoever he was—whom you were hurrying off to crucifixion, a man who was a complete stranger to you, ought to have been entitled, when he stated that he was a Roman citizen, to obtain from you, the governor, if not release, then at least a stay of execution, by his mention of citizenship and his appeal to it?

[167] Humble men of obscure birth sail the seas and travel to places they have never seen before. They are unknown there, and often do not have people with them who can vouch that they are who they say they are. Nevertheless, they have complete confidence in their status as Roman citizens, and they count on being safe not only in the presence of our magistrates, who are restrained by fear of the law and of public opinion, nor only in the presence of other Roman citizens, with whom they have language, rights, and a thousand other things in common: no, wherever they go, they believe that this status they enjoy will protect them. [168] Remove this belief, remove this protection for Roman citizens, decree that the words 'I am a Roman citizen' should confer no benefit, decree that governors and anyone else may inflict whatever punishments they like on those who state that they are Roman citizens and get away with it, simply because they do not know who they are: if you accept that defence, you will have debarred Roman citizens from every province, from every kingdom, from every free state, and in fact from every place in the world to which our people above all others have always hitherto had access.

And if Gavius mentioned the name of Lucius Raecius, a Roman equestrian who was in Sicily at the time, was it really so difficult to send a letter to Panhormus? You would have had the man safe in the custody of your friends at Messana, chained and locked away, until such time as Raecius arrived from Panhormus. If he identified the man, you could have imposed as a punishment something less than execution; and if he failed to identify him, then you could, if you liked, have established a precedent that a man who was not known to you and could not produce a reliable person to confirm his identity would be liable to crucifixion, even though he might be a Roman citizen.

[169] But why should I keep on about Gavius? That would imply that your hostility was directed specifically at him, whereas in reality you were the enemy of the whole class of Roman citizens, their title, and their rights. You were implacably opposed, I tell you, not to that particular individual, but to the freedom of everyone. If this is not the case, then why did you order the people of Messana, after they had erected the cross in their usual spot on the Pompeian Way behind the city, to move it to a site overlooking the strait? And why did you then add—something you cannot possibly deny, since you said it openly and many people heard you—that you had particularly chosen that site because you wanted the man, since he claimed to be a Roman citizen, to be able to see Italy from his cross, and make out his own home in the distance? That is the only cross, gentlemen, to have been erected in that place since Messana was founded.* Verres deliberately chose a spot within sight of Italy so that Gavius, while dying in dreadful agony, might appreciate how narrow the strait was that separated freedom from slavery, and that Italy might see her own son nailed to a cross and paying the most terrible and extreme punishment that can be inflicted on slaves.

[170] It is an outrage to shackle a Roman citizen, an abomination to flog him, and all but parricide to kill him—so what can I say about crucifying him? Words do not exist to describe so wicked an act. But Verres was not content to leave it even at that. 'Let him look out over his country,' he said. 'Let him die within sight of the laws and freedom.' It was not just Gavius, not just one ordinary man whom you subjected to torture and crucifixion, but the freedom common to all Roman citizens. But now consider the man's audacity! Surely he must have been disappointed that he could not erect that cross for Roman citizens right here in the forum, in the place of assembly, and on the rostra itself, seeing that the place in his province that he

selected was the one that was geographically nearest to Rome, and most similar to it in the amount of traffic it receives. He wanted that monument to his wickedness and criminality to stand within sight of Italy, at the entrance to Sicily, and above the strait where travellers by sea pass in each direction.

[171] Suppose I were to make these protests and lamentations not before Roman citizens, nor before people who are our country's friends, nor before people who have heard of the Roman people but never seen them; suppose I were speaking not to human beings at all but to animals; or, to go a step further, suppose I were in some empty desert and were addressing the rocks and boulders—then even such mute and inanimate objects could not fail to be moved by such awful, undeserved cruelty. But since the people I am in fact addressing are senators of the Roman people and the originators of our laws, courts, and civic rights, I ought to be confident that Verres will be judged to be the only Roman citizen who deserves to be crucified, and that no one else will be judged as meriting a fate of this kind.

[172] Just a few minutes ago we were all shedding tears over the dreadful, undeserved deaths of the ships' captains, and were upset— and rightly so—at the plight of our innocent allies. How, then, should we react when it is a case of our own flesh and blood? For the blood of all Roman citizens should be thought of as shared: not only truth, but considerations of our common safety demand this. All Roman citizens, those who are here in court and those elsewhere, now look to your strictness, appeal to your honour, and beg for your help. They are convinced that all their rights, privileges, and safe-guards, in short their very freedom hangs on the verdict you are about to deliver.

[173] From me, they already have what they wanted. But if the verdict goes the wrong way, they will get more from me, perhaps, than they are asking for. For suppose that Verres by some act of force manages to escape your strictness—something I am not worried about, gentlemen, nor consider remotely possible. But suppose I am mistaken, and he does escape: the Sicilians will complain that they have lost their case and will be unhappy about it, as indeed will I; but the Roman people, since they have given me the power of bringing cases before them,* will quickly, by 1 February at the latest, recover their rights by voting against Verres in an action brought by myself. If you want to know how this affects my reputation and career

prospects, gentlemen, it will do me no harm at all if Verres escapes from me in this court and then stands trial before the Roman people. Indeed, that type of prosecution carries prestige. For me, it would be an appropriate form of procedure, and a convenient one; as far as the people are concerned, it would be satisfying and agreeable. Now you may think that I have wanted to advance myself at the expense of this one man: that is not the case at all. But if he is acquitted, it is true that I will be in a position to advance myself at the expense of many, since it is impossible that he should be acquitted without many people breaking the law themselves.* But—by Hercules!—for your sake and that of the country, gentlemen, I would not want to see so serious a crime committed by this select jury. I would not want jurors that I myself have chosen and approved* walking around our city so tainted by their acquittal of Verres that they would look as though they were smeared not so much with wax as with mud.*

[174] For this reason, Hortensius, I would like to offer you, too, a piece of advice—if, that is, it is appropriate for a prosecutor to offer advice to a defence advocate. Look very carefully at what it is that you are doing and reflect upon it—where it is leading you, what sort of man you are defending, and by what means you are defending him. I do not want to limit in any way your scope for competing honestly with me in intelligence and oratorical ability. But if you think that you can manage this trial in private from outside the court, if you imagine that you can organize things by trickery, plotting, power, influence, or Verres' money, then I strongly advise you to abandon the idea. And as for the actions of that nature which Verres has already attempted and set in motion, which I have now tracked down and investigated, I advise you to put a stop to them and see that they go no further. Any misconduct on your part in this trial will place you in serious danger—more serious than you imagine.

[175] Of course, you may think that now you have held all your offices and been elected to the consulship, you no longer have to worry about what people will think of you. But believe me, it is just as difficult to hold onto those honours and favours which are conferred by the Roman people as it is to attain them in the first place. This country has put up with your and your friends' tyrannical domination of the courts* and of politics as long as it could manage, as long as it had to; it has put up with it. But on the day that the Roman people got their tribunes of the plebs back,* all of this power,

though you may not yet realize it, was taken away and stripped from
you. Now the eyes of the world are turned on each one of us, to
observe how honourably I prosecute, how honestly the jurors return
their verdicts, and how you go about your defence. [176] And with
each of us, if we deviate ever so slightly from the straight and narrow,
the result will not be that silent disapproval which we have hitherto
been content to ignore, but the strong, unequivocal censure of the
Roman people.

Verres is not a relation of yours, Quintus,* nor is he your friend. In
the past you have come up with various reasons to explain away your
excessive partiality in this or that trial, but none of them applies in
this case. When he was governing Sicily he used to say publicly that
he was doing what he was doing because he had confidence in you.
Now you need to take great care to prevent people concluding that
he was justified in that confidence. [177] As far as my own obligations are concerned, I am satisfied that even my worst critics will
accept that I have now discharged them. In the few hours that the
first hearing lasted, I secured Verres' conviction at the bar of public
opinion. What now remains to be judged is not my honour, since
that has been proved, nor Verres' conduct, since that has been
condemned: it is the jurors, and, to tell the truth, it is yourself.

But in what kind of context is that judgement going to take place?
This is a point which needs the most careful consideration, because
in politics, as in everything else, the mood and tenor of the times is a
factor of the utmost importance. The context, then, is one in which
the Roman people, as you must be aware, are looking for a different
class of men and a different order to sit on juries; indeed, the text of
a bill on new courts and juries has been published.* Now the person
who is really responsible for publishing this bill is not the man whose
name it bears. It is this defendant, this man I tell you, who is its true
author: by his hopes of acquittal, and his belief that you could be
bribed, he ensured that the bill came to be drafted and published.
[178] When this case began, the bill had not been published. When
he became alarmed by your evident strictness and gave every impression that he was not going to put up a defence at all, not a word was
said about any bill. But after he seemed to take heart and get his
hopes up, the bill was immediately published. Your integrity is a
strong argument against the necessity for this bill; but his unfounded
hopes and conspicuous arrogance argue greatly in its favour. At the

point we have now reached, if any member of the jury behaves at all improperly, one of two things will happen: either the Roman people will put that juror on trial* after having already voted that senators are not fit to be jurors; or the men who will try him will be the new jurors appointed under the new law to judge the old jurors whose administration of the courts caused such outrage.

[179] As for myself, is there anyone who needs me to tell them how far I ought to pursue this case? Will I be able to hold my tongue, Hortensius, will I be able to seem unconcerned—when our country has received so serious a wound, when a province has been ransacked, our allies persecuted, the immortal gods plundered, and Roman citizens tortured and killed—if the man who did all this, when I have prosecuted him, escapes unpunished? Will I be able either on leaving this court to lay down this great responsibility of mine, or continue to shoulder it and say nothing? Surely I must not let the matter rest? Surely I must bring it out into the open? Surely I must appeal to the Roman people's sense of honour? Surely I must summon to court and to the risks of a trial all those who have descended to such depths of criminality that they have either allowed themselves to be bribed or else have bribed the court themselves?

[180] Now someone may perhaps ask me, 'So are you really going to take on such an onerous task, and make an enemy of so many people?' Not—by Hercules!—with any particular enthusiasm, or even willingly. But I do not enjoy the same advantages as those who were born into noble families, on whom are conferred all the honours of the Roman people without them even having to get out of bed.* The terms and conditions of my political existence bear no similarity to theirs. I am reminded of the wise and observant Marcus Cato.* He saw that it was his ability, not his birth, that recommended him to the Roman people, and he wanted to be the founder and ancestor of a famous family of his own. But despite this, he still made enemies of the most powerful men of his day, and through his great efforts lived an extremely long and extremely glorious life. [181] And then what about Quintus Pompeius,* a man of low and obscure origin? He made many bitter enemies, did he not, while nevertheless obtaining the highest honours, as a result of his willingness to work hard and take risks? More recently we have seen Gaius Fimbria, Gaius Marius, and Gaius Coelius* making important enemies but nevertheless achieving by their hard work those same honours which

you have attained by living a life of amusement and inattention. This is the direction and path along which men like me have to proceed; we follow their line and example.

We are well aware of the degree to which certain nobles look on the talent and application of the new men with jealousy and detestation. If we take our eye off the ball for just one second, they are there to catch us out. If we lay ourselves open to any suspicion or charge, they will attack us without hesitation. We know that we have to be always on the alert, always hard at work. [182] We have enemies: let us face them. Work to do: let us crack on with it. We have more reason to be afraid of silent, hidden enemies than open and declared ones. Hardly any of the nobles looks kindly on the hard work we put in. It is impossible for us to secure their favour by any services that we might perform.* They are at variance with us in spirit and in sympathy, as if they were a race apart. So what harm can it do us if they are our enemies, when they regard you with hostility and jealousy even before you have done anything to offend them?

[183] I therefore hope, members of the jury, that once I have done what the Roman people expect of me, and have also discharged the obligation which my friends the Sicilians invited me to undertake, I will be able to make this prosecution my last. Nevertheless I have decided, if the confidence I have in you should turn out to be misplaced, to prosecute not just those chiefly responsible for bribing this court, but also those who share in the guilt by having accepted those bribes. Therefore, if there are any who intend to use their influence, their daring, or their cunning to corrupt this court in the present trial, they should prepare to do battle with me, and let the Roman people judge between us. And if they have found me to be sufficiently vigorous, sufficiently tenacious, and sufficiently watchful in prosecuting the man whom the Sicilians have given me as an enemy, they should reflect just how much more committed and fierce I shall be against all those whose enemy the security of the Roman people will have required me to become.

[184] Now hear me, Jupiter best and greatest, whose royal offering,* worthy of your beautiful temple, worthy of the Capitol and the citadel of all nations, worthy of its royal donors, made for you by kings, dedicated and promised to you—an offering which Verres, in an outrageously criminal act, wrenched from their royal hands; you whose holy and beautiful image* he removed from Syracuse;

hear me, Queen Juno, whose two holy and ancient shrines located on two islands of our allies, Melita and Samos,* in an act of similar criminality, he stripped of all their offerings and adornments;

hear me, Minerva, whom he robbed at two of your most famous and sacred temples—at Athens, where he took a large quantity of gold, and at Syracuse, where he took away everything except the roof and walls;*

[185] hear me, Latona and Apollo and Diana, whose shrine at Delos*—or rather, as people who respect the gods believe, their ancient seat and immortal home—he pillaged in a violent night-time burglary;

hear me again, Apollo, whom he removed from Chios;

hear me yet again, Diana, whom he robbed at Perga,* and whose holy image at Segesta, twice consecrated there, first by the devotion of the Segestans, and later by the victorious Publius Africanus,* he had taken down and carried away;

hear me, Mercury, whom Verres set up in the gymnasium of some man's private house, but whom Publius Africanus had specifically wished to be kept in the exercise-ground of the city of our allies, Tyndaris,* as the tutelary guardian of the young men of that place;

[186] hear me, Hercules, whom at Agrigentum in the dead of night, with a gang of slaves he had recruited and armed for the purpose, he attempted to remove from his base and carry away;*

hear me, holy mother of Ida,* whose sacred and revered temple at Engyium he left so completely despoiled that nothing is left there any longer, except for the name of Africanus* and the evidence of the sacrilege that was perpetrated—the victory memorials and temple adornments having been removed;

hear me, Castor and Pollux, located where the Roman people throng, who watch over and witness all that goes on in the forum—the great deliberations, the laws, and the courts—from whose temple he obtained profit and plunder* in the most scandalous fashion;

hear me, all you gods who, conveyed on carts, watch over the solemn assemblies of the games, whose route he had constructed and maintained not as a mark of respect, but for his own profit;*

[187] hear me, Ceres and Libera, whose rites, according to universal religious belief, rank far above others in grandeur and mystery;* by whom life and food, customs and laws, and gentleness and humanity are said to have originally been given to people and

communities, and spread among them; and whose observances, adopted and taken over from the Greeks, the Roman people celebrate with such public and private devotion that you would think that those rites had spread to Greece from Rome rather than to Rome from Greece: these were then so violated and polluted by this one man that the image of Ceres in her shrine at Catina, which it is sinful for all but women to touch or even look at, was wrenched from its position and carried away on this man's orders—not omitting to mention that other image of Ceres which he removed from its rightful home at Henna,* an image so realistic that when people saw it they thought that they were gazing either at the goddess herself, or at an image of her not made by human hand, but descended from the sky; [188] hear me again and again, I implore and call on you, most holy goddesses who inhabit the lakes and groves of Henna and who are protectors of the whole island of Sicily that has been entrusted to me to defend, and whose discovery of corn, made available to the entire world, has filled all peoples and nations with awe of your divinity;

and I implore and beseech all the other gods and goddesses against whose temples and worship the defendant, inspired by some reckless, criminal madness, has constantly waged impious and sacrilegious war!

If, in dealing with this case and this defendant, my conduct has been determined solely by the safety of our allies, the status of the Roman people, and my own sense of obligation, if all my care, vigilance, and planning has been directed at nothing but the claims of duty and honour, then I pray that the intention I had in accepting the case and the sense of obligation I felt in seeing it through may be your guiding motives, too, in judging it. [189] If, moreover, Gaius Verres' actions consist entirely of unprecedented and unique examples of crime, violence, treason, lust, avarice, and brutality, then I pray that your verdict may produce an outcome that reflects his life and actions. Finally, I pray that Rome, and my own sense of obligation, may be satisfied with this single prosecution that I have undertaken, and that from now on I may be allowed to defend good men instead of being compelled to prosecute bad ones.

# DE IMPERIO CN. POMPEI
## ('ON THE COMMAND OF GNAEUS POMPEIUS')

*De imperio Cn. Pompei* ('On the command of Gnaeus Pompeius'), alternatively known as *Pro lege Manilia* ('For the Manilian law'), is Cicero's
first deliberative speech (i.e. a speech involving the recommendation of a
course of action in a deliberative assembly), and the earliest surviving
example of a deliberative speech from ancient Rome. It was delivered from
the rostra in the forum to an assembly of the people in 66 BC, the year in
which Cicero held the praetorship. The course of action which it recommends was a highly popular one—that the Roman people vote for a bill of
the tribune Gaius Manilius to give Pompey (as Gnaeus Pompeius is
known in English) command of the long-running war against Mithridates,
the king of Pontus. This law would doubtless have been passed whether or
not Cicero advocated it, but by publicly associating himself with it, and
with Pompey, Cicero helped to ensure that he would have the political
support necessary to secure his own election to the highest regular office
of state, the consulship, in 64. The speech was therefore more important
for its effect on Cicero's career than for its effect on Roman history.
Nevertheless, it is for us a historical source of prime importance for the
workings of politics at Rome and for Roman policy and government in the
eastern Mediterranean—as well as being a particularly fine example of
Cicero's oratory before the people.

To explain the circumstances of the speech, it is best to begin, as Cicero
does (§ 4), with the person whose actions brought the whole situation
about, Mithridates VI Eupator, king of Pontus, and Rome's most formidable enemy in the first century BC. Mithridates inherited the throne of
Pontus (the eastern third of the southern coast of the Black Sea) from his
father Mithridates V Euergetes in 120 BC, when he was about 11 years of
age. Mithridates V had been a loyal friend of the Romans and had helped
them against Carthage, and as a result had been allowed to acquire a
number of the neighbouring kingdoms to the south without challenge. He
inherited Paphlagonia and took Galatia; the Romans added Phrygia; and
in Cappadocia, he installed his son-in-law as king. When he was assassinated in 120, his widow Laodice acted as regent for her two sons, Eupator
and Chrestus. By *c.*113, however, Eupator had removed his mother and
brother and established himself as Mithridates VI (Laodice, who may have
tried to kill him, was imprisoned, and Chrestus was executed). Soon after
his father's death, the Romans had removed Phrygia and the additional
kingdoms from Mithridates' control; this seems to have been the origin of
his long-standing hatred of the Romans.

Mithridates wished to enlarge his kingdom, and began by successfully taking over Armenia Minor and the eastern coast of the Black Sea (Colchis), and then the Crimea and the territories on the northern coast; these acquisitions greatly increased the resources available to him, and put him in a strong position for war. Next, he turned his attention to his father's former possessions in Asia Minor. He allied himself with Nicomedes III, king of Bithynia, and together the two kings took Paphlagonia and Galatia (108–7); but they fell out over Cappadocia, which was briefly occupied by Nicomedes before Mithridates brought about the murder of the rightful king Ariarthes and replaced him with his own son (*c.*101). Nicomedes made representations to the senate at Rome, which ordered both kings to keep out of Paphlagonia and Cappadocia. Mithridates attempted to get round this by marrying his daughter Cleopatra to Tigranes I 'the Great', the king of Armenia; Tigranes then occupied Cappadocia in Mithridates' interest, whereupon in 92 Lucius Cornelius Sulla, as governor of Cilicia, ejected him and restored Ariarthes' rightful successor, Ariobarzanes.

Meanwhile, Nicomedes III had died in 94 and had been succeeded by his son Nicomedes IV. In 90 Nicomedes IV was driven out of his kingdom by Mithridates, but was restored the following year by a Roman commission under Manius Aquillius (the consul of 101), who then forced him to invade Pontus. This action precipitated the First Mithridatic War (88–85 BC). Taking advantage of the fact that the Romans were otherwise preoccupied with the Social War (91–87 BC) in Italy, Mithridates seized Bithynia and Cappadocia, and then invaded the Roman province of Asia. Aquillius was captured, publicly humiliated, and executed by having molten gold poured down his throat—to punish the Romans for their greed. In Asia, Mithridates ordered the massacre of an alleged 80,000 Roman and Italian men, women, and children on a prearranged day (the so-called 'Asiatic vespers', 88); this consolidated his hold on the province (since the perpetrators of the atrocity could hardly change sides afterwards). Continuing westwards, Mithridates failed to capture Rhodes, but in Greece most cities, including Athens, declared themselves for the king—a striking indication of the unpopularity of Roman rule at this time.

In 88 Sulla, now consul, was given the command against Mithridates; this was then transferred to his rival Gaius Marius, whereupon Sulla occupied Rome, killed or exiled his Marian opponents, and had the command transferred back to himself. In 87 he arrived in Greece with five legions and laid siege to Athens. The city fell the following spring, after which Sulla defeated Mithridates in two major battles, at Chaeronea and Orchomenus. In his absence, however, the Marians had taken Rome (though Marius himself had died shortly after entering upon his seventh consulship in 86), and so Sulla was anxious to return to Italy at the earliest opportunity. He therefore agreed a treaty, the Treaty of Dardanus (85), with Mithridates. The king surrendered Asia to the Romans, gave up seventy ships, and paid an indemnity; and Nicomedes and Ariobarzanes were restored to their respective thrones in Bithynia and Cappadocia. In return, Mithridates was formally recognized as king of Pontus, and was also allowed to retain his northern Black Sea possessions. Never had such a dangerous enemy of Rome been let off so lightly. Sulla settled Asia (84) and then returned to Italy (83), leaving Lucius Licinius Murena in charge of Asia.

Mithridates' northern possessions soon began to revolt, and so he prepared a large force against them. Then Murena, either because he was genuinely concerned that Mithridates would use this force against Cappadocia, or because he simply wanted the glory of a military victory, invaded Pontus. He maintained that this was not a violation of the Treaty of Dardanus because the treaty had not yet been signed. But he was heavily defeated by Mithridates, and was ordered by Sulla, who in the meantime had retaken Rome and made himself dictator, to withdraw to Asia. This episode is known as the Second Mithridatic War (83–81 BC). Notwithstanding his shameful failure, Murena was granted a triumph on his return to Rome. He did not, however, go on to hold the consulship.

Sulla died in 78. Mithridates tried and failed to persuade the senate in Rome to ratify the treaty; clearly they were intending to renew the war at their own convenience. The king's response was once again to send his son-in-law Tigranes of Armenia to occupy Cappadocia in his interest. He also conducted negotiations, perhaps in the winter of 76–75, with Quintus Sertorius, the Marian leader who was holding Spain against the central (largely Sullan) government: Mithridates offered him ships and money in return for recognition of his territorial claims. Sertorius sent him a commission to instruct him in Roman methods of warfare, and recognized all his territorial claims except that over Asia (Asia being a Roman province). At this point, in late 75 or early 74, Nicomedes died, bequeathing the kingdom of Bithynia to Rome. Mithridates responded by invading both Bithynia and Cappadocia, thus precipitating the Third Mithridatic War (73–63 BC).

Rome sent out both of the consuls of 74, Lucius Licinius Lucullus to Asia and Marcus Aurelius Cotta to Bithynia—an indication of the seriousness with which the situation was viewed. Hostilities began the following year. Mithridates defeated Cotta in a naval battle off Chalcedon, invaded Asia, and besieged Cyzicus (73); but Lucullus broke the siege and destroyed Mithridates' army, and then pursued the king to Amisus in Pontus (72). Over the next two years, he captured Amisus (71) and Sinope (70), forcing Mithridates to abandon Pontus and take refuge with

Tigranes in Armenia. By the end of 70, Lucullus held Pontus and Armenia Minor. During that year, he also took the opportunity to reorganize
the finances of the province of Asia, which had been treated with great
severity by Sulla, and passed measures for the reduction of debts. These
actions earned him the hostility of the *equites* at Rome, whose rapacious
tax-farming and moneylending activities had been the chief cause of
Rome's unpopularity. In revenge, they sought to undermine Lucullus
by claiming that he was deliberately prolonging the war. The next year
Lucullus, without the permission of the senate, advanced through
Cappadocia into Armenia, inflicted a devastating defeat on Tigranes
(some sources say 100,000 of the enemy were killed), and captured the
latter's new capital at Tigranocerta.

During 68, Lucullus advanced further into Armenia. But as the year
wore on, discontent among his troops grew (stoked up by a member of his
staff, his brother-in-law Publius Claudius Pulcher, to become famous a
decade later as the tribune Clodius). The soldiers objected to the severity
of Lucullus' discipline, his reluctance to allow them to plunder cities, and
the distance he was taking them into unfamiliar lands. Late in the year
they mutinied, refusing to march on to the old capital of Armenia,
Artaxata. When this situation became known at Rome, the *equites* pressed
for the appointment of a new commander. They had already succeeded in
having Asia withdrawn from Lucullus' command in 69; now Cilicia too
was withdrawn. Then in 67, the tide of the war changed. Mithridates
returned to Pontus and inflicted a crushing defeat on Lucullus' legate,
Gaius Valerius Triarius, at Zela. Lucullus, when he finally arrived on the
scene, was unable to engage Mithridates in a battle. It was at this point
that his remaining commands, Bithynia and Pontus, were taken away from
him, by a law of the tribune Aulus Gabinius, and assigned instead to the
consul Manius Acilius Glabrio (the man who as praetor in 70 had presided
over the trial of Verres). Glabrio turned out to be unequal to the task,
however, and would not stir beyond Bithynia. Mithridates, meanwhile,
recovered most of Pontus, while Tigranes retook Cappadocia.

It is at this point that the spotlight moves to Pompey, the greatest
general of the age. He was born in the same year as Cicero, 106 BC. He
served under his father Gnaeus Pompeius Strabo, the consul of 89, in the
Social War, and secured Sicily and Africa for Sulla following the latter's
return to Italy in 83. Although he was not yet a member of the senate, his
demand for a triumph was grudgingly agreed to by Sulla (81). After
Sulla's death, Pompey and Quintus Lutatius Catulus (the consul of 78)
together suppressed the rising of Catulus' consular colleague, Marcus
Aemilius Lepidus (78–77). When this had been done, Pompey was
ordered by Catulus to disband his army, but refused; so the senate sent

him to put down the Marian forces which were holding out in Spain under Sertorius. Success there was slow in coming, but victory was eventually achieved after the assassination of Sertorius by his subordinate Marcus Perperna Veiento in 72. While on his way back to Rome in 71, Pompey was able to mop up the remnants of Spartacus' slave revolt (73–71), which had been crushed by Marcus Licinius Crassus; Pompey's claiming of the credit for completing this war soured relations permanently between the two men. When he arrived back in Rome he held a second triumph, and, although still an *eques*, persuaded the senate to agree to his standing for the consulship of 70. He and Crassus then held the consulship together in that year—in Pompey's case seven years before the legal minimum age, and without having held any previous magisterial office (in contravention of Sulla's laws). During their consulship, the two men restored the powers of the tribunes of the plebs, severely curtailed by Sulla, and revived the office of censor. Also during this year the *lex Aurelia* was carried. This abolished the senatorial juries prescribed by Sulla, instead making juries effectively two-thirds equestrian and one-third senatorial (this is a live issue in Cicero's *Verrines*).

After his year of office, Pompey did not go out to govern a province, but waited in Rome for another extraordinary command to come up. In 67 Aulus Gabinius proposed a bill to create a three-year command against the pirates in the Mediterranean; the proposed powers were unprecedented, and covered the whole Mediterranean and its coasts to a distance inland of 50 miles. The bill made no mention of Pompey, but it was obvious that the command was intended for him. The senate, led by the senior and highly respected Catulus (whom Pompey had offended in 77 when he refused to disband his army) and Quintus Hortensius Hortalus, the consul of 69, argued vigorously against the proposal; only Caesar spoke in favour. Nevertheless, the bill was forced through amid great popular enthusiasm, and became the *lex Gabinia*. Pompey was given the command.

The campaign proved a brilliant, and unexpectedly rapid, success: in just three months, during the summer of 67, piracy throughout the Mediterranean was entirely eradicated. Politically, it now became much harder to argue that Pompey should not be entrusted with further commands. In the summer of 66, another tribune, Gaius Manilius, proposed that Pompey be put in command of Cilicia, Bithynia, and Pontus, and of the war against Mithridates. It was an attractive proposal: not only was he obviously the best man for the task (seeing that Lucullus had lost the support of his troops and had in any case been replaced), but he was already in the area where he would be needed. Caesar supported the proposal. Catulus and Hortensius, who were friends of Lucullus, naturally opposed it; but this time they had less support in the senate, and had no realistic chance of preventing the appointment.

This was the year in which Cicero was praetor, and Manilius duly invited him to address the people on the subject of the bill. Cicero had not previously spoken before an assembly of the Roman people: at Rome, all his speeches had been delivered in the lawcourts. No doubt his decision to confine himself to forensic oratory up to this point had been to some extent simply a matter of personal preference. But that decision had also enabled him to avoid committing himself politically. Deliberative speeches generally involved taking one side against another, and hence potentially alienating larger groups of people than would normally be the case in a trial or a lawsuit (in a trial, if an advocate acted for the defence, he did not necessarily alienate anyone at all). For example, if a speaker sought the favour of the people by taking a 'popular' line in a deliberative speech, elements in the senate might afterwards try to block his election to higher political office; but if he took too conservative a line, he might fail to win the support of the people. Similarly, if he supported the senate, he might alienate the *equites*, and vice versa. In the case of Gabinius' bill the previous year, the senate and the people had been violently opposed, and Cicero had wisely expressed no opinion. But with Manilius' bill there was little likelihood that he would do himself serious political damage by supporting Pompey. Most people were in favour of the bill. The Roman people (both from the city of Rome itself and from Italy) supported it because Asia was the empire's most important source of revenue, and trade and the import of grain depended on the eastern Mediterranean remaining peaceful and under Roman control. So they would be likely to vote for the bill whatever Cicero (or anyone else) might say on the subject. The *equites* supported it because they wanted to continue their ruthless exploitation of Asia through tax-farming and moneylending, and could not do so if the province was not in Roman hands. The majority of the senate probably supported it as well, not unnaturally regarding Mithridates as a more serious threat than Pompey; Cicero gives us the names of four distinguished ex-consuls of the 70s who supported it (§ 68). Of those against the bill, on the other hand, Catulus and Hortensius are the only names we have. No doubt there were other, less vociferous, opponents of Pompey whom Cicero does not mention; but it does not appear that they were in the majority.

Cicero therefore accepted Manilius' invitation, knowing that he would be advocating a popular bill. In particular, the equestrian tax-farmers had asked him to speak in favour of it (§ 4), and it was very much in his interests to keep them on his side (apart from the electoral support which the equestrian order could give him, they now supplied two-thirds of every jury—a factor which might well count in his favour when he appeared in court). The gratitude of Pompey himself might also, of course, prove useful to him. He therefore delivered, and afterwards published, *De imperio Cn. Pompei*. In the speech he gratified the supporters of the bill, and public opinion, by showering praise on Pompey: 'my subject is the outstanding and unique merit of Gnaeus Pompeius' (§ 3; cf. *Orat.* 102, written twenty years later, 'when discussing the Manilian law, my task was to glorify Pompeius'). But he also went out of his way to compliment Lucullus (§§ 5, 10, 20–1, 26), who was in fact a close friend of his (Plut. *Luc.* 41.3, 42.4), and to treat Hortensius and particularly Catulus with marked respect. Thus he was able to reap the maximum political benefit from the speech while minimizing the damage it would do him from the bill's opponents.

The *lex Manilia* was passed, by all thirty-five tribes, and Pompey began operations against Mithridates. But at Rome, the political battles continued. As soon as Manilius left office in December (the tribunician year ran from 10 December one year to 9 December the next), he was attacked by Pompey's enemies. He was prosecuted under the extortion law; he had not been a provincial governor, so presumably he was being charged as an accessory. The case came before Cicero, as praetor in charge of the extortion court, and he scheduled the trial to begin on the last day of the year. His reason for doing this is uncertain; he may have wanted to place himself in a position in which he would not have to support either side. If he were too closely identified with Manilius, he might further incur the hostility of the conservatives in the senate (it is quite possible that Manilius himself was more offensive to conservative opinion than his bill was; Cicero avoids talking about him in *De imperio*, mentioning him only at § 69). The supporters of Manilius, however, objected that the date set by Cicero did not allow for the customary ten-day interval between the formal bringing of the charge and the opening of the trial. They therefore had the trial postponed until early in 65, and forced Cicero to agree to act as Manilius' defence counsel. When the trial finally took place, the charge had been changed to treason. It is unclear whether in the event Cicero did speak for the defence. The trial aroused strong feelings; there were violent demonstrations, and the senate asked the consuls to attend and keep order. Manilius was condemned; he is never heard of again.

Meanwhile, in the east, Pompey had forced Mithridates to flee from Pontus to the Crimea. He then compelled Tigranes to surrender Armenia (66), organized Bithynia and Pontus as a single Roman province (65–64), annexed Syria (which had been under the control of Tigranes) and organized it as a province (64–63), and finally occupied Judaea, capturing Jerusalem (63). During 63, just before he arrived at Jerusalem, he received news that Mithridates had been overthrown by his son Pharnaces, and had committed suicide. According to the standard version (which is, however, open to question), Mithridates had attempted to kill himself with poison, but had been unable to do so because, by taking minute doses over many years, he had made himself immune; so instead he had ordered a Celtic bodyguard to run him through with a sword.

Cicero maintained good relations with both Pompey and Lucullus, and was elected in 64 to the consulship of 63. In 63 he proposed that a thanksgiving to the gods be held in Pompey's honour, and also arranged for Lucullus to celebrate his long-delayed triumph. Lucullus then helped Cicero during the Catilinarian crisis, and Cicero set aside time during it to take on the defence of one of Lucullus' relations, Lucius Licinius Murena, the consul-elect of 62 and the son of the Murena who had fought the Second Mithridatic War. He also defended, in 62, a client of Lucullus', the poet Archias, who had written a historical poem in several books on Lucullus' war against Mithridates. Pompey returned to Rome at the end of 62, disbanded his army, and held a triumph. The senate, however, was persuaded by Lucullus not to ratify the arrangements that Pompey had made for the settlement of the new eastern provinces and the client kingdoms beyond, and this drove him in 60 to form the alliance with Caesar and Crassus known as the 'first triumvirate'. Pompey's settlement was then ratified *en bloc* in 59. In that year Lucullus retired from public life; in 58 he was the only one of Cicero's friends to advise him against going into exile. In his later years he was famous for his luxurious living. But at the end of his life he fell victim to mental illness (possibly Alzheimer's disease), and he died in 57 or 56. In 45 Cicero made him the central character of the second book of his *Academica*, entitled *Lucullus*.

Scholars have traditionally criticized Cicero and the senate for putting too much power into one man's hands, and so destabilizing the republic and hastening its end. But it is difficult to see what else could have been done: other commanders had all failed, and the situation was critical. Moreover, the results surely justified the appointment. Pompey's defeat of Mithridates and settlement of the east was an extraordinary achievement, the greatest of his career; and when he returned to Rome he did not seize power, as Sulla had done, or revenge himself upon his enemies, or insist on further commands. When civil war finally broke out in 49, he was on the side of the legitimate government. So even though the republic was in due course to collapse, Cicero's judgement in 66 that Pompey should be appointed to the Mithridatic command—however opportunistic that judgement may have been—was surely the correct one.

# DE IMPERIO CN. POMPEI

[1] Although I have always particularly enjoyed the sight of you thronging this place, and have always thought that the spot where I am now standing* is the most distinguished one in which a magistrate may transact business with you and the most honourable one in which a private citizen may address you, nevertheless, citizens, this means of becoming famous, which has always been fully available to every decent citizen, has until now been closed to me, not because of any wish of mine to avoid it, but rather because of the path I set myself when I embarked upon my career. For until now I have never dared to speak from this place of influence, and I was determined that I should never present anything here that was not the fruit of my mature powers and the product of long practice: hence I judged that I would do better to devote the whole of my time instead to defending my friends in their hour of need.* [2] So, while this place has never been short of men ready to defend your interests, my exertions, which have been honestly and irreproachably devoted to defending private citizens, have now received the highest possible reward through the choice that you yourselves have made. For when, because of successive reruns of the election, I was formally declared, three times over, as the first of the candidates to be elected to a praetorship, and by the votes of all the centuries,* then it was made very clear to me, citizens, both what you had concluded about me personally and what you were recommending to others. Now, since I possess as much authority as, by electing me to this office, you have wished me to have, and since I also possess as much skill in legal advocacy as anyone who is reasonably energetic could acquire from almost daily practice in speaking in the courts, I will accordingly deploy whatever authority I have among those who have bestowed it upon me, and similarly, if I can achieve anything by my oratory, I will display it before those people particularly who in choosing me have judged that that art too is deserving of some reward. [3] And I am aware that I have especially good reason to be happy because, despite having no experience of making the type of speeches that are required from those who stand before you on this platform, the subject on which I now have the opportunity to address you is one on

which no one could fail to be eloquent. This is because my subject is the outstanding and unique merit of Gnaeus Pompeius—a subject on which it is more difficult to finish speaking than to begin. In making my speech, therefore, my task will not be to strive after abundance so much as moderation.

[4] I will begin at the point from which this whole situation came about. A serious and dangerous war, directed against your revenue-payers and allies, is being pursued by two extremely powerful kings, Mithridates and Tigranes, of whom the former has been left unpunished and the latter provoked to aggression, while each believes that he has been offered a golden opportunity of taking over Asia.* Every day the Roman equestrians, men of honour who have great sums invested in the collection of your revenues, receive letters from Asia; and because I am closely connected with that order, they have brought to me their concerns about the danger to the national interest and to their own property. [5] They have told me that in Bithynia, which is now a province of yours,* settlements have been burnt to the ground; that the kingdom of Ariobarzanes,* which borders with territories that pay you revenue, is entirely in enemy hands; that Lucius Lucullus, having achieved great things, is retiring from the war; that his successor* is not adequately equipped to undertake a war on such a scale; that one man is wanted and demanded by all our allies and the citizens there as commander for this war; that this same one man is dreaded by the enemy; and that he is the only person to whom this applies

[6] So you can see what the situation is; and now you must decide yourselves what is to be done. It seems to me best first to discuss the character of the war, then its scale, and finally the choice of a commander.

The character of this war is such as ought particularly to stir your hearts and set them ablaze with a determination to see the matter through to the end. It is a war in which the glory of the Roman people is at stake—a glory handed down to you from your ancestors, a glory conspicuous in all areas of life, but particularly so in the military sphere. A war in which the safety of our friends and allies is at stake—something for which your ancestors undertook many great and important wars in the past. A war in which the largest and most reliable revenues of the Roman people are at stake, the loss of which would entail the loss of both the means of enjoying peace and the means of making war. A war in which the property of many of your fellow-citizens is at stake—something which you ought to have regard for, for the sake of the individuals concerned and also for the sake of the country.

[7] More than other peoples, you have always sought after glory and been eager for renown. It is therefore imperative that you wipe out that mark of disgrace incurred in the earlier Mithridatic war, which has now stained the reputation of the Roman people deeply and for much too long. For disgrace it is that that man* who, on a single day in so many cities throughout the whole of Asia, by a single message and a single word of command ordained that the Roman citizens in Asia should be killed and butchered, has not only still paid no penalty commensurate with his crime, but more than twenty-two years later is still sitting on his throne. And as king, he is not content to hide away in some dark corner of Pontus or Cappadocia, but wishes to break out from the kingdom he inherited and range over the territories that pay you revenue—in the bright light, that is, of Asia. [8] What has happened is that our commanders in their struggle with that king have so far brought back only the trappings of victory, not victory itself. Lucius Sulla held a triumph over Mithridates, and so did Lucius Murena*—both men of courage and outstanding commanders—but the result of their triumphs was that the king, though driven back and defeated, nevertheless remained on his throne. All the same, these generals should be given praise for what they achieved and pardon for what they left un-achieved, seeing that Sulla was recalled from that war to Italy by the national interest, and Murena by Sulla.*

[9] Mithridates, however, devoted all the time that followed not to effacing the memory of the first war, but to making preparations for a fresh one. He constructed and fitted out enormous fleets and assembled vast armies from whatever countries he could, and made out that he was preparing for a war against the kingdom of the Bosporus,* which adjoined his own territory. He then sent envoys with letters all the way to Spain to the chiefs* with whom we were then at war: his intention was that war would be conducted accord-ing to a single plan by two enemy armies on land and sea in the two places in the world that are the furthest apart and most different from each other, and that you, engaged in a struggle on two fronts, would find yourselves fighting for possession of the empire itself.

[10] However, the danger in the west, from Sertorius in Spain, which was much the tougher and more intractable of the two, was repelled by the inspired strategy and outstanding bravery of Gnaeus Pompeius. In the east, on the other hand, the war was managed by the eminent Lucius Lucullus in such a way as to suggest that his great and glorious achievements in the early stages were due not to luck but to his own abilities, while the more recent happenings there should be attributed not to any fault on his part but to bad luck. But I am going to talk about Lucullus later on, citizens, and you will find that my words will neither deny him any of the glory that belongs to him nor attribute to him any that does not.

[11] As for the honour and glory of your empire, since that is the point with which I began, please consider what your feelings on this subject ought to be. Our ancestors often undertook wars merely because our merchants and ship-owners had been somewhat roughly handled: so how, I ask you, ought you to feel when so many thousands of Roman citizens have been killed at a single command and on a single occasion? Merely because their envoys had been a little insolently addressed, your forefathers wanted Corinth, the light of all Greece, to be extinguished:* will you, then, allow a king to go unpunished who put a legate of the Roman people, an ex-consul, in chains, flogged and subjected him to every kind of torture, and then killed him?* They could not tolerate the freedom of Roman citizens being limited: will you ignore the fact that their lives have been taken from them? They took action when the rights of an embassy were violated by mere speech: will you overlook the torture and murder of a legate? [12] It was an achievement of the most glorious kind for them to hand down to you so magnificent an empire: you must now ensure that you do not incur a corresponding disgrace by proving unable to protect and safeguard what you have inherited.

Again, when the lives of your allies are placed in extreme, critical danger, how, I ask you, should you react? King Ariobarzanes, the friend and ally of the Roman people, has been driven out of his kingdom; two kings,* sworn enemies not just of yourselves but of your friends and allies too, threaten the whole of Asia; and all the cities throughout Asia and Greece are compelled by the scale of the danger to look to you for help. They do not dare to ask you for one particular commander, especially seeing that you have already sent someone else.* Indeed, they are convinced they would get into serious trouble if they suggested it. [13] And yet they see and feel, just as you do, that there is one man who possesses the highest qualifications, and that he is nearby—which makes them all the more distressed at being without him. His mere proximity and his reputation, even though it is for a naval war that he has come,* has resulted, they feel, in the enemy's onslaughts being checked and slowed down. These people are unable to speak openly, and so it is in silence that they ask you to decide that they also are worthy of having their safety put in the hands of this great man. Moreover, they ask you this all the more fervently because the commanders we send to other provinces tend to be the sort of men whose arrival in allied cities, even where they do protect them from the enemy, scarcely differs from a hostile assault—whereas this man, as the allies had heard before but now see with their own eyes, displays such moderation, such kindness, and such humanity that they have come to the conclusion that the people who are the luckiest are those with whom he delays the longest.

[14] So if our ancestors fought wars against Antiochus, Philip, the Aetolians, and the Carthaginians* purely for their allies' sake, having received no injury themselves, just think how eager you ought to be to defend the safety of your allies and the prestige of your empire when you *have* been injured—and especially when your most important revenues are at stake! The revenues of the other provinces, citizens, are scarcely large enough to make it worth our while governing those provinces; but Asia, on the other hand, is so rich and fertile that it easily surpasses all other territories in the productiveness of its soil, the variety of its crops, the extent of its pasturage, and the size of its exports. Therefore, citizens, if you wish to hold on to something that is useful in time of war and desirable in time of peace, you must defend this province not just from disaster but also from the fear of disaster. [15] In other areas of life, loss occurs only when a disaster actually takes place; but in the case of revenues, it is not just the occurrence of some evil but the actual fear of it that brings disaster. For when an enemy army is not far away, even if there has as yet been no incursion, the livestock is abandoned, the soil is no longer cultivated, and merchant shipping comes to a halt. As a result, the harbour duty, the tithes, and the grazing tax* produce no revenue; and so a single rumour of danger, a single foreboding of war, can often cause the loss of an entire year's income. [16] What,

then, do you suppose are the feelings of those who pay us the revenues or those who farm and collect them, when two kings are nearby with enormous armies, when a single cavalry raid can in an instant carry off an entire year's revenue, and when the tax-farmers conclude that it is extremely dangerous to keep on the large staffs that they maintain in the salt-works, in the fields, in the harbours, and in the guard-posts?* Do you really think you can continue to enjoy these benefits without keeping those who procure them for you free not only, as I have just said, from disaster, but also from the fear of disaster?

[17] There is another point you must not overlook, one I left until last when I started to discuss the character of the war. This relates to the property owned by many Roman citizens—whose interests, citizens, you in your wisdom must take carefully into account. First of all, those honourable and distinguished gentlemen, the tax-farmers, have moved their business and their funds to that province, and their property and interests ought in themselves to be a concern of yours. For if we have always believed that our revenues are the sinews of the state, then we certainly ought to describe the order which farms those revenues as the mainstay of the other orders. [18] Secondly, there are energetic and industrious people from the other orders, some of whom do business in Asia in person—and you ought to protect their interests while they are away—while others have large sums invested in the province. It will therefore be a mark of your humanity to save this large number of citizens from ruin, and a mark of your wisdom to appreciate that the national interest would be affected by the ruin of so many of them.

In the first place, you should not imagine that a military victory at a later date will enable you to recover the revenues that the tax-farmers have lost: because of the disaster they have suffered, they are in no position to bid for a fresh contract, and new bidders, in view of what has happened, will be deterred from coming forward. [19] In the second place, we should remember the lesson that this same Asia and this same Mithridates taught us at the beginning of our hostilities with him,* since we learned it the hard way. What happened was that a great many people lost large sums in Asia, and their resulting inability to meet their financial obligations caused a collapse of credit at Rome. It is in fact impossible for many people in the same country to lose their fortunes without dragging still more people down with them, and you should take action to protect the state from this danger. Believe me, and believe the evidence of your own eyes! This whole system of credit and finance which operates here at Rome, here in this very forum, is tied up with and inseparable from the money invested in Asia: if that is lost, then our finances here are inevitably involved in the same general collapse.

Decide, therefore, whether you should hold back from pursuing this war with all possible vigour—a war to defend the honour of your name, the safety of your allies, your most important revenues, and the fortunes of a great many citizens, fortunes inseparable from those of the state.

[20] Now that I have spoken about the character of the war, I want to say a few words about its scale. For some people might argue that while the war is necessary and must be fought, nevertheless it is not so serious that we need be unduly alarmed by it. On this point my main concern is to prevent the possibility of your making light of matters about which you ought in fact to be taking the most careful precautions. Furthermore, I would like everyone to understand that I attribute to Lucius Lucullus all the praise that is due to a valiant soldier, a man of wisdom, and a great commander. I would therefore stress that at the time he arrived in Asia the forces of Mithridates were enormous, and equipped and supplied with everything they could possibly require; that Mithridates himself was besieging Cyzicus, the most famous city in Asia and the one most friendly to us, with a vast army, and had attacked it with terrible ferocity; and that Lucius Lucullus, by his courage, persistence, and intelligence, succeeded in liberating that city from the siege and all its attendant dangers. [21] A large and well-equipped fleet, puffed up with fanatical hatred, captained by men from Sertorius' forces, and making for Italy at top speed, was defeated and sunk by this same commander.* Moreover, in numerous battles he destroyed vast enemy hordes, and so opened up Pontus to our legions, when previously it had been closed to the Roman people from every side. Sinope and Amisus, which contained royal residences supplied and stuffed with every kind of provision, together with a great many other cities in Pontus and Cappadocia, were taken at the very moment of his approach and arrival.* The king, stripped of the territories ruled by his father and grandfather before him, was forced to take refuge as a suppliant with other kings in other countries;* and

while all these achievements were being carried out, the allies of the Roman people were kept safe and their revenues intact. I trust that this is praise enough, and I am sure you will agree, citizens, that none of those who oppose this law and course of action have praised Lucius Lucullus as highly as I have from this platform.

[22] At this point someone may perhaps ask how, if this is how things stand, there could be much of a war left still to fight. I will tell you, citizens, since it seems a reasonable question. In the first place, Mithridates fled from his kingdom in just the same way as the famous Medea* is said to have once fled from that same kingdom of Pontus. As she was making her escape, the story goes, she scattered her brother's limbs along the route where her father would follow her, so that he would lose time as he stopped in his pursuit to collect the scattered remains and grieve over them. Similarly, Mithridates, making his escape, left behind in Pontus the whole of his vast store of gold, silver, and treasures of every description which he had either inherited from his forefathers or else plundered from all over Asia in the earlier war* and amassed in his own kingdom. While our men were collecting all these rather too carefully, the king himself slipped through their hands. Medea's father was held up in his pursuit by grief; but our people were held up by joy.

[23] The terrified Mithridates took refuge with Tigranes, the king of Armenia, who comforted him in his despair, raised his shattered spirits, and rescued him from his disaster. Lucius Lucullus then entered that country with his army, whereupon still more peoples rose against our commander. Nations which the Roman people had never had any thought of attacking or provoking took fright; and there was also a damaging and strongly held belief which had taken hold among the barbarian peoples that our army had come to that region specifically for the purpose of plundering a certain extremely wealthy and much venerated temple.* As a result, many large nations were stirred up by this alarming new threat. Our own troops, despite their capture of one city from Tigranes' kingdom* and their other successes in battle, became concerned at how far they were from home and from their loved ones. [24] At this point I will say no more; for the way it turned out was that our troops were more eager for an early return from that region than for a march deeper into it.

Mithridates meanwhile had built up his forces once again, and in addition numerous kings and nations helped him by providing strong reinforcements from abroad. Indeed, this is what we find normally happens: kings who are in trouble have no difficulty obtaining help and sympathy from many quarters, particularly from other kings or from people who live as subjects of a king, since to them the name of king is something great and venerated.* [25] The result was that Mithridates, after his defeat, was in a position to achieve things he never dared hope for before it. He returned to his kingdom, and then, not content with merely setting foot in the land he had been driven out of and never thought he would see again, launched an attack on our renowned and victorious army. Allow me, citizens, to do at this point what poets who write about Roman history do, and pass over our disaster*—a disaster so terrible that the commander received news of it not from any survivor of the battle, but from the circulating rumour.

[26] At this point, in the hour of disaster and at the worst setback of the war, Lucius Lucullus, who might perhaps have been capable of recovering the situation to some degree, was ordered by yourselves—since you wanted to follow tradition and set some limit to the tenure of his command—to disband those of his troops who had completed their service, and hand over the remainder to Manius Glabrio. I am passing over a great deal on purpose; but please try to supply the omission for yourselves by contemplating the significance of a war in which powerful kings join forces, nations are roused to renew hostilities, peoples not previously involved flock to the cause, and a new commander of ours is appointed after the former army's defeat.

[27] I think I have said enough about why the character of this war makes it necessary, and its scale dangerous. It remains, I think, to speak about the choice of a commander, and his appointment to this major undertaking. I only wish, citizens, that you had so many brave men of spotless reputation at your disposal that you would find it difficult to decide which of them you would prefer to put in charge of such a major undertaking, and such a great war! But as it is, Gnaeus Pompeius, and he alone, has by his own merit surpassed in glory not only everyone who is alive today, but also all the great figures of the past. In this case, then, is there anything that could possibly make any of you hesitate?

[28] To my way of thinking, there are four qualities that a great commander must possess: military knowledge, ability, authority, and

luck. Who, then, has there ever been who had, or potentially had, greater military knowledge than he? This is a man who went straight from school and from his childhood education to his father's army and to military training in a major war against formidable enemies;* who at the end of his childhood served as a soldier in the army of a great commander,* and at the beginning of his youth was himself the commander of a great army;* who fought the enemy more often than anyone else has quarrelled with any personal opponent, has fought more wars than others have read about, and has carried out more commissions than others have coveted; and whose youth was trained in military knowledge not by the teaching of others but by personal experience of command, not by setbacks in war but by victories, and not by periods of service but by triumphs. In short, what type of war can there be in which the fortune of the state has not made use of him? Civil, African, Transalpine, Spanish (a war involving both citizens and exceptionally warlike tribes), slave, and naval wars,* wars and enemies different in character and locality, wars not only undertaken by this one man but also completed by him—all these demonstrate that there is no aspect of military experience which can escape the knowledge of this man.

[29] As regards the ability of Gnaeus Pompeius, what speech could possibly do justice to it? What could anyone say that would not be unworthy of him, already known to you, or familiar to everyone? For the attributes of a great general do not consist only of those that are commonly thought of as such: dedication in one's duties, courage in danger, thoroughness in undertaking the task in hand, speed in accomplishing it, foresight in planning—qualities that are as evident in this single man as in all the other commanders, put together, that we have ever seen or heard of. [30] Italy is witness to it—which the victorious Lucius Sulla himself conceded owed its liberation to Pompeius' ability and the assistance he provided. Sicily is witness to it—which he rescued from the many dangers which surrounded it not by the terrors of war but by the speed of his strategy. Africa is witness to it—which had been crushed by the large enemy forces and was overflowing with their blood. Gaul is witness to it—through which, by a massacre of Gauls, a route was opened for our legions to march on to Spain. Spain is witness to it—which repeatedly saw countless enemies defeated by him and laid low. Italy again and again is witness to it—which, when it was being threatened by the terrible

danger of the slave war, looked to him in his absence for help: the expectation of his arrival reduced the war and scaled it down, and his arrival itself left it dead and buried. [31] And now every shore is witness to it, every land, every people, every nation, and finally every sea—both the open seas and every inlet and harbour on every individual coast.

Was there any place at all on any coast during those years that was either so well defended that its safety could be guaranteed or so well hidden that it would never be noticed? Who ever travelled by sea without exposing himself to the danger of being killed or enslaved—having to choose between sailing in winter or sailing when the sea was infested with pirates? Who ever thought that a war so large-scale, so humiliating, so long-standing, and so spread out and dispersed could be completed either by any number of commanders in a single year or by a single commander in any number of years? [32] Was there a single province that you* succeeded in keeping free of pirates in all those years? Was there any revenue of yours that was secure? Was there any ally that you kept safe? Did your navy protect anyone? How many islands do you imagine were abandoned, how many cities of your allies emptied by fear or captured by the pirates?*

But why am I talking about things that happened far away? There was once a time when the Roman people used typically to conduct their wars in distant lands, and use the bulwarks of their power for the defence of their allies, not of their own homes. Do I need to point out that the seas were closed to your allies during those years, when your armies never made the crossing from Brundisium* except in the depths of winter? Do I need to bewail the fact that people sent to you from foreign countries were taken prisoner, when even envoys of the Roman people were ransomed? Do I need to point out that the sea was not safe for merchants, when twelve axes* fell into the hands of the pirates? [33] Do I need to mention the famous cities of Cnidus, Colophon, or Samos, or the countless others that were captured, when you are well aware that your own ports—those ports through which you draw life and breath—have been in the hands of the pirates? Can you be unaware that the busy port of Caieta, when it was full of ships, was sacked by the pirates under the eyes of the praetor, while the children of a man who had previously fought a war against the pirates were kidnapped by pirates at Misenum?* Why should I bewail that setback at Ostia* which brought shame and disgrace on our country, when virtually under your very eyes a fleet actually commanded by a consul of the Roman people was captured and sunk by the pirates?

Immortal gods! Is it really possible that the astonishing, super-human ability of a single mortal man has brought such a beacon of light to our country, and in so short a time, that you, who only recently looked out on an enemy fleet at the mouth of the Tiber, now hear that there is not a single pirate ship within the mouth of Ocean?*
[34] You have seen for yourselves the speed with which he achieved this; even so, I should not omit to mention it. For who in their eagerness for doing business or making money ever managed to visit so many places or complete so many long journeys in as short a time and as rapidly as, under Gnaeus Pompeius' leadership, that unstop-pable force of war sailed across the seas? Although it was not yet the season for navigation, he nevertheless went to Sicily, reconnoitred Africa, and took his fleet to Sardinia, and, by means of strong gar-risons and fleets, secured those three bread baskets for Rome. [35] Next, after strengthening the two Spains and Transalpine Gaul with garrisons and ships and sending further ships to the coast of Illyricum and to Achaea and the whole of Greece, he returned to Italy and fortified the seas on either side with the largest fleets and the strongest garrisons; and after that, on the forty-ninth day after his departure from Brundisium, he personally added the whole of Cilicia to the empire of the Roman people. All pirates, wherever they were, were either taken prisoner and executed or else surrendered to his—and only to his—power and authority. When he was in Pamphylia, people from as far away as Crete* sent envoys to him to ask for mercy: he did not deny them the chance of surrendering, but demanded hostages from them. And so this war, so vast, so long-standing, so widely dispersed, unleashed against all peoples and nations, was planned by Gnaeus Pompeius at the end of winter, begun at the beginning of spring, and completed by midsummer.*

[36] Such is his astonishing, superhuman ability as a commander. But to turn to his other qualities, which I began to discuss a few moments ago, how great and how numerous they are! In an ideal, perfect commander, we should not look only for military abilities: there are many other excellent qualities which support and go with them. In the first place, what integrity commanders should have; then what moderation in everything they do, what good faith, what

graciousness, what intelligence, what humanity! So let us briefly look at these qualities as they are found in Gnaeus Pompeius.

He possesses them all, citizens, to the highest degree possible—but they can be recognized and understood more from a comparison with others* than by being viewed on their own. [37] For what commander can count as a commander at all when centurions' commissions in his army are and have been sold? What noble, patriotic ideals can we suppose are held by someone who has been so eager to hold on to his command that he has divided out among the holders of public office funds allotted to him by the treasury for fighting the war, or so greedy that he has lent out these funds at interest at Rome? I can tell from your muttering, citizens, that you know who the men are who have done these things. For my part, I am naming no one—so no one can be angry with me without admitting that he is one of those I am referring to. But is there anyone who does not know that this greed on the generals' part has caused our armies to spread utter devastation wherever they go? [38] Just think of the tours which our commanders have made in Italy in recent years, through the countryside and the Roman citizen communities, and you will easily be able to infer how they act among foreigners. In recent years, do you think that more enemy cities have been destroyed by the arms of your soldiers, or allied states by their obligation to quarter them during the winter? No commander can control an army if he is not also capable of controlling himself; nor can he be strict in passing judgement if he is not willing to submit to the strict judgement of others. [39] It is said that, once his legions had arrived in Asia, no one who submitted to Gnaeus Pompeius was harmed by the hand, or even the footstep, of a single soldier in his whole army. Can we be surprised, then, that he surpasses all other commanders so completely? As for the way in which his soldiers behave in winter quarters, verbal and written reports reach us every day to the effect that not only is no one forced to spend money on the troops, but no one is allowed to even if he wants to. For our ancestors intended that the houses of our friends and allies should serve as a shelter from the winter weather, not as a shelter for greed.

[40] But think how much moderation he shows in other matters too. From where do you think he got his extraordinary rapidity, his astonishing speed in travelling? It was not because his rowers were unusually strong or because of any hitherto undiscovered method of

navigation or any new winds that he reached the most distant places as quickly as he did, but rather because he was not held back by the things that hold other commanders back. Greed did not deflect him from his chosen course and cause him to chase after plunder, nor did passion cause him to seek pleasure, or beautiful surroundings luxury, or famous places sight-seeing, or indeed work rest; and as for the statues, paintings, and other works of art which are found in Greek cities and which other commanders think are theirs for the taking,* he did not even consider them worth going to see. [41] The result is that everyone in those places now regards Gnaeus Pompeius not as having been sent out from Rome, but as having come down from heaven. Now at last they have started to accept that there did once exist Romans who possessed the self-control that he does—something which foreign peoples had begun to suppose impossible, a myth without foundation. Now the splendour of your empire is beginning to shed its light on those peoples as well. Now they have come to understand that it was not for no reason, when we had magistrates of Gnaeus Pompeius' moderation, that their ancestors preferred to be subjects of the Roman people than to rule others themselves.

Again, it is said that he makes himself so freely available to private citizens, and allows them such liberty to complain of the wrongs done to them by others, that although his standing is higher than that of princes, in his accessibility he seems on a par with the humblest in society. [42] His wisdom, too, and the authority and eloquence of his oratory—which is an element of the authority of a commander—you, citizens, have frequently had occasion to observe in this very place. As for his good faith, what store do you think our allies set by it when all our enemies, of every race, have judged it inviolable? And such is his humanity that it would be difficult to say which was greater—the enemy's fear of his valour while they were fighting him or their gratitude for his mercy once they had been defeated. So will anyone hesitate to entrust this great war to him—a man who seems destined by some divine intelligence for the purpose of terminating all the wars of our time?

[43] Now authority is another factor of prime importance in the management of warfare and the command of armies; and I am sure no one doubts that the commander we are considering is pre-eminent in this too. Who is not aware how vitally important it is to

the management of a war what our enemies and our allies think of our generals—because we know that in such critical situations people are made to experience fear, contempt, hatred, and devotion just as much by talk and rumour as by rational calculation? What name, then, has ever been more famous throughout the world than his? Whose achievements have equalled his? On whom else have you bestowed such great and conspicuous marks of esteem—which more than anything else establish authority? [44] Do you imagine there is any region anywhere that is so remote that word has never reached it of that great day on which the entire Roman people packed the forum, together with all the temples which afford a view of this place, in order to insist that Gnaeus Pompeius, and he alone, be appointed commander in a war that affected all peoples?* I do not intend to say any more, or use other commanders to demonstrate the importance of authority in war: Gnaeus Pompeius himself can be taken as the perfect example of every good quality.

On the very day on which you appointed him commander of the war against the pirates, grain, which had been extremely scarce and expensive, suddenly dropped in price and became as cheap as could hardly have happened in a time of prolonged peace and exceptional harvests—all as a result of one man's reputation and the hopes he inspired. [45] And now, after the catastrophic defeat in Pontus which I reluctantly referred to a short while ago,* when our allies were in a state of panic, the enemy's resources and morale had recovered, and the province* was left without adequate defences, you would have lost Asia, citizens, had not the good fortune of the Roman people so providentially brought Gnaeus Pompeius into the area at the critical moment. His arrival checked Mithridates, elated by his unaccustomed victory, and slowed the progress of Tigranes, who was threatening Asia with large forces. So who will doubt what his action will accomplish, when his authority has already produced such results? Who will doubt that with an official command and an army he will easily save our allies and revenues, when he has already protected them merely by his name and reputation?

[46] But look what it tells us about the authority of Gnaeus Pompeius amongst the enemies of the Roman people,* when in so short a space of time they have all surrendered to him, and to him alone, from places so far away and so far apart; and when envoys from the assembly of Cretan states, when there was already a

commander of ours with an army in their island, travelled almost to the ends of the earth to find Gnaeus Pompeius and tell him that it was to him that all the states of Crete wished to surrender!* And did not Mithridates himself send an envoy all the way to Spain, again to Gnaeus Pompeius?* (Pompeius always considered the man an envoy, although those who resented that he had been sent expressly to Pompeius* preferred to consider him a spy.) So you are now in a position to decide, citizens, what effect you think this authority will have on those kings,* and on foreign peoples, heightened as it has been by his subsequent achievements and by the great marks of esteem which you have conferred upon him.

[47] It remains for me to speak about the quality of luck— something that no one can guarantee in his own case, but which we may nevertheless call to mind and take note of in the case of another. As is appropriate for a man speaking about something that is under the control of the gods, I will speak briefly and diffidently. In my judgement, it was not only because of their ability, but very often because of their good fortune that Maximus, Marcellus, Scipio, Marius,* and the other great generals were granted armies and commands. For it is certainly the case that some men of distinction were helped towards their attainment of honour, glory, and great achievements by a kind of heaven-sent good fortune. But with respect to the luck of the man about whom I am now speaking, I am going to be careful not to claim too much. I shall avoid saying that good fortune was within his control, but instead will make it look as if I am doing no more than noting what has happened in the past, and expressing the hope that things will continue in the same way in the future. If I do that, the immortal gods will not view what I say as offensive or ungrateful. [48] I am therefore not going to proclaim his great achievements at home and on campaign, on land and at sea, and point out the luck that has accompanied them—how it is not just the case that his fellow-citizens have always agreed with his wishes, our allies always complied with them, and our enemies always obeyed them, but even the winds and the weather have always fallen in with them. This, though, I will say, very briefly, that no one has ever had the presumption to dare to ask the immortal gods, even privately in his own heart, for favours as numerous and substantial as those which the immortal gods have showered upon Gnaeus Pompeius. And not only for the sake of our common security and our

empire, but for the sake of the man himself, you ought to hope and pray, citizens, as indeed you do,* that the luck that he enjoys should remain associated with him for ever.

[49] Therefore since this war is so important that it cannot be ignored, and so large in scale that it must be managed with especial care, and since it is open to you to put in command of it a man who possesses unrivalled knowledge of warfare, exceptional ability, outstanding authority, and extraordinary good fortune, can you hesitate, citizens, to accept this great blessing, which the immortal gods have offered and granted to you, and use it to protect and enhance our country? [50] Suppose that Gnaeus Pompeius were at this moment a private citizen at Rome: he would still have to be selected for a war of this importance, and sent out. But as it is, in addition to all his other qualifications, he has the further advantage that he is already in the area where he is needed, has an army, and can immediately take over the other armies from those currently in command of them. So what are we waiting for? What is to stop us following the guidance of the immortal gods and entrusting this war against Mithridates to the same man to whom we have, to the greatest benefit of the state, entrusted everything else?

[51] However, the illustrious and patriotic Quintus Catulus, a man to whom you have awarded the highest honours that are in your power to bestow, and Quintus Hortensius,* who possesses supreme gifts of position, fortune, merit, and talent, hold a different view. For my part, I admit that their authority has influenced you strongly on many occasions in the past, as indeed it should. But in this particular case, although, as you know, the authority of these valiant and illustrious gentlemen stands against me, we can still set that authority to one side and arrive at the truth by a logical consideration of the facts. And it will be all the more easy to do this because my opponents admit the truth of everything I have said so far—that the war is an important one and large in scale, and that Gnaeus Pompeius alone possesses all the necessary qualities in the fullest measure.

[52] What, then, is Hortensius' position? It is that if everything is to be put in the hands of one man, then Pompeius is the most appropriate person; but that everything should *not* be handed over to one man. This argument is now out of date: it has been refuted much more by the course of events than by words. For it was you yourself, Quintus Hortensius, who with your matchless fluency

and unrivalled eloquence made a long, impressive, and highly
wrought speech in the senate opposing the valiant Aulus Gabinius,*
when he had published his bill to appoint a single commander
against the pirates; and from this place too you spoke at length
against the bill. [53] So, by the immortal gods, if the Roman people
had chosen at that time to pay more heed to your authority than to
their own welfare and their true interests, would we still be in possession today of our present glory and our world empire? Or do you
imagine that we actually had an empire at a time when envoys,
quaestors, and praetors of the Roman people were regularly kidnapped, when communication both official and non-official with any
province was out of the question, and when all the seas were so
closed to us that it was in fact impossible for us to transact any public
or private business at all?

[54] Was there ever any state in the past—I do not mean Athens,
which is said at one time to have had a fairly extensive command of
the seas, nor Carthage, with its navy and considerable maritime
strength, nor Rhodes, whose naval discipline and success has never
been forgotten—was there any state in the past, I repeat, so weak and
insignificant that it was unable by itself to defend its own harbours
and fields and some portion of its territory and coast? And yet—by
Hercules!—for a number of years prior to the passing of the Gabinian law, the great Roman people, who have preserved their reputation for invincibility in naval warfare right down to our own times,
were deprived of a large—in fact the largest part not just of their
own resources, but of their prestige and their empire. [55] Our
ancestors overcame King Antiochus and King Perseus* at sea, and
defeated the Carthaginians,* the most experienced and best-equipped
seafarers, in every naval engagement they fought with them; but we,
by contrast, were nowhere a match for the pirates. In earlier times
not only did we keep Italy safe, but we were able to guarantee the
safety of all our allies, however far off, simply through the prestige of
our empire. The island of Delos,* for example, far away from us in the
Aegean Sea, was a place to which people used to come from all over
with their cargoes of merchandise. It was crammed with riches, and
it was small, with no city wall; but despite all this its inhabitants were
never afraid. We, on the other hand, were deprived of access not just
to our provinces and the coasts of Italy and our ports, but even to the
Appian Way!* At that period the magistrates of the Roman people

must surely have felt ashamed to mount this very platform,* given that our ancestors had handed it down to us decorated with naval trophies and spoils taken from enemy ships!

[56] The Roman people recognized that you, Quintus Hortensius, and the others who put forward the same view, were speaking with the best of intentions in expressing that view. Nevertheless, when our country's security was at stake, the Roman people preferred to pay heed to the wrong done to them rather than to your authority. The result was that a single law, a single man, and a single year not only released you* from the grievous and humiliating situation you were in, but also brought about one in which you seemed at last genuinely to be master of all other peoples and nations on land and sea.

[57] This, in my opinion, makes it all the more unbecoming that there should have been opposition to the request, the most urgent request, of Gnaeus Pompeius that Aulus Gabinius should be appointed as his legate*—whether this opposition was instigated in order to attack Gabinius or Pompeius, or most likely both of them. Is the man who is requesting a legate of his own choice for a war of this importance an unsuitable person to be granted what he asks for, when other commanders going off to rob our allies and plunder our provinces have taken with them whatever legates they chose? Or should the man who carried the law which brought security and honour to the Roman people and all other peoples be permitted no connection with the commander and army which were appointed as a result of his advice and his willingness to put himself at risk? [58] Or take Gaius Falcidius, Quintus Metellus, Quintus Coelius Latiniensis, and Gnaeus Lentulus,* whose names I mention with the greatest respect: after they had been tribunes of the plebs, they were allowed to serve as legates the following year. So are people going to insist on the letter of the law only in the case of Gabinius—someone who was surely entitled to special consideration? After all, the war was being conducted under a 'Gabinian law', and it was Gabinius himself who, through your vote, was responsible for the appointment of the commander and the army. I hope that the consuls will bring the question of his appointment to a legateship before the senate. If they drag their feet or refuse, I undertake to raise it there myself. I will allow no one's hostility to deter me from relying on your support and defending your right to appoint whomsoever you choose to office, nor will I pay attention to any obstruction short of a tribunician veto—and

anyone who threatens to interpose a veto will have to think long and hard, I believe, about how far they may go. In my opinion, citizens, Aulus Gabinius has a unique right to be treated as the partner of Gnaeus Pompeius in the war against the pirates and in his other achievements, seeing that one of these men, through your votes, entrusted the conduct of that war to a single person, whereas the other one took on what had been entrusted to him and carried it out.

[59] It remains, I think, for me to say something about the authoritative view held by Quintus Catulus. When he asked you on whom you would place your hopes if you put everything into Gnaeus Pompeius' hands and something then happened to him, it was a great tribute to his merit and position that you answered, almost to a man, that you would place them on him. His ability is, it is true, so outstanding that, no matter how large or difficult the undertaking, his intelligence could master it, his integrity safeguard it, and his merit accomplish it. But on the present question, I disagree with him most emphatically, because I believe that the more short and uncertain human life is, the more the state ought to take advantage of the life and qualities of someone who is truly great—for as long, indeed, as the immortal gods will allow.

[60] 'But no departure should be made from the precedents and principles of our ancestors.' I shall not point out here that our ancestors invariably followed custom in time of peace, but expediency in war, and that they invariably responded to emergencies with new ways of doing things. I shall not point out that two very serious wars, the Punic war and the Spanish war, were terminated by one and the same commander, and that the two powerful cities which above all others threatened our empire, Carthage and Numantia, were both destroyed by the same man, Scipio.* I shall not remind you that not so long ago it seemed appropriate to you and your fathers to rest all the hopes of the Roman empire in Gaius Marius alone, appointing him to conduct a war against Jugurtha, and another against the Cimbri, and another against the Teutoni.*

In the case of Gnaeus Pompeius—in which Quintus Catulus opposes any departure from precedent being made—just think how many departures from precedent have already been made with Quintus Catulus' full support! [61] Was anything so unprecedented as for a mere youth, holding no public office, to raise an army at a time of national crisis?* Yet that is what he did. For him to command it? He did command it. To succeed brilliantly in that command? He did succeed. Was anything such a departure from custom as for a man who was barely grown up and much too young to qualify for senatorial rank* to be given a command and an army, and to be put in charge of Sicily and Africa and entrusted with the management of a war there? In these duties he displayed exceptional ability, responsibility, and integrity; in Africa he terminated a war of the greatest importance, and brought his army home victorious. Was anything so unheard of as for a Roman equestrian to hold a triumph? Yet the Roman people did not merely witness that triumph: they thought that everyone ought to go and see it and celebrate it together with enthusiasm. [62] Was anything so unusual as for a Roman equestrian, even though there were two illustrious and valiant consuls* available, to be sent to a great and terrible war with a consul's authority? He was indeed sent. There were at the time one or two in the senate who argued that it was wrong to send with the authority of a consul someone who was only a private citizen; but then Lucius Philippus is said to have replied that as far as he was concerned, he was voting not to send him with a consul's authority, but with that of both the consuls!* Indeed, such was the general confidence that he would serve the country well that a task that would normally be assigned to two consuls was entrusted to the abilities of a single youth. Was anything so unparalleled as for him to be exempted from the laws by senatorial decree and made consul at an age when he was not yet legally qualified to hold any curule office?* Was anything so incredible as for a Roman equestrian to be awarded a second triumph by senatorial decree?* In fact if you count up all the departures from precedent that have been allowed to everyone in history, there are fewer of them than we have witnessed in the case of this one man. [63] And all these numerous instances, so significant and so unparalleled, were approved, to the benefit of this same person, with the full endorsement of Quintus Catulus and other eminent men of equal standing.*

Let them therefore make sure that we do not have a situation in which you have always approved their decisions about the standing of Gnaeus Pompeius, but they reject your own judgements, and the decisions of the Roman people, about him. This would be seen as unjust and intolerable—particularly given that the Roman people are now in a strong position to defend their own decision about him in the face of all who disagree. Indeed, you have every right to defend that decision, seeing that when you chose him, and him alone, out of many possible contenders, to appoint to the war against the pirates, a chorus of protest was heard from precisely the same people who are protesting now. [64] If you appointed him to that command for frivolous reasons or without considering the national interest, then those men are right to try to use their wisdom to temper your enthusiasm. But if it was in fact you who had a clearer view of the national interest than they did at that time, if it was you who, by yourselves and in the face of their opposition, brought self-respect to our empire and safety to the world, then these leading men should finally admit that they and everyone else have now no option but to defer to the unanimous authority of the Roman people.

This war, citizens, relates to Asia, and to kings. It therefore calls not only for the unique military ability that Gnaeus Pompeius possesses, but also for many other fine moral qualities. It is not easy for a Roman commander to pass through Asia, Cilicia, Syria, and the kingdoms of the interior, and think only of the enemy and of honour. Then again, there may be some commanders who have feelings of decency and self-control and are restrained in their behaviour; but because so many of the rest are utterly rapacious, no one actually believes that the decent ones exist.

[65] It is impossible to exaggerate, citizens, the degree to which we are detested by foreign peoples, because of the greed and corruption of the men we have sent out to govern them in recent years.* In all those lands, do you think there is any shrine that our magistrates have treated as sacred, any state they have treated as inviolable, or any private house they have treated as closed and barred to them? On the contrary, they actually go searching for rich and flourishing cities that they can find an excuse for declaring war on: that gives them their opportunity of plundering them. [66] I would gladly discuss this face to face with the eminent and illustrious Quintus Catulus and Quintus Hortensius: they know well the wounds that have been inflicted on our allies, they can see the disasters that have befallen them, they can hear their lamentations.* When you send out armies, do you think it is to defend your allies from the enemy, or to use the enemy as an excuse for attacking your friends and allies? Is there any state in Asia that is capable of restraining the spirit and determination of a single military tribune, let alone of a legate or a commander?

So even if you have a commander who seems capable of defeating the armies of kings in a pitched battle, still, unless he is also capable of keeping his hands, his eyes, and his thoughts off the allies' property, their wives and children, the art works of their shrines and cities, and the royal gold and treasure, he will be unfit to be sent to a war in Asia, and against kings. [67] Do you imagine that there is any state at peace with Rome that remains rich? Do our opponents consider any state that remains rich to be at peace with Rome? Citizens, the coastal districts asked for Gnaeus Pompeius not just because of his military reputation, but because of his self-restraint. For they saw that all but a few governors every year were enriching themselves at public expense, and that all we seemed to be doing with our so-called fleets was incurring more and more losses and so adding to our disgrace. I can only conclude, then, that those who object to everything being put in the hands of one man are unaware of the avarice of those who assume provincial commands, the money they spend to acquire them, and the deals they do to be assigned them— as if we did not see that Gnaeus Pompeius is 'great'* not only because of his own virtues, but because of others' vices! [68] So do not hesitate to entrust the supreme command to this one man, the only man in many years that our allies, when he arrives at their cities with his army, are happy to receive.

But if you think that my proposal, citizens, needs to be backed up by men of authority, you will see that it is being supported by someone who has considerable expertise in all types of warfare as well as in important matters of state, Publius Servilius:* his achievements on land and sea are so outstanding that, when you are considering questions of war, you ought to pay more heed to him than to anyone else. It also has the support of Gaius Curio,* on whom you have conferred exceptional honours, a man of the greatest achievements, and of exceptional talent and wisdom. It has the support of Gnaeus Lentulus,* in whom you will all recognize exceptional intelligence and exceptional decorum, in keeping with the highest honours that you have conferred upon him. And it has the support of Gaius Cassius,* a man of unparalleled integrity, uprightness, and resolution. See, then, how the authority of these men allows me to answer the arguments of those who oppose me!

[69] Since that is how things stand, Gaius Manilius, I would first like to applaud and strongly support your law, your intention, and your proposal; and then I would like to urge you, since you have the

authority of the Roman people behind you, to stand by that proposal, and not be deterred by violence or threats from any quarter. In the first place, I am sure you possess the required courage and determination. Secondly, when we see such a large and enthusiastic crowd assembled here for a second time to appoint the same man as before, how can we be in any doubt about either what is proposed or our ability to see it through?

For my own part, whatever energy, wisdom, industry, and talent I may possess, whatever influence I have by virtue of the praetorship which the Roman people have bestowed upon me, and whatever I can accomplish by means of authority, loyalty, and resolution, all this I pledge and devote to you and to the Roman people, for the purpose of carrying this proposal through. [70] And I call all the gods to witness—especially those who preside over this hallowed spot, who can see right into the minds of public figures—that I am not supporting this proposal because anyone has asked me to, or because I suppose that by doing so I would gain the favour of Gnaeus Pompeius, or because I am looking to use any great man's position to gain for myself protection from attack or help in attaining office.* After all, any attack will easily be repelled (insofar as a mere human may guarantee it) by the protection of innocence, and as for office, that will come to me, if you wish it so, not from any individual, or as a result of speeches given here, but from my own hard work in the career I have been following.*

[71] So whatever burden I have taken on with regard to this issue, citizens, I declare that I have done it entirely for the sake of the national interest. Indeed, far from seeming to have done it in order to win popularity, I am aware that it has actually made me quite a few enemies, both open and undeclared; and I could well have done without this, although it would not have been in your interest for me not to have acted as I have done. But the conclusion I came to, citizens, was that since I was holding this high office* which you were kind enough to bestow upon me, I had a duty to put your wishes, the dignity of Rome, and the security of our provinces and allies before considerations of my own private interest.

# IN CATILINAM
## ('AGAINST CATILINE')

In 64 BC Cicero achieved his life's ambition and was elected consul, together with Gaius Antonius Hybrida. Their year of office, 63, turned out to be one of the more eventful years of the late republic: an attempted *coup d'état*, the Catilinarian conspiracy, took place. The leader and figure-head of this was Lucius Sergius Catilina ('Catiline' in English), a patrician with an unsavoury past who had finally despaired of being elected consul, and had decided instead to seize power—a consulship, rather than a dicta-torship or worse—by unconstitutional means. A rising of Catiline's followers in Rome was nipped in the bud by Cicero; a related rising in Etruria, led by Catiline, was put down by an army under the command of Antonius. Cicero was more alive than his fellow senators to the very real threat which Catiline presented: the senators were more inclined to believe a patrician ex-praetor than a consular new man, and would take no action against Catiline without proof of his guilt. But Cicero provided that proof: he exposed the conspiracy, won over public opinion (thereby saving potentially thousands of lives), and then suppressed the rising in the city by the controversial execution of five ringleaders who had admit-ted their guilt before the senate—but had not been formally tried. In a series of speeches, *In Catilinam* ('Against Catiline') or, as they are more familiarly known, the *Catilinarians*, he provoked Catiline into open revolt, informed the senate and people of important developments, and debated the fate of those arrested. The careful but decisive manner in which he dealt with the crisis and removed the threat ensured that there were no adverse long-term consequences for Rome. The consequences for himself, however, were disastrous: in 58 he was exiled by his enemy Publius Clodius Pulcher for what he regarded, with justification, as his greatest public achievement.

The Catilinarian conspiracy was a serious, if short-lived, emergency in the final decades of the republic. Cicero's four *Catilinarians*, together with Sallust's *Catiline*, a historical account of the conspiracy written two dec-ades later (*c.*42 BC), make this the most fully attested event in Roman history. It was also the central event in Cicero's life: many of his sub-sequent public utterances were made, implicitly or very often explicitly, with reference to the conspiracy and the actions which he took at that time. Moreover, the *Catilinarians* are the most famous, most exciting, and most read of Cicero's speeches—thrilling from beginning to end, and compelling examples of the use of oratory in a fast-developing political crisis.

Catiline's family was of no political importance—it had produced no consul for more than 300 years—and his patrician birth, though it gave him considerable social distinction, did not lead automatically to high office. His career began with military service under Gnaeus Pompeius Strabo in the Social War, and under Sulla in *c.*82–80. During the latter period he made use of the opportunities presented by the civil war and by Sulla's proscriptions to amass vast wealth: in the competitive world of the post-Sullan era, money was essential if one was to succeed in politics— and also, in Catiline's case, avoid conviction in the courts. The sources claim that he murdered various members of his family at this time (his brother, his wife's brother, and his sister's husband) or at other times (his wife and son), but these allegations are best explained as arising from the character-assassination to which he was subjected in the 60s (the best-attested allegation, the murder of his wife's brother Marcus Marius Gratidianus, dissolves upon close inspection; cf. B. A. Marshall, *CQ*, NS 35 (1985), 124–33). Nevertheless, he appears to have committed a number of murders outside his own family; we have the names of four alleged victims. After a further period of military service (it is not known where) in the early 70s, he is next heard of in 73, when he was prosecuted for adultery with a Vestal virgin, Fabia, a half sister (or cousin) of Cicero's wife Terentia. However, various consulars, including the highly respected Quintus Lutatius Catulus (the consul of 78), submitted testimonials in his favour, and the charge was withdrawn.

In 68 he was praetor, and in 67–66 he served as governor of Africa. During his governorship, embassies came to Rome to protest against his rapacity, and in the summer of 65 a charge of extortion was brought against him. Cicero, not yet his enemy, considered defending him (*Att.* 1.2.1; cf *Cael.* 14), despite believing him to be guilty (*Att.* 1.1.1): clearly Catiline was still respectable (and had done nothing to injure Cicero's family in the affair over Fabia). When the case came to trial, he was supported by the consul Lucius Manlius Torquatus and was acquitted— allegedly after collusion with the prosecutor Publius Claudius Pulcher (the future Clodius).

The trial, however, had delayed his plans to stand for the consulship. He first attempted to stand in 66 when he returned from Africa and found that the consulships of 65 had unexpectedly become vacant. Publius Cornelius Sulla and Publius Autronius Paetus had been elected for 65, but had then been convicted of electoral malpractice and deprived of their prospective consulships. Catiline therefore applied to stand in the supplementary election that would be held to fill the vacancies: if he were elected, this would neatly allow him to escape his likely prosecution for extortion (since magistrates could not be prosecuted while holding a senior public office). However, the consul presiding over the supplementary election, Lucius Volcacius Tullus, refused to accept his candidature on the grounds that he had not submitted his nomination within the specified period (meaning, presumably, that he had not been a candidate in the original election). The next year, 65, was (again, presumably) the year in which Catiline had originally intended to stand; but at that point his extortion trial was under way, and so he had to defer his candidature until 64.

The political situation at the end of 66 and beginning of 65 was volatile. There was a rumour that Sulla and Autronius were planning to recover their forfeited consulships by violence: they may have demonstrated against the incoming consuls, Lucius Manlius Torquatus and Lucius Aurelius Cotta, on 1 January 65. Secondly, there were popular disturbances over the impending trial of Gaius Manilius, the tribune of 66 who had proposed the *lex Manilia* putting Pompey in command of the war against Mithridates. Cicero, as praetor in charge of the extortion court in 66, had scheduled the trial for the last day of the year, but had then been forced to postpone it until 65; when it finally took place, the senate asked the consuls to attend and keep order. What role Catiline may have played in these events is unclear. He is said to have appeared in the forum, armed, on the last day of 66, and also to have put off his plans until 5 February 65; these incidents could conveniently be explained as being connected with the deferred trial of Manilius (if this is correct, Catiline is more likely to have been acting against Manilius, not for him). In later accounts by Cicero, however, as well as in the credulous accounts of Sallust and later historians, Catiline is implicated in the events relating to Sulla and Autronius, and his involvement is blown up into a 'first Catilinarian conspiracy', a plot to murder the consuls and leading senators and seize power (as rumour claimed, absurdly, that Sulla and Autronius intended to do). Had Catiline really intended to do anything of this nature he would not, of course, have been supported by the consul Torquatus at his extortion trial in 65 (nor would Cicero have considered defending him); but once Catiline had resorted to conspiracy in 63, he was thought to have been capable of anything. The 'first Catilinarian conspiracy' of 66 and/or 65 has been one of the great red herrings of Roman history, and was fully exposed as a fiction only in 1964 (by two scholars independently, R. J. Seager, *Historia*, 13 (1964), 338–47, and R. Syme, *Sallust* (Berkeley etc., 1964), 86–102).

It was in the election of 64, then, that Catiline stood for the consulship for the first time. He had six rivals: Cicero, Antonius, and four minor figures with no realistic chance of election (Lucius Cassius Longinus, the future Catilinarian conspirator, was one of them). It was a weak field. Antonius' only claim to consideration was that he was the son of Marcus Antonius the orator, the consul of 99 BC. Like Catiline, the younger Antonius had enriched himself in the Sullan proscriptions; he had then been expelled from the senate by the censors in 70 (for extortion, contempt of court, and debt), but had quickly secured readmission, becoming tribune in *c.*68 and praetor in 66. In the praetorian elections for 66, Cicero was the first of the candidates to be elected: he then gave his support to Antonius, with the result that Antonius rose from last place to third. In 64, Antonius and Catiline were the establishment choice for the consulship, and apparently enjoyed the support of Crassus and Caesar. Despite the fact that Antonius owed Cicero a debt of gratitude for his support three years earlier, he and Catiline decided to join forces in order to defeat him. Their bribery was so extensive that the senate considered proposing fresh legislation to impose severer penalties; the proposal was vetoed by a tribune. Cicero then made a strong attack in the senate on Antonius' and Catiline's character and record, in a speech entitled *In toga candida* ('In a whitened toga', a whitened toga being the dress worn by candidates for election; this is the origin of the word 'candidate'). This speech, of which only fragments survive today, is the origin of the myth of the 'first Catilinarian conspiracy', and of the allegation that Catiline was responsible for the murder of Gratidianus. (*In toga candida* did not attack the other four candidates.) Catiline and Antonius replied to the speech by attacking Cicero's lack of senatorial ancestors. When the election came, Cicero was once again elected first, and Antonius narrowly beat Catiline to second place. (It is interesting to reflect how history might have been different if Catiline had instead beaten Antonius. For one thing, we would not have the *Catilinarians*.)

After the elections, Catiline was prosecuted again, this time for murders committed during the Sullan proscriptions (i.e. the murder of persons who had not been proscribed, since the proscriptions themselves were legal). His uncle, Lucius Bellienus, had been convicted of this same offence just before the elections. But Catiline was supported once again by the consulars (though not this time by Torquatus), and was acquitted.

Cicero, then, had an ally of Catiline for his colleague as consul. Early in 63, he did a deal with Antonius. In the allocation of provinces for the consuls of 63, Cicero had been assigned Macedonia, which offered an unscrupulous governor opportunities for considerable self-enrichment, while Antonius received the much less lucrative Cisalpine Gaul. Cicero had no wish to govern a province and be absent from Rome, and so he bought Antonius' allegiance by exchanging provinces with him. Some months later he publicly renounced Cisalpine Gaul, and so, unusually, did not proceed to a province when his year as consul was at an end. (Cisalpine Gaul was assigned instead to the praetor Quintus Caecilius Metellus Celer, the future consul of 60.) With hindsight, this was the

wrong decision. If he had been absent for a year or two after his consulship, he might have avoided the attacks he was to endure for his execution
of the ringleaders of the conspiracy. (On Cicero's exchange of provinces,
see W. Allen, Jr., *TAPA* 83 (1952), 233–41.)

In the summer, Catiline was standing for the consulship for the second
and final time. The other candidates were Decimus Junius Silanus, who
had been one of the candidates in 65, Lucius Licinius Murena, and
Servius Sulpicius Rufus, who was a leading jurist and friend of Cicero;
Sulpicius and Catiline were both patricians and so it was impossible for
both of them to be elected (every year at least one consul had to be a
plebeian). During the campaign bribery was once again rife—probably all
the candidates except Sulpicius engaged in it—and once again the senate
attempted to suppress it. First, a senatorial decree was passed, on Cicero's
proposal, clarifying the terms of the law on electoral malpractice, the *lex
Calpurnia* of 67; afterwards, on Sulpicius' insistence, Cicero and Antonius
together carried a new law, the *lex Tullia*, regulating electoral practices,
defining malpractices more specifically, and adding a ten-year exile to the
penalties laid down by the *lex Calpurnia*. Marcus Porcius Cato, recently
elected to the tribunate for 62, threatened to prosecute any candidate for
the consulship who engaged in bribery—though he would, he added,
make an exception of his brother-in-law Silanus (whom we can probably
therefore assume to have been guilty). In the senate a few days before the
consular elections (in the second half of July), Cato specifically threatened
Catiline with prosecution. Catiline replied enigmatically that if he were
ruined by a conviction in the courts, he would see that he brought the
whole country down with him.

Shortly before the election was due to take place, Catiline gave an
inflammatory address at his house, recommending himself as someone
who was prepared to go to any lengths on behalf of the poor and desperate, among whom he included himself. He is represented in the sources as
having depended for his support on three groups of people: those of all
levels of society who were suffering as a result of debt; Sullan veterans
who had been rewarded with land but had fallen on hard times; and people
who had been dispossessed in Sulla's confiscations (the first group obviously overlapped to some extent with the other two). The fact that he
rallied his supporters under a silver eagle used by Marius in the war
against the Cimbri (see *Cat.* 1.24, 2.13; Sal. *Cat.* 59.3) would suggest that
he appealed more to the third group, dispossessed Marians, than to
the second: Cicero would then have exaggerated, in order to increase
Catiline's unpopularity, the extent to which he relied on Sullan veterans
(a group with whom few probably had much sympathy). But on the other
hand, Catiline's ally Manlius was a Sullan veteran; so there must have

been at least an element of the second group among his following. (See
further W. V. Harris, *Rome in Etruria and Umbria* (Oxford, 1971), 289–94.)

The difficulties faced by these groups were considerable. Italian agri-
culture was still suffering as a result of Sulla's civil war, confiscations, and
settlements (82–81), and as a result of Spartacus' revolt (73–71). Up and
down Italy, the men who had had their land taken away by Sulla and the
men to whom he had given it lived in close proximity: there must have
been a great deal of localized violence and unrest. Moreover, during the
previous decade the Third Mithridatic War (73–63) and the pirates (to 67)
had prevented Roman financiers lending money abroad, and they had
instead lent it in Italy. But with Pompey's defeat of Mithridates in 63 and
his settlement of the eastern provinces, there was a rush to lend money
overseas. (The situation became so serious that the senate this year banned
the export of gold and silver from Rome; Cicero took steps to enforce the
ban.) At home, creditors immediately called in their loans. This spelled
ruin for the urban plebs and for heavily indebted members of the upper
class alike. To many, their only hope appeared to be a one-off cancellation
of debts (*novae tabulae*): at the end of his life, in 44, Cicero was to remark
that pressure for this had never been greater than in his consulship (*Off.*
2.84). For the upper class, unprecedented political and social competition
caused by Sulla's rigid 'sequence of offices' (*cursus honorum*), with its ever
decreasing number of positions available at each stage in a senator's career,
had led to an explosion of bribery and indebtedness. Aediles, for instance,
were required to put on games at their own expense: the games would
need to be more spendid than the previous ones if the magistrate were to
rise higher, but even so he would have no guarantee that he would ever
gain the provincial governorship which would allow him to recoup his
outlay. After Caesar gave his aedilician games in 65 he was allegedly in
debt for 25 million sesterces; the sum was not paid off until he had
conquered Gaul. (See further Z. Yavetz, *Historia*, 12 (1963), 485–99; and
on debt in this period, M. W. Frederiksen, *JRS* 56 (1966), 128–41.)

Prior to his last attempt at the consulship, Catiline appears to have
shown no interest in addressing Rome's social problems; but the plight of
so many of his contemporaries now presented him with an opportunity.
During his campaign he was escorted by a large group of supporters from
Arretium and Faesulae in northern Etruria, one of the areas that had
suffered most from Sulla's confiscations and settlements. This group,
led by Gaius Manlius, a former Sullan centurion, consisted mainly of
discontented Sullan colonists, but also included a number of the dispossessed. (That is what Cicero says at *Mur.* 49; but it is possible, as we have
seen, that the Sullan colonists were in fact in the minority. Manlius'
presence in Rome is attested by Plutarch (*Cic.* 14.2).) To these men and

his other supporters, Catiline offered the policy they longed for—cancellation of debts. It was precisely the policy to win him the support of the desperate from all ranks of society—and one that no respectable politician was prepared to offer.

Once the content of Catiline's election address at his house had been reported to Cicero, Cicero persuaded the senate to postpone the elections in order that they could discuss the speech Catiline had made. So the senate met, and Catiline, called upon to justify himself, far from denying what he had said, made another speech in the same vein. To Cicero's dismay, the senate then declined to take any effective action, and the election therefore went ahead without further delay (there is no good reason for thinking it was postponed until October). Catiline attended with a gang of armed men. Cicero, who was presiding, came with a bodyguard, and ostentatiously wore a large cuirass. He did this partly to register his disagreement with the senate about the nature of the threat posed by Catiline, and partly to bring home to the people the danger that Catiline represented. The voting took place, and Silanus and Murena, the two plebeians, were elected. Sulpicius and Cato then launched a prosecution of Murena under the *lex Tullia* for electoral malpractice.

Despairing of gaining power by conventional means, Catiline now started his conspiracy. He could have chosen instead to wait for Murena's conviction and then stand against Sulpicius at the supplementary election which would follow: he did not this time face the difficulty he had faced in 65 of not having been a candidate in the original election. But he had evidently run out of patience, hope, and cash.

We know little of what happened in August and September. In September the senate seems to have discussed Catiline's conspiracy (on the rather dubious evidence of Suetonius, who says that they were discussing it on the day when the future emperor Augustus was born); but there was as yet no hard evidence against him. On the night of 19 (or perhaps 18) October, however, Crassus came to Cicero's house at midnight, accompanied by Marcus Claudius Marcellus (the future consul of 51 and subject of Cicero's *Pro Marcello*) and Quintus Caecilius Metellus Pius Scipio Nasica (the future consul of 52), and handed him a set of letters that had been delivered to his house. Crassus had opened only the one addressed to himself: it was anonymous, and warned him of an impending massacre by Catiline and advised him to leave Rome in secret. The next morning Cicero convened the senate and had the rest of the letters read aloud by their addressees (we are not told who they were); all the letters carried the same message as the letter to Crassus. After this, on 20 October (and therefore either at this same meeting of the senate or at another a day later), Quintus Arrius, an ex-praetor, reported that news had come from

Faesulae that Manlius was preparing an armed rising. The senate therefore passed the emergency decree (*senatus consultum ultimum* or 'SCU'),
first used against Gaius Gracchus in 121 BC, urging the consuls to take
whatever action they considered necessary for the security of the state (the
date of the SCU, usually given as 21 October, but given here as 20 October, is very uncertain: it was either eighteen or seventeen days before the
date of the *First Catilinarian*, which is itself uncertain).

A week later (27 October), Manlius, having heard of the passing of the
SCU, was in open rebellion. Some modern scholars have suggested that
his rising was in origin independent of Catiline. But there is no suggestion
of this in the ancient sources (except an ironic rejection of the idea by
Cicero at *Cat.* 2.14); and Manlius had supported Catiline during the
election campaign. The deal between Manlius and Catiline seems to have
been that Manlius would help Catiline achieve his ambition of being
elected consul if Catiline would then redress his men's grievances and give
them relief from their debts. Once Catiline had decided, after the election,
that he would continue to seek the consulship by other means, Manlius
must have made a decision that it was in his best interest to continue the
arrangement. (On Manlius' connection with Catiline, see F. J. Phillips,
*Historia*, 25 (1976), 443–4.)

Cicero now took a number of security measures, as he had been urged
to do by the senate's decree. He made arrangements for the defence of
Rome, and also of Praeneste, which he believed the conspirators were
planning to seize on 1 November. Early in November, news came from
Faesulae that Manlius' rebellion had begun, and there were reports of
slave revolts at Capua and in Apulia. To meet these threats, two generals
who were outside the city waiting to be awarded triumphs, Quintus
Marcius Rex (the consul of 68) and Quintus Caecilius Metellus Creticus
(the consul of 69), were sent to Faesulae and Apulia respectively. In addition, two praetors, Quintus Pompeius Rufus and Metellus Celer, were
sent respectively to Capua and Picenum. Rewards were offered to anyone
who came forward with information about the conspiracy. No one did so.

All this time Catiline remained in Rome. There was as yet no real
evidence to incriminate him: the letters sent to Crassus had been anonymous, and so proved nothing. Lucius Aemilius Paullus, however, gave notice
that he intended to prosecute Catiline for violence. Catiline responded by
offering to place himself in the custody first of Manius Aemilius Lepidus
(the consul of 66), then of Cicero, then of Metellus Celer (who presumably had not yet left for Picenum), then of a Marcus Metellus (possibly the
praetor of 69); but of these the first three refused to accept him, and
the fourth presumably refused also, since Catiline remained a free man.
The case never came to trial.

Quintus Marcius Rex, meanwhile, had arrived in Etruria. Manlius sent him a message stating his supporters' grievances, to which Marcius replied that the men should lay down their arms and put their trust in the senate's mercy. Understandably, they declined to take this advice. (It is interesting that Manlius should have attempted to make terms with Marcius: this would appear to show that his support for Catiline was merely the means to an end, and that Catiline's consulship was in itself a matter of indifference to him.)

On the night of 6 November, Catiline held a secret meeting in Rome with his chief supporters at the house of one of them, the senator Marcus Porcius Laeca, in the scythe-makers' quarter. Arrangements were made for Catiline himself to go to Manlius' army, and for other conspirators to go and take charge of the risings elsewhere in Italy. Those who remained would organize assassinations and the firing of various parts of the city. (Cicero makes much of the Catilinarians' alleged intention to burn Rome, and it was largely this claim which enabled him to turn the urban plebs against the conspiracy. It is incredible, however, that Catiline should have intended a general conflagration—though quite possible that he planned specific, localized fires, and was foolish enough to imagine that they would not spread.) Finally, two conspirators, Gaius Cornelius (an *eques*) and Lucius Vargunteius (a man who had been tried for electoral malpractice and probably expelled from the senate), would call on Cicero at his house early the next morning and assassinate him. (Antonius, of course, was Catiline's ally of old, and the conspirators did not plan to kill him.)

Cicero was well provided throughout the conspiracy with spies and informers, and so he was usually one step ahead of Catiline. One of his informers was Fulvia, the mistress of one of the conspirators, Quintus Curius (an ex-senator, expelled in 70). She told him of the meeting at Laeca's house and the plot to assassinate him, and so on the morning of 7 November Cornelius and Vargunteius found the consul's house closed to callers and strongly defended.

Cicero immediately called a meeting of the senate, in the temple of Jupiter Stator. (Some modern accounts place this meeting a day later, on 8 November; but it seems most unlikely that Cicero would have waited a day. On 3 December he would have no trouble summoning the senate for an immediate meeting. For further discussion of this point, see second note on *Cat.* 1.1 below, pp. 302–3.) To the surprise of many, no doubt, Catiline attended; but no one would sit near him. Cicero then stood up and denounced him in his *First Catilinarian* (*In Catilinam* I)—a speech aptly described by Sallust (who is not on the whole particularly interested in Cicero) as 'brilliant, and of service to the state' (*Cat.* 31.6). (The scene is well imagined in a famous nineteenth-century fresco by Cesare Maccari in the Palazzo Madama in Rome.) At some point Catiline offered to go into voluntary exile, if the senate would pass a decree to that effect; but Cicero would have none of it. When Cicero had finished, Catiline bravely replied, protesting his innocence and pointing out that he was a patrician whereas Cicero (being from Arpinum) was a mere squatter—a thoroughly Roman line of argument. This defence was not well received, however, and Catiline rushed out of the temple. (This is Sallust's version; Cicero was to claim in 46 BC that Catiline said nothing (*Orat.* 129).)

That night he slipped out of Rome—but without taking his followers with him. He left behind letters for several consulars in which he again protested his innocence, and claimed that he had left for exile in Massilia (Marseilles, the refuge of Verres) in order to spare his country a civil war. The road he took, the Via Aurelia, was indeed the road to Massilia, not the one to Faesulae. But on the other hand he had already sent ahead a military force and a consignment of arms to wait for him at Forum Aurelium on the Via Aurelia (*Cat.* 1.24, 2.13), and from there he would be able to cut across to the Via Cassia, and follow it (as in the event he did) through Arretium to Faesulae. In view of this, it is unrealistic to suppose that he had any intention of going into exile, whether permanently, or merely until Murena was convicted and a supplementary consular election announced. Instead, his choice of the Via Aurelia, and the letters he left behind, must have been intended to deceive public opinion, in order to minimize the chances of a force being sent after him.

However, he also sent a 'very different letter' (as Sallust says) to Catulus (the ex-consul who had helped him out at his adultery trial in 73). In this letter he stated that he had taken the action that he had taken (which was not spelt out, and could refer to either insurrection or exile) because he had been robbed of office, that he was following his normal custom of championing the oppressed, and that his financial situation was capable of recovery; and he asked Catulus to look after his wife, Aurelia Orestilla. This letter differed from the other ones that he sent in that this one did not unequivocally state that he had gone into exile; hence he cannot have decided firmly on that course of action. The letter is preserved in Sallust's account (*Cat.* 35); it gives the impression of a man who is proud, impetuous, and doomed. Catulus read it out in the senate.

Next day, 8 November, Cicero addressed the people at a public meeting while the senate were being summoned: this speech is the *Second Catilinarian* (*In Catilinam* II). In it he informs the people of Catiline's flight and describes the types of people who support the conspiracy— though taking care to exclude his audience themselves from his analysis (Sallust says that initially the entire plebs supported Catiline: see *Cat.* 37.1; 48.1).

A week or so later, news reached Rome that Catiline had arrived in Manlius' camp. There could now be no further doubt as to his guilt. The senate declared him and Manlius public enemies; Antonius was given the command against them, and Cicero was to defend the city. An amnesty was offered to any of Catiline's followers who surrendered before a certain date, but no one took up the offer.

It was at this point, in late November, that Sulpicius' and Cato's prosecution of Murena for electoral malpractice came to trial. To Sulpicius' disappointment and annoyance, Cicero undertook the defence, along with Quintus Hortensius Hortalus, and Crassus. Cicero's argument was that whether or not Murena had broken the *lex Tullia*—and he of course argued that he had not—Murena ought to be acquitted because of the threat from Catiline. He and Antonius were due to step down in a month's time, and it was absolutely necessary that there should be another two consuls ready to take over from them. Moreover, Murena was a military man whereas Sulpicius was a jurist, and in the current emergency it was the soldier who was needed. This argument persuaded the jury and Murena was unanimously acquitted. Afterwards Cicero published his speech, *Pro Murena*, one of his most entertaining and brilliant defences.

Shortly after the trial was over, Cicero, by an extraordinary stroke of good fortune, was given the chance to acquire the evidence that he needed to prove the guilt of Catiline's leading associates in the city. The Allobroges, a tribe from Narbonese Gaul who were suffering from exploitation and debt, had sent envoys to Rome to put their case before the senate, but the senate had rejected their appeal. Shortly afterwards, the envoys were approached by a freedman called Publius Umbrenus, who was acting on the instructions of the most senior of Catiline's followers, the patrician Publius Cornelius Lentulus Sura—the former consul of 71, who had been expelled from the senate in 70 (along with Antonius and Curius), and was now praetor. Umbrenus told the envoys that if they supported the conspiracy, they would get what they wanted. They were then introduced to a conspirator of equestrian rank, Publius Gabinius Capito, and were told the names of others who were in the plot. After debating among themselves what to do, the envoys decided to report what they had learned to their tribe's patron, Quintus Fabius Sanga (who was presumably the person who had put their case before the senate); and he went straight to Cicero. Seeing this as an opportunity to acquire incriminating evidence, and well aware of the propaganda value of the Catilinarians being caught conspiring with Rome's traditional enemy, the Gauls, he told Fabius to direct the Allobroges to ask the ringleaders for written statements which they could show to their people. Three of the conspirators complied: Lentulus, a patrician senator Gaius Cornelius Cethegus, and another *eques*, Lucius Statilius. A fourth conspirator, Lucius Cassius Longinus, a praetor with Cicero in 66 and one of the unsuccessful candidates for the consulship of 63, suspected a trap and replied that since he was going to Gaul anyway he need not put anything in writing—then promptly left Rome. The plan that was agreed was that the envoys would leave Rome by the Mulvian Bridge, just outside Rome to the north (on the road leading to the Via Cassia); they would be escorted as far as Faesulae by Titus Volturcius, a native of Cortona in Etruria; and then, after a meeting with Catiline, they would complete their journey to Gaul on their own. In addition to the statements which the Gauls were to take with them, Volturcius would take a personal letter from Lentulus to be delivered to Catiline, saying that Catiline ought to enlist slaves—something that he had always refused to do, since his rising was not a slave revolt and it would be highly damaging to his cause if it were perceived as being one, or could be represented as one. (The purpose of this letter must have been to give Catiline a means of assuring himself that Volturcius was not a spy, since Volturcius had joined the conspiracy only after Catiline's departure from Rome. One scholar has suspected that the letter was in fact a plant by Cicero; but Lentulus would later acknowledge in the senate that the handwriting was his.)

The envoys duly informed Cicero of the plan that had been arranged. He then ordered two of the praetors, Lucius Valerius Flaccus and Gaius Pomptinus, both military men, to place an ambush at the Mulvian Bridge on the appointed night, that of 2 December. In the early hours of the 3rd, the envoys and Volturcius walked into the trap. The envoys immediately surrendered. Volturcius made some resistance and then he too surrendered. The praetors took them, together with the incriminating letters, to Cicero.

Armed with this evidence (still kept sealed), Cicero gave orders that five of the conspirators—Lentulus, Cethegus, and Statilius, who had given letters to the envoys, together with Gabinius, whom the envoys would be able to identify, and a further conspirator, Marcus Caeparius of Tarracina—should be brought to him at once. The first four were fetched (they would not have known of the ambush at the Mulvian Bridge), and at the same time a cache of arms was removed from Cethegus' house. Caeparius, however, had heard of the discovery of the plot and had left for Apulia, where he was intending to instigate a slave revolt among the shepherds (evidently Metellus Creticus had been successful in putting down the earlier rising there). (We know nothing about Caeparius or what the evidence was which justified Cicero in ordering his arrest; perhaps he was named in the letters given to the envoys, and Cicero knew this.)

Cicero meanwhile had called a meeting of the senate in the temple of

Concord, and had given orders for the building to be surrounded by an armed guard. Out of regard for Lentulus' status as a praetor and fellow magistrate, he led him into the building by the hand; the other three conspirators followed under guard, and the meeting began. Volturcius was questioned first. Initially he denied all knowledge of the conspiracy; but when he had been promised immunity from prosecution in return for his evidence, he revealed what he knew, and named, besides the five conspirators whose arrest had been ordered, Autronius (the consul-elect of 65 who had been convicted of malpractice), Servius Cornelius Sulla (a senator and distant relation of the dictator Sulla), Vargunteius (one of the men who had attempted to assassinate Cicero on the morning of 7 November), and many others. Next, the envoys told their story, which corroborated Volturcius' evidence but may not have added much to it— although they did mention Cassius, who had declined to give them a letter and then fled. After this, the three conspirators whose letters had been captured were made to acknowledge their seals, and the letters were opened and read out. The contents were found to be sufficiently incriminating, and the men admitted their guilt; Gabinius also admitted his guilt, though he had written no letter. Lentulus was denounced by his brother-in-law, Lucius Julius Caesar, the consul of 64.

At the end of the meeting, the senate passed a decree. Cicero was thanked in the most generous terms for having saved Rome from extreme danger; the two praetors who carried out the ambush were thanked; and Antonius was thanked for having severed his connection with the conspirators (this must have been well meant, but inevitably sounds damning). Lentulus was to resign his office, and each of the five men whose arrest Cicero had ordered was to be placed in the custody of a senator: Lentulus was taken by the aedile Publius Cornelius Lentulus Spinther (the future consul of 57), Cethegus by an ex-praetor Quintus Cornificius, Statilius by Caesar, Gabinius by Crassus, and Caeparius (who appears to have been brought back to Rome at the end of the day) by Gnaeus Terentius. A further four conspirators—Cassius, Umbrenus, and two others, a Sullan colonist from Faesulae called Publius Furius, and a senator, Quintus Annius Chilo—were also to be placed in custody as soon as they were captured. (It is strange that only four people fell into this category, and not, for instance, Cicero's two would-be assassins, Cornelius and Vargunteius; the senate must have decided only to proceed against those against whom the evidence was unimpeachable). Finally, a thanksgiving was to be offered to the gods in Cicero's name—the first time such a thing had ever been done in honour of a civilian. In addition (not part of the decree), Catulus hailed Cicero as the father of his country, and Lucius Gellius Poplicola (the consul of 72 and censor of 70, whose good judgement in expelling Lentulus from the senate had just been dramatically confirmed) declared that in his view Cicero deserved the civic crown (a decoration normally awarded only to soldiers who had saved a citizen's life in battle). The senate certainly made amends for its failure to heed Cicero's warnings about Catiline earlier in the year.

By the time the meeting ended, it was evening. Cicero walked out of the temple, stepped a few paces forward into the forum, and there gave the people a full account of everything that had taken place. This speech, the *Third Catilinarian* (*In Catilinam* III), caused a complete turn-around in public opinion. Until now, the urban plebs had supported Catiline. Now, thanks largely to Cicero's revelation of Catiline's plans for burning parts of the city, the people cursed him and lauded Cicero to the skies. Sallust says they reacted as if they had been freed from slavery (*Cat.* 48.1–2).

The next day, 4 December, an informer, Lucius Tarquinius, gave information in the senate incriminating Crassus, but was disbelieved and imprisoned. It is certainly inconceivable that a man of Crassus' wealth, and an ally of the equestrian financiers, should have supported a move-ment for the cancellation of debts, and in any case Crassus had earlier demonstrated his loyalty by giving Cicero the letters which had been delivered to his house. Later Crassus suspected that Cicero was behind the allegation; but this is unlikely since Cicero refused to accept a false allegation made against Caesar by Catulus (whom Caesar had recently defeated in the election for *pontifex maximus*) and Gaius Calpurnius Piso (the consul of 67). The meeting also voted rewards for Volturcius and the envoys of the Allobroges. Finally, the nine conspirators whose cases were discussed the day before were declared to have acted against the interests of the state (like their earlier declaration that Catiline and Manlius were public enemies, this was a formulaic expression of disapproval, but one without generally accepted constitutional significance). While the senate was meeting, the followers of Lentulus attempted to gather a force together to set him free, and Cethegus urged his own followers to do the same for him.

On 5 December ('the Nones of December') a third meeting of the senate was held, in the temple of Concord, to decide what should be done with the five conspirators who were being held in custody, and the other four, should they be caught. Cicero was later to say (at *Att.* 12.21.1, written in 45 BC) that he had already made (i.e., presumably, expressed) a judgement on their fate before he consulted the senate on 5 December, but he does not say what judgement, or when (it has been suggested that he may have said something in the spoken version of the *Third Catili-narian*). In any case, the debate of 5 December was a full and free exchange of views, with many individual changes of mind as powerful and persuasive speeches were made, in a situation in which there was (as modern scholarship abundantly confirms) no right answer.

Cicero first called on Silanus, the consul-elect, for his opinion. Silanus said that the men deserved 'the extreme penalty', which everyone not unnaturally took to mean execution—a punishment which would certainly have had a deterrent effect on Catiline's supporters, but would not have been legal, since citizens could not be put to death without trial, and the senate was not at this date a criminal court (the senate's various decrees, such as the SCU, could not alter the fact that the conspirators were citizens and were entitled to citizens' legal rights). Next Cicero called the other consul-elect, Murena: he expressed the same opinion as Silanus; and so did fourteen ex-consuls. After that it was the turn of the praetors-elect to give their opinion. Caesar was called, and proposed a quite different punishment. Pointing out the dangerous precedent that execution would set, and hinting at the legal difficulties, he proposed instead life imprisonment: each conspirator would be held in a strongly fortified Italian town, and no one would ever be allowed to raise the question of their release. The proposal was completely impractical, as Cicero was quick to point out, and was in fact no more lawful than execution was. But it cleverly allowed Caesar to present himself before the senate as an implacable enemy of the conspirators, and then to appear before the people as the man who had attempted to save their lives. In this way he was able to enhance his status as a popular politician, an upholder of the rights of the people against the arbitrary power of magistrates. (Crassus, who was also believed to be sympathetic to Catiline, avoided committing himself to any view by staying at home.)

After this, it was no longer at all clear what was the right thing to do, and various speakers sided either with Silanus or with Caesar; an ex-praetor, Tiberius Claudius Nero, proposed putting off a decision until Catiline had been defeated. Cicero then intervened: in his *Fourth Catilinarian* (*In Catilinam* IV), he reviewed the two proposals, made clear (but did not explicitly state) his own preference for that of Silanus, and pressed the senate to come to a decision before nightfall. He also asked it not to be influenced by the possible consequences of their decision for himself. Since the senate was technically only an advisory body, the responsibility for any action taken would lie entirely with Cicero—though a senatorial vote would naturally give him considerable moral backing. (Later, for example at *Phil.* 2.18, he would sometimes claim that he had merely obeyed the senate's orders: this falsifies the constitutional position. His view that the conspirators had by their own actions forfeited their legal rights was equally spurious, though perhaps widely shared.)

At this point Silanus made a second speech, and feebly explained that by 'the extreme penalty' he had really meant life imprisonment: effectively, he withdrew his proposal. Speaker after speaker then gave their support to Caesar's proposal; one of these was Cicero's brother Quintus, a praetor-elect, who did not want his brother to have an illegal course of action forced upon him. So a consensus emerged in favour of life imprisonment. Only Catulus seems not to have wavered in his support for execution.

It was only now that the tribunes-elect, relatively junior members in the hierarchy, were called on to speak; and Cato, a young man who had recently demonstrated his uncompromising views at the trial of Murena, stood up. Castigating his brother-in-law Silanus for changing his mind (as a strict Stoic, Cato believed that changes of mind could not be justified), he bitterly attacked Caesar's proposal, accused him of being in league with Catiline, reproached the senators for their squeamishness, and argued vigorously for execution as being in accordance with the spirit of Roman tradition (even though the situation itself was unparalleled). It was an extraordinary performance, all the more remarkable in view of Cato's junior rank, and it marked him out to his contemporaries as a man of greatness. In his *Catiline* (51–2), Sallust gives his own versions of the speeches of both Caesar and Cato (he ignores the other ones, including Cicero's, in order to concentrate on these two), and allows the reader to infer that these two men—utterly different, but equally brilliant—will go on to become the two defining talents of the closing era of the republic. (Plutarch, *Cat. Mi.* 23.1–2 is also an important source for Cato's speech: it differs significantly from Sallust's account, and is probably closer to the truth. Details have been taken from both sources in the summary given above.)

When Cato sat down, the senate burst into applause. All the ex-consuls and a large number of others changed their minds and agreed with him. The question was put to a vote, and Cato's proposal was carried overwhelmingly. Even Cethegus' brother is said to have voted for execution. A further proposal from Caesar, that the conspirators' property should not be confiscated, nearly caused a riot, and some *equites* who had come in support of Cicero drew their swords on Caesar as he was leaving the building. (Cicero himself made sure afterwards that the men's property was not confiscated.)

By this time it was evening, and Cicero put the senate's decree into effect without delay. The five conspirators were fetched from where they were being held and led through the forum towards the state prison. Again, Cicero personally escorted Lentulus, since he, though no longer a praetor, was still an ex-consul; the other four were escorted by praetors. One after another the men were taken into the prison and lowered, by a rope, into a squalid subterranean execution chamber, the Tullianum, where they were immediately strangled. When the last of the men was dead, Cicero turned round to face the crowd and announced, 'They have lived' ('Vixere', the odd formulation being chosen to avoid bad luck). The crowd, silent until now, erupted into a state of euphoria. As Cicero made his way back through the forum to his house, the people crowded round him applauding him and calling him the saviour and founder of his country. Women holding lamps stood on the rooftops watching the scene. (This account of Cicero's warm reception in the forum comes from Plutarch, *Cic.* 22.5–7; but given that his source will be Cicero's lost account of his consulship, written in 60, there may be some exaggeration in Cicero's favour.) Cicero had overwhelming public backing for the action that he had taken, and he had undoubtedly saved the city from a bloody conflict. But he had broken the law, and the responsibility was his alone.

On 10 December the new tribunes entered office. One of them, Quintus Caecilius Metellus Nepos, lost no time in speaking out against the executions and threatening to veto Cicero's retiring speech, declaring that one who had punished others without allowing them the right to speak in their own defence ought not to be allowed the right to speak himself. On 29 December, Cicero's last day as consul, he carried out his threat: he and another tribune, Lucius Calpurnius Bestia, who was allegedly a Catilinarian conspirator, vetoed the speech, allowing Cicero to do no more than swear the traditional oath that he had obeyed the laws during his tenure of office. But Cicero neatly altered the wording of the oath, swearing instead that he had saved the state; and the people responded with an oath affirming this themselves. This incident seriously damaged Cicero's relations with Nepos' brother, Metellus Celer, who had been sent to Picenum, but had now moved up to his province of Cisalpine Gaul, the province Cicero had turned down (and which he may have helped Celer to obtain in the hope of buying off his brother's opposition); an awkward exchange of letters between the two is preserved at *Fam.* 5.1–2 (January 62 BC).

On 1 January 62 Silanus and Murena became consuls; Caesar and Quintus Cicero were among the praetors. Nepos persisted in his campaign against Cicero, and attacked him in the senate; but the senate passed a decree granting immunity from prosecution to anyone involved in the punishment of the conspirators. Nepos was opposed in particular by Cato, his colleague as tribune; Cato harangued the people and persuaded them to vote Cicero greater honours than those the senate had voted, including that of father of his country (an appellation applied by Catulus to Cicero on 3 December, but not part of the senate's decree). (The conflict between Cicero and Cato over the trial of Murena appears to have been quickly put aside.) Next, Nepos proposed a bill, with Caesar's support, to recall Pompey from the east to save Rome from Catiline (Nepos' half-sister Mucia was Pompey's wife). Together with another tribune, Quintus Minucius Thermus, Cato vetoed the proposal: Thermus physically stopped Nepos' mouth as he was reciting the bill, violence ensued, and Murena stepped in to save Cato from Nepos' armed supporters. The senate then passed the SCU a second time, whereupon Nepos left Rome, with threats of revenge, to join Pompey in the east. Caesar was suspended from his praetorship, but was soon reinstated.

It was at around this time, at the beginning of January 62, that Catiline was finally defeated. The approach of Antonius from the south at the end of November had made him abandon his camp at Faesulae and take to the mountains. Then news came of the executions at Rome: this prompted most of his followers to desert, reducing his force from 10,000 to 3,000 (there is no good reason to think that at the end he abandoned his policy of refusing the help of slaves). The suppression of the conspiracy in the city made a march on Rome out of the question, and the planned outbreaks in other parts of Italy had come to nothing. Catiline therefore decided there was nothing for it but to cross the Apennines into Cisalpine Gaul, and then make for Narbonese Gaul, where he would perhaps find the Allobroges, whose grievances had not been redressed, sympathetic to his cause. But to the north he found his way blocked by the three legions of Metellus Celer (who was probably at Bononia). Deciding that he would do better against his old ally Antonius, who might perhaps not fight too hard, he turned back to face him at Pistoria (24 miles north-west of Faesulae). He was right in thinking that his friend did not relish the contest: pleading an attack of gout, Antonius handed over the command to his legate Marcus Petreius, a professional soldier of more than thirty years' experience. In the ensuing battle of Pistoria, Catiline's army fought long and hard (he had Sullan veterans on his side), but in the end was annihilated. Manlius was one of the first to fall; there were no survivors. Sallust tells us that when Catiline's body was found, he was still just breathing, and his face retained the fierce look that had characterized it during his life. Antonius had the head cut off and sent to Rome as proof that Catiline was no more. (On Catiline's movements, see G. V. Sumner, *CP* 58 (1963), 215–19; we cannot be sure, however, how the chronology of Catiline's defeat relates to the chronology of events in Rome.) After the battle, further risings elsewhere in Italy were crushed by the praetors, among the Paeligni (in the centre of Italy, to the east of Rome) by Marcus Calpurnius Bibulus, the future consul of 59, and in Bruttium by Cicero's brother Quintus.

Back in Rome, trials of suspected Catilinarians began to be held under the *lex Plautia de vi* (Plautian law concerning violence); these lasted several months. The prosecutions were all instigated by private individuals, as was normal at Rome: neither Cicero nor the senate took any further action against the conspirators. In fact, one of those accused, Publius Sulla, the nephew of the dictator and consul-elect of 65, was defended (as Murena had been) by Cicero and Hortensius, and acquitted: in *Pro Sulla*, which survives, Cicero argues that, as the consul who suppressed the conspiracy, he would have known had Sulla been involved. (The prosecutor was Lucius Manlius Torquatus, the son of the man who had gone on to hold the consulship of which Sulla had been deprived.) All the other defendants, however, were convicted and went into exile. These included Laeca; Cicero's two would-be assassins, Cornelius and Vargunteius; Autronius; and Servius Cornelius Sulla and his brother Publius. In most cases or in all, Cicero gave decisive evidence for the prosecution. (We hear nothing of the other four men—Cassius, Umbrenus, Furius, and Annius—who were covered by the senate's decree of 5 December. It is most likely that all four left Rome as soon as their arrest was ordered on 3 December, fled to Catiline, and died with him at Pistoria; it is possible that Furius was the man from Faesulae whom Sallust says commanded the left wing of Catiline's army (*Cat.* 59.3).)

After defeating Catiline, Antonius went off to the province Cicero had given him, Macedonia, where he remained governor until 60. There he suffered military defeat, and oppressed the provincials; on his return to Rome, he was prosecuted in 59, probably for extortion, by the young Marcus Caelius Rufus (Cicero's future client). For the rest of Cicero's life, his view of other politicians was determined by their actions at the time of the Catilinarian conspiracy, or their attitude to it, and during the 50s he defended in court a number of people who had helped him during the crisis. Antonius was the first of these: although Cicero had no personal liking for him—indeed, he can hardly have looked on him with anything but disgust—he nevertheless believed that the man who was nominally responsible for the defeat of Catiline ought not to be allowed to fall victim to their political enemies. So he defended him with vigour, and lost. (On the trial, see E. S. Gruen, *Latomus*, 32 (1973), 301–10.) On the day of Antonius' conviction, a group of Catilinarian sympathizers met at Catiline's tomb, decorated it with flowers, and held a funeral dinner. Antonius went into exile, in Cephallenia (not far, in fact, from Autronius, who had chosen Epirus as his place of exile); and he remained there until he was recalled by Caesar in the 40s. In 42 he was made censor, a surprising appointment for a convicted criminal, and especially for a man whom the censors of an earlier year had expelled from the senate—but then he was Mark Antony's uncle.

As tribune in 62, Cato persuaded the senate to help the urban plebs by extending the distribution of subsidized grain, more than doubling the cost to the treasury. At the end of the year, Pompey returned to Italy; but he did not seize power, or attack the senatorial establishment. Instead, he disbanded his troops, and divorced his wife, Metellus Nepos' half-sister. Also this year the Allobroges rebelled, having received no relief from their troubles, in spite of the great service they had done Rome. They were crushed in 61 by the governor of Transalpine Gaul, Gaius Pomptinus (the praetor whom they had previously encountered at the Mulvian Bridge).

As time went by, Cicero found it increasingly necessary to defend the action that he had taken in 63, especially once he had made an enemy of Clodius—a more dangerous opponent than Nepos—at Clodius' trial for sacrilege in May 61. In 60 he decided on a propaganda campaign, and published (i) all the political speeches of his consulship which he had not already published (*Pro Murena* was not included, so presumably was already in the public domain); (ii) a prose account of his consulship in Greek (later used by Plutarch as his main source for the Catilinarian conspiracy, but now lost); and (iii) an epic poem on his consulship in Latin (*Consulatus suus*, parts of which survive). The evidence for (i) is given in a letter to his friend Atticus (*Att.* 2.1.3, written in June 60 BC), where the twelve speeches are listed; they include the four *Catilinarians*. Cicero makes it clear (*a*) that he has just committed these speeches to paper and (*b*) that Atticus has not seen them before; so this must be their first publication, and not a reissue. The question therefore arises whether our four *Catilinarians* are a true record of what Cicero said on the several occasions in 63, or whether they merely give us what in 60 he wanted people to think he had said. Are they purely a production of 63, intended to influence the events of that year, and with no awareness of what was to follow? Or are they a production of 63 that has subsequently been modified to provide an additional slant, reacting to the author's concerns in 60 and providing a retrospective justification of his political actions? Because Cicero has not introduced into the speeches any indisputable anachronisms (although some passages, such as *Cat.* 3.15 and 4.21, come very close), we cannot say that they *must* reflect the situation of 60. There is certainly a pervasive element of apologia in the speeches, which would serve Cicero's purposes in 60, and would seem surprising in a context in which the executions of 5 December had not yet taken place. But on the other hand, it is not impossible that Cicero was aware from the beginning of the crisis that the actions he would be called upon to take might prove controversial (indeed, the biographer Cornelius Nepos comments at *Atticus* 16.4 on his prophetic powers). So the question cannot be answered with certainty. Nevertheless, Cicero first gave these speeches to the world in 60, and presented them as part of a larger body of work, a corpus of his consular speeches. It would therefore be unwarranted to treat them purely as productions of 63, and dismiss out of hand (as some scholars have done) any possibility of later revision (the fact that the four speeches are almost identical in length may be a further factor in favour of revision). A more judicious approach would involve taking them as productions of 60, accepting that they provide an account of the events of 63 that is historically accurate in such matters as chronology and fact, but at the same time recognizing that there is a high likelihood that in some passages (e.g. *Cat.* 1.4, 3.14, 3.15, 3.26–29a, 4.1–3, 4.19–24) they respond to the historical situation of the years after Cicero stepped down from his consulship.

In the short term, Cicero's propaganda campaign must be judged a failure: in 58 Clodius became tribune and succeeded in driving him into exile for his execution of citizens without trial. He was recalled by a united senate the following year (Nepos, now consul, was with difficulty persuaded to give his consent); but the blow to his prestige remained with him for the rest of his life. As a result, he never passed up any opportunity of reminding people in his speeches of how as consul he had saved Rome—how it had been as a civilian, not as a general, that he had done it, and how it had been achieved by the deaths of a mere five criminals. In the words of the younger Seneca a century later, he praised his consulship 'not without justice, but without end' (*Dialogues* 10.5.1). He reacted in this way not because he was an egomaniac, but because it was never universally accepted that he had done the right thing. There would always be enemies ready to attack his record and to turn public opinion against him; hence he always felt it necessary to fight his corner. His suppression of the conspiracy at Rome was undoubtedly a great achievement, and it is difficult to identify any point at which he made the wrong decision. But he himself paid a high personal price.

Although in the short term the *Catilinarians* did not save Cicero from criticism, in the longer term they proved overwhelmingly successful: they turned Catiline into one of the great villains of history. There are signs in Cicero's own works that Catiline may not have been wholly bad. As we have seen, Cicero considered defending him at his extortion trial in 65, and in *Pro Caelio* (56 BC) he is forced to admit that he did have some admirable qualities, and a certain allure (*Cael.* 12–14):

For Catiline had, as I am sure you remember, a great many indications of the highest qualities—not fully developed, mind you, but sketched in outline. He mixed with numerous individuals of bad character; yet he pretended to be devoted to the best of men. He had the effect of degrading those around him; yet he could also stimulate them to effort and hard work. The fires of passion burned within him; yet he was a keen student of military affairs. For my part I do not think the world has ever seen a creature made up of such contrary, divergent, and mutually incompatible interests and appetites.

Who was more agreeable, at one particular time, to men of high rank, and who more intimate with scoundrels? Who at one time a more patriotic citizen, and who a more loathsome enemy of this country? Who more corrupt in his pleasures, and who more able to endure hard work? Who more avaricious in rapacity, and who more lavish in generosity? That man, gentlemen, had many features that were paradoxical. He had a wide circle of friends, and he looked after them well. What he had, he shared with everyone. He helped all his friends in times of need with money, influence, physical exertion, even, if necessary, with recklessness and crime. He could adapt and control the way he was to suit the occasion, and twist and turn his nature this way and that. He could be stern with the serious, relaxed with the free-and-easy, grave with the old, affable with the young, daring with criminals, and dissolute with the depraved. And so this complex, ever-changing character, even when he had collected all the wicked traitors from far and wide, still held many loyal, brave men in his grasp by a sort of pretended semblance of virtue. Indeed, that dastardly attempt to destroy this empire could never have come into being had not that monstrous concentration of so many vices been rooted in certain qualities of skill and endurance.

But that view, though it had some influence on Sallust's portrayal in the *Catiline*, never took hold. It was instead the uniformly negative portrait that we find in the *Catilinarians* that captured the imagination of posterity. By the time of Virgil, a generation after Cicero, the *Catilinarians* had already become literary classics. Cicero's invective had become unanswerable: Catiline was the archetypal traitor. In the *Aeneid*, Virgil twice presents Catiline as a figure in Tartarus, paying the penalty for his crimes. In the first of these passages the reference is oblique, and refers to Catiline's alleged marriage to his own daughter, one of the wilder claims included by Cicero in *In toga candida* in 64: 'This one forced his daughter's bed and a marriage forbidden' (6.623; for the identification of Catiline, see D. H. Berry, *CQ*, NS 42 (1992), 416–20). In the second passage, Virgil has been describing the scenes from Roman history that Vulcan has depicted on the shield he has made for Aeneas, and continues (8.666–9):

> Away from these he had added
> The abode of Tartarus, the tall portals of Dis,
> The punishment of crime, and you, Catiline, clinging
> To an overhanging cliff, and trembling before the faces of the Furies.

In the modern era, the invective of the *Catilinarians* continued to cast its spell. As late as 1894, one of the scholarly commentators on these speeches, A. S. Wilkins, could write, 'Swept away in the eddy of the universal immorality, in early youth Catilina flung himself into all possible pleasures and excesses which, without undermining his gigantic strength, blunted his moral feelings, and, through his inclination to ambition, led him into a chain of awful crimes, through which his name stands out in history as one of the monsters of mankind' (p.ix). In the twentieth century, some scholars tried to break free from Cicero's presentation by arguing that Catiline was set up by Cicero, and that he had nothing to do with Manlius' rising and/or the conspiracy in the city. But not even they seriously attempted to defend Catiline's character. In the end, it has proved impossible to escape from the power of Cicero's denunciation.

In reality, Catiline's conspiracy was not so very different from the many other outbreaks of civil disorder which occurred in the unstable world of the late republic: it bears a strong resemblance, for instance, to the rising of Marcus Aemilius Lepidus in 78–77. What made it unique was that it took place in the consulship of Cicero. If it had occurred a year earlier, it might have become a much more serious affair, and we might well know little about it. But by delivering and then publishing the *Catilinarians*— one of the greatest productions of Latin literature—Cicero ensured that Catiline and his conspiracy would always be remembered, provoke debate, and fascinate.

# IN CATILINAM I

[1] How far, I ask you,* Catiline, do you mean to stretch our patience? How much longer will your frenzy continue to frustrate us? At what point will your unrestrained recklessness stop flaunting itself? Have the nightly guards on the Palatine, have the patrols in the streets, have the fears of the people, have the gatherings of all loyal citizens, have these strongly defended premises in which this meeting is being held, have the faces and expressions of the senators here had no effect on you at all? Do you not realize that your plans have been exposed? Do you not see that your conspiracy has been arrested and trapped, now that all these people know about it? Which of us do you think does not know what you were up to yesterday evening, what you were up to last night,* where you were, whom you collected together, and what plan of action you decided upon? [2] What a decadent age we live in! The senate is aware of these things, the consul sees them—yet this man remains alive! Alive, did I say? He is not just alive: he actually enters the senate, he takes part in our public deliberations, and with his eyes he notes and marks down each one of us for assassination. We meanwhile, brave men that we are, think that we have done enough for our country if we merely get out of the way of his frenzy and his weapons.

You, Catiline, ought long ago to have been taken to your death, and on a consul's order. It is on yourself that the destruction which you have long been plotting for all of us ought to be visited. [3] The distinguished chief pontiff, Publius Scipio, as a mere private citizen killed Tiberius Gracchus,* when Gracchus was causing a mild disturbance in our country: so are we, as consuls, to put up with Catiline, when he is aiming to devastate the entire world with fire and slaughter? I will pass over precedents that are too old, such as Gaius Servilius Ahala, who killed Spurius Maelius* with his own hand when Maelius was contemplating an uprising. Gone, gone is that one-time public virtue which led men of courage to punish a citizen traitor more severely than the deadliest foreign enemy. But in fact we have a decree of the senate* against you, Catiline, that is stern and authoritative. So it is not the national deliberations or the resolution of the senate that is wanting: it is we, we the consuls, I tell you, who are failing to act!

[4] The senate once decreed that the consul Lucius Opimius should see to it that the state came to no harm.* Not a night intervened. Gaius Gracchus, despite his illustrious father, grandfather, and ancestors, was killed on suspicion of stirring up dissension; and the ex-consul Marcus Fulvius was also killed, together with his children. A similar senatorial decree put the state into the hands of the consuls Gaius Marius and Lucius Valerius*—and did even a single day then elapse before death and the state's vengeance overtook the tribune of the plebs Lucius Saturninus and the praetor Gaius Servilius? But we for twenty days now* have been allowing the edge of the senate's authority to become blunt. We have a senatorial decree like those earlier ones, but it is filed away, as if hidden in a sheath—but on the strength of that decree, you, Catiline, should have been instantly killed. You remain alive, and yet you live on not to put aside your recklessness, but to increase it. Conscript fathers, my only wish is to be compassionate,* my only wish is not to appear remiss in the midst of a national emergency, but already I find that I am guilty of doing nothing, and doing wrong.

[5] There exists in Italy a military camp, hostile to the Roman people, in the mountain passes of Etruria. Each and every day, the number of the enemy increases. The commander of that camp, and the leader of that enemy, you can see inside the city walls, and even in the senate, plotting some form of ruin for our country each day from within. If I now order your arrest, Catiline, and if I order your execution, I suppose what I shall have to be afraid of is not that every loyal citizen will accuse me of being slow to act, but that someone will say I have been too severe! But as it happens, there is a particular reason why I am still not bringing myself to do what I ought to have done long ago. You will be executed only when no one can be found so criminal, so wicked, and so similar to yourself as to deny the justice of that course of action. [6] As long as there remains a single person who has the temerity to speak up for you, you will remain alive—and live in the way you do now, surrounded by the many strong guards I have posted, and prevented from moving against your country. In addition, the many eyes and ears that you are not aware of will continue, as in the past, to track your every move and keep guard against you.

What is the point, Catiline, in waiting any longer, when night cannot cloak your criminal plots in darkness, when a private house cannot confine conspiratorial voices inside its walls—if everything is exposed to the light of day, everything breaks out into the open? Take my advice: call off your plans, and stop thinking of assassination and arson. Whichever way you turn, you have been thwarted. Your plans are all as clear as day to me. Let me take you through them.

[7] Do you remember that I declared in the senate on 21 October that Gaius Manlius, your sidekick and partner in crime, would take up arms on a certain day, and that that day would be 27 October? And was I not correct, Catiline, not just about the rising, so large, terrible, and extraordinary as it was, but also—and this is much more remarkable—about the actual date? I also informed the senate that you had deferred your massacre of leading senators until 28 October, although by that time many of our national leaders had already abandoned Rome, not so much from a desire to save their lives as because they wanted to thwart your plans. Surely you cannot deny that, when that day arrived, my vigilance, together with the guards I posted, successfully prevented you from taking action against the country? Or that you kept on saying that even though the others had left, you were quite happy with massacring only those of us who remained behind? [8] And when you were confident that you were going to seize Praeneste* on 1 November by a night attack, did you have any idea that the town had been fortified on my orders with troops, guards, and watchmen? Nothing that you do, nothing that you attempt, and nothing that you contemplate takes place without me not only hearing about it, but actually seeing it and being fully aware of it.

Now go over with me what happened last night; you will see that I am much more vigilant in defence of the country than you are for its destruction. I declare that yesterday evening you went to the scythe-makers' quarter—I will be absolutely precise—to the house of Marcus Laeca,* and that you met there a number of your accomplices in this criminal lunacy in which you are all engaged. Do you dare to deny it? Why do you say nothing? If you deny it, I shall prove it. In fact, I notice that there are here in the senate several of those who were with you. [9] Immortal gods! Where in the world are we? What country do we inhabit? In what city do we live? Here, conscript fathers, here amongst our very number, in this, the most revered and important council in the world, there exist men who are plotting the massacre of all of us and the destruction of this city—and even of the entire world. I, the consul, see them; I ask for their opinion on matters of state; and men who ought by rights to be put to the sword I am not even wounding, as yet, with my words.*

So you were at Laeca's house last night, Catiline. You parcelled out the regions of Italy. You decided where you wanted each man to go. You selected those you were going to leave behind in Rome and those you were going to take away with you. You designated the parts of the city to be burnt. You confirmed that you were on the point of leaving Rome yourself. But you added that you would nevertheless have to stay just a little longer—because I was still alive. Two Roman equestrians* were found to relieve you of that particular concern: they gave their word that they would assassinate me in my bed the very same night, just before dawn. [10] I discovered all this almost as soon as your meeting had broken up. I protected and strengthened my home by increasing the guards, and I denied entry to the men whom you yourself had sent to call on me first thing in the morning—and who did indeed come at that time, as I had meanwhile told numerous prominent people that they would.

In view of this, Catiline, finish what you have started: leave the city at long last. The gates are open: go. For too long now have Manlius and that camp of yours been waiting for you to assume command of it. And take all your followers with you; or if you cannot take them all, take as many as you can. Purge the city. As for me, you will release me from the great fear I feel, if only there is a wall separating us. At all events, you cannot stay any longer with us: I will not tolerate it, I will not endure it, I will not allow it.

[11] We owe a great debt of gratitude to the immortal gods and especially to this Jupiter Stator,* the god who from the earliest times has stood guard over our city, for enabling us time and again to escape this pestilence, so foul, so revolting, and so deadly to our country. But we cannot go on forever allowing the survival of the state to be endangered by a single individual. As long as you, Catiline, set traps for me while I was consul-elect, I used private watchfulness, not public guards, to defend myself. Then at the last consular elections,* when you wanted to kill me, the consul, together with your fellow candidates in the Campus Martius, I foiled your abominable plot by

the protection and services of my friends, without declaring any public state of emergency. In short, whenever you went for me, I stood up
to you on my own—even though I was aware that if anything were to
happen to me, it would be a terrible disaster for our country.

[12] But now you are openly attacking the country as a whole. You
are calling to destruction and devastation the temples of the
immortal gods, the houses of the city, the lives of all Roman citizens,
and finally the whole of Italy. Even so, I will not yet venture to carry
out my first duty and act as befits my office and the strict traditions
of our ancestors: instead, I shall act in a way which is more lenient,
but also more conducive to the national security. For if I order your
execution, all the other members of the conspiracy will remain
within the state; but if you leave Rome, as I have long been urging
you to do, the voluminous, pernicious dregs of society—your
companions—will be flushed out of the city.

[13] Well, Catiline? Surely you cannot be hesitating to do on my
orders what you were already doing anyway of your own free will?
The consul orders a public enemy to get out of Rome. Into exile, you
enquire? That is not what I am ordering—but if you ask my opinion,
it is what I advise.

At Rome, Catiline, what is there, at the present time, that can
possibly give you any pleasure? Aside from your degraded fellow
conspirators, there is not a single person in this city who does not
fear you, not a single person who does not hate you. Is there any
mark of disgrace with which your private life has not been branded?
Is there any dishonour in your personal affairs that does not
besmirch your reputation? From what lust have your eyes, from what
crime have your hands, from what outrage has any part of your body
ever abstained? Is there any youth that you have ensnared with the
enticements of corruption whom you have not then gone on to provide with either a weapon to commit crime or a torch to fire his lusts?
[14] Or again, when you recently made your house ready for a new
bride by bringing about the death of your previous wife, did you not
compound this crime with yet another that is quite incredible?* But
I will pass over this and let it be veiled in silence, because I do not
want such a monstrous crime to appear either to have been committed in our country, or to have been committed and not punished. I
will also pass over the financial ruin which you will find hanging over
you on the 13th of this month.*

I come now to matters which relate not to the shame of your personal immorality, nor to the disgraceful state of your financial affairs, but to the supreme interests of Rome, and the lives and survival of each one of us. [15] Can this light of day, Catiline, or this fresh air afford you any pleasure, when you are aware that nobody here is ignorant of the fact that on 29 December in the consulship of Lepidus and Tullus you stood in the assembly armed with a weapon, that you had formed a body of men to kill the consuls and the leaders of the state, and that it was not any change of mind or failure of nerve on your part that prevented you from carrying out your insane crime, but simply the good luck of the Roman people?* But there is no need to go on about that: after all, those crimes are well known, and you have committed a good many others since. But how many times you have attempted to assassinate me as consul-elect, and how many times as consul! How many seemingly inescapable thrusts of yours I have dodged by a slight swerve and, as they say, by sleight of body! You achieve nothing, you accomplish nothing, but that does not deter you from trying and hoping. [16] How many times that dagger of yours has been wrenched from your hands, how many times it has dropped by some lucky chance and fallen to the ground! But you still cannot manage without it. With what special rites you must have consecrated and dedicated it I do not know, for you to plunge it into the body of a consul.

But as for the present, what sort of life are you living? You see, I shall talk to you in a way that will not seem motivated by the hatred I ought to feel for you, but by the pity you certainly do not deserve. A short while ago, you walked into the senate. Who out of that packed gathering of people, and out of so many of your friends and connections, offered you a single word of greeting? If no one else in history has ever been treated like that, do you really wait for the insult to be expressed in words, when you have been crushed by the strongest verdict—that of utter silence? And what about the fact that, when you entered the chamber, these benches suddenly emptied? That all the consulars, men whom you had many times marked down for assassination, left the area of benches near you empty and unoccupied the moment you took your seat?* How, I ask you, do you feel about that?

[17] By Hercules, if my slaves were as afraid of me as all your fellow-citizens are of you, I would certainly think I ought to leave my

house—so don't you think you ought to leave Rome? And if I saw my fellow-citizens looking at me, even without justification, with such deep hatred and suspicion, I would prefer to remove myself from their sight than remain before the hostile gaze of all of them. But you, knowing the crimes you have committed and so being aware that the hatred everyone feels towards you is merited and has long been your due, do you hesitate to remove yourself from the sight and presence of those whose minds and feelings you are injuring? If your very own parents feared and hated you, and it was absolutely impossible for you to become reconciled with them, surely, I think, you would withdraw to somewhere where they could not see you. But now your own country, which is the common parent of us all, hates you and is frightened of you, and has long ago come to the conclusion that you are contemplating nothing but her destruction. Will you not then respect her authority, defer to her judgement, or fear her power?

[18] Your country, Catiline, addresses you, and, though silent, somehow speaks to you in these terms: 'For years now, no crime has been committed that has not been committed by you, and no crime has been committed without you. You alone have killed many citizens, and have oppressed and plundered our allies, while escaping punishment and remaining free.* You have managed not merely to ignore the laws and the courts, but to overturn and shatter them. Your previous crimes, intolerable as they were, I put up with as best I could. But now I am racked with fear solely because of you; whenever there is the slightest sound, it is Catiline that people fear; and it seems inconceivable that any plot can be formed against me without your criminality being the cause of it. That this should be so is unendurable. Therefore depart, and release me from this fear! If my fear is justified, your departure will save me from destruction; but if it is not, it will at long last spare me my alarm.' [19] If your country were to address you just as I have done, ought she not to be granted what she asks, even though she could not force you?

But what of the fact that you gave yourself into custody—that, to allay people's suspicions, you said that you were prepared to live at Manius Lepidus' house?* When he would not have you, you even had the audacity to come to me and request that I keep an eye on you in my own home! But I gave you the same answer as he did, that I could hardly consider myself safe within the walls of the same house as you, when I was already in considerable danger being within the same city walls. So off you went to the praetor Quintus Metellus.* And when he had sent you packing, you made your way to your dear friend, the excellent Marcus Metellus,* whom you obviously thought would be very conscientious in guarding you, very quick in suspecting you, and very active in punishing you! But how far away from prison and chains do you think a man ought to be who has already himself come to the conclusion that he needs to be kept under guard?

[20] In this situation, Catiline, if you cannot bring yourself to die, surely you cannot hesitate to flee to some other country, and surrender that life of yours—which you have saved from a whole series of just and well-deserved punishments—to exile and solitude?

'Put the question to the senate,' you say. That is what you demand; and if this order should pass a decree saying that it wishes you to go into exile, you undertake to comply. I am not going to put it to the senate: it would not be my practice to do so.* All the same, I will allow you to see what view these senators take of you. Get out of Rome, Catiline. Free the country from fear. Go into exile—if that is the term you are waiting to hear. Well then? Don't you hear, don't you notice the senators' silence? They agree, and say nothing. Why then do you hold out for a spoken decision, when you can clearly see their silent preference?

[21] Now if I had spoken to this fine young man here, Publius Sestius,* or to the valiant Marcus Marcellus,* in the way I have just been speaking to you, the senators would have physically assaulted me, consul though I am, and in this temple too; and they would have been fully justified in doing so. But in your case, Catiline, their inaction denotes approval, their acquiescence a formal decree, and their silence applause. And this does not apply only to the members of the senate, whose opinions you clearly value highly, even if you hold their lives cheap: what I say applies equally to those Roman equestrians, fine and honourable men that they are, and to the rest of the citizens, men of great courage who are surrounding this building, whose numbers you could see, whose feelings you could observe, and whose shouts you could hear only a moment ago. For a long time I have only just managed to keep their hands and weapons away from you; but I am sure I shall have no difficulty persuading them to escort you all the way to the city gates, if you now decide to forsake everything that you have for so long been desperate to destroy.

[22] But why am I saying this? Do I imagine that *your* resolve could be broken? That *you* could come to your senses? That *you* could think of escape? That *you* could consider exile? How I wish the immortal gods would put *that* idea into your head! And yet, if my words did frighten you so much that you were driven to contemplate exile, I can see what a storm of unpopularity would break over me— not necessarily immediately, when the memory of your crimes was still fresh, but at a later date. It would be worth it, however, so long as the consequences only affected me, and did not put the state at risk. But that *your* character should be reformed, that *you* should be deterred by the penalties of the law, or that *you* should put your country before yourself—that is too much to ask. For you are not the man, Catiline, to be turned from disgrace by a sense of decency, or from danger by fear, or from madness by reason.

[23] Therefore go, as I have said often enough now. If I am your enemy, as you say I am, and your aim is to whip up hostility towards me, then go straight into exile. If you do this, it will be hard for me to endure what people will say about me; if you go into exile at the consul's command, it will be hard for me to bear the burden of the odium that will fall on me. If, on the other hand, your aim is to enhance my glory and reputation, then leave with your desperate gang of criminals, take yourself off to Manlius, stir up the bad citizens, separate yourself off from the loyal ones, make war on your country, and revel in banditry and wickedness! If you do that, it will look not as if I have driven you into the arms of strangers, but as if you have been invited to go and join your friends.

[24] Yet why should I be urging you, when I already know that you have sent a force ahead to wait for you under arms at Forum Aurelium,* when I know that you have agreed a prearranged day with Manlius, and when I know that you have also sent ahead that silver eagle* to which you have dedicated a shrine at your house, and which I trust will bring only ruin and disaster to you and all your followers? How, after all, could you go without the object to which you used to pay homage each time you set out to commit a murder, when you would touch its altar with your sacrilegious right hand before using that same right hand straight afterwards to kill Roman citizens?

[25] You will go, at long last, where your unrestrained, insane ambition has long been driving you; nor will this cause you any regret, but, on the contrary, a sort of indescribable delight. It was for

madness such as this that nature created you, your own desire trained you, and fortune preserved you. Not only have you never wanted peace, but you have never wanted war either—unless it was a criminal one. Drawing on the worst of society, you have scraped together a gang of traitors, men entirely abandoned not just by fortune, but even by hope. [26] What delight you will take in their company, what joy you will experience, what pleasure you will revel in, seeing that from so sizeable a gathering you will be able neither to hear nor to see a single decent man! Those physical powers of yours* we hear so much about have set you up for a life of this kind: the ability to lie on the bare ground has prepared you not just for launching sexual assaults but for committing crime, the capacity to stay awake not just for cheating husbands in their sleep but for robbing unsuspecting people of their property. Now you have an opportunity to show off your celebrated capacity to endure hunger, cold, and the lack of every amenity—hardships which you will shortly find out have finished you off! [27] When I prevented you from attaining the consulship,* I at least managed to ensure that you would be in a position only to attack the country as an exile, not to devastate it as consul, and that the criminal enterprise you would undertake would only go under the name of banditry, and not war.

Now, conscript fathers, I want to avert and deflect a particular complaint that our country might—almost with reason—make against me. So please pay careful attention to what I am going to say, and store it deep inside your hearts and minds. Imagine that my country, which is much more precious to me than my own life, imagine that all Italy, imagine that the entire nation were to address me like this: 'Marcus Tullius, what are you playing at? Are you going to permit the departure of a man whom you have discovered to be a public enemy, who you see will be a leader in war, who you are well aware is awaited in the enemy camp as their commander, a man who is an instigator of crime, the leader of a conspiracy, and the mobilizer of slaves* and bad citizens—so that it will look as if you have not driven him out of the city, but let him loose against it? Surely you are going to give orders that he be cast into chains, led away to execution, and made to suffer the ultimate penalty? [28] What on earth is stopping you? The tradition of our ancestors? But in this country it has very often been the case that even private citizens have punished dangerous citizens with death. Or is it the laws that have been passed relating to the punishment of Roman citizens?* But at Rome people who have rebelled against the state have never retained the rights of citizens. Or are you afraid that history will judge you harshly? Although you are known only for what you have done yourself, and do not have distinguished ancestors to recommend you, the Roman people have nevertheless seen fit to raise you, and at so early an age, through all the magisterial offices and elevate you to the supreme power. Fine thanks you will be paying them in return, then, if you neglect the safety of your fellow-citizens through concern for your reputation or fear of any kind of danger! [29] But if you are afraid of being judged harshly, being criticized for showing severity and resolution is no more to be dreaded than being criticized for criminal neglect of duty. Or, when Italy is ravaged by war, her cities destroyed, and her homes on fire, do you imagine that your own reputation will be exempt from the flames of hatred?'

To these most solemn words of our country, and to all individuals who share the feelings she expresses, I will make this brief answer. Had I judged that punishing Catiline with death was the best course of action, conscript fathers, I should not have given that gladiator a single hour of life to enjoy. For if it is the case that our most distinguished and illustrious citizens did not merely not damage their reputations when they killed Saturninus, the Gracchi, Flaccus,* and many other figures of the past, but actually enhanced them, then certainly I had no need to fear that killing this murderer of Roman citizens would do any harm in the future to my own reputation. But even if there was considerable danger of its doing me harm, I have always been of the opinion that unpopularity earned by doing what is right is not unpopularity at all, but glory.

[30] And yet there are not a few members of this order who either fail to see what is hanging over us or pretend not to see it. These people have fed Catiline's hopes by their feeble expressions of opinion, and have given strength to the growing conspiracy by their reluctance to believe in its existence. Their authority is such that, had I punished Catiline, many people—not just traitors, but people who do not know any better—would say that I had acted in a cruel and tyrannical manner. But as it is, I know that if he goes to Manlius' camp, as he means to, there will be no one so stupid as not to see that the conspiracy exists, and no one so wicked as not to acknowledge that it exists.

But if he, and he alone, is killed, I know that this cancer in the state can be repressed only for a short time: it cannot be suppressed permanently. On the other hand, if he removes himself and takes all his followers with him, and brings together in one place all the other castaways he has collected from here and there, we will be able to wipe out and expunge not only this cancer which has grown up in our midst, but also the root and seed of future ills.

[31] We have been living for a long time now, conscript fathers, amid the dangers of a conspiracy and the attempts on our lives, but somehow or other all this criminal activity and this long-standing violence and frenzy has come to a head during my tenure of the consulship. If, out of so many brigands, only this man here is removed, we will perhaps be under the impression, briefly, that we have been freed from our fear and anxiety. But the danger will remain, enclosed deep within the veins and vitals of the state. It is like when people who are seriously ill toss and turn with a burning fever: if they have a drink of cold water, they initially seem to find relief, but are afterwards much more seriously and violently ill than they were before. In the same way, this disease from which our country is suffering will initially seem to abate if this man is punished, but will then break out much more violently, as the other conspirators will still be alive.

[32] Therefore let the traitors depart. Let them detach themselves from the good citizens, gather together in one place, and, as I have said many times now, be separated from us by the city wall. Let them stop attempting to assassinate the consul in his own home, thronging round the tribunal of the city praetor,* besieging the senate-house with swords, and preparing fire-arrows and torches to burn the city. Finally, let it be inscribed on the forehead of every citizen what he thinks about his country. I promise you this, conscript fathers, that we the consuls will show such conscientiousness, you will show such authority, the Roman equestrians will show such courage, and all loyal citizens will show such solidarity that, once Catiline has departed, you will see everything revealed, exposed, crushed, and punished.

[33] With omens such as these, Catiline, and for the sake of the survival of the state, the death and destruction of yourself, and the ruin of those who have linked themselves to you in every type of crime and murder: be off to your sacrilegious and wicked war! And

you, Jupiter, who were established by the same auspices as those by which Romulus founded this city, whom we rightly call the 'Stayer'* of this city and empire, may you drive him and his associates away from your temple and the other temples, away from the buildings and walls of the city, and away from the lives and fortunes of all the citizens! And on these men who are the opponents of decent citizens, the enemies of their country, brigands of Italy, and linked together in an unholy alliance and syndicate of crime, on these, living and dead, may you inflict everlasting punishment!

# IN CATILINAM II

[1] At long last, citizens, Lucius Catilina,* crazed with recklessness, panting with criminality, treacherously plotting the destruction of his country, and menacing you and this city with fire and the sword—this criminal we have expelled from Rome; or released; or followed with our farewells as he was leaving of his own accord. He has gone, departed, cleared off, escaped.* No longer will that grotesque monster plan the demolition of our city walls from inside those very walls. And we have indisputably beaten the one man who is at the head of this civil war. No longer, then, will that dagger of his be twisted between our ribs. In the Campus Martius, in the forum, in the senate-house, and in our own homes we will have nothing to fear. When he was driven from the city, he was dislodged from his point of vantage. So now we will be fighting a proper war in the open against an external enemy, with nothing to stop us. Without a doubt we destroyed him and won a magnificent victory when we turned him from secret plots to open banditry. [2] He has not taken with him, as he wished, a dagger covered in blood; he has departed with me still alive; I have wrenched his sword from his hand; and he has left the citizens unharmed and the city still standing—so just think of the sense of grief that must have overwhelmed and crushed him! He now lies prostrate, citizens, and realizes that he has been struck down and laid low. Again and again, surely, he is turning his eyes back towards this city, bewailing the fact that it has been snatched from his jaws. The city, on the other hand, seems to me delighted that it has vomited forth such a pestilence and spewed it out.

[3] But it may be that some of you will take the view that ought really to be the view of everyone, and criticize me severely for what my speech boasts of and glories in—the fact that I did not arrest so lethal an enemy, but allowed him to escape. However, the blame for that, citizens, lies not with me, but with the circumstances. Lucius Catilina ought long ago to have paid the supreme punishment and been executed, as the tradition of our ancestors, the strictness of my office, and the national interest demanded of me. But how many people do you think there were who refused to believe my allegations, how many who even spoke up for the offenders, how many

who were so stupid as to imagine that the conspiracy did not exist, and how many who were so wicked as to give it their support? If I judged that by removing Lucius Catilina I could free you completely from danger, I would long ago have risked not only my popularity but even my life to remove him. [4] But at that time not even all of you were sufficiently convinced of the existence of the conspiracy, and I saw that, if I punished him with the death he deserved, I would make myself so unpopular that I would not be in a position to take action against his accomplices. Instead, therefore, I brought matters to a point where you would be able to fight in the open, and also to see clearly who the enemy was.

As to how frightened we ought to be of such an enemy now that he is in the open, you will be able to divine my own feelings on this, citizens, from the fact that I am disappointed that he has taken so few of his fellow conspirators from the city with him. Indeed, I wish that he had marched out of Rome at the head of his entire force! I find that he took with him Tongilius,* a man he had first had sexual relations with when Tongilius was a boy, and also Publicius and Minucius, men whose unpaid restaurant bills were hardly likely to destabilize the state. But those he has left behind are quite another matter. What debts they have, what power, what noble birth!

[5] When I think of our legions in Gaul, and the levy which Quintus Metellus* has held in Picenum and on the Umbrian coast, and also of the forces that we are building up day by day, I feel such contempt for that army of his, made up as it is of superannuated no-hopers, prodigal farmers, rural bankrupts, and men who would rather jump bail than desert his ranks. I need not go so far as to present such people with our army's line of battle: all I will have to do is to show them the praetor's edict* and they will fall to the ground!

As for those I notice rushing around the forum, standing in front of the senate-house, even coming into the senate, gleaming with lotions, resplendent in purple—I would rather he had taken these with him as his soldiers. But they are still here; and we should remember that it is not so much his army that we should be afraid of as those who have deserted it. In fact, we should be all the more alarmed by their behaviour, because they are aware that I know what they are up to, but they are not bothered by it. [6] I see who has been allotted Apulia, who has Etruria, who Picenum, who the Umbrian coast, and who has demanded responsibility for Rome itself, with the plans for assassination and arson. They are aware that all their plans of the night before last have been reported to me. I revealed them in the senate yesterday. Catiline himself took fright and fled. These men, on the other hand—what are they waiting for? They are gravely mistaken if they suppose that the leniency I have shown hitherto will last for ever.

I have now achieved my objective, to make all of you see that a conspiracy has been openly formed against the state—unless, of course, there is anyone who thinks that people of Catiline's ilk will not share his views! Leniency, then, is no longer appropriate: the situation demands firmness. But even at this late hour, I shall make one concession: they can still leave, still depart—so as to prevent poor Catiline pining away because he misses them so much! I shall even show them the way: he took the Via Aurelia, and if they get a move on, they will catch him up by this evening.

[7] How lucky Rome would be, if it could indeed get rid of this urban trash! By Hercules, with Catiline alone flushed away, our country already seems refreshed and restored! Or can you think up or invent any evil or crime that he has not conceived of himself? What poisoner anywhere in Italy, what gladiator, what brigand, what cut-throat, what assassin, what forger of wills, what swindler, what glutton, what spendthrift, what adulterer, what loose woman, what corrupter of the young, what corrupt man himself, what degraded individual can be found who does not admit to having lived on the closest terms with Catiline? For years now, what murder has been committed without his involvement, what disgusting sexual outrage without his participation? [8] What other man has ever presented such great temptations to young men as he? Some of them he had sex with in the most disgraceful way, while with others he scandalously submitted himself to their own sexual impulses.* To some he promised whatever it was they hankered after, to others the death of their parents*—and not merely by urging them on, but by giving active help. And how quickly he succeeded in assembling a vast crowd of the worst of society—not only from the city, but from the countryside as well! Not only at Rome, but even in the furthest corners of Italy, there was not a single debtor whom he failed to recruit to this extraordinary criminal alliance. [9] So that you can appreciate the diversity of his interests and the full range of his

activities, there is no gladiator in a training school who inclines ever
so slightly to crime who does not also boast of his close relationship
with Catiline—and, on the other hand, there is no actor* at all fickle
and useless who does not also claim to be just about his dearest
friend. Catiline himself, as a result of his repeated sexual misconduct
and criminal activities, had acquired the ability to endure cold,
hunger, thirst, and lack of sleep, and was therefore hailed as a hero
by people of this sort. However, his sexual excess and criminal
behaviour actually tended to dissipate his physical energy and mental
power.

[10] If his companions follow where he has gone, if those herds
of desperate criminals clear out of the city, how happy we will be,
how lucky Rome will be, how highly praised my consulship will be!
For theirs is no ordinary depravity, their boldness not natural or
tolerable. They think of nothing except murder, except arson, except
pillage. They have squandered their inheritances, mortgaged their
properties. Their money ran out long ago, and now their credit has
begun to run out as well; but those tastes they had in their days of
plenty remain the same. If, in all their drinking and gambling, they
were concerned only with revelling and prostitutes, they would
indeed be beyond hope, but we could put up with them. But who
could possibly put up with cowards plotting against men of courage,
fools against the wise, drunks against the sober, sluggards against the
wakeful? Reclining at their banquets, embracing their whores, heavy
with wine, stuffed with food, wreathed with flowers, drenched with
perfume, and worn out by illicit sex, they belch out their plans for
the massacre of decent citizens and the burning of Rome.

[11] For my part, I am certain that these men are going to meet
their doom, that the punishment long due for their treachery, wickedness, criminality, and self-indulgence is either imminent or at the
very least on its way. My consulship cannot cure these men; but if
it removes them, it will have extended the life of our state not for
some short period, but for many centuries to come. There is no
foreign people we need be afraid of, no king capable of making war
on the Roman people: on land and sea, one man's valour* has brought
universal peace. The internal war is all that remains: the plots are
within, the danger is within, the enemy is within! Our struggle is
against decadence, against madness, against crime. Let me tell you,
citizens, I am assuming the leadership of this war. I am taking on the

hostility of these criminals myself. Whatever can be cured, I will somehow cure; but whatever has to be cut out, I will not allow to remain as a cancer within our state. So let them either leave or stay in peace—or, if they stay but keep their present intentions, let them expect what they deserve!

[12] But there are some who say, citizens, that I have forced Catiline into exile. But if I could produce that effect with just a word, I would do the very same to those who are accusing me of this. Of course, Catiline was so timid or even bashful that he could not endure the consul's voice, and as soon as he was ordered to go into exile, off he went! But yesterday,* citizens, when I had narrowly escaped being assassinated in my own home, I summoned the senate to the temple of Jupiter Stator and put the entire matter before the conscript fathers. After Catiline had arrived, what senator spoke to him? Who greeted him? Who even looked on him as merely a bad citizen, and not as the deadliest of enemies? In fact they went further: the leading senators moved away from the area of benches where he had taken his place, and left it empty and unoccupied.* [13] Then I, the stern consul who forces citizens into exile with a mere word, asked Catiline whether or not he had spent the night in a meeting at the house of Marcus Laeca. To begin with, the criminal, aware of his guilt, declined to answer: so I revealed further details. I explained what he had done during the night, where he had been, what he had planned for the following night, and how he had drawn up his strategy for the entire war. He hesitated: he was trapped. I therefore went on to ask him what was keeping him from setting out on the journey for which he had long prepared—since I had information that he had sent ahead arms, axes, rods of office,* trumpets, military standards, and also that silver eagle* to which he had even dedicated a shrine at his house. [14] So how could I be said to be forcing into exile a man whom I saw had already entered upon war? Manlius, the centurion who has set up a military camp in the territory of Faesulae, was, I suppose, acting on his own authority when he declared war on the Roman people;* and that camp is not in fact waiting at this very moment for Catiline to join it as its leader; and Catiline himself— forced into exile!—has actually taken himself off to Massilia, as is claimed, and not to this camp!

What a wretched business it is, not simply running the country, but even saving it. For suppose that Lucius Catilina, trapped and

thwarted by the measures I have taken, the labours I have under-
gone, and the risks I have run, now suddenly takes fright, changes his
mind, abandons his supporters, gives up his plans for war, and turns
from the path of crime and war to flight and exile. In that case,
people will say not that I have torn from him the arms of criminality,
or that my precautions have paralysed him with terror, or that he has
been forced to give up his hopes and his attempt, but that an innocent man has been driven into exile without trial by the violent
threats of the consul. And if he does follow that path, there will be
people who will regard him not as criminal but as pitiable, and will
regard me not as an exceptionally diligent consul, but as the cruellest
of tyrants! [15] But it will still be worth my while, citizens, to brave
the storm of this false and unjust calumny, just so long as you are
spared the danger of this horrifying, unspeakable war. So by all
means let it be said that I have forced him into exile—just so long as
that is where he goes.

But, trust me, he will not go there. Never, citizens, for the sake of
being spared hostility, will I pray to the immortal gods for you to
receive news that Lucius Catilina is at the head of an enemy army
and is mobilizing his troops. But I am afraid this is indeed the news
you will be hearing within three days*—and I am much more concerned about possible future criticism for having let him go than for
having driven him out. As for those who claim that he was driven
out, when in fact he left by his own choice, just think what they
would be saying if I had executed him! [16] Yet those who keep
saying that Catiline is on his way to Massilia are not so much
aggrieved that he is doing this as afraid in case he is. None of
them is so kind-hearted that they really wish him to go to Massilia
rather than to Manlius. And as for Catiline himself, even if—by
Hercules!—he had never previously contemplated what he is now
doing, he would still prefer to be killed in brigandage than live in
exile. As it is, everything has gone for him exactly as he wished and
planned, except that he did not manage to assassinate me before he
left Rome. We ought therefore to hope that he is going into exile
rather than complain that he is.

[17] But why have I been talking for so long about a single enemy,
an enemy who now admits that he is an enemy, and one whom I have
no fear of, because, as I have always hoped, the city wall now lies
between us? And why am I saying nothing about those who conceal

the fact that they are enemies, who have not left Rome, and who are here in our midst? I should prefer not to have to punish these men if I can help it, but instead cure them and reconcile them with their country—something which should not be impossible, so long as they are prepared to listen to what I have to say. Let me set out for you, citizens, the types of men from which these forces are drawn; I will then give each group, if I can, the medicine of my advice and persuasion.

[18] The first group consists of people who have large debts and more than enough property to pay them off, but who are so attached to that property that nothing can set them free. They have every appearance of respectability, because they are in fact rich, but their intentions and principles are utterly scandalous. Do you really think you can be wealthy and well provided with land, properties, silver, slaves, and everything else, and yet hold back from selling some of your possessions to improve your credit? What, then, are you waiting for? War? Really? And do you seriously imagine that amidst the general devastation your own property will be sacrosanct? New books,* then? Those who expect that from Catiline are mistaken. By my generosity, new books will indeed be provided—auctioneers' catalogues! That, I tell you, is the only thing that is going to save those who do have property. Indeed, if they had been prepared to do this earlier, instead of stupidly trying to pay the interest on their debts with the income from their estates, they would today be both richer and better citizens. But this is actually the group we need be frightened of least, because either they can be persuaded to change their views or, if they do not, they will be more likely, I think, simply to say prayers against their country than to take up arms against it.

[19] The second group consists of those who, despite being over-whelmed with debt, look forward to ruling, are hungry for power, and think that with the country in turmoil they will be able to obtain offices they have no hope of obtaining when the country is at peace. To these people, I think I should give this advice—the same advice, in fact, as I give to all the others—that they should abandon all hope of attaining their goal. First of all, they need to be aware that I am keeping watch over the country, am on hand to defend it, and am looking out for it. Secondly, the loyal citizens are showing great courage; the populace, vast as it is, is showing complete unity; and on top of this, our military forces are strong. Finally, the immortal gods

will bring help in person to this unconquered people, this glorious empire, and this fairest of cities against the terrible criminal violence that we face. But imagine that these men achieve what they so furiously desire. Surely, amid the ashes of the city and the blood of citizens, which in their wicked and criminal hearts they long for, they will not aspire to become consuls, dictators, even kings? Surely they must see that, if they succeed in obtaining the offices they covet, they will only end up having to hand them over to some runaway slave or gladiator?

[20] The third group consists of men who are quite old now, but who have kept fit and are still strong. Manlius, the man Catiline is taking over from, is a member of this group. They are the men from the colonies Sulla founded. Now I recognize that in the main these colonies consist of loyal, courageous men; but all the same there are some colonists who, on suddenly being given money they never expected to have, have been throwing it around in a prodigal and high-handed manner. Building as if they were aristocrats, delighting in coaches, litters, armies of servants, and sumptuous banquets, they have fallen so deeply into debt that, if they are ever to become solvent again, Sulla would have to be brought back from the dead! They have also driven quite a few poor and needy farmers into hoping, as they do, that the plundering of former times* is going to be repeated. Both these classes of people I treat as belonging to the same group—plunderers and thieves—but I advise them to give up their insane thoughts of proscriptions and dictatorships. The horror of that time is branded so deeply on our national psyche that today not only men but even, I think, dumb animals would refuse to countenance its return.

[21] The fourth group is certainly varied, mixed, and unruly. These are people who went under long ago, who have never got their heads above water, who partly through laziness, partly through business failures, and partly also through extravagance stagger on with long-standing debts, and who have given up in the face of bankruptcy summonses, hearings, and sequestrations—a very large group of people who are reported to have abandoned Rome and the country districts for that military camp. These people I would class not so much as keen soldiers as lazy backsliders. If they cannot stand on their own two feet, it would be much better if they fell as soon as possible, just so long as they do not disturb the state—or even their

immediate neighbours. For I cannot see why, if they are incapable of living honourable lives, they should want to die in dishonourable circumstances,* or why they imagine death will be less distressing to them if they meet their end along with many others than if they do so on their own.

[22] The fifth group consists of murderers, cut-throats, and every other type of criminal. I do not want these men to abandon Catiline; and in fact they cannot be made to do so. Let them be killed as brigands, since there are far more of them than the prison* can cope with.

The final group is last not just in number but also in character and way of life. This is Catiline's very own, his elect, his special band of lovies. They are the ones you see with carefully arranged hair, moisturized faces, either too young to shave or else with full beards, with tunics down to their wrists and ankles, and wearing dresses not togas. All the energy of their lives, and the labour of their waking hours, is devoted to dinners that last till dawn. [23] In this clique, every gambler, every adulterer, and every filthy pervert is to be found. These boys, so elegant and refined, have perfected the art not just of sex, active and passive, nor just of singing and dancing, but of wielding the dagger and poisoning food. Unless they leave Rome, unless they die (even if Catiline himself should die), I tell you that they will be a spawning-ground of future Catilines in our country. But what is it those pathetic creatures want? Surely they are not going to arrive at the camp with their fancy women in tow? Yet how will they manage without them, especially during these long winter nights? How will they endure the frost and snow up there in the Apennines? Perhaps they expect to endure the glacial temperatures more easily because they have had plenty of practice dancing naked at dinner parties? [24] What a truly terrifying war this is going to be, with Catiline in command of this praetorian cohort of poofs!

Now, citizens, prepare your own armies and your own defences to fight these crack troops of Catiline's! First, pit your consuls and generals against this exhausted and wounded gladiator. Then lead out the flower and pride of all Italy to fight this banished and enfeebled collection of castaways. The towns and colonies of Italy are more than a match for the hills and forests of Catiline. Nor is there any need for me to compare the other resources, equipment, and defensive forces that you possess with that brigand's total lack of such advantages. [25] But if we leave on one side all the things that we are supplied with and he lacks—the senate, the Roman equestrians, the Roman people, the city, the treasury, the revenues, all of Italy, all the provinces, foreign countries—if, leaving all these on one side, we choose to make a comparison of the actual principles that are in conflict, we will be able to tell from that alone how inferior their position is. On our side fights decency, on theirs depravity; on ours modesty, on theirs perversion; on ours honesty, on theirs deceit; on ours duty, on theirs crime; on ours steadfastness, on theirs hysteria; on ours honour, on theirs disgrace; on ours self-restraint, on theirs self-indulgence; on ours, justice, self-control, courage, prudence, and all the virtues, fighting against injustice, extravagance, sloth, recklessness, and all the vices; finally, wealth is fighting against poverty, good principles against bad, reason against madness, and well-grounded confidence against absolute despair. In a conflict and battle of this kind, even if human strength were to fail, would the immortal gods themselves not step in to ensure that these outstanding virtues triumph over those many, extreme vices?

[26] Under these circumstances, I urge you, citizens, as I did before, to defend your homes and guard them vigilantly. For my part, I have taken all the necessary steps to ensure that the city is properly protected without disturbing you, and without declaring a state of emergency. I have informed all your fellow-citizens in the towns and colonies of Catiline's departure last night, and they will easily be able to defend their towns and territories. The gladiators, a force Catiline thought he could rely on absolutely— although they are more loyal to the country than some of our patricians are—will be kept under guard on my authority. Quintus Metellus,* whom I sent in advance to the Umbrian coast and Picenum for precisely this purpose, will either crush Catiline or put a stop to all his movements and plans. As to all the other matters to be decided, put into action, and carried out, I shall now consult the senate, which as you see is being convened.

[27] But now to those who have stayed behind in Rome—or rather to those whom Catiline has deliberately planted in Rome to destroy the city and each one of you—I will keep repeating the following warning; after all, they may be enemies today, but they were born as Roman citizens. If anyone has felt that I have been too lenient up until now, it was because I have been waiting for what was still

hidden to burst out into the open. But for the future, I can no longer forget that this is my country, that I am your consul, that it is my duty either to live with you or give my life for you. The gates are unguarded, and there is no ambush on the road: so if anyone wishes to leave, I am prepared to turn a blind eye. But if anyone makes a move inside the city, if I discover any plan or scheme—let alone any act—against our country, that person should be aware that Rome has all-seeing consuls, it has outstanding magistrates, it has a strong senate; it has weapons—and it has a prison,* which our ancestors ordained as a punishment for serious and flagrant crimes.

[28] In all these measures, citizens, I shall make sure that this serious crisis is put down with the least possible disturbance, this extreme danger put down without a state of emergency being declared, and this biggest and most brutal civil war in history put down with a single civilian—myself—as your leader and commander. In managing the situation, I shall make sure, citizens, so far as is possible, that not a single traitor inside the city shall pay the penalty for his crimes. But if the extent of manifest crime, if the scale of the danger hanging over our country compels me to deviate from this policy of leniency, then I shall certainly make sure—and this is something one hardly dare hope for in such a major, hazardous war—that no good citizen loses his life, and that all your lives are saved by the punishment of only a few individuals.

[29] When I make you this promise, citizens, I do it not on the basis of my own intelligence or of any human wisdom, but as a result of many unambiguous signs from the immortal gods, under whose guidance I have arrived at these hopes and this policy. They do not guard us from afar, as in days gone by, against a distant foreign enemy, but here present among us now they are defending their temples and the houses of the city with the protection of their divine power. Your duty, citizens, is to pray to them, to worship them, and to implore them, now that all the forces of our external enemies have been defeated on land and sea,* to defend this city, which they have ordained should be the most beautiful, the most prosperous, and the most powerful city in the world, from the unspeakable criminality of citizen traitors.

# IN CATILINAM III

[1] The country, citizens, together with the lives of each one of you, your property, your fortunes, your wives and children, this glorious seat of empire, this most blessed and most beautiful of cities—all these today, as a result of the great love that the immortal gods feel for you, and also as a result of my own physical toil, mental effort, and readiness to accept personal risk, you can see snatched from fire and the sword and the very jaws of death, preserved for you, and restored to you. [2] We consider the day on which we are saved to be at least as jubilant and joyful as the day on which we are born: when we are saved, our happiness is assured, whereas when we are born, we cannot take anything for granted; and also, of course, we are born with no feelings, but feel pleasure when we are saved. Surely then, since we have elevated the founder of this city* to the immortal gods by our gratitude and praise, you and your descendants ought also to honour the man who has saved this same city once it had already been founded and grown to greatness. For what I have done is to extinguish the fires that were being set to the whole of the city, the temples, the shrines, the houses, and the walls, and were about to engulf them; and I have beaten back the swords that had been drawn against the state, pushing away their tips as they were held to your throats. [3] Since all this plotting has been discovered, exposed, and revealed to the senate by me, I will now give you, citizens, a brief account of it. This will enable you to find out what you currently do not know, but are eager to learn—how serious it is, how flagrant it is, and the means by which it has been detected and demonstrated.

First of all, then, when Catiline escaped from Rome some days ago,* he left behind in the city his partners in crime, the most danger-ous leaders of this unspeakable war. Accordingly, I have been con-stantly on the alert, citizens, and have been looking to see how, amid such widespread and well-concealed plotting, our safety might best be ensured. For at the time when I expelled Catiline from the city—and I am no longer afraid of making myself unpopular by using that word, because I ought now to be more frightened of being criticized for letting him leave alive—at that time, when I wanted to get him out of Rome, I imagined that either the rest of the conspirators would leave with him or else those who remained behind would be weak and powerless without him. [4] But when it became clear to me that those whom I knew to be the fiercest and most extreme criminals had stayed behind in Rome and were still in our midst, I spent all my time, night and day, trying to find out and see what it was they were doing and what it was they were planning.* Since I realized that the extraordinary scale of their criminal intentions would incline you to doubt what I was telling you when you merely heard it through your ears, I therefore found out as much as I could, intending that when you actually saw the conspiracy with your eyes you would then at last apply your minds to taking steps to ensure your own safety.

I discovered, then, that Publius Lentulus* had tampered with the envoys of the Allobroges for the purpose of stirring up a war beyond the Alps and a revolt in Gaul; that the envoys had been sent back to their own people in Gaul with letters and instructions, and on their way there were to visit Catiline; and that an escort, Titus Volturcius,* had been assigned to them, and had been given a letter for Catiline. It seemed to me that this was just the opportunity I needed—one very hard to come by, and yet one I had hoped all along the immortal gods might send me—an opportunity that would provide clear proof of the whole business not just to me, but to the senate and your-selves. [5] So yesterday I sent for the praetors Lucius Flaccus and Gaius Pomptinus,* both of them valiant men and true patriots. I explained the situation to them, and told them what I wanted them to do. They, being men of absolutely unswerving loyalty towards their country, accepted the task without the slightest objection or delay. At dusk, they secretly arrived at the Mulvian Bridge, and there they split their force into two parts, placing them in the nearest houses on either side of the bridge over the Tiber. Without anyone suspecting a thing, they had brought with them a large number of brave followers, while I myself had sent some hand-picked young men from the prefecture of Reate,* armed with swords, whom I have been making regular use of for the defence of the country.

[6] Towards the end of the third watch,* the envoys of the Allobroges and their entourage,* together with Volturcius, began to cross the Mulvian Bridge, and immediately came under attack. Swords were drawn on both sides. Only the praetors knew what was going on: no one else had been told. A fight broke out; but Pomptinus and Flaccus intervened and stopped it. The letters which the men

were carrying were all handed over to the praetors, their seals unbroken. The men themselves were arrested and brought to me just as dawn was breaking. I immediately sent for the villain who had co-ordinated this criminal plan, Cimber Gabinius,* before he could suspect that anything was amiss. Then I also summoned Lucius Statilius,* and after him Gaius Cethegus.* Lentulus was very slow in coming—I imagine because, unusually for him, he had stayed up late into the night writing letters.*

[7] A large number of the most senior and illustrious men of our city, having heard the news, came to visit me this morning. They wanted me to open the letters before putting them before the senate, in case they contained nothing incriminating and I should then be accused of having created a state of national alarm without good reason. But I replied that in a situation involving public danger I could not do other than place the matter just as it was before the public council. Even, citizens, if the information which had been reported to me turned out not to be contained in the letters, I nevertheless believed that, when our country was in such grave danger, I had nothing to fear from being over-zealous.

As you saw, I quickly called a full meeting of the senate. [8] While it was being summoned, I did as the Allobroges advised me and immediately sent the valiant praetor Gaius Sulpicius* to Cethegus' house and asked him to confiscate any weapons he should find there. He duly removed from there an immense quantity of daggers and swords.

I brought Volturcius into the senate without the Gauls. On the orders of the senate, I gave him immunity from prosecution. Then I encouraged him not to be afraid and to tell us what he knew. When he had more or less recovered from his terror, he said that he had a letter and instructions from Publius Lentulus to Catiline—that Catiline should enlist slaves, and that he and his army should march on Rome as soon as possible. The plan was that, when those in Rome had set fire to every part of the city, in accordance with the directions and dispositions already made, and had massacred an unlimited number of citizens, Catiline would appear on the scene to mop up anyone who had escaped from Rome, and would then join forces with these leaders in the city.

[9] Next the Gauls were brought in. They said that an oath and letters had been given to them by Lentulus, Cethegus, and Statilius

to take back to their people. They had been told by these three and by Lucius Cassius* to send cavalry to Italy as soon as possible: there was not going to be a shortage of infantry. Lentulus, moreover, had said to them that, according to the Sibylline books and the responses of the soothsayers, he was the third Cornelius who was destined to rule Rome and exercise dominion over it, the first two being Cinna and Sulla.* He had also said that this year, being the tenth year after the acquittal of the Vestal virgins* and the twentieth after the burning of the Capitol, was destined to be the year in which this city and empire would be destroyed. [10] The Gauls added that Cethegus had had a difference of opinion with the other conspirators: Lentulus and the others had wanted the massacre and the burning of the city to take place during the Saturnalia,* but Cethegus had thought that too long to wait.

To cut a long story short, citizens, I ordered the letters allegedly given by each of the men to be produced. First I showed Cethegus his, and he acknowledged his seal. I cut the string and read what was inside. In the letter, which was written in his own hand and addressed to the senate and people of the Allobroges, he undertook to do what he had promised to their envoys, and he requested them to do in return what the envoys had promised to him. Just before this, Cethegus, when asked about the discovery of the swords and daggers at his house, had managed a reply: he said that he had always been a connoisseur of fine weaponry. But now when his letter was read out, he suddenly seemed weakened and crushed by his sense of guilt, and fell silent. Statilius was brought in, and acknowledged both his seal and his handwriting. His letter, saying much the same as the previous one, was read out, and he confessed. Then I showed Lentulus the next letter and asked him whether he recognized the seal. He nodded. 'It is indeed,' I told him, 'a well-known seal, a portrait of your illustrious grandfather,* who surpassed everyone in his love for his country and for his fellow-citizens: though it cannot speak, this seal surely should have called you back from so terrible a crime.' [11] His letter, written along the same lines to the senate and people of the Allobroges, was read. I gave him the opportunity of commenting on it; he initially declined. But shortly afterwards, when the evidence had been set out and presented in its entirety, he stood up and asked the Gauls what business they had had with him to cause them to come to his house; and he put the same questions to

Volturcius. They replied briefly and emphatically, telling him through whom* and how many times they had come to see him, and asking him whether he had not said anything to them on the subject of the Sibylline prophecies. Then, suddenly driven mad by his crime, he showed what a guilty conscience can do. Although he could have denied what they had said, all of a sudden to everyone's surprise he confessed that it was true.* Not only did his intelligence and the oratorical skill in which he has always excelled* fail him, but so too did his unparalleled insolence and wickedness—such was the effect of his being caught red-handed committing his crime.

[12] Volturcius, however, suddenly demanded that the letter which Lentulus had given him for Catiline should be produced and opened. Lentulus was deeply shaken at this, but nevertheless acknowledged both his seal and his handwriting. The letter bore no name, but ran as follows: 'The person I have sent to you will tell you who I am. Make sure you act like a man, and remember how far you have gone already. See to whatever you need, and make sure you accept the help of anyone that offers it, however lowly.'* Then Gabinius was brought in and, although at first he tried to brazen it out, in the end he denied none of the Gauls' allegations.

[13] Let me add, citizens, that although I thought the letters, seals, handwriting, and finally the confession of each person were totally convincing arguments and evidence of their guilt, still more convincing were their pallor, the looks in their eyes, the expressions on their faces, and their silence. So stunned were they, so intently did they stare at the ground, and so furtively did they steal occasional glances at each other that they looked not as if they had been incriminated by others, but as if they had incriminated themselves.

When the evidence had been set out and presented, citizens, I asked the senate what action it wished to be taken in the supreme interest of the state. The leading members then made firm and courageous proposals, which the senate adopted without amendment. The decree which it passed has not yet been written out, so let me tell you from memory, citizens, what was decreed.

[14] First of all, I am thanked in the most generous terms, that thanks to my courage, wisdom, and foresight the country has been saved from the most extreme danger. Secondly, the praetors Lucius Flaccus and Gaius Pomptinus are justly and deservedly praised for the brave and loyal assistance they gave me. Praise is also given to my

valiant colleague* for excluding the members of this conspiracy both
from his own affairs and from affairs of state. They voted too that
Publius Lentulus, after resigning his praetorship, should be placed in
custody, and that Gaius Cethegus, Lucius Statilius, and Publius
Gabinius, who were all present, should likewise be placed in custody.
This was also to apply to Lucius Cassius, who had insisted on being
given responsibility for the burning of the city; to Marcus Caeparius,*
who was identified as the man chosen to raise the shepherds of
Apulia in revolt; to Publius Furius,* one of the colonists settled by
Lucius Sulla at Faesulae; to Quintus Annius Chilo,* who, together
with this man Furius, was constantly engaged in these dealings with
the Allobroges; and to Publius Umbrenus,* a freedman who was
shown to have introduced the Gauls to Gabinius. Moreover, citizens,
the senate displayed such leniency as to take the view, in spite of the
size of the conspiracy and the number of domestic enemies involved,
that all that was needed to save the country was the punishment of
a mere nine traitors, and that that would be enough to bring the rest
to their senses.*

[15] In addition, a thanksgiving has been decreed to the immortal
gods in my name for the exceptional favour they have bestowed on
us. This is the first time in the history of our city that such an
honour has been granted to a civilian, and the wording of the decree
runs: 'because I had saved the city from burning, the citizens from
massacre, and Italy from war'. And if you compare this thanksgiving
with the other ones that have been decreed in the past, you will find
that there is this difference, that the others were given for services
towards the state, whereas this one alone was given for saving it.

What needed to be done first has been done and dealt with.
Although the senate judged, once the evidence had been revealed
and his confession made, that Publius Lentulus had forfeited the
rights not only of a praetor but of a citizen, he was nevertheless
permitted to resign his office.* This has the effect of freeing us from
any religious scruple in treating him as a private citizen when we
come to punish him—although no such scruple prevented the illustrious Gaius Marius from killing the praetor Gaius Glaucia* without
his being named in any decree.

[16] So, citizens, you have captured and are now holding under
arrest the criminals who have been at the head of this exceptionally
wicked and perilous war. Now that the dangers which threatened our

city have been averted, you would be justified in concluding that all
Catiline's army, all his hopes and resources have collapsed into nothing. When I was driving him out of the city, I foresaw, citizens, that
once he was out of the way I would have nothing to fear from the lazy
Publius Lentulus, or the obese Lucius Cassius, or the reckless,
insane Gaius Cethegus. Out of all of them, he was the only one to be
afraid of—and only for so long as he remained inside the city walls.
He knew everything; he could get through to anybody. He had the
ability and the nerve to accost anyone, to sound them out, to push
them to revolt. His mind was predisposed to crime—and in whatever
direction his mind went, his tongue and hand would be sure to
follow. He had particular people selected and assigned for particular
tasks. But when he delegated something, he did not suppose it
already done: there was nothing that he did not personally attend to,
take in hand, watch over, toil over. He could endure cold, thirst,
hunger. [17] He was keen, so bold, so well prepared, so clever, so
vigilant in committing crime, and so thorough in depravity that
if I had not succeeded in driving him away from his plots inside
the city and towards armed rebellion—I give you my real opinion,
citizens—then it would have been no easy task for me to remove so
great an evil from over your heads. Had I not driven him away, he
would not have let us off until the Saturnalia, nor would he have
given such advance notice of the date of the country's doom and
destruction, nor would he have let his seal and letter fall into our
hands as unmistakable evidence of his guilt. As it is, he has not been
here, and as a result things have been so badly bungled that no
burglary of a private house has ever been so clearly proved as this
terrible conspiracy against the state has been unmistakably detected
and stopped. Had Catiline remained in Rome until now, even though
I pre-empted and prevented all his plots for as long as he was here,
we would have had a fight on our hands, to say the very least. As long
as he remained an enemy inside the city, we would never have been
able to deliver the state from such awful danger in such peace, such
calm, and such silence.

[18] And yet, citizens, the way I have managed everything would
seem to suggest that the action that has been taken and the foresight
that has been shown derive from the will and wisdom of the
immortal gods. We can assume this partly because it hardly seems
possible that human thought could have directed such momentous

events, but more particularly because the gods have brought us help and aid during these times in so manifest a form that they have almost been visible to our eyes. To say nothing of the burning torches that have appeared at night in the western sky, to pass over the bolts of lightning and the earthquakes, to say nothing of the other phenomena that have appeared during my consulship so frequently that the immortal gods appeared to be prophesying the events which are now unfolding—all the same, citizens, I must not pass over or leave out what I am about to tell you.

[19] You will recall that during the consulship of Cotta and Torquatus* various objects on the Capitol were struck by lightning. Images of the gods were toppled, statues of men of olden times were knocked down, the bronze tablets of the laws were melted, and even the founder of this city, Romulus, was struck—you will remember it,* a gilded statue on the Capitol of an unweaned baby gaping at the udder of a wolf. At that time the soothsayers, summoned from every corner of Etruria,* predicted murder, arson, the destruction of the laws, internal and civil war, and the fall of Rome and our empire unless the immortal gods were appeased by every possible means, and used their power virtually to alter fate. [20] In response to the soothsayers' warnings, games were held for ten days, and nothing that could possibly serve to appease the gods was left undone. The soothsayers also ordered a larger image of Jupiter to be erected and positioned on an elevated site facing east, the opposite direction to that in which the previous one had faced. Their hope, they said, was that if the statue which you can now see faced towards the rising of the sun, the forum, and the senate-house, then the plots that had been secretly formed against the city and the empire would be illuminated and made visible to the senate and people of Rome. So the consuls made a contract for the erection of a new statue. But the work proceeded so slowly that the statue was not erected under the last consuls, or in my consulship—until this very day!*

[21] Citizens, which of us here can be so blind to the truth, so impetuous, so deranged as to deny that everything we see, and particularly this city, is controlled by the will and power of the immortal gods? When the soothsayers had given their warning that murder, arson, and the destruction of the state were being plotted, and by citizens too, some people refused to believe that criminality on such a scale was possible—but you found out that wicked citizens

had not merely planned it, but begun to put their plans into action. And surely what happened this morning was so striking that you would have to conclude that Jupiter Best and Greatest was responsible—that at the very moment when the conspirators and the witnesses against them were being led on my orders through the forum to the temple of Concord,* the statue was set up? Once it had been put into position and turned towards yourselves and the senate, the senate and yourselves then saw all the plots which had been made against the lives of everyone revealed and laid bare.

[22] The conspirators are all the more deserving of hatred and punishment in that they have attempted to cast their detestable, deadly firebrands not just onto your houses and homes, but onto the temples and shrines of the gods. But if I were to claim that it is I who have stopped them, I would be being intolerably presumptuous: it is Jupiter, Jupiter who has stopped them, Jupiter who has saved the Capitol, Jupiter who has saved these temples, Jupiter who has saved the whole city, and Jupiter who has saved each one of you! It is under the guidance of the immortal gods that I have shown the determination and purpose necessary to come upon these conclusive proofs of guilt. Surely the attempt to recruit the Allobroges would never have taken place, surely Lentulus and the other enemies in our midst would never have been so reckless as to entrust matters of such importance to barbarians they did not know, and actually give letters to them, unless the immortal gods had taken away their senses while they were in the act of perpetrating such wickedness? Again, that Gauls, from a country scarcely at peace with us, the only people left who seem to be both able and not unwilling to make war on the Roman people, that they should forgo the prospect of immense power and wealth offered to them without their asking by patricians, and place your safety higher than their own advantage—do you not think that this is the work of the gods, especially when those Gauls did not have to fight us in order to overpower us, but merely to keep silent?

[23] Therefore, citizens, since a thanksgiving has been decreed at all places of worship, you should spend the days devoted to it celebrating with your wives and children. Often in the past, honours have been justly and deservedly paid to the immortal gods—but never more justly than now. You have been rescued from the cruellest and most wretched of deaths, and rescued without a massacre

and without bloodshed. Without an army, without fighting, and as civilians, and with me alone, a civilian, as your leader and commander, you have been victorious.

[24] Think, citizens, of all the civil wars, not only the ones you have heard of, but the ones you have personally witnessed and remember. Lucius Sulla crushed Publius Sulpicius.* Gaius Marius, the guardian of this city, and many valiant men he either exiled or killed. The consul Gnaeus Octavius expelled his colleague from the city by force of arms: where we are standing now was piled with bodies and overflowing with the blood of citizens. Afterwards Cinna and Marius gained the upper hand, and with the deaths of our most illustrious citizens the light of our country was put out. Later Sulla avenged the brutality of that victory: I do not need to remind you how many citizens lost their lives and what a catastrophe it was for Rome. Marcus Lepidus quarrelled with the illustrious and valiant Quintus Catulus, though Lepidus' death was not so deeply mourned as those of the others.*

[25] And yet all those conflicts were concerned not with destroying the state, but only with changing it. Those people I mentioned did not want there to be no country, but a country in which they were the leading men; they did not want to burn this city, but to do well in it. Yet all those conflicts, none of which was aimed at the annihilation of the state, were settled not by the restoration of harmony, but by the murder of citizens. In this war, on the other hand—the most serious and brutal one in history, a war such as has never taken place within any barbarian tribe, a war in which Lentulus, Catiline, Cethegus, and Cassius ruled that all who were capable of living in safety in a city that was itself safe should be counted as enemies—in this war, citizens, I have secured the safety of you all. Your enemies predicted that the only citizens to survive would be those who were still left after an endless massacre, and the only parts of the city those that the flames could not reach; but I have kept both city and citizens unharmed and intact.

[26] In return for this great service, citizens, I shall ask you for no token of merit, no badge of honour, no monument of praise—except that you remember this day for ever.* It is in your own hearts that I would like all my triumphs, all my decorations of honour, monuments of glory, and badges of praise to be founded and grounded. Nothing that is mute will satisfy me, nothing that is silent, and

nothing that is attainable by men less worthy than I. My achievements, citizens, will be nurtured by your remembering them, will
grow by people talking about them, and will mature and ripen by
being recorded in literature. I know that the same length of days—
which I hope will be without end—has been ordained for the memory of my consulship as for the survival of Rome, and that at one and
the same moment our country has produced two citizens, one of
whom* has carried the frontiers of your empire to the borders not of
earth, but of heaven, while the other has preserved the home and
centre of that empire.

[27] The nature and consequences of my achievement, however,
differ from those of the achievement of people who have fought
foreign wars: I have to live with the people I have defeated and
suppressed, whereas they have left their enemies either dead or sub-
jugated. It is therefore up to you, citizens, to see that, if others
profit—and rightly—from what they have done, I never come to
harm as a result of what I have done. I have ensured that the vile
criminal plots of traitors cannot harm you: you must now ensure that
they do not harm me.

Even so, citizens, they cannot now do me harm. Strong is the
defence provided by loyal citizens, a defence I can count on for all
time; strong is the authority of the state, ever my silent defender; and
strong also is the power of a guilty conscience, which will lead those
who ignore it, in their eagerness to attack me, to implicate themselves. [28] It is not in my nature, citizens, to give way in the face of
anyone's criminal actions; on the contrary, I will always strike the
traitor first. But if the attacks of internal enemies,* which you have
been saved from, come to be directed exclusively at me, then you will
have to consider, citizens, what you want to happen in the future to
people who, in order to secure your safety, expose themselves to
unpopularity and great danger.

For myself, though, what else can now be added to life's rewards?
Neither in the honours which you can bestow nor in the glory that
is won by virtue can I see any higher peak of eminence to which I
might wish to climb. [29] But what I shall most certainly do, citizens,
is to defend and enhance, as a private citizen, the achievements of my
consulship, so that if any odium should arise from my preservation
of our country, it will harm those who hate me, and increase my
glory. In short, my policy will be always to keep in mind what I have

achieved, and to ensure that those achievements are attributed to my own merit and not simply to chance.

Citizens, night has fallen. Worship Jupiter, the guardian of this city and of yourselves. Go home, and, although the danger has now been averted, defend your homes and guard them vigilantly, just as you did last night. I shall make sure that you do not have to do this for much longer, and that you can live in lasting peace, citizens.

# IN CATILINAM IV

[1] I see, conscript fathers, that the eyes and faces of all of you are turned in my direction: I see that you are concerned not just about the danger to yourselves and the country, but also, if that is averted, about the danger to me.* Your goodwill towards me comforts me in my troubles and relieves my pain, but—by the immortal gods!—put aside that goodwill and forget my safety, and think instead of yourselves and your children! As far as I am concerned, if I was given the consulship on condition that I should have to endure every kind of suffering, every kind of pain and torture, then I will bear it not just bravely but even gladly, so long as my efforts result in security and honour for you and the Roman people.

[2] I am a consul, conscript fathers, for whom neither the forum, which is the home of all justice,* nor the Campus Martius, sanctified as it is by the consular auspices, nor the senate-house, the supreme protection for all nations, nor the home, which is every man's refuge, nor the bed,* usually a place of rest, nor finally this curule chair, the seat of honour, has ever been free of plots and mortal danger. There is much that I have said nothing about, much that I have endured, much that I have forfeited,* and much that I have put right, at no little personal cost, to relieve your fear. But if the immortal gods intend this to be the outcome of my consulship, that I should rescue you and the Roman people from a pitiless massacre, your wives and children and the Vestal virgins* from brutal rape, the temples and shrines and this beautiful homeland of each one of us from the most loathsome fire, and the whole of Italy from war and devastation, then I am willing to submit, alone, to whatever fortune may have in store for me. And if Publius Lentulus was persuaded by the soothsayers to believe that his name would spell destruction for our country,* why should I not rejoice that my consulship should spell deliverance for the Roman people?

[3] Therefore, conscript fathers, consider your own interests, take thought for your country, save yourselves, your wives, your children, and your property, and defend the name and security of the Roman people—but stop sparing me trouble and worrying on my behalf. In the first place, I should venture to hope that all the gods who protect

this city will reward me so far as I deserve; and secondly, if anything happens to me, I shall die calm and prepared. For a man of courage, death cannot be shameful; for a man who has reached the consulship, it cannot be untimely;* and for a wise man, it cannot be pitiable. But I am not so iron-hearted as to remain unmoved by the grief of my dear beloved brother* who is with us, or by the tears of all these men you can see surrounding me.* Often my thoughts turn towards my home, whenever I see my wife, beside herself with worry, my terror-stricken daughter, my baby son, whom I think the country is holding to its bosom as a hostage for my consulship, and also my son-in-law,* whom I can see standing outside, waiting to see what the rest of today will bring. All these factors have an influence on me—but only to make me wish that, even if I myself should meet a violent end, at least my family and you may all be safe, instead of both they and us dying together amid the destruction of our country.*

[4] Therefore, conscript fathers, apply yourselves to the security of the country, and keep a look out for all the storms that threaten it unless you take preventive action. This is not Tiberius Gracchus precipitating a crisis and running up against your severe judgement because he hoped to become tribune of the plebs a second time; or Gaius Gracchus because he stirred up those who wanted land reform; or Lucius Saturninus because he killed Gaius Memmius.* No, the men that are held are people who have remained behind to burn the city, to massacre you all, and to receive Catiline into Rome. Their letters, seals, handwriting, and a confession from each one of them is also held. The Allobroges are approached, the slaves are roused to revolt,* Catiline is sent for. And a plot has been formed to ensure that, once everyone has been murdered, there should be no one left even to mourn the name of the Roman people or lament the destruction of so great an empire.

[5] All this informers have proved to you, the accused have admitted, and you have already pronounced upon in numerous judgements. First, you have thanked me in unprecedented terms, stating that it was by my courageous and painstaking efforts that a conspiracy of traitors has been exposed. Secondly, you have required Publius Lentulus to resign his praetorship. Thirdly, you have decreed that he and the others about whom you gave your judgement should be taken into custody. Most importantly, you have voted a thanksgiving to be held in my name, an honour never previously granted to a

civilian. Finally, you yesterday granted the most handsome rewards to the envoys of the Allobroges and to Titus Volturcius. All these actions go to show that the named men who have been placed in custody have been visibly and indisputably condemned by you.

[6] Nevertheless I have chosen to refer the matter to you, conscript fathers, as if it were still an open question: I want you to give your verdict on what has been done and decree the punishment. But I shall first say what as consul I ought to say. It is a long time now since I first observed that a great insanity had arisen in our country, and that a new kind of evil was being concocted and stirred up; it never entered my head, however, that such an extensive and deadly conspiracy as this was the work of citizens. But now whatever happens, and however you are disposed to think and vote, you must make up your minds before nightfall. You can see the magnitude of the crime that has been reported to you. If you think that only a few people are implicated in it, you are completely mistaken. The evil has been sown more widely than you suppose: it has not only seeped through Italy but has crossed the Alps and, creeping on its way unnoticed, has already taken over many of our provinces. Delay and procrastination will do nothing to check it: so whatever punishment you choose to impose, that punishment must come quickly.

[7] I see that so far we have two proposals, one from Decimus Silanus,* who proposes that those who have attempted to destroy Rome should be punished by death, and one from Gaius Caesar, who rules out the death penalty but recommends the strictest penalties otherwise available. Each of them proposes a punishment of the greatest severity, as befits his own standing and the scale of the crime that has been committed. Silanus believes that those who have attempted to kill all of us, to kill the Roman people, to destroy the empire, and to obliterate the name of Rome should not be allowed to enjoy life and breathe the air that is common to all for a single second, and he recalls that Rome has often imposed this punishment on traitors in the past. Caesar, on the other hand, feels that the immortal gods have not ordained death as a punishment, but as a natural and inevitable end or as a release from pain or misfortune: that is why wise men have never been loath to meet their deaths, and men of courage have often been happy to die. Being cast into chains, on the other hand, and for life, is undeniably an exemplary punishment for a wicked crime. So he wants the men distributed among the

towns of Italy. Now that course of action would appear to be unjust, if you intend to order the towns to take the men, and problematic, if you merely ask them to. But if that is what you want, go ahead and decree it. [8] I shall do as you direct, and I am sure I shall manage to find someone* who does not consider himself honour-bound to refuse to carry out your wishes—which will, after all, have been decided on for reasons of national security. Caesar also proposes that the towns should be severely punished should any of the traitors escape; and he specifies a formidable guard appropriate to their crimes. He stipulates that no one should be permitted to reduce the penalties imposed on the men he is condemning, whether by decree of the senate or by vote of the people; and so he even takes away their hope, which is the sole consolation of those in adversity. He further orders that their property be confiscated, and so leaves those wicked individuals with only their lives. And if he were to take that too away from them, the effect would be to spare them considerable mental and physical torment, as well as all punishment for their crimes. That is why, to give criminals some reason to be afraid while they are alive, past generations wanted there to be comparable punishments awaiting evildoers in the underworld, because they clearly saw that without such punishments death in itself would be nothing to be frightened of.

[9] Now, conscript fathers, I can see where my own interest lies. Suppose you adopt the proposal of Gaius Caesar. Since he has taken what is reckoned to be the 'popular' path in politics, it may be that I will have less reason to worry about being attacked by popular politicians, given that it was he who formulated and advocated the proposal. But if you adopt the other one, I fear that that may entail more trouble for me. Even so, the national interest ought to prevail over considerations of my own safety.

So we have from Caesar, as his own standing and the distinction of his ancestors* demand, a proposal which may serve as a pledge of his everlasting goodwill towards our country. It clearly shows what a difference there is between the fickleness of demagogues* and the truly popular spirit which has the people's interests at heart. [10] In fact I notice that one of those who wish to be considered popular politicians* is absent from our meeting, evidently so as not to have to vote on the life or death of Roman citizens. Yet this is the man who two days ago gave Roman citizens into custody and voted me a thanksgiving, and then yesterday voted generous rewards to the informers. When a man has authorized custody for the defendant, thanks for the investigator, and rewards for the informer, no one, surely, can be in any doubt as to what verdict he has arrived at regarding the whole question and the issue at stake.

But to return to Gaius Caesar: he recognizes that the Sempronian law* relates to Roman citizens; that someone who is an enemy of the state cannot conceivably be viewed as a citizen; and that the man who carried the Sempronian law himself paid the penalty to the state by the will of the people. He is also not prepared to accept that Lentulus, in spite of his lavish expenditure of money, can be described any longer as a man of the people, given that he has so brutally and cruelly plotted the massacre of the Roman people and the destruction of this city. So although Caesar himself is the mildest and gentlest of men, he does not hesitate to consign Publius Lentulus to eternal darkness and chains, and he stipulates that no one should ever be permitted to attract attention to himself by reducing his punishment or ever to win popularity by bringing ruin on the Roman people. Finally, he proposes that his property be confiscated, so that he should be subjected to every kind of mental and physical torment and be reduced to poverty and destitution.

[11] If you adopt this proposal, then, you will be giving me a popular and well-liked companion to take with me to the public meeting.* If, on the other hand, you prefer to adopt Silanus' proposal, the Roman people will readily release both you and me from the accusation of cruelty, and I shall maintain that this proposal was in fact much the more lenient of the two.

In any case, conscript fathers, how can we call it cruelty when the crime we are punishing is so monstrous? My view springs from how I feel. It is true that I wish to be able to enjoy, together with yourselves, our country that has been saved. But it is no less true, insofar as I am having to take a firm line on this issue, that I am motivated not by vindictiveness—for who has a milder nature than I?—but by an exceptional sense of humanity and compassion. I imagine this city, the light of the world and the citadel of every nation, suddenly being burnt to the ground. I see in my mind's eye pitiful heaps of citizens unburied, in a country that has itself been buried. There appears before my eyes a vision of Cethegus, crazily revelling over your corpses. [12] And when I imagine Lentulus ruling over us as king, as he told us himself the soothsayers had given him reason to hope,* and Gabinius arrayed in oriental splendour, and Catiline on hand with his army, I cannot help but shudder at the thought of mothers weeping, girls and boys running for their lives, and Vestal virgins being raped.* It is precisely because this prospect seems to me so dreadfully pitiful and pitiable that I am taking a firm and resolute stance against those who would perpetrate such atrocities.

Let me ask you, if a head of a family were to find his children killed by a slave, his wife murdered, and his home burnt, and failed to inflict the greatest punishment possible on the slave responsible, would he be thought compassionate and merciful, or utterly cruel and inhuman? For my part, I would consider a man perverse and iron-hearted if he did not seek to reduce his own pain and torture by inflicting pain and torture on the person who had injured him. It therefore follows that in the case of these men who have plotted to butcher us, our wives, and our children, who have attempted to destroy the homes of each one of us and this home of the whole nation, and who have done this for the specific purpose of settling the tribe of the Allobroges upon the final traces of this city and upon the ashes of an empire that has been destroyed by fire, if we then act with severity, we shall surely be thought of as merciful. But if instead we choose to show leniency, we can only expect, amid the destruction of our country and its citizens, to acquire a reputation for the most terrible cruelty.

[13] I do not suppose that anyone thought that that valiant lover of his country, Lucius Caesar,* was showing excessive cruelty two days ago when he declared that his brother-in-law—the husband of his most excellent sister—deserved to be put to death. He said this in the man's presence and hearing too, adding that his own grandfather had been killed on a consul's order, and that his grandfather's son, a mere boy who was acting as envoy for his father, had been thrown into prison and executed. Had *they* done anything resembling what these men have done? Had *they* hatched a plot to destroy their country? The time to which Caesar was referring was one in which there was a desire for the state to provide handouts, a time when there was an element of factional strife.* Moreover, Lentulus' illustrious grandfather* took up arms and went after Gracchus. He even sustained a serious wound in his efforts to ensure the preservation of the national interest—whereas this Lentulus, by contrast, calls in the

Gauls to overturn the foundations of the state, rouses the slaves to revolt, summons Catiline, and assigns us to Cethegus to be butchered, the rest of the citizens to Gabinius to be killed, the city to Cassius to be burnt, and the whole of Italy to Catiline to be plundered and laid waste. You are afraid, I take it, that in the case of such a monstrous and unspeakable crime as this, people may think your reaction excessive! On the contrary, we ought to be much more afraid of people thinking that by sparing punishment we have been cruel towards our country than that by applying it with severity we have been over-harsh towards our bitterest enemies.

[14] But I cannot pretend, conscript fathers, that I am not hearing whispers. I can hear what people are saying, and it sounds as if they are worried that I do not have the resources to implement whatever decision you come to today. But let me assure you, conscript fathers, that everything has been anticipated, planned, and arranged, partly by the extremely careful precautions which I have taken myself, but partly also by the much stronger determination of the Roman people to defend their sovereignty and hold on to all that they have. Everyone has come here today, people of every order, every class, and every age. The forum is packed, the temples surrounding the forum are packed, the entrances to this temple where we are now are all packed. This is the only issue since the foundation of our city on which everyone holds exactly the same opinion—excepting only those who realize that they must die, and so prefer to die along with everyone else rather than on their own. [15] I for my part am quite happy to make an exception of such people and treat them as a special case: I would not class them as wicked fellow-citizens, but as the deadliest external enemies.

But as for everyone else—immortal gods!—how numerous they are, how determined they are, and how nobly they have united in defence of our common safety and honour! Do I of all people* have to remind you at this point of the Roman equestrians? While they yield to you the first place in rank and deliberation, they are your rivals in their love for their country. Now, after many years of conflict, this day and this issue unite them with you, calling them back into alliance and harmony with this order.* And if we can make this national unity, forged in my consulship, permanent, then I can promise you that no internal civil disturbance will ever again affect any part of our national life. I see that the treasury tribunes have courageously come forward with no less determination to defend the country. I see also that the entire body of scribes,* who happen to have come to the treasury today in considerable numbers, have turned their attention from the allotment of their posts to the national security. [16] All the free-born citizens are here, even the poorest of them, in one vast crowd. In fact, is there a single person here who does not regard these temples, the sight of our city, the possession of freedom, and indeed this light of day and the very soil of our shared homeland as not just dear to him, but a source of joy and delight? It is worth your while, too, conscript fathers, to take note of the feelings of the freedmen. They by their own merit have obtained the rights of citizens, and sincerely consider this their home—while certain others who were born here, and born to the best families, have thought of it not as their homeland, but as an enemy city. But why do I mention these orders and individuals when their private fortunes, their common political interest, and—what is sweetest of all—their very freedom has roused them to defend their country in its hour of danger? There is no slave, so long as his existence is at least endurable, who does not shudder at the criminality of citizens, who does not wish Rome to remain standing, and who does not apply himself as hard as he dares and as hard as he can to preserve the national security.

[17] So if any of you happen to be worried by what people are saying, that a particular pimp of Lentulus' is going round the shops hoping that he can use money to corrupt the minds of the poor and naive, then let me tell you that the man did indeed try this and make the attempt. But he failed to find anyone so down at heel or so criminally inclined as not to wish to preserve his work-place, job, and livelihood, his couch and his bed, and the easy routine of his life. On the contrary, the vast majority of shopkeepers, in fact the entire class (it must be said) is absolutely committed to peace. All their capital, employment, and profits are dependent on a supply of customers, and rely on peaceful conditions. If their profits fall when their shops are closed, what will be the effect on those profits, do you think, when their shops have been set on fire?

[18] Conscript fathers, that is how the matter stands.* The support of the Roman people does not fail you: so you make sure that you do not appear to be failing the Roman people. You have a consul who has been allowed to escape from a great many dangers and plots and from the jaws of death not for the sake of his own life, but to ensure

your safety. All the orders are united in heart, mind, determination, courage, and voice to save our country. Beset by the torches and weapons of a diabolical conspiracy, our common homeland stretches her suppliant hands to you. To you she commends herself, to you she commends the lives of all her citizens, to you she commends the citadel and the Capitol, to you she commends the altars of her household gods, to you she commends yonder eternal fire of Vesta,* to you she commends the temples and shrines of all the gods, and to you she commends the walls and houses of the city. And it is on your own lives, on those of your wives and children, on your property, on your homes, and on your hearths that you must today reach your decision.

[19] You have a leader who is thinking of you and not of himself— something you do not always have. You have a situation in which all the orders, all men, and the entire Roman people are all of one mind—something which, on a domestic issue, we have never seen before today. Just think what enormous effort was involved in creating our empire, what valour in establishing our freedom, what divine favour in increasing and building up our prosperity—and how a single night* almost destroyed all of this. Your task today is to make sure that such a thing can never again be contemplated, let alone brought off, by citizens. And the reason I have said this is not to rally you—indeed, you have almost overtaken me in determination—but simply so that my voice, which ought to be the chief voice in the state, will be seen to have fulfilled its consular duty.

[20] Now before I ask you once again for your views, I should like to say a word about myself. You can see for yourselves how many people are members of this conspiracy—a great many. And I can see for myself how many personal enemies I have made—the same number. I believe, however, that these people are base, weak, contemptible, and craven. But if that gang should ever again be stirred up by the insanity of some criminal, and succeed in overpowering your authority and that of the state, I shall never, conscript fathers, regret the actions and the line I have taken. Death they may threaten me with; but we are all going to die. In life, on the other hand, no one has ever received such honours as you have voted me in your decrees. Others have received your thanks for having served the country well—but I alone for having saved it.

[21] Let Scipio have his fame,* since by his intelligence and courage

he forced Hannibal to leave Italy and return to Africa; let the second Africanus be showered with the highest praise for destroying the two cities most hostile to this empire of ours, Carthage and Numantia; let Paullus be judged outstanding, since his triumph was adorned by the most noble and once the most powerful of kings, Perseus; let Marius have everlasting glory for twice liberating Italy from occupation and the prospect of slavery; and let Pompeius be rated higher than all of these, since his achievements and merits are bounded by the same borders and limits as the course of the sun. But amid the praise due to these men there will surely be some space left for my own glory— unless perhaps it is a greater achievement to open up provinces for us to go out to than to ensure that those who have gone out to them have a country to which they can return in triumph.*

[22] In one respect, however, a victory abroad is preferable to one at home: foreign enemies either are crushed and turned into subjects or are admitted* and consider themselves bound by ties of gratitude. But once citizens have been corrupted by some kind of lunacy and have become traitors to their country, you may be able to stop them destroying the state, but you can never constrain them by force or conciliate them by kindness. It is obvious to me, therefore, that the war that I have undertaken against traitors must be unending. I trust, however, that with your help and that of all loyal citizens, and with the recollection of the terrible dangers to which we have been exposed—a recollection which will always be retained not only among our own people who have themselves been saved, but in the minds and conversation of people of all nations—I and those who are with me shall easily drive back the forces that assault us. Certainly, there is no force that is strong enough to subvert and undermine the bond between yourselves and the Roman equestrians, and the absolute unanimity that exists among all loyal citizens.

[23] Since that is how the matter stands, instead of a command, instead of an army, instead of the province I have given up,* instead of a triumph and the other marks of honour that I have forfeited in order to keep guard over Rome and your own safety, instead of the new friends and clients that I would have acquired in a province (although in my work at Rome I devote just as much effort to maintaining my existing connections as I do to acquiring new ones), instead of all these benefits that would otherwise come to me, and in return for the exceptional efforts I have made on your behalf, and in

return also for this conscientiousness with which, as you can see, I have protected the country, I ask you for nothing whatsoever—except that you hold on to the memory of this moment and of my whole consulship. As long as that memory remains fixed in your minds, I shall feel that I am defended by the strongest of walls. But if the power of traitors deceives and triumphs over my hopes, then I commend my little son* to you: he will surely receive the protection necessary to ensure not just his survival, but his standing in the state—just so long as you remember that his father was a man who saved Rome at his own unique personal cost.

[24] Therefore on the survival of yourselves and the Roman people, on your wives and children, on your altars and hearths, on your shrines and temples, on the houses and homes of all of the city, on your dominion and freedom, on the safety of Italy, and on the entire state you must now make your decision carefully, as you have begun to do, and courageously. You have a consul who will not hesitate to obey whatever you decree, and who will defend your decision, and answer for it personally, for the rest of his days.

# PRO MARCELLO
## ('FOR MARCELLUS')

In *In Catilinam* IV we saw a free exchange of views taking place in the senate in a free republic, with Cicero presiding as consul. *Pro Marcello* was also delivered in the senate—but we have moved forward in time to 46 BC. In that year, the free republic had fallen, and Caesar was dictator for ten years. The republicans, led by Pompey, had been defeated at Pharsalus (9 August 48), and Pompey was dead. Most of the surviving republicans had then either made their peace with Caesar or gone on to suffer defeat at Thapsus (6 February 46). Cato, true to his Stoic principles, had committed suicide rather than submit to a tyrant—thus winning for himself eternal glory as a republican martyr. The senate was packed with Caesar's supporters, and pardoned Pompeians were careful what they said. Cicero himself, pardoned in 47 after a year's anxious wait, attended the senate only in order not to appear to be refusing to recognize its legitimacy, and did not speak. (His main preoccupation during this period was not politics, but literature: he completed the *Brutus*, a history of Roman oratory, early in 46, and the *Orator*, a discussion of oratorical style, by about September of the same year.) He had not spoken in public for nearly six years, since his successful prosecution of his enemy Titus Munatius Plancus Bursa (a tribune of 52) in, probably, January 51. The speech *Pro Marcello*, delivered in the senate in mid-September of 46, was the speech in which he finally broke his silence.

*Pro Marcello* is a speech of thanks to Caesar for agreeing to pardon his most die-hard republican enemy, Marcus Claudius Marcellus, the consul of 51. It is in fact misnamed: the title *Pro Marcello* ('For Marcellus') leads one to expect a forensic speech, a defence of Marcellus in a court of law. Instead this is an epideictic (display) speech, a speech in praise of Caesar (technically, a panegyric), and would more correctly be called *De Marcello* ('On Marcellus'), the title it is given by two Latin writers of the fourth century AD, Arusianus Messius and Servius. But the manuscripts of the speech call it *Pro Marcello*, and scholars (with one recent exception) have not seen fit, or dared, to alter that title. We do not know what title, if any, Cicero gave it.

Marcus Claudius Marcellus, although not a patrician, belonged to one of Rome's most noble and aristocratic families. The most famous member of that family had been the Marcus Claudius Marcellus who held the consulship five times, won the *spolia opima* ('spoils of honour') in 222 BC for killing a Gallic chief in single combat, and went on in 211 to capture Syracuse from the Carthaginians after a two-and-a-half-year siege. The family maintained its distinction in our period too: the subject of this speech held the consulship in 51, his cousin Gaius Marcellus held it in 50, and his (Marcus') brother Gaius Marcellus held it in 49. The consul of 50 was married to Octavian's sister Octavia; their son Marcus Marcellus was to be Augustus' successor of choice before dying in 23 BC and being immortalized by Virgil in the *Aeneid*.

Little is known, however, of the early career of our Marcellus. Twelve years younger than Cicero, he held the quaestorship in 64, and supported him during the Catilinarian conspiracy. We know of his involvement in four court cases in the 50s, always on the same side as Cicero: in 56, when he supported Titus Annius Milo against Publius Clodius Pulcher; in 54, when he spoke for Marcus Aemilius Scaurus (Cicero's *Pro Scauro* survives); and in 52, when he supported Milo after the murder of Clodius, both in the preliminary summons of Milo's slaves and in Milo's actual trial. In the *Brutus* (248–50), the interlocutor Brutus is made to speak highly of Marcellus' oratory, emphasizing its similarity to that of Cicero himself; since the *Brutus* otherwise deals, with the sole exception of Caesar, only with orators no longer living, Marcellus' inclusion in that work is, like that of Caesar, an exceptional compliment.

In 51, then, Marcellus held the consulship. His colleague was Cicero's close friend Servius Sulpicius Rufus, the brilliant jurist who is patronized so entertainingly in *Pro Murena* (63 BC), and whose obituary is the *Ninth Philippic* (43 BC). Sulpicius had had a long wait for the consulship (his first attempt had been in 63); in the election, he had defeated Cato, his partner in the Murena trial.

In 51, Caesar was coming to the end of his conquest of Gaul, and at Rome the most pressing political issue was whether and under what circumstances he could be induced to give up his command, which he had held since 58. The 'first triumvirate' had come to an end in 53 with the death of Crassus. That left just two men dominating the political scene, Pompey and Caesar; but they had become estranged, with Pompey increasingly (since his third consulship in 52) siding with the senate. Caesar was vulnerable to prosecution, since the laws of his consulship in 59 had been passed by violence; but he was exempt from prosecution so long as he held an official command. His aim was therefore to hold on to his command in Gaul until he had fully settled the new province, and then step straight from his command to a second consulship (to enable him to do this, a 'law of the ten tribunes' in 52 had given him permission to stand for the consulship in absence; but a later law in the same year had left its status doubtful). Caesar's enemies, on the other hand, were determined to prevent him from having his way by removing him from his command at the earliest opportunity, and then prosecuting him. These men, who were generally the most hardline of republicans (and who included aristocrats like the Marcelli), saw Pompey as a means of countering him, but would have preferred ideally to be rid of both men—then the supremacy of the senate would be assured. Cicero, by contrast, like the vast majority of senators, was prepared to appease Caesar in order to prevent the very real danger of civil war. The date at which Caesar's command was supposed to end is uncertain, and may never have been made explicit (this has been one of the big questions of Roman historical scholarship). But a law had been passed in Pompey's second consulship in 55 to the effect that the question of a successor to Caesar should not be raised in the senate before 1 March 50 (alternatively, the law may have specified that as the terminal date of his command).

On becoming consul, Marcellus announced that he intended to raise the question of a successor to Caesar in Gaul. But his colleague Sulpicius opposed such provocation. Then Marcellus went further. One of the laws passed during Caesar's consulship in 59 had set up a colony of Roman citizens at Novum Comum (modern Como) in Transpadane Gaul. In order to make the point that he did not recognize the law—or, more importantly, the *lex Vatinia* of the same year under which Caesar had been appointed to his Gallic command—Marcellus had a citizen of the place flogged (a punishment which could not legally be inflicted on Roman citizens), telling him to go and show his wounds to Caesar. (There was some doubt as to whether or not the man was an ex-magistrate of his town, as he may have claimed; if he was, then the punishment was illegal even if the claim of the people of Novum Comum to Roman citizenship was not valid.) In a letter to his friend Atticus, Cicero called Marcellus' action 'ugly' (*Att.* 5.11.2). The threatened debate on the question of a successor to Caesar finally took place after much delay at the end of September, and it was decided to put the matter on the senate's agenda for the following 1 March. If Caesar were removed from his command on that day, it would then be impossible for him to step straight from his command to a consulship.

When 1 March came, the proposed debate was vetoed. Meanwhile, the new consul Gaius Marcellus continued his cousin's policy of active hostility to Caesar. In December, a proposal that Caesar and Pompey should each give up their commands (Pompey had a command in Spain, which he governed through legates) was approved by the senate by a large majority (370 to 22), but not acted upon. The consul Marcellus then tried and failed to have Caesar declared a public enemy, after which both consuls went to Pompey and formally instructed him to take command of the forces of the state. On 1 January 49—the day on which Marcellus' brother Gaius became consul—a proposal arrived from Caesar that he and Pompey should each give up their commands simultaneously: if this were not accepted, Caesar would resort to force. The proposal was not put to a vote; instead, Pompey's father-in-law, Quintus Caecilius Metellus Pius Scipio Nasica, proposed that if Caesar did not lay down his arms by a certain date, he should be declared a public enemy. This proposal was carried but then vetoed; and on 7 January the hard-liners persuaded the senate to pass the emergency decree (*senatus consultum ultimum* or 'SCU'). On 10 or 11 January Caesar then crossed the frontier of his province, the Rubicon, and invaded Italy.

Once the Civil War had begun, those who were not committed to Caesar had to consider what they should do. Cicero, who had returned to Rome from his governorship of Cilicia only at the beginning of 49—too late to try to prevent the war—delayed in Italy until June, before reluctantly deciding to join Pompey in Greece. Gaius Marcellus, the consul of 50, remained in Italy, and succeeded in obtaining Caesar's pardon. The brothers Marcus and Gaius, on the other hand, both joined Pompey— more out of fear of Caesar than commitment to his opponent (*Att.* 9.1.4). Gaius, the consul of 49, was put in command of the Rhodian section of Pompey's fleet, but seems to have died by the time of Pharsalus. After Pharsalus, Cicero (who was not present at the battle) returned to Italy to wait for Caesar's pardon, but Marcus Marcellus would do nothing so humiliating. Instead, he retired to Mytilene, on the island of Lesbos, where he took lessons from Cratippus of Pergamum, a leading Peripatetic philosopher. (Pompey also visited Mytilene after Pharsalus, and complained to Cratippus at the turn fortune had taken.)

To the surprise of many, no doubt, the policy Caesar chose to adopt towards his enemies was one of clemency (*clementia*). There were no proscriptions. Generally speaking, Caesar wanted those of his former opponents who were not sworn enemies to return to Rome and take their place in his senate. When he pardoned Cicero in September 47, he showed him conspicuous public respect. Then while he was away fighting the republicans in Africa, Cicero found himself treated with the greatest civility by Caesar's friends, who took lessons from him in oratory and invited him to their dinner parties; and they undertook to put in a good word for him on Caesar's return in July 46. While Cicero had no liking for dictators (he had lived through the Sullan period), by 46 this dictatorship was proving on the whole to be benevolent and even enlightened— greatly preferable, in fact, to whatever might have been expected had the republicans succeeding in recovering Italy.

Throughout this period Cicero corresponded with republican exiles, encouraging them to ask for Caesar's pardon and return to Rome, as he himself had done; among other considerations, their return would help to justify his own early submission to Caesar. In the summer of 46 he wrote three such letters to Marcellus, using every conceivable argument to try to persuade him to return (*Fam.* 4.7, 4.8, 4.9). Then at a meeting of the senate in mid-September, Caesar's father-in-law, Lucius Calpurnius Piso Caesoninus (the consul of 58 whom Cicero had attacked in his invective *In Pisonem* of 55 BC), happened to mention Marcellus' name (not necessarily in connection with his restoration). At the mention of the name, Marcellus' cousin Gaius, the consul of 50, threw himself at Caesar's feet, and the entire senate rose and approached the dictator in supplication. Caesar responded by criticizing Marcellus' bitterness towards him and contrasting it with the fair-mindedness and good sense shown by Marcellus' colleague Sulpicius (who, like Cicero, had reluctantly supported Pompey and obtained Caesar's pardon, and was now serving as governor of Achaea). But then he unexpectedly declared that he would not refuse the senate's request: apart from anything else, he said, to refuse it would augur ill for his future relations with them. The senators were invited in order of seniority to express their opinion (why this was necessary is unclear, unless Caesar simply wished to hear himself praised); all except one expressed thanks to the dictator for what he had done. The dissentient was Lucius Volcacius Tullus, the consul of 66, who was evidently hoping to ingratiate himself with Caesar by showing spite towards his enemy. When it was Cicero's turn to be called, he was so struck by Caesar's magnanimity and the senate's solicitude that he decided to break his long silence, and gave an impromptu speech of thanks to Caesar. Our source for these events is *Fam.* 4.4, a letter which Cicero wrote to Sulpicius in Greece soon afterwards: in this letter he says that he had felt that he was witnessing 'some semblance of reviving constitutional freedom', and that he had decided that he would henceforward make speeches from time to time, just often enough to keep Caesar satisfied with him. (One scholar has suggested that the pardon of Marcellus was stage-managed by Caesar; that is not impossible, but seems unlikely from Cicero's account.) Afterwards Cicero wrote up and published the speech he had given—our *Pro Marcello*. We should not automatically assume that he revised it when he wrote it up, since he was well capable of producing a perfect speech without advance preparation and then remembering what he had said (alternatively, his words may have been taken down as he spoke). In the letter to Sulpicius he says that his speech in the senate was a long one, and so there is at any rate no reason to think that he expanded what he had said for publication (as for example the younger Pliny would much later do with his *Panegyricus*).

   *Pro Marcello* is, like any speech delivered before an autocrat (or, indeed, any poem written under one), difficult to interpret. The first question we should consider is Cicero's sincerity. Here the letter to Sulpicius, and another written in the same period to the former Pompeian Aulus Caecina (*Fam.* 6.6.10), provide the answer: Cicero was genuinely moved by Caesar's pardon of Marcellus, and saw it as a sign that everything might just come right after all. Caesar's clemency towards his former enemies was something truly remarkable—quite different from the way in which, in Cicero's own lifetime, Marius and Sulla, for example, had behaved. Caesar's unexpected pardon of Marcellus, his most implacable republican enemy, was an extraordinary concession, and not at all the act of a tyrant. The two letters just cited show that Cicero considered that this was the moment for him to break his silence and come to an accommodation with a regime which was not (he supposed) going to go away, and which was turning out much better than he had ever dared hope. As for the effusiveness with which he expresses his gratitude, this should not cause surprise: he was, after all, addressing an autocrat, and anything less would have appeared grudging. In any case, this was an important moment for him: he had not spoken in public for almost six years, and he must have wanted to rise to the occasion with a speech that would demonstrate that he could still produce great oratory.

The second question to ask is whether Cicero attempts in the speech to put pressure on Caesar to follow any particular course of action. The speech does not urge him to adopt specific policies which he has not already adopted (the very general proposals mentioned at §§ 23 and 27 are matters which he already had in hand). It is not, therefore, a manifesto. On the other hand, it does urge him to promote peace, and to continue pardoning his enemies—in other words, to continue his existing policy of clemency. Moreover, panegyric by its nature always does contain an element of pressure (particularly if the speech is afterwards widely circulated): by enumerating his subject's virtues, the orator lays a continuing obligation on him to give evidence of those virtues. *Pro Marcello*, then, does seek to put pressure on Caesar; but in view of the weakness of Cicero's political position, such pressure did not perhaps amount to very much.

The third question is whether Cicero sees any political role for himself under the new regime. At §§ 32 3 he presents himself as the spokesman of the senate, and there is little doubt that that is what he intended his role to be: he would speak for the senate before Caesar, and in particular would mediate between Caesar and the former Pompeians. Unlike Cato, Cicero was a realist, and in times when he did not enjoy political independence he could be surprisingly eager to take on the role of adviser to those in power. We have a graphic demonstration of this from 62 BC in the letter he sent to Pompey shortly before Pompey returned to Rome from his conquests in the east. In that letter (*Fam.* 5.7) Cicero recommends himself to Pompey as a friend and political ally, 'a not much lesser Laelius to a far greater Africanus'. In *Pro Marcello*, the language is different (and much more sophisticated), but the message the same: Cicero would like to be admitted to the role of adviser and confidant. Moreover, the particular stylistic brilliance of the speech would have been intended to make it clear to Caesar—who was himself an orator of the first rank—just how useful a supporter and advocate he could potentially be.

A radically different interpretation of the speech has, however, been proposed (by R. R. Dyer, *JRS* 80 (1990), 17–30). On this interpretation, our *Pro Marcello* bears little relation to whatever Cicero may have said in the senate on the occasion of Marcellus' pardon, but is a tract probably dating from May or June of the following year. Its purpose is, first, to provoke outrage among its senatorial readers at Caesar's despotism and, secondly, to warn Caesar that if he does not restore the republic he will be liable to assassination. The view that the speech is to be read ironically as an attack on Caesar is cited by an ancient scholiast, the Scholiasta Gronovianus (295–6 Stangl), only to be dismissed, and so far has not persuaded modern scholars either (the fullest rebuttal is that of M. Winterbottom in J. F. Miller *et al.* (eds.), Vertis in Usum: *Studies in Honor of Edward Courtney* (Munich, 2002), 24–38). One argument against it is that it depends in large part on the assumption that the exercise of clemency would of itself arouse the senators' resentment; yet clemency is generally viewed as an unambiguously good quality in the literature of the period (as, for example, at *Cat.* 1.4, where Cicero attributes the quality to himself as consul). Moreover, it is surely most improbable that Cicero should have intended as a call to tyrannicide a speech which most contemporary readers must, in view of its original context (whether or not it was rewritten later), have taken at face value as a speech in praise of Caesar.

Marcellus heard of his pardon first from his cousin Gaius and then from Cicero, and agreed to fall in with their joint wishes. His reply to Cicero (*Fam.* 4.11) was warm and extremely generous. It was, as E. D. Rawson has remarked, 'such a letter as Cicero's heart must have swelled at receiving from so great a noble' (*Cicero: A Portrait* (London, 1975), 219). Even so, Marcellus expressed no great enthusiasm for returning to Rome. In around December Cicero wrote to him again urging him to hurry up and come home (*Fam.* 4.10). Then in the following summer he received sad news from Sulpicius (who was still governor of Achaea; in March 45 he had sent Cicero his famous consolation on the death of Cicero's daughter Tullia (*Fam.* 4.5) ). In a letter written at Athens on 31 May 45 (*Fam.* 4.12), Sulpicius reported that Marcellus had been murdered. The letter is worth quoting from at length (trans. D. R. Shackleton Bailey):

On 23 May I took ship from Epidaurus to Piraeus, where I met my colleague Marcus Marcellus, and spent the day there to be with him. I took leave of him the following day, intending to travel from Athens to Boeotia and wind up what remained of my assizes. He proposed, as he told me, to sail round Cape Malea towards Italy. Two days later I was about to set out from Athens, when about three o'clock in the morning a friend of his, Publius Postumius, arrived to tell me that my colleague Marcus Marcellus had been attacked with a dagger by Publius Magius Cilo, a friend of his, after dinner, and had received two wounds, one in the stomach and one in the head behind the ear. It was hoped, however, that there was a chance for his life. Magius had later committed suicide, and he himself had been sent to me by Marcellus to tell me what had occurred and ask me to send him doctors. Accordingly, I collected some doctors and set out straight away for Piraeus as day broke. I was not far away, when a boy of Acidinus' met me on the road with a note which stated that Marcellus had breathed his last shortly before dawn. So a very eminent man has been tragically murdered by a villain. He was spared by the respect of his enemies only to meet his death at the hand of a friend.

The rest of the letter describes the arrangements Sulpicius made for Marcellus' funeral. Writing to Atticus shortly afterwards, Cicero speculated on the reason for the murder: Magius must have been bankrupt, asked Marcellus to help him, been given a rather blunt refusal, and then attacked him in a fit of rage (*Att.* 13.10.3). At any rate, there was no reason to believe the rumour that Caesar was responsible (a theory which, apart from anything else, would fail to account for the suicide of Magius).

Nine months later Caesar himself was murdered, by a group of more than sixty conspirators consisting of pardoned Pompeians and Caesarians alike. He had done little towards the work of reconstruction that Cicero had vaguely alluded to in *Pro Marcello*, nor had he formulated any kind of constitutional settlement; instead, his behaviour had become increasingly despotic—some would say megalomaniac. He seems to have been aware of the offence he caused: after Cicero was kept waiting to see him one day, he was said to have remarked, 'Can I doubt that I am detested, when Marcus Cicero has to sit waiting instead of being able to come and see me at his convenience? And if anyone is easygoing, he is. I am sure he must really hate me' (*Att.* 14.1.2). Since the time of *Pro Marcello*, Cicero had indeed become disappointed in him, and he rejoiced at his demise.

Caesar's assassination precipitated the final, bloody chapter of the republic. Once more, senators found themselves free to say what they liked. Cicero chose to make full use of that freedom, in his *Philippics*—and then paid for it with his life.

# PRO MARCELLO

[1] The long silence, conscript fathers, which I had maintained for all this time—not from any fear, but out of a mixture of grief and diffidence*—has today been brought to an end; and today has also brought a return to my former practice of freely expressing my wishes and opinions. For such exceptional kindness, such unprecedented and unheard of clemency, such extraordinary moderation in someone who has attained absolute power over everything, and such astonishing and, one might almost say, superhuman wisdom—these are things I cannot possibly pass over in silence. [2] Now that Marcus Marcellus, conscript fathers, has been returned to yourselves and to the state, I feel that it is not just his, but my own voice and standing that have been preserved and restored to yourselves and to the state. For I was grieved and deeply distressed, conscript fathers, to see that so great a man as he, who had espoused the same cause as I myself had, did not enjoy the same good fortune; and I could not bring myself, nor did I think it right, to continue in that career which we once shared, after he, my rival and imitator in my work* as in my other interests—indeed I might say my partner on life's journey—had been torn from my side.

So what you have done for me, Gaius Caesar, is to open up my former way of life from which I had become debarred, and for all the others here present, to raise a standard,* as it were, for optimism regarding the future of our country. [3] For it has become apparent to me in the cases of many individuals and particularly in my own case—just as it became apparent to everyone else just now when, after reminding us of how Marcus Marcellus had wronged you,* you nevertheless gave him back to the senate and the state—that you pay more heed to the authority of this order and the dignity of the state than you do to the real or imagined wrongs done to yourself.

Today Marcellus has indeed reaped the greatest possible reward for his past life, both through the unanimous acclamation of the senate and through your own important and impressive decision. And from this you must certainly understand how praiseworthy it is to bestow a favour, when there is such glory in being granted one. [4] He is indeed fortunate, in that his restoration has brought almost as much joy to everyone else as it will to him when he comes to hear of it. And it is an honour that he has rightly and deservedly obtained: for who is there who can surpass him in noble birth, integrity, learning, blamelessness of life, or in any kind of claim to praise?

There is no stream of genius large enough, no tongue or pen forceful or fluent enough I will not say to embellish your achievements, Gaius Caesar, but even to record them.* But I do nevertheless maintain, and with your permission declare, that there is no glory in all those achievements greater than that which you have this day attained. [5] I often keep in my mind's eye, and gladly go out of my way to tell others, that all the achievements of our own commanders, all those of foreign countries and the most powerful peoples, and all those of the most illustrious kings fall short of what you have achieved, if they are compared with the scale of the campaigns you have undertaken, the number of your battles, the geographical diversity of the places in which you have fought, the speed with which you have completed your conquests,* and the variety of your wars— and, moreover, that no one could have marched through such widely separated territories in less time than you have I will not say raced across them, but conquered them.

[6] If I refused to concede that these achievements are greater, almost, than the human mind or understanding can grasp, I would be out of my mind myself; even so, there are other achievements still greater. Some people are inclined to depreciate military glory, withholding it from the leaders and sharing it instead among the rank and file, so that it no longer belongs exclusively to the commanders. It is true that in warfare the courage of the soldiers, the natural advantage of the ground, allied assistance, fleets, and supplies all make a significant contribution. Fortune, too, claims for herself, almost as of right, the greatest share; and when anything turns out favourably, she considers the success almost entirely due to herself. [7] But in the glory which you have acquired by your present action, Gaius Caesar, you have no partner: all of it, however great it may be (and it is indeed the greatest possible), all of it, I repeat, is yours. No centurion, no prefect, no cohort, no troop can take any of it for themselves, and even that mistress of human affairs, Fortune, does not offer herself as your partner in *this* glory: she yields it to you, and admits that it is wholly and exclusively yours. For accident is never an element in wisdom, nor is chance a component of sagacity.

[8] You have subdued nations barbaric in ferocity, innumerable in population, unlimited in territory, and abounding in every kind of resource: but the things which you conquered were in their nature and situation amenable to conquest. After all, no power is so strong that it cannot be weakened and broken by steel and force. But to conquer one's own temper, to check one's anger, to show moderation towards the conquered, to take a fallen enemy pre-eminent in birth, character, and virtue, and not merely raise him up, but actually enhance his former standing—that is the act of someone whom I would not rank with the greatest of men, but would judge akin to a god.

[9] Your military glories, Gaius Caesar, will be made famous by the pens and tongues not only of ourselves, but of virtually every nation: no age will ever cease to sing your praises. But still, deeds of that sort, even when one reads about them, somehow seem to be drowned out by the shouts of soldiers and the sound of trumpets. On the other hand, whenever we hear or read of some act of clemency, kindness, justice, moderation, or wisdom—especially when it is performed at a moment of passion, which is the enemy of good judgement, or in the hour of victory, which is by nature arrogant and proud—how we are set ablaze with approval, irrespective of whether the story is fact or fiction, so that often we find ourselves loving someone that we have never actually seen! [10] But you we do see here in front of us. We perceive your thoughts, emotions, and expression—and they tell us how you wish to see the preservation of whatever part of our state the fortune of war has spared. With what praise, then, shall we extol you, with what devotion attend you, and with what affection embrace you? I call heaven to witness that I believe the very walls of this senate-house are yearning to thank you for the fact that that great personage* will shortly take up his place here where he belongs, and where his ancestors belonged before him. For my part, when like all of you I witnessed just now the tears of the excellent Gaius Marcellus,* whose devotion to his family is so remarkable, my heart was filled with the memory of all the Marcelli: even though they are dead, by saving Marcus Marcellus you have given them back their honour, and rescued from the verge of extinction a family of the highest nobility whose numbers are now severely reduced.

[11] It is right for you to esteem this day more highly than the

countless major thanksgivings* that have been decreed in your honour. For this act belongs to Gaius Caesar alone: all the other
achievements which took place under your leadership, great as they
were, were nevertheless accomplished with the help of a large and
mighty following. But in this case you are simultaneously leader and
follower. What you have done is so outstanding that, although time
will eventually wear away your trophies and monuments (after all,
there is nothing that is created by human handiwork that age does
not destroy and devour), [12] this act of fairness and gentleness will
blossom more fully with every day that passes. So the more that time
undermines your works, the more it will add to your praise. You had
already, it is true, vanquished all other victors of civil wars in justice
and mercy: today, however, you have yourself vanquished yourself.
I am afraid that my attempt to express what I feel may be only
imperfectly understood by those who are listening to what I say: but
you seem to have vanquished victory, since you have given back
to the vanquished what had been taken from them. For when, by
the universal law of victory, we had all been vanquished and had
perished, we were saved by your decision to show clemency. Rightly,
therefore, you alone are invincible, since you have utterly vanquished
the nature and power of victory itself.

[13] Now as for this decision of Gaius Caesar, conscript fathers,
consider how widely it applies. All those of us who were driven by
some sad and deadly fate of our country to take up arms, even
though we were guilty of human error, have at all events been acquitted of any crime. When, in response to your appeal, he saved Marcus
Marcellus for his country, and when, although no one had appealed,
he restored me to myself and to my country, and similarly all the
other eminent men to themselves and to their country (if you look
around you, you will see how numerous and distinguished they
are)—when he did this, he did not admit enemies into the senate-
house: on the contrary, he judged that most of us had resorted to war
more from ignorance and from empty and ungrounded fears than
out of motives of avarice or cruelty.

[14] In the Civil War, I always thought that proposals for peace
should be listened to, and I always regretted that not only peace,
but even the arguments of those who advocated it, were rejected. I
myself did not take up arms in that or any other civil war: my policy
was always directed towards peace and the toga,* not towards war and

arms. It was a particular individual* that I followed, from personal allegiance rather than public duty; and so heavily did the loyal memory of a grateful heart weigh with me that, with my eyes open and with full awareness of what I was doing, without avarice and without even the slightest expectation of success, I hurried to—how shall I put it?—a self-chosen doom. [15] This policy of mine was not something I kept to myself. Before the war began I often spoke in the senate in favour of peace, and while we were at war I continued to advocate it, even at the risk of my life. No one, therefore, could be so unreasonable a commentator as to question Caesar's attitude to the war, seeing that he did not hesitate to reinstate those who had advocated peace, while being less conciliatory towards the others. This policy of his was perhaps less surprising at a time when the final result was still uncertain and the fortune of war doubtful. But when a victor in war shows favour to those who have advocated peace, he surely leaves little doubt that he would have preferred not to fight at all than to emerge victorious.

[16] On this point I can testify to how Marcus Marcellus feels, since our views coincided during the war just as they had always done in peacetime. How often, and with what bitter pain, have I observed his dismay at the overbearing behaviour of certain individuals and the savagery they would have shown in victory!* We who actually witnessed that behaviour have all the more reason to feel grateful, Gaius Caesar, for your generosity. For it is not any more the principles of either side that we have to weigh up, but the victories. [17] We have seen your victory concluded with your battles: the sword unsheathed within the city we have not seen. The fellow-citizens we have lost were struck down by the violence of Mars, not by the anger of victory; and no one should doubt that Gaius Caesar, if he could, would raise many of them from the dead, seeing that he saves as many as he can of those who belonged to the same side as they did. As for that side, I will do no more than express what we all feared, that if they had won, their victory would have been vindictive. [18] Some of them made threats not merely against those who had taken up arms, but sometimes against the non-combatants, saying that it was not a man's politics that counted, but his physical location.* So it seems to me, then, that even if it was in order to punish the Roman people for some offence or other that the immortal gods provoked so terrible and tragic a civil war, they have

now at any rate been appeased or sated, and have at long last transferred all hope of safety to the clemency and wisdom of the victor.

[19] Take pleasure, therefore, in this outstanding deed that you
have done. Reap the reward not only of your good fortune and glory,
but of your natural disposition and character: it is that from which
wise men derive the greatest pleasure and satisfaction. When you
look back over the other things that you have achieved, you will very
often give thanks for your own talents—but most often for your luck.
On the other hand, when you reflect on us, whom you have desired
to join you in matters of state, you will also have reason to reflect on
your extraordinary acts of kindness, your astonishing generosity, and
your unprecedented wisdom—qualities which I would venture to
describe not as the highest virtues, but as the only ones. For there is
such splendour in genuine glory, and such nobility in magnanimity
and sagacity that it seems as if these particular qualities are the gifts
of virtue, and other ones merely the loans of luck.

[20] So do not grow tired of saving good men—especially since
they have erred not as a result of selfishness or any moral failing, but
from a conception of their duty that was foolish perhaps, but by no
means criminal, and from a certain illusion of what the country
required of them. For it is no fault of yours if some people have been
afraid of you; on the contrary, it is greatly to your credit that they
came to the realization that they had nothing to fear.

[21] I come now to that extremely serious complaint, that awful
suspicion that you have expressed*—something which all citizens,
and especially those of us whom you have restored, must guard
against no less than you yourself must. Though I trust that it is
groundless, I will not for a moment make light of it, since any precautions that are taken for your security are taken for ours too, and if
one is going to err on one side or the other, I would far sooner appear
excessively fearful than insufficiently careful. But who is there so
insane? Someone from among your supporters? Yet who are more
well disposed to you than the people to whom you have granted a
salvation they did not expect? Or someone from among those who
have been with you from the start? It is inconceivable that anyone
could be so savage as not to value above his own life the life of the
leader through whom he attained the pinnacle of his desires. But if
your friends are plotting no crime against you, should you take precautions against your enemies doing so? What enemies? It is a fact

that all those who were your enemies have either lost their lives through their own stubbornness* or kept it through your own mercifulness, so that either none of your enemies survive, or if any do they are now your most loyal friends.

[22] But still, given that men's minds do contain dark corners and hidden recesses, let us by all means increase your suspicion—for that way we shall also increase your vigilance. After all, is there anyone so ignorant of the world, so politically naive, and so oblivious to his own safety and that of his fellow men that he fails to appreciate that his own survival is bound up with yours, and that the lives of everyone depend exclusively on yours? Spending my days and nights thinking about you, as I am bound to do, I shudder only at the risks to which all humans are subject, the uncertainty of good health, and the frailty of our bodily constitution—and I grieve at the fact that our country, which ought to be immortal, is dependent on the life of a single mortal. [23] But if, in addition to the risks to which humans are subject and the uncertainty of health, there should also be a conspiracy for criminal and treacherous ends, then what god do we imagine would have the power, even if he had the desire, to rescue our country?

It is your task, Gaius Caesar, and yours alone, to restore everything that you can now see lying battered and shattered (as was unavoidable) by the violence of war. Courts must be established, credit restored, self-indulgence checked, the birth-rate raised,* and everything which has become disintegrated and dissipated reorganized by means of stringent legislation. [24] In such a terrible civil war, amid such stirrings of spirits and swords, it was inevitable that the stricken state, whatever the final result, would lose many ornaments of its prestige* and many bulwarks of its security, and that each leader would do many things under arms that he would not have permitted in peacetime. It is your task now to heal all these wounds of war, which no one but you is capable of treating.

[25] That is why I was disappointed when I heard you make that admirable remark, so full of wisdom, 'I have lived long enough for nature, or for glory.'* Long enough perhaps for nature, if you like; and, I will add, for glory, if that is what you want; but—and this is the crucial point—by no means long enough for your country. So please do not show the wisdom of philosophers in despising death: do not be wise at our peril! It is always being reported to me that you

keep saying, much too often, that as far as you are concerned you have lived long enough. I do not doubt your sincerity; but I would approve the sentiment only if you were living for yourself alone, or had been born for yourself alone. But as it is your achievements have to do with the safety of all the citizens and the entire country—and you are so far from completing your greatest works that you have not yet even laid the foundations* of what you are contemplating.

So, having reached this point, do you really intend to fix the limit of your life not according to what the country needs but according to the equanimity you have attained? And what if the limit you have fixed turns out to be insufficient for glory? You must admit that, although you are a philosopher, you do hanker after that! [26] 'But is the achievement I will leave behind me,' you will ask, 'not enough?' It would certainly be enough in the case of any number of others— but for you it is too little. For anything that exists, however great it may be, is too little, if something else exists that is greater. But if the result of your immortal achievements, Gaius Caesar, is that, after vanquishing your opponents, you leave the country in its present state, then please make sure that your superhuman ability does not produce merely wonder rather than actual glory—assuming, of course, that glory consists of a brilliant, widespread renown resulting from great services to one's friends, one's country, or the human race. [27] This part therefore still awaits you, this act of the drama remains, this is what you must work at—to place the country on a sound footing, and, yourself above all others, to reap its benefits in peace and tranquillity. Then and only then, when you have both discharged your obligations to your country and satisfied nature herself with your full fill of life, say, if you wish, that you have lived long enough.

In any case, what is this 'long', which has some final stopping point? When that point comes, all past pleasure counts for nothing, because there is none to follow. And yet that spirit of yours has never been content to stay within the confines that nature has given us to live in: it has always burned with the desire for immortality. [28] But we must not consider your life as consisting merely of what is contained within your body and your breath: your life, I tell you, is what will flourish in the memory of every age, it is what posterity will nurture, it is what eternity itself will always preserve! So it is eternity to which you should devote yourself, eternity to which you should reveal yourself: it has long had much from you to wonder at, but now is also looking to you for deeds to praise.

Future generations will surely be astounded to hear and read of your commands, your provinces, the Rhine, the Ocean, the Nile,* your numberless battles, your unbelievable victories, monuments, games, and triumphs. [29] But unless you bring stability to this city through reform and legislation, your renown will just wander far and wide, without acquiring a settled home and fixed habitation. Among those yet to be born, there will be great differences of opinion, as there have been among us. Some will praise your achievements to the skies, while others will perhaps find something missing*—and that the most essential thing of all—unless you now proceed to extinguish the flames of civil war by the rescue of your country, and thereby prove the former to have been the result of fate, but the latter the result of policy. Submit, therefore, to the judgement of those who, many centuries from now, will judge you, and may well do so with less partiality than we do: for they will judge you without passion and without self-interest on the one hand, and without envy and without malice on the other. [30] And even if, as some mistakenly believe,* you will be beyond caring about all that when the time comes, you are surely not at this time beyond caring whether you are, in truth, a man whose fame will never be obscured by oblivion.

Our fellow-citizens were divided in their loyalties, and differed in their opinions. We diverged not only in our policies and ideals, but in weapons and camps. The situation was far from clear. The dispute was between leaders who were both men of the highest distinction. Many were unsure as to what was for the best, many as to what was in their interest, many as to where their duty lay, and some also as to what was lawful. [31] The country endured this wretched war which fate had forced upon it. The victor was one who did not let his good fortune stoke up the hostility felt towards him, but instead let his goodness assuage it; nor did he judge all those with whom he had been angry as deserving in addition exile or death. Some laid down their arms; others were disarmed. Ungrateful and unjust is the citizen who, though freed from the danger of arms, nevertheless keeps his spirit armed: even the one who did not give up his cause, but fell in battle and there poured out his spirit is better.* For although some will regard such conduct as obstinacy, others will view it as constancy.

[32] But at the point at which we are now, all dissension has been crushed by force of arms, and extinguished by the fairness of the victor: the result is that all those who possess some degree not necessarily of wisdom, but merely of sanity, desire the same thing. We cannot be secure, Gaius Caesar, unless you too are secure, and unless you also continue to follow the policy which you have followed in the past and particularly today. Therefore all of us who desire Rome to remain secure both urge and beseech you to take care of your life and your personal safety; and since you believe that there is some hidden danger which you need to take precautions against, we all promise you (if I may express also on behalf of others the feeling which I experience myself) not only sentinels and bodyguards, but the protection of our own lives and limbs.

[33] But, to conclude my speech at the point at which it began, we all offer to you, Gaius Caesar, our profoundest thanks—while feeling even greater gratitude in our hearts. We are all of one mind, as you could see from everyone's prayers and tears. There is no need for everyone to stand and make a speech; but they all wish me at least to do so, since it is in a way necessary that I should do so. The most appropriate reaction to your restoration of Marcus Marcellus to this order, to the Roman people, and to the country is, I can see, actually taking place. For I can see that everyone is overwhelmed with a joy that does not arise only from the salvation of one individual, but from the salvation of every one of us. [34] My own reaction, on the other hand, is one of absolute goodwill—a goodwill towards Marcellus, which was always well known, and which I would judge scarcely inferior to that of his excellent and devoted cousin Gaius Marcellus,* and inferior to that of no one besides him—a goodwill which, since I expressed it for so long through my worry, my anxiety, and my exertions on his behalf as long as his fate was in doubt, I should without question also, now that I have been liberated from that dreadful anxiety, trouble, and grief, continue to express. Therefore, Gaius Caesar, I offer you my thanks. I owe to you, wholly and completely, not only my preservation, but the position of honour which I now hold. I never supposed that anything more was possible—and yet the countless personal favours which you have conferred on me have been gloriously crowned by what you have done today.

# PHILIPPIC II

Like *Pro Marcello* (46 BC), the *Second Philippic* is an epideictic (display) speech set in the senate. But there the resemblance ends. *Pro Marcello* dates from the period of Caesar's dictatorship; the *Second Philippic* from two years later, six months after his assassination. *Pro Marcello* is a short panegyric; the *Second Philippic* a lengthy invective. And *Pro Marcello* was delivered on a real occasion, in Caesar's presence; the *Second Philippic*, like that other masterpiece of Cicero's, *Pro Milone* (52 BC), and like *In Verrem* II.1–5, was never delivered. Most importantly, however, with the *Second Philippic* we have entered a new world—a world of fear and uncertainty in which powerful men made competing appeals to Caesar's veterans, and republicans, reinvigorated by their act of tyrannicide but unprepared for the consequences, began to reckon up the terrifying forces ranged against them.

In this world, in September 44, the major figures were Marcus Antonius (in English, Mark Antony), the dead Caesar's consular colleague, and the 18-year-old Gaius Julius Caesar Octavianus (Octavian), Caesar's great-nephew, principal heir, and adoptive son. For Cicero, it was the first of these who presented the greater danger. He had not wished to cross swords with Antony; but when Antony, with all the authority of a consul, bitterly attacked him in the senate in his absence, he felt impelled to write, in pamphlet form, a comprehensive rejoinder. This rejoinder, the *Second Philippic*, marked the point of no return in Cicero's deteriorating relationship with Antony, while also confirming Cicero's status as Rome's greatest orator. Written in a simpler style than most of his previous speeches, particularly the elaborate *Pro Marcello*, it is an utterly devastating attack. Later orators and critics regarded it as the classic invective, and the fact that its author was murdered for writing the *Philippics* certainly added to its fascination. In the early empire it was also of political interest in that Antony was Octavian's great rival—the enemy in Augustan ideology as well as in Ciceronian rhetoric. The speech did much to determine the way Antony was viewed by posterity: it was used by Plutarch for his *Life of Antony* (*c.* AD 110–15), which in turn provided the historical basis for Shakespeare's *Antony and Cleopatra*. Nearly two centuries after its composition, the satirist Juvenal, himself a past master in the art of denigrating others, would label it 'the divine *Philippic*' (10.125).

Cicero's *Philippics* (there are fourteen of them in existence, four dating from 44 and the rest from January to April 43) are more properly known as *In Antonium* ('Against Antonius'). But in a lost letter to Brutus, Cicero

jokingly suggested that they might be described as his 'Philippics', and in
a reply of 1 April 43 (*Epistulae ad Brutum* 2.3.4) Brutus good-humouredly
approved the title, which then stuck (as Plutarch testifies at *Cic.* 48.6). The
title *Philippics* is a reference to the four (extant) speeches which the Athenian orator Demosthenes composed against Philip II of Macedon between
351 and 340. Cicero's *Philippics*, like those of Demosthenes, set out to
defend the freedom of the state against an aggressor who threatened it.
But apart from that, Cicero's speeches have little in common with their
Greek namesakes, and contain no verbal allusions to them. In choosing the
title, Cicero did not mean to suggest any complex relationship between the
two sets of speeches: all he was doing was making a light-hearted comparison between himself and Greece's most famous orator. Indeed, when
he published his corpus of consular speeches in 60, he wrote to Atticus
comparing the speeches, in an equally light-hearted way, with Demosthenes' *Philippics* (*Att.* 2.1.3), and it is perhaps only an accident of
history that it is his speeches of 44–43 that have come to be known as the
*Philippics* rather than those of 63. The *Second Philippic*, however, does
have something in common with Demosthenes' greatest speech, *De corona*
('On the crown', 330 BC): both speeches review at length the careers of the
orator and an opponent (in Demosthenes' case, his enemy Aeschines), and
Cicero's speech contains six allusions to its Demosthenic counterpart. But
even so, the influence of Demosthenes is not strongly felt: Cicero does not
allow imitation of an admired literary predecessor to deflect him from his
central purpose of abusing his opponent.

Let us review the political developments which resulted in Cicero's
composition and publication of the speech. On the morning of the Ides
(15th) of March 44, the consul and dictator Gaius Julius Caesar was
assassinated in the senate by a large group of conspirators, some of them,
like Marcus Junius Brutus and Gaius Cassius Longinus, republicans who
objected to tyranny, others Caesarians who for one reason or another had
turned against their leader. They had chosen their moment carefully: in
three days' time Caesar had been due to leave for a three-year expedition
against the Parthians, to avenge Crassus' defeat at Carrhae in 53. The
other consul, Antony, was taken to one side just before the deed was done:
the conspirators had decided to kill Caesar alone (a basic error which
Cicero later claimed that, had he been invited to join the conspiracy,
he would have pointed out; cf. *Fam.* 10.28.1, 12.4.1). In the afternoon, the
conspirators, who described themselves as 'liberators', addressed the
people in the forum and then, after being received with a stony silence,
took refuge on the Capitol.

Two days later, on 17 March, Antony called a meeting of the senate and
a compromise was agreed by which an amnesty was granted to Caesar's

assassins, but the dictator's acts, including those not yet made public, were ratified. Caesar had wanted Publius Cornelius Dolabella (who from 50 to 46 had been Cicero's son-in-law) to take over from him as consul when he left for Parthia; Antony, although he had previously resisted this, now gave way, and Dolabella was appointed as his colleague. The conspirators were then persuaded to come down from the Capitol.

Caesar's funeral took place on *c.*20 March. Antony gave the oration, but his words so stirred up the crowd (whether intentionally or not) that they burned the body themselves on an improvised pyre in the forum, instead of allowing it to be taken to the pyre that had been prepared in the Campus Martius. There was considerable violence, and attacks were made on the houses of the conspirators. (The chaotic scenes must have recalled those which had accompanied the impromptu cremation of Publius Clodius Pulcher in the senate-house in 52.) Antony brought the situation under control, however, and soon afterwards won the approval of Cicero and other republicans by proposing that the office of dictator be abolished. But it was no longer safe for the conspirators to remain in Rome: Brutus and Cassius withdrew from the city on *c.*12 April (in Brutus' case, special permission was required, since he was city praetor), and others left to take up the provincial governorships assigned to them by Caesar (Brutus' cousin Decimus Junius Brutus Albinus went to Cisalpine Gaul). Cicero himself, although he had not been a conspirator, left Rome on 7 April to visit his country estates.

By mid-April, Antony had already started abusing his position as consul and custodian of Caesar's papers (these had been handed over to him by the dictator's widow Calpurnia as early as the night of 15 or 16 March). Since the ratification of Caesar's acts had extended to those not yet made public, Antony took the opportunity of forging documents in Caesar's name in return for massive bribes. He also helped himself to the vast treasury that Caesar had deposited in the temple of Ops (possibly for use in the Parthian campaign), and he bought Dolabella's acquiescence with funds taken from the same source. These actions appalled Cicero, but he did not make his feelings public, and Antony treated him throughout this period with a show of respect. The senate, however, decreed that from 1 June all of Caesar's purported acts should be subject to scrutiny by a special commission set up for the purpose.

On 18 April, Octavian arrived at Naples (at the time of Caesar's death, he had been at Apollonia in northern Greece, preparing to join his great-uncle for the Parthian campaign). Large numbers of Caesar's veterans had been settled in Campania, and Octavian presented himself to them as Gaius Julius Caesar, the dictator's adoptive son. (He also presented himself to Cicero, who at this time was staying at his villa in Puteoli.) A week or so after this, Antony left for Campania himself, ostensibly to oversee the settlement of further veterans, but partly no doubt also to secure his own hold over the soldiers. Once he had left the capital, his colleague Dolabella, in a demonstration of independence, demolished an altar and column that had been set up on the spot where Caesar had been cremated, and summarily executed the people who were worshipping there. At the beginning of May, however, Octavian arrived in Rome and announced his intention to claim his inheritance, pay Caesar's legacies to the Roman people, and hold games in Caesar's honour.

On *c.*18 May, Antony returned to Rome with a large bodyguard of Caesar's veterans; Octavian asked him to hand Caesar's property over to him, but he refused. On 1 June, Antony convened a meeting of the senate, but the senators were intimidated by his soldiers and few attended. Next (on 2 or 3 June), he went to the assembly and carried laws—illegally, since no notice had been given—to extend his and Dolabella's governorships of Macedonia and Syria respectively from two to five years (even though two years had been the limit set by Caesar for such appointments). Finally, he exchanged his province of Macedonia for Gaul, while nevertheless retaining command of five legions which had been sent to Macedonia in preparation for the Parthian campaign. For him, the advantages of Gaul were, first, that it would allow him to take over three legions which were under the command of Decimus Brutus and, secondly, that he would then be in a position, like Caesar in 49, to cross the Rubicon and invade Italy, should he feel the need to do so.

Brutus and Cassius, meanwhile, were eager to return to Rome and resume their duties as praetors. On 5 June, Antony, who wanted the pair kept out of political life, persuaded the senate to appoint them to a grain commission, to be held in Asia and Sicily respectively; considering this demeaning, they at once began lobbying to have the commission repealed. For himself, on the other hand, Antony secured the establishment of a powerful Board of Seven, charged with distributing public land in Italy among Caesar's veterans and the poor; he, his brother Lucius Antonius, and Dolabella (whose allegiance, of course, he had bought) were all to be members.

On 6–13 July, Brutus sponsored the Apollinarian Games, although he did not dare attend (nor did Cicero, though Brutus wanted him to). The games earned him considerable popularity, as he had hoped—but this popularity lasted scarcely longer than the games themselves. On 17 July, Cicero, despairing of the political situation, started out on a voyage to visit his son, who was studying in Athens; he intended to return to Rome only when Antony's consulship was over. Towards the end of the month, Octavian held his promised games in Caesar's honour, despite the fact that

Antony had not allowed him access to the funds he needed to pay for them; he was forced to borrow the money instead. During the games, a comet appeared for seven days, and was interpreted as a sign of Caesar's divinity. The popularity which Octavian acquired from these games, and from the legacies which he started to pay to the Roman people (again, with borrowed money), caused relations between him and Antony to deteriorate so much that their soldiers, fearing civil war, forced them to meet on the Capitol and be publicly reconciled to one another.

On 1 August, Antony convened the senate. Brutus and Cassius had counted on opposition to him being expressed, but only Lucius Calpurnius Piso Caesoninus, the consul of 58 and Caesar's father-in-law, spoke out. Antony and Brutus and Cassius then issued edicts attacking each other. At around this time, Brutus and Cassius were assigned new provinces, Crete and Cyrene respectively (hardly prestigious appointments, but an improvement on the grain commission), and set sail for the east. Cicero, meanwhile, had attempted to sail to Greece, and had actually got as far as Syracuse, but had been forced back by contrary winds to Leucopetra (six miles south of Regium). There he heard that the situation in Rome had apparently improved, and that his absence was being criticized; so he changed his plans and turned back towards the capital. On 17 August, he met Brutus at Velia (on the coast between Naples and Regium), and learned from him more accurate news of the situation in Rome. Each of them then continued on their way, never to meet again.

On 1 September, Cicero arrived back in Rome, and was welcomed by enthusiastic crowds. But he soon learned that the senate was meeting that day in order to vote honours to Caesar: Antony was proposing to add an extra day in the dictator's honour to all the festivals of thanksgiving to the gods. Cicero therefore sent his apologies, explaining that he was tired after his journey. Antony responded by attacking him in the senate and threatening to destroy his house. The next day Cicero attended the senate (this time Antony was absent), and delivered the speech which came to be known as the *First Philippic*. This was outwardly respectful and conciliatory, but nevertheless enumerated the illegalities committed by Antony as consul. The result was that Antony made a public declaration of hostility to Cicero, and then set to work preparing an invective against him, demanding his presence in the senate on 19 September (the next day on which the senate could meet). When the appointed day came, Cicero judged it too dangerous for him to attend, and stayed away. The meeting was held in the temple of Concord (in which Cicero had held the famous debate on the Catilinarian conspirators nineteen years earlier): Antony brought in armed men, locked the doors, and delivered the invective that he had prepared. In that speech, which does not not survive, he accused

Cicero of ingratitude and unfriendly behaviour towards himself, and went on to criticize Cicero's consulship and whole career, blaming him for, among other things, the murder of Clodius, the Civil War, and Caesar's assassination. It was a comprehensive attack: he even found space in it to ridicule Cicero's poetry.

Naturally enough, perhaps, Cicero immediately began work on a written rebuttal—the *Second Philippic*. This was essentially the speech that he would have given in reply to Antony had he been able to: it is written exactly as if delivered in the senate on 19 September, and scrupulously avoids reference to events that happened later. At the end of October, Cicero sent a draft of it to his friend Atticus: it was to be shown only to people who would be sympathetic, and was not to be given a wider circulation until such time as the republic had been restored. Cicero was fully aware that it would have been folly to publish it under the conditions then existing. In public, he did not dignify Antony's attack on him with a reply.

While Cicero was thus engaged, relations between Antony and Octavian were rapidly worsening. Early in October, Antony accused Octavian of plotting to assassinate him. When Antony then went to Brundisium to take command of the five legions which were being transferred to him from Macedonia, Octavian raised an army from Caesar's veterans and, on 9 November, briefly occupied Rome. Antony quickly returned to the city; but when two of his Macedonian legions defected to Octavian, he nominated a new set of provincial governors and then set out for Cisalpine Gaul early on 29 November. On 20 December, the senate received a letter from Decimus Brutus, the governor of Cisalpine Gaul, in which he announced his refusal to hand over his province, with its three legions, to Antony. Cicero therefore delivered the *Third Philippic*, in which he persuaded the senate to approve Decimus Brutus' action and to rule that all the existing governors should retain control of their provinces until further notice. The *Fourth Philippic*, delivered before the people on the same day, contained further praise of Decimus Brutus and argued that Antony was now in effect a public enemy. It was probably at this point, when he was irrevocably committed to a course of opposition to Antony, that he released the *Second Philippic* into public circulation.

So began Cicero's 'finest hour', in which, through the remaining *Philippics* (January to April 43), he directed the senate in its war against Antony. Decimus Brutus, after being besieged and relieved at Mutina, was eventually killed by Antony. Dolabella was declared a public enemy, was besieged by Crassus in Syria, and committed suicide. Octavian marched on Rome, seized the consulship (aged 19), and revoked the amnesty that had been granted to Caesar's assassins—thus unleashing the further civil war in which Brutus and Cassius would perish. Finally, in November 43,

228        *Philippic II: Introduction*

Antony, Octavian, and Marcus Aemilius Lepidus (Master of the Horse at
the time of Caesar's assassination, and governor of Narbonese Gaul and
Nearer Spain) came together to form the 'second triumvirate', thus effectively ending the republic. Their proscription lists, agreed in advance, were
immediately published; and Cicero was murdered on 7 December. His
head and hands—the hand that had written the *Philippics*—were displayed, on Antony's orders, on the rostra at Rome. There people saw,
according to Plutarch (*Cic.* 49.2), 'not the face of Cicero, but an image of
Antony's soul'.

# PHILIPPIC II

[1] To what fate of mine, conscript fathers, should I attribute the fact that, over the past twenty years,* there has not been a single enemy of the state who did not at the same time declare war on me also? I need not name names: you will recall them yourselves. Those enemies paid me penalties greater than I would have wished: I am surprised, Antonius, that when you copy their deeds you do not also shudder at their ends. I was less surprised in the case of the others. After all, none of them set out to become my enemy: in each case, it was because they attacked the state that they encountered my opposition. You, on the other hand, though I had never said so much as a word against you, attacked me with unprovoked abuse—so you could present yourself as more reckless than Catiline, more demented than Clodius; and you calculated that your alienation from me would serve as a recommendation for you in the eyes of disloyal citizens.

[2] So what am I to make of this? Should I conclude that he despises me? But I cannot see anything in my private life, in my reputation, in my record, or in these moderate abilities of mine that would merit the contempt of— Antonius! Or was it that he thought the senate the place where I could most easily be disparaged? Yet this is a body which has borne testimony in the case of many illustrious citizens that they served their country well—but in my case alone that I saved it.* Or did he wish to vie with me in oratory? How kind of him! After all, what richer or more rewarding theme could I possibly have than to speak both for myself and against Antonius? No, the only possible conclusion is this—that he felt he had no chance of convincing those like himself that he really was an enemy of his country unless he were also an enemy of mine.

[3] Before I reply to his other points, I want to say a few words about the friendship which he accused me of having violated, since I consider this a charge of the utmost seriousness.

He complained that at some time or other I appeared in court against his interests. Was I really not free to appear in opposition to a stranger on behalf of an extremely close friend?* Not free to appear in opposition to influence that had been acquired not by the prospect of virtue, but by pretty-boy looks? Not free to appear in opposition to

an injustice which he* had contrived by securing an utterly scandalous veto in his favour, instead of by a praetor's judgement? But I
think you brought up this matter in order to recommend yourself to
the dregs of society, since everyone would remember that you were
the son-in-law of a freedman, and that your children were the
grandchildren of a freedman, Quintus Fadius.*

But you had been my pupil, you said, and a regular visitor at my
house. If this were true, it would have been better for your reputation, better for your morals! But it is not true, and even had you been
desperate to come to me, Gaius Curio* would not have let you out of
his sight.

[4] You said that you had declined to stand for the augurate* as a
favour to me. What astonishing effrontery, what outrageous cheek!
At the time when Gnaeus Pompeius and Quintus Hortensius, at the
request of the entire college, put my name forward (no one was
permitted to have more than two sponsors), you were bankrupt and
saw no way out for yourself except through revolution. Besides,
could you have stood for the augurate at a time when Curio was
not in Italy, or, when you were later elected, could you have carried a
single tribe without Curio's backing? Friends of his were actually
convicted of violence for being over-zealous on your behalf.

[5] But I was done a favour by you. And what favour was that? As
it happens, I have always openly acknowledged what it is you are
referring to: I have preferred to say that I am in your debt than let
people who do not know any better suppose me ungrateful. But what
was the favour? That you did not kill me at Brundisium?* Could you
in fact have killed a man whom the victor himself—who, as you used
to boast, had made you the chief of his band of brigands—had
wanted kept unharmed, and had actually ordered to go to Italy in the
first place? Suppose you could have. How else can brigands confer a
favour, conscript fathers, except by asserting that they have granted
life to those from whom they have not taken it away? But if this were
truly a favour, those who assassinated the man who had saved them,*
men whom you yourself were in the habit of calling 'illustrious',
would never have won the glory they did. And what sort of 'favour'
is it to have refrained from committing a horrific crime? Under the
circumstances, I should not have been so much pleased at not having
been killed by you as dismayed that it was within your power to do so
with impunity.

[6] But let us agree to call it a favour, since brigands cannot grant anything greater: where can you say I have been ungrateful? Are you really saying that I should not have complained at the destruction of the state, in case I appeared to show you ingratitude? Yet in that complaint,* sorrowful and grief-stricken as it was—but also necessary for me to make, in view of this rank in which the senate and people of Rome have placed me—did I say anything offensive, did I say anything intemperate, did I say anything unfriendly? What self-control it required, when complaining about Marcus Antonius, to refrain from abuse—particularly when you had scattered to the winds the last remnants of the state; when at your house everything was up for sale in the most disgraceful of markets;* when you admitted that laws that had never been promulgated had been enacted both by yourself and in your own interest;* when as augur you had abolished the auspices, and as consul the right of veto; when to your shame you were going around with an armed escort;* and when, worn out with wine and fornication, you daily indulged, within that shameless house of yours, in every type of perversion. [7] But I behaved instead as if my quarrel were with Marcus Crassus,* with whom I have had many serious disagreements in my time, rather than with a supremely worthless gladiator. I made a deeply felt complaint about the state, but said not a word about the man. For this reason I will make him understand today how great was the favour that he on that occasion received from me.

He even read out a letter* he claimed I had sent him  thereby showing his lack of good manners and his ignorance of the common courtesies. After all, has anyone with the slightest understanding of how gentlemen behave towards one another ever produced a letter sent to him by a friend with whom he subsequently had had a disagreement and read it out in public? What does such behaviour amount to but the abolition of the bonds of society, the abolition of communication between absent friends? How many jokes are put in letters which, if published, would seem inappropriate—and how many confidences that ought never to be divulged!

[8] So much for his lack of manners: but look at his astonishing stupidity. What would you have to say to me in reply, O man of eloquence that you are—or at least appear to be to Mustela Seius and Tiro Numisius?* And since, even as I speak, those two are standing armed with swords in full view of the senate, I shall certainly join

them in reckoning you eloquent—if, that is, you can explain how you are going to get them off when they are put on trial for bearing arms in public! Come on, then, what would you have to say to me if I told you that I never sent you that letter in the first place? How would you prove me wrong? By the handwriting—your knowledge of which has been so lucrative?* But how could you? The letter is in the hand of a secretary. How I envy your teacher,* who has taught you such ignorance in return for an enormous fee, the size of which I shall shortly reveal! [9] For what could be less intelligent for any person—let alone an orator—than to bring up a point against his opponent which, if it were countered with a simple denial, could not be taken further?

But as it happens I do not deny it—and on this issue I thereby prove you guilty not just of bad manners, but of madness. For is there a single word in that letter that does not betoken civility, respect, and goodwill? Indeed, your accusation consists of nothing other than that in that letter I did not think badly of you, and that I wrote to you as if to a citizen, as if to a man of honour, and not as if to a criminal and brigand. But for my part I am not going to publish your letter, even though, since you attacked me first, I would be perfectly within my rights to do so. In that letter you ask for my consent to the recall of some exile, and assure me that you will not recall him unless I agree to it. I then agreed to what you asked. After all, why should I stand up to your criminal behaviour, when neither the authority of this order nor the views of the Roman people nor any of the laws could hold it in check? [10] But why did you need to ask me in the first place, if the man's recall had really been authorized by a law of Caesar's? Of course, he wanted the credit for the favour to be mine*—even though, if the law really had been carried, there would be no credit even for himself!

Conscript fathers, I have something to say in my own defence and much to say against Marcus Antonius. As to the former theme, I ask you to listen to me sympathetically as I defend myself; as to the latter, I shall myself make sure that you pay me close attention while I speak against him. At the same time I beg of you: if you agree that my whole life and particularly my public speaking have always been characterized by moderation and restraint, then please do not think that today, when I give this man the response he has provoked, I have forgotten my true nature. I am not going to treat him as a consul any more than he has treated me as a consular. And whereas he cannot in any sense be regarded as a consul, either in his private life, or in his administration of the state, or in the manner of his appointment,* I am beyond any dispute a consular.

[11] So to let you appreciate what sort of consul he professes himself to be, he attacked my consulship. Now that consulship, conscript fathers, was mine in name only: in reality it was yours. For what decision did I arrive at, what action did I take, what deed did I do other than by the advice, authority, and vote of this order?* And now do you, as a man of wisdom, not merely of eloquence, dare to criticize those proceedings in the very presence of those by whose advice and wisdom they were transacted? But who was ever found to criticize my consulship except you and Publius Clodius? Indeed, Clodius' fate awaits you, just as it did Gaius Curio, since you have at home the thing which did for both of them.*

[12] Marcus Antonius does not approve of my consulship. But Publius Servilius* approved of it—of the consulars of that time I name him first, because his death is the most recent. Quintus Catulus approved of it, a man whose authority will always remain a living force in this country. The two Luculli, Marcus Crassus, Quintus Hortensius, Gaius Curio, Gaius Piso, Manius Glabrio, Manius Lepidus, Lucius Volcacius, and Gaius Figulus approved of it. Decimus Silanus and Lucius Murena,* who were then consuls-elect, approved of it. Like the consulars, Marcus Cato* approved of it—a man who in taking leave of life showed great foresight, especially in that he never saw you become consul. But Gnaeus Pompeius* above all approved of my consulship in that, the moment he saw me on his return from Syria, he embraced me and congratulated me, saying that it was thanks to me that he would once again set eyes on his country. But why do I mention individuals? A packed senate approved my consulship* so strongly that there was no one who did not thank me as if I were his parent, and who did not put it down to me that he was still in possession of his life, his property, his children, and his country.

[13] But since the many distinguished gentlemen whom I have just named are all now lost to our country, I turn to the living. Out of the body of consulars, two are still with us. The gifted and judicious Lucius Cotta* proposed a thanksgiving in the most complimentary terms for those very actions which you criticize, and the consulars

I have just named, together with the entire senate, accepted the proposal—an honour which I was the first civilian since the foundation
of our city to receive. [14] Lucius Caesar,* your uncle—what eloquence, what resolution, what authority he showed as he denounced
his sister's husband, your stepfather! He was the man you should
have had as your guide and mentor in all your decisions throughout
your life—and yet you chose to model yourself on your stepfather
rather than your uncle! Although unrelated to him, I as consul
accepted Caesar's guidance—but did you, his sister's son, ever ask
his advice on any public matter at all?

Immortal gods, whose advice, then, *does* he ask? Those fellows, I
suppose, whose very birthdays we are made to hear announced.
[15] 'Antonius is not appearing in public today.' 'Why ever not?' 'He
is giving a birthday party at his house outside the city.' 'Who for?' I
will name no names: just imagine it's now for some Phormio or
other, now for Gnatho, now for Ballio* even. What scandalous disgrace, what intolerable cheek, wickedness, and depravity! Do you
have so readily available to you a leading senator, an outstanding
citizen, and never consult him on matters of public interest—while
all the time consulting people who have nothing of their own, but
sponge off you instead?

Your consulship, then, is a blessing, and mine was a curse. Have
you so lost your sense of shame, together with your decency, that you
dare to say such a thing in the very temple* where *I* used to consult
the senate in its days of greatness, when it ruled the world—but
where *you* have now stationed thugs armed with swords? [16] But
you even dared (is there anything you would not dare?) to say that
in my consulship the Capitoline path* was packed with armed slaves.
I was, I suppose, preparing violence to force the senate to pass those
wicked decrees! You despicable wretch—whether you do not know
what happened (since you know nothing of anything good) or
whether you do—you who talk with such utter lack of shame before
such men as these! When the senate was meeting in this temple, did
any Roman equestrian, did any young noble except you, did anyone
of any class who recalled that he was a Roman citizen fail to come to
the Capitoline path? Did anyone fail to give in his name?* And yet
there were neither enough clerks nor enough registers to record all
the names that were offered. [17] After all, traitors were admitting
to the assassination of their homeland, and were compelled by the

testimony of their accomplices, by their own handwriting, and by the
almost audible sound of the words they had written to confess that
they had conspired to set fire to the city, to massacre the citizens, to
devastate Italy, and to destroy their country. In such a situation, who
would not be roused to defend the national security—particularly at
a time when the senate and people of Rome had the sort of leader*
under whom, if we had a similar leader now, you would have met the
same fate that those traitors did?

He claims I refused to hand over his stepfather's body for burial.
But not even Publius Clodius ever accused me of that, Clodius, who
to my regret (because I had good reason to be his enemy) has now
been outdone in every kind of vice by you. [18] But how did it occur
to you to remind us that you were brought up in the house of Publius
Lentulus? Was it that you were afraid we might find it impossible to
believe that you could have turned out so bad by nature, unless
nurture also were added? So obtuse were you that throughout your
entire speech you were at issue with yourself, making statements that
were not merely incoherent but actually inconsistent and incompatible: the result was that you seemed to be not so much in dispute
with me as with yourself. You admitted that your stepfather was
implicated in that terrible crime, and yet you complained that he was
punished for it. Thus you praised what is properly mine and blamed
what is entirely the senate's. For I arrested the guilty men, but the
senate punished them.* What a clever orator this man is, since he fails
to grasp that he is praising his opponent and criticizing his audience!

[19] Now here is a sign, I will not say of his impudence, since he
wants to be called impudent, but of the last thing he wants to have
ascribed to him, his stupidity—a quality in which he surpasses
everyone else. He talked of the Capitoline path—and this at a time
when armed men are patrolling our benches, and when soldiers,
sword in hand, stand posted within this very sanctuary of Concord
(immortal gods!), this actual sanctuary in which, during my consulship, the salutary measures which have ensured our survival to this
day were proposed! Accuse the senate! Accuse the equestrian order,
which at that time was united with the senate!* Accuse all classes, all
citizens—so long as you admit that this order at this very moment is
being besieged by Ituraeans!* It is not impudence which causes you to
make such shameless accusations, but your failure to see the extent
to which you contradict yourself. Obviously, then, you are ignorant.

For if you yourself have taken up arms in order to destroy your country, what is more insane than to reproach someone else for doing so in order to preserve it?

[20] But at one point you even attempted to be witty. Good gods, it didn't suit you at all! You must carry some of the blame for this yourself—after all, you could always have borrowed some jokes from your actress wife.* 'Let arms to the toga yield.'* Yes? And didn't they? But at a later point the toga yielded to your arms. We ought therefore to enquire whether it was better for the arms of criminals to yield to the freedom of the Roman people or for our freedom to yield to your arms. But I will not reply to you further about the verses. I will, though, make this brief observation—that you have no understanding of this or any literature at all, whereas I, without ever failing in my duty either to the state or to my friends, have nevertheless managed to devote my spare time to producing works in every literary genre, and by these compositions of the night I have succeeded in bringing some profit to the young and some credit to the reputation of Rome. But this is not the moment for this; let us pass on to more important matters.

[21] You said that I instigated the killing of Publius Clodius.* Now what would people think if he had been killed at the time when you, sword in hand, chased him across the forum in full view of the Roman people? Indeed, you would have finished him off were it not for the fact that he threw himself beneath the stairs of a bookshop and, barricading himself in there, halted your attack.* I admit that I supported you on that occasion; but not even you say that I put you up to it. But as for what Milo did, I did not have any opportunity of supporting him, since the deed was done before anyone had any notion it was going to take place. Nevertheless, you say I put him up to it. I suppose Milo's character was such that he was incapable of being of service to his country unless someone were egging him on! But you say I was pleased at what happened. So? When the whole of Rome was celebrating, should I alone have had a long face? [22] Anyway, an inquiry* was held into Clodius' death—an inquiry rather inadvisedly set up, it is true. After all, what was the point of passing a law to establish a new court for murder when a legally constituted court already existed? Anyway, an inquiry was held; and the allegation that no one made against me while the trial was taking place* you now turn up and make after so many years have elapsed.

[23] You dared to claim, and at enormous length too, that it was thanks to me that Pompeius was detached from Caesar's friendship, and that it was therefore my fault that the Civil War happened. In this you were not entirely wrong; but you were wrong about the timing, and that is the most important thing. In the consulship of that outstanding citizen Marcus Bibulus* I left no stone unturned in my efforts to win Pompeius away from his alliance with Caesar. But Caesar was more successful that I was: he won Pompeius away from his friendship with me. But after Pompeius had completely given himself over to Caesar, why should I try to draw him away from him? It would have been stupid to make the attempt, impertinent to advise it. [24] However, there were two occasions on which I did advise Pompeius against Caesar. Do blame me for them, if you can. The first was when I advised him not to extend Caesar's command for a further five years, and the second when I advised him not to allow him to be given permission to stand for office in absence.* Had I succeeded in persuading Pompeius on either of these points, we should never have reached the pitiful state we are in now.

But after Pompeius had handed over all his own resources and those of the Roman people to Caesar,* and had at long last started to become aware of what I had long foreseen, and after I saw myself that an appalling war was descending on our country, I never ceased in my efforts to promote peace, harmony, and mediation. Indeed, many people know what I kept on saying at the time: 'How I wish, Gnaeus Pompeius, that you had either never entered into an alliance with Gaius Caesar or else had never broken it off! The first course would have attested to your steadfastness, the second to your prudence.' These, Marcus Antonius, have always been my policies regarding Pompeius and the state. Had they prevailed, our country would still be standing; and you, as a result of your crimes, your debts, and your disgrace, would have fallen.

[25] But all that is ancient history. Turning to the more recent past, you said that I instigated the killing of Caesar. On this I am afraid, conscript fathers, that you may think me guilty of the shocking offence of having arranged for a sham prosecutor to bring a charge against me—someone who would not only laud me with praises that rightfully belong to me but also load me with ones that properly belong to others. For who ever heard my name mentioned as one of the partners who carried out that glorious deed?* And of

those partners, whose name has been kept secret? Kept secret, do I say? Whose name was not immediately broadcast? I would sooner venture that there were some who had not been in the plot, but whose boasts gave the impression that they had been, than that anyone had been in the plot and was anxious to conceal his involvement. [26] Moreover, how likely is it that among so many people, some of whom were virtually unknown and some mere youths—not the sort of people one could shelter behind—a name such as mine could have gone unnoticed?

Besides, if those who acted to liberate their country needed others to activate them, would I really be needed to urge on the Bruti, both of whom saw the mask of Lucius Brutus every day, and one of whom also that of Ahala?* Would these men, with these ancestors, really look to outsiders for guidance instead of to their own families, would they look far afield instead of to their own houses? And what about Gaius Cassius?* Born into a family which could not endure anyone's influence, let alone their tyranny, he really must have needed me, I suppose, to show him the way! Even without his illustrious companions, he would have finished the job off in Cilicia,* at the mouth of the river Cnydus, if Caesar had only moored his boat on the bank on which he had originally planned, and not on the opposite one. [27] Was Gnaeus Domitius* inspired to regain his freedom not by the killing of his illustrious father, nor by the death of his uncle, nor by the deprivation of his public career—but by my prompting? Or did I persuade Gaius Trebonius?* I should not have dared even to advise him. The country therefore owes him an even greater debt of gratitude in that he put the freedom of the whole Roman people before his friendship with an individual, and preferred to overthrow a tyranny than to participate in it. Or did Lucius Tillius Cimber* follow my prompting? I was much more astonished that he did that deed than hopeful that he might—astonished because he forgot the favours he had received, but remembered his country. And what about the two Servilii—Cascas should I call them, or Ahalas?* Do you think they were inspired by my prompting rather than by their own patriotism? It would take too long to go through all the rest: their sheer number is a blessing for the state, and a glory for themselves.

[28] But remember how my intelligent adversary proved his point against me. 'As soon as Caesar had been killed,' he said, 'Marcus Brutus, raising aloft his bloodstained dagger, called out to Cicero by

name, and congratulated him on the recovery of freedom.' But why me in particular? Because I was in the plot? Don't you think the reason he called out my name was this—that since he had just done a deed comparable with what I myself had done,* he called on me to witness the fact that his glory now rivalled my own?

[29] And do you not understand, you utter moron, that if it were a crime to have wished Caesar dead, which is what you accuse me of, then it must also be a crime to have rejoiced once Caesar was dead? For what difference is there between someone who urges an action before it is done and someone who applauds it afterwards? What does it matter whether I wanted it done or was pleased that it had been done? Well then, is there anyone—besides those who were glad that he had turned into a king—who did not want this deed to happen, or failed to approve of it afterwards? So all are guilty. All loyal citizens, so far as was in their power, killed Caesar. Not everyone had a plan, not everyone had the courage, not everyone had the opportunity—but everyone had the will.

[30] But consider the doziness of this man—this sheep, rather. These were his words: 'Marcus Brutus, whose name I mention with respect, called out to Cicero as he held the bloodstained dagger—which should make it clear that Cicero was in the plot.' So you call me a criminal because you have a suspicion that I suspected something, whereas the man who held up his dagger dripping with blood 'is mentioned with respect'. All right, then. We'll put up with this doziness in your words—since that in your actions and opinions is so much greater! Determine at long last, consul, the position you want to apply to the Bruti, Gaius Cassius, Gnaeus Domitius, Gaius Trebonius, and the rest. Sleep off your drunkenness, I tell you; belch it out! Or must we bring flaming torches to wake you up, asleep on an issue as important as this? Are you ever going to understand that you have got to make up your mind whether the men who carried out that deed are murderers or champions of freedom?

[31] Pay attention for a moment. Try to think like a man who is sober, just for a second. I am their friend, as I freely admit, their partner, as you accuse me of being; and I tell you that there is no middle way. If they are not liberators of the Roman people and saviours of the state, then I admit that they are worse than cutthroats, worse than murderers, worse even than parricides—if it is indeed a more wicked crime to kill the parent of one's country* than

one's own parent. What do you say then, you man of wisdom and judgement? If you consider them parricides, why have you always mentioned them with respect, both here in the senate and before the Roman people? Why was Marcus Brutus on your proposal granted exemption from the laws in the event of his being absent from Rome for more than ten days?* Why was such astonishing honour shown to Marcus Brutus when the Apollinarian Games* were held? Why were provinces given to Brutus and Cassius, why were quaestors assigned, why was the number of legates increased?* And all this was done through you. Not murderers, therefore. It follows that they must, on your reckoning, be liberators, since there is no third possibility. [32] What is the matter? Surely I am not confusing you? Perhaps you cannot fully grasp a disjunctive argument. However that may be, this is what my conclusion amounts to: since you have freed them of guilt, you have also judged them to be deserving of the highest rewards.

I therefore now retract what I said. I shall write to them and tell them that if anyone should happen to ask them whether what you accuse me of is true, they are not to deny it. I am afraid, you see, that either their having kept me in ignorance of the plot will reflect discreditably on them, or else my having been invited but refused to join it will reflect utterly disgracefully on me. Holy Jupiter, has there ever been any action, not just in this city but in the whole world, more significant, more glorious, or more worthy to be remembered for all time? And do you* include me as a partner in that enterprise, together with its leaders, as in a Trojan horse? [33] I do not decline. I even thank you—whatever your intention was. It was an enterprise so heroic that I prefer the unpopularity which you seek to stir up against me to any praise. After all, does anyone enjoy a happier fate than those whom you declare you have driven out and exiled? What land is so deserted or so inhospitable as not to seem to greet them with welcoming words on their arrival? What people are so savage as not to think, when they catch sight of them, that they have reaped the greatest harvest that life can offer? What future generation will be so forgetful, what history books so ungrateful as not to celebrate their glory with everlasting remembrance? By all means, then, enrol me in their number!

[34] But I am afraid that there is one thing of which you may not approve: if I had indeed been in their number, I should have

removed not just the king, but kingship itself from the state. And if that pen* had been mine, as is claimed, then believe me, I should have finished off not just one act, but the entire play.

And yet, if it is a crime to have wished Caesar dead, then please consider, Antonius, what ought to happen to you. For everyone knows that you and Gaius Trebonius plotted to kill him at Narbo;* and your involvement in that plot is the reason why Trebonius, as we saw, drew you to one side while Caesar was being killed. For my own part (and note the generosity with which I deal with you), I praise you for the noble intentions you once had; I thank you for not turning informer; and I forgive you for not acting. After all, the task called for a real man.

[35] But if anyone takes you to court and applies Cassius' famous test, 'Who stood to gain?',* then please take care you are not caught. It is true, as you yourself used to point out, that everyone who did not want to be a slave profited from Caesar's death; but you gained more than anyone, because now not only are you not a slave, you are a king. You freed yourself of your colossal debts at the temple of Ops.* You made use of the account books held there to squander an unimaginable sum of money. You had a large part of the contents of Caesar's house transferred to yours.* And you have a highly profitable factory set up at your own house to produce forged notebooks and memoranda*—a scandalous market of estates, towns, exemptions, and revenues. [36] What, except Caesar's death, could possibly have rescued you from your poverty and debts? You seem a little put out. Surely you are not worried that this charge may be seen as relating in some way to you? Let me free you from your fear: no one will ever believe you were involved. Serving your country well is not what you do; and our country already has illustrious men who performed that noble act. All I claim is that you were pleased it happened: I am not maintaining that you were responsible.

I have replied to the most serious charges. Now I must answer those that are left.

[37] You have brought up Pompeius' camp against me, and that whole period.* If at that time, as I have already said,* my advice and authority had prevailed, you today would be poor, we would be free, and the country would not have lost all those leaders and armies. I foresaw exactly what was going to happen; and I admit that it made me as unhappy as it would certainly have made all the other patriots

had they foreseen it too. I was stricken with grief—stricken with grief, conscript fathers—when I reflected that our country, once saved by your efforts and mine,* would very soon be destroyed. I was not so unphilosophical or ignorant of the world as to feel crushed from a desire to cling onto life—a life which, as long as it continued, was likely only to consume me with anguish, but which, once ended, would free me from all my unhappiness. No, what upset me was that I wanted all those brilliant luminaries of our nation to stay alive—all those consulars, all those praetorians, all those honourable senators, all the flower of our young nobility, and those armies of patriotic citizens. If they had only stayed alive, however harsh the terms of peace (and I thought any kind of peace with fellow-citizens preferable to civil war), our country would still exist today. [38] If my opinion had prevailed, and if those people whose lives I was anxious to preserve had not, in their excitement at the prospect of victory, taken the lead in opposing me, then (to say nothing of any other consequences) you would certainly never have kept your place in this order—or in this city.

You say I forfeited Pompeius' goodwill because of the things I said. But was there anyone he was more fond of? Anyone he was more ready to talk to and discuss his plans with? This was indeed 'great',* that we could disagree in politics and yet remain friends. Each of us saw the other's point of view and understood his outlook. My primary concern was for the lives of our citizens; we could think about principle later. He on the other hand put principle first. Each of us knew what he wanted to pursue, and that made our difference of opinion more tolerable. [39] What that brilliant and almost super-human man thought of me is known to those who accompanied him from Pharsalus to Paphos.* He never mentioned my name except in the most honourable terms, terms full of friendly feeling and regret that I was not with him; and he admitted that while he had had the higher hopes, I had had the greater foresight. So do you have the impertinence to attack me in that man's name, while at the same time conceding that whereas I was his friend, you are the purchaser of his property?*

But let us pass over that war, in which you did better than you deserved. I shall not even comment on the joking you claimed I indulged in in the camp. That camp was in a state of anxiety; but human beings, even in times of crisis, do sometimes unwind, if they are human at all. [40] However, the fact that I am criticized for my gloom one moment and for my light-heartedness the next is a sure sign that I showed restraint in both.

You said that I never receive any inheritances. Would the charge were true! Then more of my friends and connections would still be alive. But what put it into your head to bring this up? After all, my accounts do in fact show that I have received more than twenty million sesterces in inheritances. But I concede that in this area you have been luckier than I. Me nobody made his heir unless he was a friend of mine; so that along with the material benefit, if there was any, there also came a degree of sadness. You, on the other hand, were the heir of Lucius Rubrius of Casinum,* a man you never once set eyes on. [41] And observe how fond of you he was, this man who could have been black or white as far as you knew. He passed over the son of his brother Quintus Fufius,* an honourable Roman equestrian with whom he was on the best of terms, and the son whom he had publicly proclaimed as his heir he did not even name in his will. You, on the other hand, whom he had never seen, or at least never spoken to, he made his heir. Please tell me, if it is not too much trouble, what Lucius Turselius* looked like, how tall he was, which town he came from, and which tribe. 'I have no idea,' you will say, 'I only know what farms he owned.' So that is why he disinherited his brother and made you his heir instead! Furthermore, Antonius seized many other private fortunes, the property of people he had nothing to do with, posing as their heir and using force to drive away the real heirs. [42] And yet the thing that surprised me most was that you dared to bring up the subject of inheritances in the first place, after you yourself had declined to accept that of your father.*

Was it to formulate arguments such as these, you utter lunatic, that you spent day after day declaiming in a country house that rightfully belongs to someone else?* Though, as your closest friends are always saying, the reason you declaim is to help you belch up your wine, not to sharpen your intelligence. But you retain, for your own amusement, a master elected by yourself and your fellow-drinkers, a rhetorician* whom you have given leave to say what he likes against you, a witty fellow by all accounts—but of course the task of finding suitable subject matter with which to attack you and your friends is hardly a difficult one. Observe what a difference there is between you and your grandfather:* he weighed his words and said what would benefit his case; you gabble irrelevances. [43] But what a fee your rhetorician received! Listen, listen, conscript fathers, and learn what wounds our country has sustained! You assigned two thousand *iugera** of the plain of Leontini to the rhetorician Sextus Clodius, and tax-free as well: that is the enormous price the Roman people had to pay so that you could learn to be a fool. Surely, you criminal, you did not find this gift, also, in Caesar's notebooks? But I shall be talking later* about the land at Leontini and in Campania, land which Antonius stole from the state and profaned with the most scandalous occupants.

I have now said as much as I need to in reply to his charges. But I still ought to say something about my censorious critic himself. I am not going to pour forth everything that could be said on the subject: after all, if we cross swords often, as we are bound to, I will always need to have fresh material. But even so, the sheer number of his crimes and misdemeanours affords me ample scope.

[44] Would you like us, then, to look at your record from your childhood onwards? Yes, I think so: let's start at the beginning. Do you remember how when you were still a child you went bankrupt?* 'That was my father's fault,' you will say. I grant it: your defence is a model of filial duty! But what reflects your own effrontery is that you sat in the fourteen rows, when under the Roscian law* there was a specific place set aside for bankrupts—regardless of whether their bankruptcy was their own fault or the result of bad luck.

Then you assumed the toga of manhood—and immediately turned it into a toga of womanhood.* First you were a common prostitute: you had a fixed rate for your shameful services, and not a low one either. But soon Curio* appeared on the scene. He saved you from having to support yourself as a prostitute, fitted you out in the dress of a married lady, as it were, and settled you in good, steady wedlock. [45] No slave boy bought for sexual gratification was ever as much in his master's power as you were in Curio's. How many times did his father* throw you out of his house! How many times did he post guards to stop you crossing his threshold! But you, with night to aid you, lust to drive you, and the prospect of payment to compel you, had yourself lowered in through the roof-tiles. Such disgrace that house could endure no longer. Are you aware that I am speaking about things of which I am exceptionally well informed? Cast your mind back to the time when the elder Curio was confined to bed by his grief. The son threw himself in tears at my feet and asked me to help you out. He begged me to protect him from his father's anger if he asked him for six million sesterces—that being the sum for which he said he had stood surety for you. As for himself, in the ardour of his passion he declared that he could not endure the pain of being separated from you, and would therefore take himself off into exile. [46] How deep were the troubles of a flourishing family which I at that time laid to rest, or rather removed altogether! I persuaded the father to pay off his son's debts;* to use the family's capital to redeem a young man of such promising character and abilities;* and to assert his rights and powers as the head of the family to prevent his son not only from being a friend of yours, but even from seeing you. When you remembered that I was responsible for all of this, would you have dared to provoke me with your insults if you did not rely on the protection of those swords which we now see in front of us?

[47] But let us now pass over his sexual crimes and depravity: there are some things I cannot decently relate. (You have more freedom of speech than I, because you have allowed things to be done to you which no opponent with any sense of modesty would ever bring himself to speak of.) So let me move on to the rest of his career. I shall touch upon this only briefly: I am keen to hurry on to his behaviour in the Civil War—a catastrophic period for our country—and his behaviour today. Now I realize that you, gentlemen, know more about this than I do;* nevertheless, I would ask you to pay me close attention, just as you are doing now. In situations such as this, our spirits should be stirred not only by discovering the facts, but also by recollecting them. Even so, we should, I think, cut short the middle of the story, so as not to be too late in reaching the end.

[48] Intimate with Clodius during his tribunate he was, this man who now recounts the favours he has done me. He was the torch that set alight all his conflagrations, and even at that time he was up to something inside Clodius' house—he knows very well what I am talking about.* Then he marched off to Alexandria, in defiance of the senate's declared wishes, and in defiance of the state and divine prohibition.* But of course Gabinius was his commander, and anything he did with *him* had to be all right! And what about his return home—what was that like? From Egypt he went straight to Furthest Gaul,* without first going home. But what home am I talking about?

In those days everyone had their own home—though you had none.*
Home, do I say? Was there anywhere in the world where you could
set foot on ground that belonged to you, with the single exception of
your place at Misenum—and that you owned jointly with others, like
some sort of Sisapo?*

[49] You returned from Gaul to stand for the quaestorship.* I dare
you to say that you called on your mother* before coming to see me.
I had received a letter from Caesar asking if I would accept your
apologies, and so I did not allow you to say a single word on the
subject of reconciliation. After that you paid me attentions, and
I kept a lookout for you in your campaign for the quaestorship. It was
then that you attempted to kill Publius Clodius in the forum before
the approving eyes of the Roman people.* Though you did this on
your own initiative, and not on my prompting, you nevertheless
declared that, as far as you were concerned, you would never make
adequate amends for the wrongs you had done me* unless you actually killed him. I am therefore astonished that you should now say
that it was at my prompting that Milo carried out that deed, since
when you offered me the same service on your own initiative I did
nothing to encourage you. In any case I preferred, should you per-
severe in your attempts, that the deed be put down to your credit
rather than to your desire to do me a favour.

[50] You were elected quaestor; then all of a sudden, without a
decree of the senate, without the lots being drawn, without any legal
justification, you ran off to Caesar.* In your view, once you had
squandered all you had to live on, that was the only place in the
world that could serve as a refuge for your poverty, debt, and profli-
gacy. But once you had stuffed yourself there with Caesar's largesse
and your own plunderings—if you can call it stuffing, when you
immediately throw up what you have just swallowed—you flew,
destitute, to the tribunate, intending to conduct yourself in that
magistracy, if at all possible, just as your husband had.*

Now please bear with me, gentlemen, while I tell you not of the
vile excesses he has perpetrated against his own self and the honour
of his family, but of the treacherous crimes he has committed against
us and our fortunes—that is to say, against the whole country. What
you will discover is that the root of all our troubles sprang from this
man's wickedness.

[51] On 1 January in the consulship of Lucius Lentulus and Gaius

Marcellus,* you were all anxious to shore up the state, tottering as it
was and threatening to collapse; and you were willing to pay due
consideration to Gaius Caesar himself, so long as he were of sound
mind. But then this man here used his tribunate, which he had sold
and made over to Caesar, to block your deliberations, and placed his
own neck beneath that axe* which has come down on many others for
lesser crimes. Against you, Marcus Antonius, the senate passed that
decree—a senate still intact, its leading lights not yet put out—that
decree which is customarily passed against a civilian enemy, according to the tradition of our ancestors. And have you dared to attack
me before the conscript fathers—this same order which judged that
I was the saviour of the state,* and you the enemy of the state?

For some time now, the matter of that crime of yours has not been
raised—but its memory is not erased. As long as the human race, as
long as the name of the Roman people shall endure—and that will be
for ever, if you allow it—so long will that pestilential veto of yours be
spoken of. [52] What self-interested action, what over-hasty decision
was being taken by the senate when you, a single youth,* prevented
that entire order from passing a decree on the national security, not
once but again and again, refusing all negotiation over the senate's
expressed wish? What was it trying to do except prevent you from
completely overturning and destroying the state? But neither the
requests of the leaders of our country, nor the warnings of your
elders, nor the representations of a packed senate could bring you to
alter a decision which you had put up for sale and knocked down to
the highest bidder. Then it was that, after many solutions had been
tried, there inevitably fell on you that stroke which fell on few before
you,* and from which none had escaped unscathed.* [53] Then it was
that the senate put weapons into the hands of the consuls and the
other holders of power, military and civil, for use against you—
weapons which you would never have escaped, had you not gone
over to those of Caesar.

It was you, yes, you, Marcus Antonius, who first gave Gaius Caesar,
desperate as he was to wreak havoc, an excuse to make war on his
country. After all, what else did he say, what other excuse did he give
for his demented intention and action than that the veto had been
disregarded, the tribunician prerogative abolished, and the freedom
of Antonius curtailed by the senate? I will not explain how specious,
how frivolous these excuses were, especially given that there can

never be any just cause whatsoever for a man's taking up arms against his country. But enough of Caesar: you surely must confess that the cause of that ruinous war was you and you alone. [54] How wretched you must be if you have grasped this! And more wretched still if you have not grasped that this is what is being recorded in history, this is what is being handed down to posterity, and this is what will be the recollection of every generation for the rest of time: that you were the sole cause of the consuls being driven out of Italy, and with them Gnaeus Pompeius, the shining glory of the empire of the Roman people, and every consular whose health allowed him to take part in that disastrous flight, the praetors, the praetorians, the tribunes of the plebs, a large part of the senate, the flower of our young manhood—in a word, the whole of the state driven out and banished from its home! [55] Just as seeds contain the origin of trees and plants, so you were the seed of this most lamentable war. Gentlemen, you grieve that three armies of the Roman people were slaughtered:* it was Antonius who slaughtered them! You mourn the loss of our most illustrious citizens: it was Antonius who robbed you of them! The authority of this order was expunged: it was Antonius who expunged it! And everything that we have seen happen since that time (indeed, what calamity have we not seen?), we shall, if we calculate correctly, attribute to Antonius alone. Just as Helen was to Troy, so was he to this city both the cause of war and the bringer of pestilence and death.

The rest of his tribunate resembled its beginning. He did everything that the senate, while the state was still intact, had made impossible. But let me tell you of a crime within a crime. [56] He restored many people who had been convicted—but never a word about his own uncle.* If he was being strict, then why not strict towards everyone? If merciful, then why not merciful towards his own family? To say nothing of all the others, he restored his gaming partner Licinius Lenticula,* who had been convicted for gambling— as if it were really the case that the man's conviction prevented him from gambling with him! No, the reason he restored him was so that he could pay off his own gambling debts by carrying a law in his friend's favour. But what explanation did you give the Roman people as to why he should be restored? It was, I imagine, that he had been prosecuted in his absence; that he had been convicted without a defence; that there had been no legally constituted court to try cases of gambling; that he had been a victim of armed violence; or that, as used to be said in your uncle's case, the jury had been bribed! No, it was none of these. But he was a good man and deserved to be a citizen. That is irrelevant; but since being convicted counts for nothing these days, I would pardon him myself if this were true. But when an utterly disreputable individual, the sort of person who would not hesitate to start gambling even in the forum, is properly convicted under the gambling law, doesn't the person who restores him reveal his own addiction in the most blatant manner possible?

[57] In this same tribunate, Caesar, on his departure for Spain, handed Italy over to this man here* for him to trample underfoot. Just think of his progress along the roads, his visitations of towns! I appreciate that I am dealing with matters that are extremely well known and much discussed, and that the events I am and will be talking about are more familiar to those who were in Italy at that time than to me who was not.* Nevertheless, I will pick out particular details, even though what I have to say cannot possibly equate to your first-hand knowledge. After all, was there ever, anywhere on earth, such scandal, such disgrace, and such dishonour? [58] A tribune of the plebs was conveyed in a gig. Lictors wreathed in laurel marched in front of him.* In their midst, an actress* was carried in an open litter; respectable people, coming from the country towns and having inevitably to meet her, addressed her not by her well-known stage name, but as 'Volumnia'. A coach-load of pimps took up the rear; and his mother, cast out, walked behind her filthy son's mistress as though that woman were her daughter-in-law. Poor mother, to have such disastrous offspring!* With the imprint of these scandals Antonius stamped on every town, prefecture, and colony, in fact on the whole of Italy.

[59] To criticize the rest of what he did, conscript fathers, is difficult and dangerous*. He took part in the war.* He drenched himself in the blood of citizens—better men than he. He met with good fortune—if there can be good fortune in crime. But since I am anxious not to upset the veterans—although their position is different from yours (they simply followed their leader, whereas you sought him out)—and do not want you to set them against me, I will say nothing about what sort of war it was.

From Thessaly you came back to Brundisium with the legions, victorious. And there you did not kill me.* What a huge favour! For I admit you could have done it, even though every single one of the people who were with you was in favour of my being spared. [60] So powerful is the love of one's country that even to your legions I was inviolable, because they remembered that the country had been saved by me. But let us allow that you granted me what you did not take away from me, and that I owe you my life because you did not deprive me of it: how could I go on acknowledging this favour of yours (as I used to do) once you had insulted me, especially since you were well aware that what you said would prompt this speech from me in return?

[61] You arrived at Brundisium, then, into the bosom and embrace of your little starlet. What's wrong? Am I not telling the truth? How distressing it is to be unable to deny what is so disgraceful to admit! If you felt no shame before the people from the country towns, what about the army veterans? Was there a single soldier at Brundisium who did not catch sight of her? A single soldier who was not aware that she had travelled for days on end to bring you her congratulations? A single soldier who was not sickened to discover so late in the day what a worthless man he had followed? [62] After that there was another trip through Italy, with the same actress in attendance. Soldiers were settled on the towns in an appallingly brutal fashion; and at Rome there was a hideous plundering of gold, silver, and especially—wine.

To crown all this, he was appointed—without Caesar's knowledge, since Caesar was then at Alexandria, but by the gift of Caesar's friends—Master of the Horse.* So he thought that gave him the right to live with Hippias, and place hired horses with Sergius the actor.* And he had chosen as his residence not the house which he is now only just holding on to, but that of Marcus Piso.* Why should I mention his decrees, his plunderings, and his seizure and bestowal of the estates of the dead? Poverty compelled him; he had nowhere to turn. He had not yet come into his enormous inheritance from Lucius Rubrius, or the one from Lucius Turselius;* and he had not yet succeeded to the fortunes of Gnaeus Pompeius and the many others who were not at Rome—an instant heir.* No, he had to live as brigands do, owning only what he had managed to rob.

[63] But let us pass over these examples of a sturdy wickedness, and talk instead of a lightweight kind of worthlessness. You with that gullet of yours, that chest, that gladiator's physique downed such a

quantity of wine at Hippias' wedding that you were forced to throw up in full view of the Roman people—the next day. What a disgusting sight—disgusting even to hear of! Had this happened to you at dinner, as you knocked back bottle after bottle, is there anyone who would not have thought it outrageous? But at a gathering of the Roman people, while conducting public business, as Master of the Horse, when a mere belch would have been shocking, he vomited, filling his lap and the whole platform with morsels of food stinking of wine! But he himself concedes that this was among his grosser achievements. Let us move on, then, to his greater ones.

[64] Caesar returned from Alexandria*—blessed by fortune, he reckoned; but to my way of thinking, no man can be fortunate who brings bad luck on his country. A spear was planted in front of the temple of Jupiter Stator,* and the property of Gnaeus Pompeius was subjected—I can hardly continue; I have no tears left, but the pain remains fixed in my heart—the property, I tell you, of Gnaeus Pompeius Magnus was subjected to the pitiless cry of an auctioneer. On that occasion, and on that occasion only, the country forgot its servitude and gasped: though their hearts were enslaved—since fear governed everything—the Roman people let out a gasp that was free. Everyone waited to see who could be so treacherous, so insane, so hostile to the gods and mankind as to dare to bid in that wicked auction. But no one came forward except Antonius—even though there were many others standing around that spear who would have stopped at nothing else: he alone came forward to dare the deed which all the other criminals had recoiled and shrunk from perpetrating.

[65] Were you so overcome by doziness, then—or, to be more accurate, by insanity—as to purchase confiscated property (a man of your birth!), and the property of Pompeius too, without appreciating that it makes you accursed in the eyes of the Roman people, an object of detestation, and the enemy of all the gods and all mankind now and for ever more? But how presumptuous was the way in which this spendthrift immediately threw himself on the property of the man whose valour caused the name of Rome to fill foreign peoples with terror, but whose fairness caused it to fill them with love!

So, drenching himself with the wealth of that great man, he danced for joy, like a character from a play, 'rags to riches'.* But, as some poet* has it: 'Ill gotten, ill spent.' [66] It is incredible and weird

how he squandered so much property in so few, I will not say
months, but days. There was a vast quantity of wine, an enormous
weight of the purest silver, valuable textiles, and a large store of
elegant and beautiful furniture from numerous houses—the belong-
ings not of a sybarite, but of a man of ample means. Within a
few days, it had all gone. [67] What Charybdis* was ever so all-
consuming? Charybdis did I say? If that ever existed, it was only a
single creature. I call heaven to witness that Ocean itself could
scarcely have swallowed up so many things, so widely dispersed in
places so far apart, in so short a time. Nothing was secured, nothing
was kept under seal, nothing was catalogued. Whole cellars were
given away to the most worthless individuals. Actors came and took
what they liked, as did actresses. The house was packed with gam-
blers, filled with drunks. Drinking went on for days on end, all over
the place. Often, too—for he is not always lucky—gambling losses
piled up; and in the slaves' cubicles you could see beds made up with
the purple bedspreads of Gnaeus Pompeius. So stop being surprised
at how quickly this property was used up. Such prodigality could
quickly have devoured not just one man's patrimony,* however rich it
was—and this was rich—but entire cities and kingdoms.

But the house itself and the property outside the city—[68]
monstrous effrontery! Did you dare to enter that house, did you dare
to cross its hallowed threshold, did you dare to show your revolting
face before its household gods? For a long time no one could set eyes
on that house, no one could pass it without weeping: are you not
ashamed to have been a lodger in it all this time? After all, in spite of
your own ignorance, there is nothing in it that can give you any
pleasure. Or when you see those naval trophies* in the forecourt, do
you suppose it is your own house that you are entering? That is
impossible. You may be without sense or feeling—indeed, you are—
but you do at least recognize yourself, your own things, your own
people. In fact, I do not believe that you can ever have a moment's
peace, awake or asleep. You may be crazed and violent—you are—
but whenever you see a vision of that unique man, you must inevitably start in terror from your sleep, and often be driven insane when
awake.

[69] For my part, I pity the very walls and roof. For what had that
house ever witnessed that was not decorous, what that was not in the
best traditions and displaying the highest moral standards? As you

are well aware, conscript fathers, that great man was as respected at home as he was famous abroad, nor did he merit higher praise for his foreign victories than he did for his domestic conduct. Yet in his house the bedrooms have now been turned into knocking-shops, and the dining rooms into greasy spoons. But Antonius these days denies it. Don't ask: he's turned frugal! He has told that woman of his to pack her bags and go, has taken away her keys as the Twelve Tables prescribe,* and has put her out into the street. What an upright citizen, what a worthy man! In the whole of his life, the most honourable thing he has ever done is to have divorced an actress!

[70] But how he keeps going on about 'both consul and Antonius'!* He might as well have said, 'both consul and libertine', or 'both consul and wastrel'. For does 'Antonius' signify anything else? If the name carried any prestige, your grandfather* would, I imagine, have referred to himself at some time or other as 'both consul and Antonius'. But he never did. My colleague, your uncle,* would have done so too—unless of course there is no Antonius but yourself!

I leave out those misdemeanours which do not relate to the part you played in attacking the country, and return instead to your own particular role—that is, to the Civil War, whose birth, formation, and nurturing were entirely your own doing.

[71] At this point* you took no part in that war, being too cowardly—and also too lustful. You had already tasted the blood of your fellow-citizens, or rather drunk deeply of it: you had fought at Pharsalus. At the head of your squad, you had killed the high-ranking and illustrious Lucius Domitius;* and you had also tracked down and brutally murdered many other fugitives from that battle whom Caesar would very possibly have spared, as he did others. After such heroic deeds as these, how was it that you did not go with Caesar to Africa, especially with so much of the war still to be fought? And how did you stand with him after his return from Africa?* How did he rate you? You had been quaestor* to him as general, Master of the Horse* to him as dictator, the originator of his war, the instigator of his cruelty, a sharer in his booty, and under the terms of his will, as you yourself used to claim, his son;* and he called on you to pay him the money you owed for the house, the suburban property, and everything that you had bought at auction.

[72] Your initial response was one of defiance. I do not want to be criticizing you in everything, so let me say that it was fair and

reasonable enough. 'Why does Gaius Caesar demand money from me? Why not I from him? Or did he win without my help? He couldn't have done. I gave him his pretext for the Civil War; I proposed pernicious legislation; I took up arms against the consuls and commanders of the Roman people, against the senate and people of Rome, against our country's gods, altars, and hearths, and against our country itself. Surely it wasn't only for his own benefit that he won? Shouldn't those who shared in the crime have a share in the spoils as well?' You were justified in asking this—but what did justice have to do with it? He was the more powerful.

[73] So your protests were brushed aside, and Caesar sent soldiers to you and your sureties. Then all of a sudden you produced that famous list. How people laughed, that in such a long list, consisting of so many properties of every kind, there was in fact nothing, except a share in that place at Misenum,* that the vendor could call his own! The auction itself was a sorry spectacle: draperies of Pompeius', several only, soiled; some silver items, also Pompeius', damaged; some filthy slaves. It made us upset that there was anything still left for us to see.

[74] However, the heirs of Lucius Rubrius,* backed by a decree from Caesar, stopped the sale from taking place. Our prodigal was stuck: he did not know where to turn. Indeed, it was at that time that an assassin sent by Antonius was allegedly arrested at Caesar's house with a dagger; and Caesar, openly attacking you, complained about it in the senate.* Then he set out for Spain,* after giving you, in view of your poverty, a few extra days to pay up. But not even then did you follow him. So fine a gladiator, and yet so quick to take your discharge? Who, then, would be afraid of this man so hesitant in standing up for his own faction—that is, for his own self-interest?*

[75] He did eventually set out for Spain; but he could not, he says, reach it in safety. So how did Dolabella* manage to get there? You should either not have joined Caesar's side, Antonius, or, once you had joined it, you should have followed it to the end. Three times Caesar fought against citizens, in Thessaly, Africa, and Spain.* In all those battles, Dolabella was at his side; and in the one in Spain he even sustained a wound. If you ask my opinion, I wish he had not taken part; but although we should fault his decision, his consistency at least was commendable. But what about you? The children of Gnaeus Pompeius were attempting in the first place to recover their

country. Very well, then; let us agree that this concerned the whole of your party equally. But they were also attempting to recover their own ancestral gods, altars, hearths, and family home—and it was *you* who had taken those. Now when they were resorting to arms to recover what was legally theirs, who had the best justification (though, in an unjustifiable situation, what justification can there be?) for fighting against the children of Gnaeus Pompeius? Who? You, of course, who had acquired their property. [76] Or was Dolabella battling on your behalf in Spain just so you could remain at Narbo* and vomit up the food your host there put in front of you?

But what a homecoming from Narbo—and he even asked why I had returned so suddenly from the journey *I* had undertaken!* I explained the other day, conscript fathers, why it was that I came back: I wanted, if possible, to be of service to the state even before 1 January. As to your enquiry about the manner of my return, first of all it was in daylight, not under cover of dark; then it was in boots and a toga, not in slippers* and a shawl. I can see you staring at me, and I can tell you are seething. But I am sure you would be friends with me again if you appreciated the shame I feel at your behaviour—although you yourself feel no shame at it. Of all the most outrageous crimes, I have never seen or heard anything more disgraceful. Though you supposed yourself to have been Master of the Horse,* though you were standing for the consulship (or rather asking Caesar for it) for the following year, nevertheless you raced through the towns and colonies of Gaul, the region where we used to campaign for the consulship in the days when that office was stood for and not asked for, in slippers and a shawl!

[77] But consider the frivolity of the man. When he reached Saxa Rubra* between three and four in the afternoon, he went into hiding in a grotty pub and lay low there getting drunk until it was dark. Then he got into a gig and sped on his way to Rome, his face muffled, and arrived at his own house. The doorman: 'Who is it?' 'A courier from Marcus.' He was taken immediately to the woman he had come to see,* and handed her a letter. While she read it, weeping—for it was written in the language of a lover (the gist of it was that he was going to have nothing further to do with that actress of his, and that he had abandoned his passion for her and made it all over to her instead)—while she was weeping copiously, the poor man could bear it no longer: he revealed his face, and threw his arms

around her. What a worthless individual! What else can I call him? I cannot think of a better description. Was it, then, so that your wife could get a surprise when she saw you, her pretty boy, when you unexpectedly revealed yourself, that you subjected Rome to a night alarm, and Italy to many days of uneasiness?* [78] Your reason within your home was one of love; but outside it your reason was even more discreditable—to prevent Lucius Plancus* selling up your sureties. And when a tribune of the plebs brought you before a public meeting and you replied that you had come on your own 'private affairs', you gave rise to all sorts of jokes at your own expense.* But that's too much about these trifles: let us pass on to more serious matters.

When Gaius Caesar came back from Spain,* you went further than anyone else to meet him. You travelled back the way you had come, to make sure that he should recognize, if not your courage, then at least your energy. Somehow or other you were readmitted to his friendship. This was how Caesar operated: if a man were utterly ruined by debt and poverty, and he recognized that he was a worthless but impulsive character, then he was quite happy to have him as one of his friends. [79] Since your own qualifications in this respect were unimpeachable, orders were given for you to be elected consul*—and as Caesar's colleague. I make no complaint about Dolabella, who was encouraged, brought forward, and then frustrated. Is there anyone who is unaware of the treachery of both of you towards Dolabella in this matter? Caesar induced him to stand and then, when he had promised him the office and guaranteed it, intervened and transferred it to himself; and you then attributed to Caesar's treachery what had in fact been your own wish all along.

The first of January arrived. We were summoned to a meeting of the senate; and Dolabella made a much fuller and better prepared attack on Antonius than I am doing now.* [80] But by the gods, what a reply he goaded Antonius into making! In the first place, although Caesar had made it quite clear that he would order Dolabella's election as consul before he himself left Rome* (he was always saying and doing things of this sort, and yet people still maintain he was not a king!)—although Caesar had said this, our fine augur here* announced that he had been elected to that priesthood so that he could use the auspices either to block or to invalidate elections, and that was what in this case he proposed to do.

In the first place, observe the astonishing stupidity of the man.

[81] How so? The action which you said you could take by virtue of being a priest—would you have been any less able to take it if you had not been augur, but *had* been consul? You could in fact have taken it even more easily. For we augurs only have the right to report omens which have actually occurred, whereas the consuls and other magistrates can watch for ones that have not. All right, then: he didn't know what he was talking about. After all, it is no use demanding professional knowledge from a man who is never sober! But consider his impudence: many months before this,* he announced in the senate that he would either use the auspices to forbid Dolabella's election or do what in the event he did.* Can anyone tell in advance what is going to be wrong with the auspices unless he has decided to watch the heavens? But that is illegal at an election; and if anyone has been watching the heavens, he has to report the fact before the elections are held, not once they have begun. But this is impudence intermingled with ignorance: he no more knows what an augur ought to know than he acts as a decent man should.

[82] Now recall his consulship from 1 January down to 15 March. Was any flunkey ever so subservient, so grovelling? He could do nothing on his own initiative; he asked permission for everything; sticking his head into the back of his colleague's litter,* he would ask him for favours that he could then go on to sell.

The day of Dolabella's election then came round. Lots were drawn to determine which century should be the first to vote:* Antonius held his peace. The result was announced:* Antonius said not a word. The first class was called; the result was announced. Then, as always happens, the six centuries of equestrians; then the second class; and all this was done faster than I can describe it. [83] After the business had been completed, our fine augur (you could call him Gaius Laelius!)* announced: 'Adjourned'. What unparalleled impudence! What had you seen? What had you felt? What had you heard? For you did not say at the time, nor do you say now, that you had been watching the heavens. So the religious objection which you had already foreseen on 1 January and foretold so far in advance duly came to pass! Therefore, by Hercules, I hope that your fabrication of the auspices will not bring catastrophe on the state, but on you instead! You implicated the Roman people in your religious crime. As augur you obstructed an augur; as consul you obstructed a consul.*

I do not wish to say any more, in case I appear to be subverting Dolabella's consular acts, which will have at some point to be referred to our college.* [84] But observe the arrogance and insolence of the man. So long as *you* wish, Dolabella's election is invalid; but the moment your wishes change, the auspices were in order.* If it means nothing when an augur makes an announcement in the words that you used, then admit that, when you used the word 'adjourned', you were drunk. But if that word does have force, then please tell me, augur to augur, what it is.

But I don't want my speech to skip over the single most glorious of all the many exploits of Marcus Antonius; so let me come to the Lupercalia.* He is not acting the innocent, conscript fathers: he looks embarrassed, and is sweating and pale. But he can do as he pleases— so long as he does not do what he did at the Porticus Minucia!* What can one say in defence of such disgraceful behaviour? I look forward to hearing, because I want to see the point at which the plain of Leontini comes into view.*

[85] Your colleague* was sitting on the rostra, dressed in a purple toga, seated on a golden chair, a wreath upon his head. You climbed the steps, you approached the chair, a Lupercus (you were indeed a Lupercus—but you should have remembered that you were also a consul)*—and you held out a diadem. Throughout the forum, there was an audible gasp. Where had you got the diadem from? You hadn't just found it on the ground and picked it up: you had brought it with you—a deliberate, premeditated crime. You kept on trying to place the diadem on Caesar's head, as the people shouted their dis- approval; he kept on rejecting it, to the people's applause. So, you criminal, you were revealed as the one and only person who, as well as setting up a tyranny and wanting to have your colleague as your master, were in addition putting the Roman people to the test to see what they would tolerate and endure.

[86] But you even made a play for sympathy: you threw yourself as a suppliant at his feet. What were you begging for? To be a slave? You should have requested that role for yourself alone, you whose manner of living since your early years showed that you would sub- mit to anything, would happily accept servitude.* You certainly had no right to make the request on our behalf, or on that of the Roman people. What magnificent eloquence you displayed—when you addressed a public meeting in the nude! What could be more

disgraceful than this, what more disgusting, what more deserving of every kind of punishment? Surely you are not waiting for us to jab you with cattle-prods?* If you have any human feeling at all, my words must tear you, must make you bleed. I am afraid that what I am about to say may detract from the glory of our greatest heroes,* but I am carried away by the grief I feel: what is more unseemly than that the man who offered the diadem should live, while the man who rejected it should by common consent have been justly killed?

[87] But he* also ordered the following entry to be added to the calendar, under 'Lupercalia': 'To Gaius Caesar, dictator for life,* the consul Marcus Antonius offered the title of King by order of the people;* Caesar declined it.' But now, now, I am not in the least surprised that you disrupt the peace; that you detest not merely the city, but even the light of day; and that you spend not just all day but every day drinking in the company of the worst of brigands. After all, in peacetime, where can you go? What place can there be for you amid those very laws and courts which you tried your utmost to abolish by means of a king's tyranny? Was it for this that Lucius Tarquinius was driven out, was it for this that Spurius Cassius, Spurius Maelius, and Marcus Manlius* were killed—so that, many centuries later, against the will of the gods, a king should be installed at Rome by Marcus Antonius?

[88] But let us go back to the auspices, the matter Caesar was on the point of raising in the senate on 15 March. Tell me: what would you have done then? My information was that you had come prepared, thinking that I was going to speak about the auspices you had fabricated, but which nevertheless had to be heeded. The good fortune of the country put an end to that day's debate. But surely Caesar's assassination did not also put an end to your view on the auspices?* However, I have now reached a point where more important matters arise than those I have begun to discuss.

What an escape you made on that glorious day, what terror you showed, and what little confidence you had that your own life would be spared, so conscious were you of your crimes! But after you had fled the scene, you secretly took refuge at your own house, thanks to the kindness of people who wanted you kept safe—if, that is, you proved to be of sound mind. [89] How accurate have my prophecies always been, yet how little believed! I spoke on the Capitol to the heroes who had liberated us. They wanted me to go to you and urge you to defend the country; but I told them that as long as you were afraid, you would promise anything they asked, but as soon as you had stopped being afraid, you would revert to your old self. So while the other consulars were going back and forth, I held to my opinion. I did not see you on that day or the next;* nor did I believe that there was any chance of making any pact which would unite the finest Roman citizens with a relentless public enemy.

Two days later I came into the temple of Tellus,* reluctantly, since armed guards had been stationed at all the entrances. [90] What a day that was for you, Antonius! Although you have suddenly become my enemy, I pity you for the damage you have done to yourself. Immortal gods, how truly great a man you would have been if you could only have maintained the stance you took on that day! We would have peace, peace made through a hostage, a boy of noble birth—the grandson of Marcus Bambalio!* Although fear was turning you into a good citizen, fear is only in the short term a teacher of duty; and that unscrupulousness of yours, which never deserts you so long as you are not afraid, has turned you into a scoundrel.

And yet at that time, when many people (but not I) thought very well of you, you behaved in an utterly criminal fashion in the way you presided over the tyrant's funeral—if funeral is what it was.* [91] Yours was that touching laudation, yours was that appeal to pity, yours was that call to action. It was you, yes, you, who lit those firebrands, both the ones with which Caesar was half-burnt and those with which the house of Lucius Bellienus* was set on fire and destroyed. It was you who launched those attacks on our houses— from criminals and, particularly, slaves—which we repelled by force of arms. Yet it was also you who, wiping the soot from yourself as it were, spent the other days on the Capitol carrying excellent decrees of the senate to the effect that no tablet granting exemption* after 15 March, or any grant, should be posted. You remember yourself what you said about exiles, and you know what you said about exemptions. But best of all was that you removed the title 'dictator' from the constitution for all time: by this action it looked as if you had conceived such a hatred of tyranny that you wanted to remove all fear of it.

[92] Some people believed that the state had been re-established, but I did not think so for a moment: with you at the helm, I was afraid of shipwreck. And I wasn't wrong, was I? That he couldn't be

false to his nature for long? Before your very eyes, gentlemen, notices were posted all over the Capitol. Exemptions were sold not only to individuals, but to whole communities.* Citizenship was no longer given out on an individual basis, but to entire provinces.* If these measures are allowed to stand—and they cannot do so without the state falling—then you have lost whole provinces, conscript fathers, and not merely the revenues but the empire of the Roman people will have been reduced by Antonius' private market.

[93b] There are countless concessions which have been bought from persons close to you,* and not without your knowledge. One stands out, however: the decree which was posted on the Capitol regarding King Deiotarus,* the loyal friend of the Roman people. When it was put up, although people were scandalized, no one could help laughing. [94] After all, did anyone ever show anyone else greater ill will than Caesar did Deiotarus? He showed him the same ill will that he showed to this order, to the equestrian order, to the people of Massilia,* and to anyone he felt loved the Roman nation and its people. And so, while from the living man King Deiotarus never obtained any justice or favour whether he was in Caesar's presence or far away, when the man was dead he got exactly what he wanted. Caesar, while in the king's presence and enjoying his hospitality,* rebuked him, made financial demands of him, assigned a part of his kingdom to a Greek he had brought with him,* and deprived him of Armenia, a country that had been bestowed upon him by the senate. All this when alive Caesar took away, but when dead he restored. [95] And in what terms! Sometimes it was 'he thought it reasonable', sometimes 'not unreasonable'. What an astonishing turn of phrase! After all, whenever we asked him for anything on Deiotarus' behalf (and it was always me who spoke for him in his absence), Caesar never once said that he thought the request 'reasonable'.

A bond for ten million sesterces was signed by the king's agents, dependable men but timid and inexperienced, without my advice or that of the king's other friends here, in the women's quarters*—a place where many things have been and are being sold. I advise you to consider seriously what action you propose to take on the strength of that bond: after all, the king, on his own initiative and without your help, and relying on no notebooks of Caesar's, recovered what belonged to him through his own military action the instant he heard that Caesar had been assassinated. [96] In his wisdom he knew that, whenever a tyrant is killed, it has always been the rule that those who have had their property taken from them by the tyrant get it back again.* Consequently, no lawyer—not even that person* whom you are alone in thinking a lawyer, who is arranging these matters on your behalf—will say that payment is due on that bond for property which had been recovered before the bond was signed. Deiotarus did not buy from you: he took possession himself before you could sell him what belonged to him anyway. He acted like a man. We, on the other hand, deserve contempt, because we hate the author but defend his acts.*

[93a] Where are the seven hundred million sesterces which appear in the accounts at the temple of Ops?* This is money with a sad provenance,* it is true; but if it is not to be returned to its original owners, it could be used to save us from having to pay tribute.* But you, Antonius, were forty million sesterces in debt on 15 March. How was it, then, that you managed to become solvent again by 1 April?

[97] And what am I to say regarding the endless notebooks, the countless memoranda?* There are actually vendors who sell them openly like programmes for the games! The mountains of coin at Antonius' house are piling up so high that the money can no longer be counted: it has to be weighed. But how blind is avarice! A notice has recently been posted exempting the extremely wealthy communities of Crete from paying tax, and it is decreed that, when Marcus Brutus' term as governor* comes to an end, Crete shall cease to be a province. Are you in your right mind? Should you not be in a straitjacket? Was it really possible that a decree of Caesar's could state that Crete should be made independent after the departure of Marcus Brutus when during Caesar's lifetime Brutus had nothing whatsoever to do with Crete? And do not imagine that nothing of significance has occurred, gentlemen: by the sale of this decree, you have lost the province of Crete. To cut a long story short, no transaction has taken place anywhere that has not involved this man here as the seller.

[98] And was it Caesar who carried the law you posted regarding exiles?* I am not seeking to make anyone's situation worse: I am simply making the point that, first, it is insulting to those whom Caesar did recall that they and the other exiles should be tarred with the same brush; and, second, I do not know why you did not do the

same for all the other exiles, since there are now no more than three or four who have not been recalled. They have all suffered equal misfortune—so why are you not being equally merciful to all of them? Why are you treating them the way you treated your uncle?* When you carried your law to recall the others, you were not prepared to include him—and you even made him stand for the censorship,* and set him on a campaign which invited ridicule and hostile criticism. [99] And why have you not held that election? Is it because a tribune of the plebs kept reporting thunder on the left?* When your own interest is involved, the auspices do not count; but when it is a matter of your relatives' interests, you suddenly become scrupulous. And didn't you also leave him in the lurch over the Board of Seven?* Someone else came along—and you were afraid, no doubt, that if you said no to that person your life would be in jeopardy!* In fact, you loaded every kind of humiliation on the man whom, if you had any family feeling, you ought to have treated as your surrogate father.* His daughter, your cousin,* you threw out of your house, after you had sought out and inspected another match. Nor is that all: you accused her, a lady of the highest virtue, of sexual misconduct. How much further could you go? And yet you did not stop there: at a packed meeting of the senate on 1 January, with your uncle sitting in his place, you had the audacity to declare that the reason you hated Dolabella was that you had discovered that he had made sexual advances towards your cousin and wife. Is there anyone who can decide whether it was more shameful of you to make such a filthy, outrageous allegation in the senate, wicked of you to make it against Dolabella,* vile of you to make it in the presence of the lady's father, or cruel of you to make it against that ill-treated lady?

[100] But let us get back to the memoranda. Did you ever formally review them? Caesar's acts were approved by the senate for the sake of peace—Caesar's genuine acts, that is, not those claimed as Caesar's by Antonius. Where do these latter spring from? On whose authority are they produced? If they are forgeries, why are they approved? If genuine, why are they sold? The senate decreed that from 1 June you and Dolabella, together with an advisory commission, should review Caesar's acts. What was this commission? Did you ever invite anyone to sit on it?* Which 1 June have you been waiting for? Was it really the 1 June for which you returned from your tour of the veterans' colonies* with an armed escort?

What a glorious trip that was that you made in April and May, when you even attempted to found a colony at Capua!* How you left that place, or rather nearly didn't leave it, everyone knows. [101] That is the city you keep threatening to attack. I wish you would try it—then I could at last leave out the 'nearly'! But what a stately progress you made! Why should I draw attention to your elaborate lunches, your wild drinking? That was your loss—but this is ours: the Campanian land, which when it was taken out of the revenues in order to be given to the soldiers* we thought left a gaping wound in the state, you set about dividing up among your lunch companions and gaming partners. I tell you that actors and actresses, conscript fathers, have been settled on the Campanian land. And after that, what is the point of protesting about the plain of Leontini? These arable lands in Campania and at Leontini used to be considered a fertile and productive part of the inheritance of the Roman people. To his doctor he gave three thousand *iugera*: how many would you have given him if he had made you sane? To his rhetorician,* two thousand: how many if he could have made you eloquent?

But let us return to his tour of Italy. [102] You founded a colony at Casilinum,* where Caesar had founded one previously. You wrote to me asking my opinion*—about Capua, it is true, but I would have given the same answer regarding Casilinum: could you legally found a new colony where there was one already existing? I replied that a new colony could not be founded legally where there already existed a colony that was duly auspicated and still functioning, but that it was possible to add new colonists to an existing foundation. But you, swept away by your own insolence, drove a coach and horses through the auspical law and founded a colony at Casilinum—a place which had already been made a colony only a few years before—raising a standard and marking out the boundaries with a plough. Indeed, with that ploughshare you just about grazed the city gate of Capua, so as to reduce the territory of that prosperous colony.

[103] Having thus turned our religious law on its head, you then proceeded to Casinum and descended on the estate of Marcus Varro,* a profoundly honourable and decent gentleman. By what right, what prerogative? 'The same,' you will say, 'as when I appropriated the estates of Lucius Rubrius' heirs, and of Lucius Turselius' heirs,* and countless other properties.' Now if you bought those estates at public auction, let the sale stand, and let the accounts stand—but they

should be Caesar's accounts, not yours, and they should record your debts, not your escape from those debts. But as for *Varro*'s estate at Casinum, who says it was sold? Who saw the spear in the ground?* Who heard the cry of the auctioneer? You claim you sent someone to Alexandria to buy it from Caesar: it was too much to expect, no doubt, that you should wait for Caesar's return.

[104] But who ever heard (and there were more people concerned for him than for anyone else) that *any* of Varro's property had been confiscated? And if it should turn out that Caesar had actually written to you ordering you to give the estate back, what words could do justice to your unparalleled impudence? Take away those swords over there, just for a moment: you will then understand that an auction of Caesar's is one thing, your brazen self-assurance another. For it is not only the master who will drive you away from that residence, but any one of his friends, neighbours, guests, or staff.

How many days you carried on your disgraceful orgies in that villa! From nine o'clock in the morning there was drinking, gambling, vomiting. Unhappy house, 'how different a master'*—although how was Antonius its master? How different an occupant, then! Marcus Varro kept that house as a retreat for study, not as a den of vice. [105] Think of the things that used to be discussed, contemplated, and written down in that villa in former times: the laws of the Roman people, the records of our ancestors,* every branch of philosophy and human knowledge. But while you squatted there (you were not its master), the whole place echoed with the shouts of drunken men, the paved floors were swimming in wine, the walls were soaking, free-born boys consorted with prostitutes, and whores with ladies of rank. People came from Casinum, Aquinum, and Interamna* to pay their respects; none was admitted. That at least was correct: after all, the insignia of rank were becoming tarnished in the hands of so shameful a person.

[106] When he had left there for Rome and was nearing Aquinum, he was approached (since Aquinum is a big place) by a pretty large crowd. But he was carried in a closed litter through the town, just like a corpse. It was stupid of the people of Aquinum to bother coming, but at least they lived on the main road. What about the people of Anagnia?* They lived off the road, but they still came down to pay their respects just as though he were a consul.* It is impossible to believe, but everyone agrees that he returned no one's greeting,

even though he had two men from Anagnia with him, Mustela and Laco,* one of whom is a master swordsman and the other a master drinker. [107] Why should I remind you of the threats and insults with which he attacked the Sidicini and bullied the people of Puteoli,* because they had chosen Gaius Cassius and the Bruti* as their patrons? And they had done so with great enthusiasm, wisdom, goodwill, and affection, and not as a result of armed force as was the case with you and Basilus* and similar types whom nobody would want as their clients, let alone as their patrons.

In the meantime, while you were away, what a glorious day your colleague had when he demolished that tomb* in the forum which you used to venerate! When the news was reported to you, as those who were with you at the time all agree, you collapsed. What happened afterwards I do not know; I suppose fear and force must have prevailed.* At any rate you dragged your colleague down from his pinnacle and made him—not like you, even now—but certainly unlike his former self.

[108] Then there was your return to Rome: what utter panic it caused throughout the city! We remembered the excessive power of Cinna, then the despotism of Sulla, and latterly we had seen the monarchy of Caesar.* If they had used swords, they had not used many of them, and they had kept them out of sight. But look at this great barbarian* entourage of yours! They follow you with drawn swords in marching order; and we see litters being carried full of shields. This has been going on for some time now, conscript fathers: we have become hardened to it.

On 1 June, when we wanted to enter the senate as arranged, we suddenly took fright and fled in terror. [109] But he, having no need of the senate, did not miss anyone's absence; on the contrary, he was delighted that we had all gone, and immediately set about doing those wonderful deeds of his. Although he had defended Caesar's memoranda for his own profit, he now overturned the laws of Caesar's that were good, because he wanted to undermine the state. He extended the tenure of provincial governorships;* then again, although he ought to have defended Caesar's acts, he actually rescinded them in matters both public and private. In public matters, nothing is more serious than a law; in private matters, nothing is more secure than a will. Regarding laws, he annulled some without giving the proper notice; and he gave notice of his intention to annul others. A will he made null and void,* though the wills of even the humblest citizens have always been upheld. The statues and paintings which, together with his gardens, Caesar bequeathed to the Roman people, Antonius had carted off, some to Pompeius' house outside the city and some to Scipio's villa.*

[110] And are you devoted to Caesar's memory? Do you love him in his grave? Did he obtain any greater honour than to be granted a couch, a sacred image, a pediment on his house, a priest?* So the deified Julius, like Jupiter, like Mars, like Quirinus, has his priest— Marcus Antonius! What are you waiting for, then? Why have you not been inaugurated? Pick a date. Choose someone to inaugurate you. We are your colleagues:* no one will turn you down! But what a revolting creature you are, whether as the priest of a tyrant or of a corpse!

Next, I would like to ask you if you have forgotten what day it is today. Don't you know that yesterday was the fourth day of the Roman Games in the circus?* And that you yourself carried a law in the assembly stipulating that a fifth day should be added in Caesar's honour? Why, then, are we not in holiday attire? Why are we allowing the honour granted to Caesar by your law to be disregarded? Can you have allowed, by your addition of a day, the thanksgivings to the gods to be polluted, and yet have been unwilling to see their couches similarly polluted?* Either get rid of religion altogether or preserve it in every particular!

[111] You ask whether I approve of the couch, the pediment on his house, the priest. I do not approve of them for a moment; but can you, who defend Caesar's acts, explain why you defend some of them, but disregard others? Of course, you may prefer simply to admit that you weigh up everything not according to Caesar's honour, but according to your own profit.

So how are you going to reply? I am waiting to hear your eloquence. I knew your grandfather* to be a fine speaker, but you have a still more open manner of speaking. After all, he never addressed a public meeting in the nude,* whereas you, simple creature that you are, unburdened yourself before our very eyes! Are you going to reply to me? Are you going to dare open your mouth at all? Are you going to find a single point from this very lengthy speech of mine that you feel confident enough to answer?

[112] But all those matters are in the past: let us leave them aside. This one day, this single day, today, this moment of time at which

I am speaking: defend it, if you can. Why is the senate encircled by a ring of armed men? Why are your henchmen listening to me sword in hand? Why are the doors of the temple of Concord not standing open?* Why are you bringing the most barbarian of peoples, Ituraeans, into the forum armed with bows and arrows? He says it is for his own protection. But surely it is preferable to die a thousand times over than to be unable to live in one's own country without an armed guard? And believe me, an armed guard is no protection: you would do better to be surrounded by the love and support of your fellow-citizens than by arms. [113] The Roman people will snatch those arms and wrest them from your grasp. I only hope we do not perish in the attempt!

But whatever you do to us, so long as you pursue your present policies, believe me, you cannot last long. For too long now has that most ungrasping of women, your wife—I mean no disrespect—owed her third instalment* to the Roman people. The Roman people have men* to whom they can entrust the helm of the state: wherever in the world they are, there is the entire defence of the state—or, rather, there *is* the state, which so far has only avenged itself, not restored itself. The state certainly has young men* of the highest rank ready to fight in its defence. Let them stay away as long as they wish, in the interests of peace: the state will call them back. Even the name of peace is sweet, and peace itself is a blessing; but there is all the difference in the world between peace and servitude. Peace is the quiet enjoyment of freedom, whereas servitude is the greatest of all evils, something to be resisted not just with war, but even with death.

[114] But if those liberators of ours have removed themselves from our sight, they have at least left behind the example of what they have done. They have done what no one ever did before. Brutus made war on Tarquinius,* who was king in the days when kings were permitted at Rome. Spurius Cassius, Spurius Maelius, and Marcus Manlius were all killed because they were suspected of having regal aspirations. But these men were the first to take up swords not against an aspirant to regal power, but against a ruling king. And just as their action is splendid and godlike on its own, so it is available for imitation—especially as they thereby acquired a glory which heaven itself seems scarcely able to contain. For though the awareness of having done so noble a deed was sufficient reward in itself, even so I do not think that mortals have the right to despise immortality.

[115] Therefore remember, Marcus Antonius, the day on which you abolished the dictatorship.\* Place before your eyes the joy of the senate and people of Rome. Now compare that with this marketing conducted by you and persons close to you,\* and you will appreciate what a gulf lies between profit and praise. But just as people who suffer from the numbness of sensation brought on by a disease are incapable of tasting food, so, I am sure, the lustful, the greedy, and the criminal cannot savour real praise. All right, then: if the prospect of praise cannot induce you to do right, cannot even fear call you away from your filthy actions? You are not afraid of the courts. If that is because you are innocent, then I approve. But if it is because you rely on violence, then you evidently do not appreciate that a person like that who has no fear of the courts has something else that he ought to be afraid of.\* [116] And if you are not afraid of brave men and loyal citizens because they are kept from you by force of arms, then, believe me, your own supporters will not tolerate you for long.\*

And what sort of a life is it to live in fear, day and night, of one's own supporters? Unless, of course, you have bound yours to you by acts of greater generosity than Caesar did in the case of certain of his assassins who were *his* supporters—if, that is, you can be compared to that man in any way at all! He had innate ability, strategic skill, a good memory, literary talent, a painstaking nature, an intelligent mind, and a capacity for hard work. His achievements in war, though catastrophic for Rome, were nevertheless great. Having aimed at monarchy for many years, he undertook great labours and ran great risks, and so achieved his goal. He won over the ignorant masses with shows, building projects, largesses, and banquets. His followers he bound to him by rewards, his opponents by an apparent clemency. In short, he succeeded in bringing a free country, partly because of its fear, partly because of its passivity, to an acceptance of servitude. [117] You I can compare to him only in lust for power; in all other respects you do not bear comparison with him.

But out of the many evils which Caesar inflicted on our country, there has come one good thing: the Roman people have now learned how far they can trust each person, whom they can rely on, and whom they should beware of. Do you not reflect on this—and realize that for brave men it is enough to have learned how noble in the act, how popular in the benefit it confers, and how glorious in the fame it brings is the assassination of a tyrant? Or do you imagine that, when people could not endure Caesar, they will put up with you? [118] Mark my words, from now on it will be a race to carry out the task: the lack of an opportunity will be no reason for delay.

Look back, I ask you, Marcus Antonius, look back at last on your country. Think of the people from whom you are sprung, not of those with whom you live. With me, do as you will: only make your peace with your country. But that is for you; I shall speak for myself. I defended this country when I was a young man: I shall not desert it now that I am old. I faced down the swords of Catiline: I shall not flinch before yours. Yes, and I would willingly offer my body, if the freedom of this country could at once be secured by my death, and the suffering of the Roman people at last be delivered of that with which it has so long been pregnant. [119] If nearly twenty years ago in this very temple I declared that death could not be untimely for a man who had reached the consulship,* with how much more truth could I now say 'for an old man'? In fact, for me, conscript fathers, death is actually desirable now that I have discharged the responsibilities of the offices I attained and completed the tasks I undertook. Two things alone I long for: first, that when I die I may leave the Roman people free—the immortal gods could bestow on me no greater blessing; and second, that each person's fate may reflect the way he has behaved towards his country.

# EXPLANATORY NOTES

Notes are cued to section numbers in the text. For recurring terms see the Glossary.

## IN VERREM I

1 *your order*: the senatorial order.

2 *Gaius Verres*: Cicero's custom in his speeches is to refer to his enemy by name as infrequently as possible, unless for special effect; normally expressions such as 'that man' (*iste*) are preferred. In this speech, Verres is referred to by name only nine times. I have tried to retain something of this reticence in the translation, though it has often been necessary to name Verres where Cicero does not (I do so nineteen times). Here Cicero does name Verres, for effect.

*which we both share*: since Cicero was a senator too.

*an embezzler . . . city jurisdiction*: Verres served under Gnaeus Papirius Carbo in Cisalpine Gaul in 83, but stole his military treasury and deserted him for Sulla; he plundered Asia and Pamphylia (part of the province of Cilicia) while serving under Gnaeus Cornelius Dolabella in 80–79, against whom he testified at the latter's extortion trial in 78 (Dolabella was convicted); and he allegedly sold justice while city praetor at Rome in 74 (*praedonem*, 'cheater', is Cicero's clever substitution for the similar-sounding *praetorem*, 'praetor').

4 *Manius Glabrio*: Manius Acilius Glabrio, the presiding magistrate. This passage suggests that the defence were hostile to Glabrio, which helps account for their eagerness to have the trial prolonged into 69 (cf. § 29). He may therefore have favoured Cicero; at any rate he allowed him to deviate from the normal procedure in his prosecution. Glabrio went on to be consul in 67, supporting his colleague Gaius Calpurnius Piso's law against electoral malpractice, and then briefly became commander in Bithynia and Pontus in 66 before being superseded by Pompey. He was possibly censor in 64. For an account of his connections and likely political opinions (not an optimate, and probably no friend of the Metelli), see L. Hayne, *CP* 69 (1974), 280–2. On his family connections, see also §§ 51–2 below, with notes.

6 *he found someone . . . to Achaea*: Cicero is reticent about the details of this other extortion trial, which delayed his own prosecution by three months (*Ver.* 2.1.30). B. A. Marshall (*Philologus*, 121 (1977), 83–9) has argued that the prosecutor in that trial may have been Quintus Caecilius Metellus Nepos (consul in 57) and the defendant Gaius Scribonius Curio, the governor of Macedonia from 75 to 72 who is mentioned below at § 18

(where see note); Achaea fell under the supervision of the governor of Macedonia.

6 *in fact . . . as far as Brundisium!*: perhaps an assistant was sent instead.

10 *the rejection of jurors*: before the trial began, both sides had the right to reject some of the jurors that had been assigned to the case; we know only that a non-senator could reject no more than three. Cicero says that it was obvious to those present (the Roman people) that the jurors Verres chose to reject were those of unimpeachable honesty, whom he would have no chance of bribing.

*what eloquence or fluency great enough*: Cicero is thinking of Hortensius (as he was at § 9 'if he had had the slightest confidence . . . in anyone's eloquence'). It suits his purpose to make much of Hortensius' powers of persuasion.

11 *by his own quaestor*: for the events referred to in this paragraph, see third note on § 2 above. Cicero emphasizes the special, enduring loyalty which a quaestor was expected to show towards the senior magistrate (consul or governor) to whom he had been assigned by lot (for a study of this loyalty, see L. A. Thompson, *Historia*, 11 (1962), 339–55); Verres betrayed both Carbo and Dolabella.

14 *our own victorious generals*: after destroying Carthage in 146, Scipio Aemilianus returned to Sicily all the statues which the Carthaginians had taken from it (*Ver.* 2.4.73–4).

16 *when the lots were cast*: i.e. the lots to decide which members of the panel assigned to the case should be selected as jurors; this was the penultimate stage in the selection of the jury, the final stage being the rejection of a set number of jurors by both prosecution and defence (see first note on § 10 above).

17 *any mark . . . on the voting-tablets*: since jurors voted by secret ballot and the voting-tablets were identical, any attempt at bribery would depend on the tablets (which were coated with wax) being marked in some way, so that the bribery-agent could check that the jurors he had bribed had fulfilled their part of the bargain.

*since the consular elections*: at which Hortensius and Quintus Caecilius Metellus were elected consuls for 69.

18 *Gaius Curio*: Gaius Scribonius Curio, consul of 76, governor of Macedonia from 75 to 72, and later censor in 61. We can infer from what follows that he was a supporter of Verres (both had done well out of Sulla's proscriptions). In 61 he supported Clodius against Cicero; Cicero wrote a pamphet attacking him, and later tried to deny authorship of it when he was in exile and needed Curio's support. See W. C. McDermott, *AJP* 93 (1972), 381–411 for a history of the relations between the two men. On the possibility that Curio was the defendant whose trial for extortion delayed Cicero's prosecution of Verres, see first note on § 6 above.

19 *the Arch of Fabius*: the triumphal arch of Quintus Fabius Maximus

Allobrogicus (consul in 121), erected in *c.*120 to commemorate Fabius' victory over the Allobroges and other tribes in Gaul. It was the first triumphal arch in or near the forum, and stood near the entry to the forum on the Sacred Way. Its inscriptions were discovered in the sixteenth century, but have since been lost.

*I formally declare*: Curio jokingly uses the same language as that used by the consul presiding over the elections when officially announcing the result.

20  *the transfer of the courts*: to the equestrian order. The people Cicero claims to be quoting, 'all the best people', were senators.

21  *were drawing lots*: to decide which praetor would be in charge of which court.

*Marcus Metellus*: Marcus Caecilius Metellus, brother of the Lucius Metellus who had succeeded Verres in Sicily and of the Quintus Metellus who had just been elected consul (with Hortensius) for 69. We learn below at § 30 that he was one of the jurors in this trial.

22  *a number of chests . . . to a Roman equestrian*: these chests of money had been used for bribery at the consular and praetorian elections which had just taken place (as the reference to these elections in the next section makes clear). The identities of the senator and equestrian are not known.

*at my election*: the impending aedilician elections, at which Verres hoped to prevent Cicero being elected aedile for 69.

23  *when he had been standing for the praetorship*: in 75.

*the Romilian tribe*: the first of the thirty-one rural tribes. Its territory lay on the right bank of the Tiber, on land said to have been taken from Veii by Romulus; see L. R. Taylor, *The Voting Districts of the Roman Republic* (Rome, 1960), 38.

24  *preoccupied and tied down by the present trial*: and therefore not in a position to prosecute them.

25  *most wholeheartedly*: Cicero was top of the poll (*Pis.* 2).

26  *Quintus Metellus*: Quintus Caecilius Metellus, consul-elect of 69, the brother of Marcus Metellus and of Lucius, Verres' successor in Sicily. After his consulship he became governor of Achaea and Crete; in Crete he defeated the pirates (68–67) and organized the island as a Roman province (66), thus earning for himself the *cognomen* 'Creticus'.

*the preliminary votes at his election*: Cicero claims that when the consular elections took place, Verres bribed the centuries that voted first (consuls were elected by the centuries in the centuriate assembly, not by the tribal assembly) to vote for Metellus; Metellus then repaid the favour by assuring Verres that he would help him out at his trial in 69. Cicero's play on words seems forced in English translation but is much neater in Latin, where *praerogativa* means both 'the century which votes first in the centuriate assembly' and also 'a forecast' (here, a forecast of Metellus' goodwill, translated loosely as 'a preliminary vote of confidence'). At elections, later centuries often took their lead from the way the first ones voted (so it made sense to target bribes at the first ones); the choice of the first century was therefore seen as a forecast of the eventual result (cf. *Phil.* 2.82).

27 *The second consul-elect*: Quintus Metellus. He was second because Hortensius was top of the poll.

*Lucius Metellus*: Lucius Caecilius Metellus, brother of Quintus and Marcus. He went on to become consul in 68, but died early in his year of office.

*'I am consul ... comes to no harm'*: this little speech conveys, as Cicero intends, a strong impression of the arrogance and power of the Metelli (note that Metellus says he is consul, although still only consul-elect). Their arrogance is borne out by a famous letter of Quintus Caecilius Metellus Celer (the husband of Clodia Metelli) to Cicero in 62: 'So I am dressed in mourning—I, who am in command of a province, in command of an army, who am fighting a war! It was not like this in our ancestors' time ...' (*Fam.* 5.1.2).

28 *the power of two praetors*: Lucius Metellus, governor of Sicily, was technically propraetor (in this translation I use the word 'governor' for ease of comprehension, though the Romans had no such term, referring instead to proconsuls and propraetors).

29 *you were made consul not by fate*: an allusion to a line attributed to Naevius (third century BC), 'By fate the Metelli become consuls at Rome' (on Naevius and the Metelli, see H. B. Mattingly, *Historia*, 9 (1960), 414–39). If Verres really made this remark, it would be one of several indications that he had a lively sense of humour (cf. § 40).

*So he will have two consuls ... on his side*: i.e. if the trial is delayed until 69.

*Manius Glabrio*: see note on § 4 above. Cicero described him as 'lazy and negligent' many years later at *Brut.* 239 (46 BC).

*the colleague of our prosecutor*: he and Cicero had been elected plebeian aediles for 69. He must have progressed to the praetorship since Cicero mentions him at *Att.* 1.1.1 as a possible rival (though not a serious one) for the consulship of 63.

*in Junius' court*: Gaius Junius had presided over a controversial trial in 74, when Aulus Cluentius Habitus had accused his stepfather Statius Abbius Oppianicus of attempting to poison him; Oppianicus was convicted by a majority of one. It was widely believed that Oppianicus was innocent of the charge and that Cluentius had obtained his conviction by bribing the jury ('the terrible corruption that took place'); Junius was afterwards fined on a technicality, his career ruined. Oppianicus died in exile, and in 66 his son accused Cluentius in turn of having poisoned him; Cicero defended Cluentius (in *Pro Cluentio*), denied that his client had been responsible for the corruption in the earlier trial (the so-called Junius trial), and secured his acquittal.

30  *Quintus Manlius and Quintus Cornificius*: Manlius' identity is uncertain.
Cornificius progressed to the praetorship and stood against Cicero for the
consulship of 63 (at *Att.* 1.1.1 Cicero views his candidature as as much of a
joke as Caesonius'). Tribunes of the plebs took up office on 10 December.

*Publius Sulpicius*: quaestor-elect; quaestors took up office on 5 December.
Since he was already a senator (all the jurors in this case were senators),
he must have been appointed to the senate by Sulla, but not yet have held
a senatorial magistracy.

*Marcus Crepereius ... Lucius Cassius ... Gnaeus Tremellius*: military
tribunes-elect (i.e. designated for the more prestigious, elected military
tribunates, not simply appointed). Gnacus Tremellius Scrofa had been
quaestor in 71; the other two were presumably also ex-quaestors.
Tremellius had military experience: he served under Crassus against
Spartacus, and was defeated and wounded, in 71. He became praetor in
the early 50s, and then probably held a provincial governorship in 51–50.
He is not to be confused with the older man of the same name who was
an agricultural authority and appears as an interlocutor in Varro's *De re
rustica*.

*Marcus Metellus' place*: Marcus Metellus, the praetor-elect who was
to assume the presidency of the court in 69, was also one of the jurors
in 70.

*virtually the entire jury will have changed*: eight jurors would have
changed. The total number of jurors in unknown, but for Cicero's statement to make sense (and allowing for some moderate exaggeration) it can
hardly have been more than twelve or fifteen.

31  *the Votive Games*: the Votive Games were held on 16 August–1 September
(August had twenty-nine days), the Roman Games on 4–18 September,
the Games of Victory on 27–31 October, and the Plebeian Games on
4–17 November. The Votive Games celebrated Pompey's victory in the
war against Sertorius in 72, and the Games of Victory Sulla's victory
over the Marians in 82. The other two sets of games were traditional
(see first note on *Ver.* 2.5.36 below).

*among the jurors I rejected*: see first note on § 10 above. In view of what
Cicero is about to say, it is surprising that he did not reject Metellus;
presumably the jurors that he did reject were even more hostile.

34  *who had previously ... to the test*: i.e. when Cicero served as a quaestor in
Sicily in 75.

35  *all my youthful energy*: Cicero was in fact 36.

36  *our entire order*: the senatorial order.

*in that place*: the rostra. Cicero is threatening to conduct prosecutions as
plebeian aedile before the plebeian assembly.

*the grandest ... spectacle of my aedileship*: aediles were expected to put on
games. During his aedileship Cicero put on three sets of games, but is not
known to have undertaken any prosecutions.

36 *Let me advise, warn, and give notice*: the traditional formula used when declaring war.

37 *the ten years*: actually eleven; the courts were transferred to the senate by the *lex Cornelia* of 81.

38 *for nearly fifty years*: actually only forty-one (or forty-two); equestrian juries in extortion trials were established by the *lex Acilia* of 122 (or 123) and abolished in 81.

*Quintus Calidius*: praetor in 79 (elected with the help of the Metelli) and governor of Nearer Spain in 78; he was convicted of extortion in 77. The jury consisted of his fellow senators, who would naturally have taken his side; those who voted against him had been bribed by the prosecution. The point of his remark was that it was understandable if the jurors voted against a fellow senator in return for a truly massive bribe, but it reflected badly on him if they did so for only a relatively modest sum.

*the senator Publius Septimius*: Publius Septimius Scaevola was convicted of extortion, apparently against the Apulians, in 72. In the assessment of damages, the amount he had to pay was increased to take account of the fact that he had allegedly accepted a bribe when serving on the jury in the trial of Oppianicus in 74 (see fifth note on § 29 above). Cf. *Clu.* 138–9, where Cicero attempts to explain away this passage by saying that he may not have said it at all, but that if he did, then he was not saying something he knew to be true, but was merely reporting a rumour.

39 *Gaius Herennius and Gaius Popillius*: the former may have been tribune in 88 or 80, and may equally have been killed while serving under Sertorius in Spain in 76 or 75; the latter is entirely unknown. The dates of their trials are also unknown.

*Marcus Atilius*: Marcus Atilius Bulbus, one of the jurors in the trial of Oppianicus. He was convicted of tampering with a legion in Illyricum; the date of the trial is unknown.

*Gaius Verres was drawing lots as city praetor*: i.e. drawing lots to decide which members of a panel assigned to a particular case that was coming up for trial should be selected as jurors (exactly as at § 16, where see note). The case Cicero is referring to, held in 74, is unknown (it is not, for once, the trial of Oppianicus, since on that occasion a 'proper trial' was indeed held).

*a senator was found*: Gaius Aelius Paetus Staienus, quaestor in 77, a juror in the Oppianicus trial.

40 *with symbols of different colours*: see first note on § 17 above. Cicero is alluding to the flagrant use of bribery at the trial of Aulus Terentius Varro for extortion in 74, at which Varro was successfully defended by his cousin Hortensius.

*a powerful friend*: Hortensius.

*those of the second to his advocates*: this was in fact technically illegal.

The *lex Cincia* of 204 BC prohibited advocates from accepting fees or gifts in return for their services; but it was regularly flouted. Verres is known to have given Hortensius a valuable bronze sphinx as payment for defending him.

41  *when the rejection of jurors was being held*: see first note on § 10 above.

44  *the restoration of the tribunes' powers*: in 81 Sulla had removed the tribunes' power to initiate legislation and to exercise limited jurisdiction, had curtailed their right of veto, and had disqualified them from holding further public office. In 75 the disqualification from office had been removed; the other powers were restored in 70 by the consuls Pompey and Crassus.

*Quintus Catulus*: Quintus Lutatius Catulus, son of the consul of 102 and himself consul in 78 and censor in 65; in 78–77 he was chiefly responsible for suppressing his colleague, the rebel Marcus Aemilius Lepidus. He was a strong defender of the Sullan settlement, and was the leader of the conservatives in the senate in the 70s and 60s, opposing the *lex Gabinia* in 67 and the *lex Manilia* in 66; he also opposed Caesar in 63. He had previously resisted the restoration of the tribunes' powers; his change of mind in 70 allowed both the restoration of the tribunes' powers and the abolition of senatorial juries to proceed without serious opposition. His sister was the wife of Hortensius.

*illustrious*: Cicero refers to senators as *clarissimi* and to *equites* (less commonly) as *splendidi*. This was a standard convention and in order to reproduce it in English I have translated these words throughout (when they refer to individuals) as 'illustrious' and 'worthy' respectively.

45  *outside the city*. Pompey still held his grant of military power (given to him for his war against Sertorius in Spain and against Spartacus' slave revolt), but in law this would be forfeited if he were to cross the city boundary and enter Rome. He did not want to give up his power because (1) this would make him ineligible for a triumph (he would no longer be a general), and (2) it would expose him to prosecution (holders of official power could not be prosecuted until their power had expired and they returned to the status of an ordinary citizen). He therefore held his triumph on the last day of December 71, and became consul (and immune from prosecution) on 1 January 70.

46  *the law about the tribunes*: the law restoring their powers, passed earlier in the year.

*of slender means*: and therefore unable to bribe his jurors. The senator's identity is unknown.

49  *a different order altogether*: the equestrian order.

50  *barring only him*: Verres.

51  *your own father's Acilian law*: the *lex Acilia*, the law of 122 (or 123) which set up a new permanent extortion court with equestrian juries. The law was part of Gaius Gracchus' legislative programme, designed in part to

win equestrian support for his agrarian scheme; it was carried by the elder Manius Acilius Glabrio, a tribune (about whom nothing else is known). A fragmentary bronze inscription, the so-called *Tabula Bembina*, gives the text of an extortion law which also prescribes equestrian juries; this law is usually presumed to be the *lex Acilia* (see M. H. Crawford (ed.), *Roman Statutes* (London, 1996), i. 39–112).

52 *your grandfather Scaevola*: Glabrio's maternal grandfather, Publius Mucius Scaevola, consul in 133, *pontifex maximus* from 130, and an eminent jurist (hence the description 'wise' above); he trained Glabrio in oratory and law. As consul he advised Tiberius Gracchus and refused to take violent action against him.

*your father-in-law Scaurus*: Marcus Aemilius Scaurus, consul in 115, censor in 109, and *princeps senatus* (leader of the senate). He was closely connected with the Metelli; he married Caecilia Metella, who after his death married Sulla. Aemilia, the daughter of Scaurus and Metella, was married first to Glabrio, and then taken from him by Sulla and married to Pompey.

53 *people who collectively refused . . . the lictors of consuls*: see §§ 25, 27.

54 *after forty days have gone by*: see § 31.

*the census*: the census was a register of all adult male citizens, compiled by the censors in theory every five years, but in practice at irregular intervals. It was abandoned in 89, held in 86 and 70, and abandoned in 65 and 64. In 70 the census recorded 910,000 names.

55 *leaders of our country*: Cicero refers to the brothers Lucius Licinius Lucullus and Marcus Terentius Varro Lucullus. Lucius was the consul of 74, who in 70 was in Asia Minor fighting Mithridates; Marcus was consul in 73, and in 71 celebrated a triumph for successes in Macedonia. Together they prosecuted one Servilius, perhaps in 91. Details of this trial are uncertain, but it is possible that it was an extortion trial, and that Servilius was convicted.

## IN VERREM II.5

1 *has openly plundered . . . public or private*: in the preceding speech, *Ver.* 2.4, Cicero recounted Verres' theft of works of art from temples and from secular places, and from communities and private individuals.

*from runaway slaves and from the threat of war*: Sicily was in serious danger from Spartacus' slave revolt in southern Italy (see first note on § 5 below); further afield, the Third Mithridatic War (73–63) was in progress in Asia Minor.

3 *Manius Aquillius*: commander of the army against the Cimbri and Teutoni in Gaul in 103 (standing in for Marius), and, as consul in 101 (with Marius), commander in the Second Sicilian Slave War (104–100). He completed the war as governor of Sicily in 100–99, killing Athenio, the

leader of the slaves, in a hand-to-hand fight. He was accused of extortion, perhaps in 97, but, although guilty (*Flac.* 98), was successfully defended by Marcus Antonius; Marius was a character witness for him. Later, in 88, he precipitated the First Mithridatic War (88–85), and was defeated, captured, and cruelly executed by Mithridates.

*Marcus Antonius*: consul in 99 and censor in 97. He was an important orator, heard and admired by Cicero (who later gave him a prominent role in his *De oratore*); he did not publish his speeches. He was murdered by the Marians in 87. (See further first note on *Imp.* 33 below.)

4 *under a specific law*: the *lex Cornelia de repetundis* (Cornelian law concerning extortion).

5 *the war against the slaves*: i.e. the war against Spartacus (73–71). This was a revolt of slaves and the rural poor in southern Italy led by Spartacus, a Thracian gladiator from Capua. There were eventually as many as 70,000–120,000 insurgents, and they were remarkably successful for two years, defeating both consuls in 72; they would have crossed into Sicily, but failed to obtain transport from the pirates. In 71 Marcus Licinius Crassus defeated most of them, crucifying the survivors (Spartacus was killed in battle); a last remnant was then destroyed by Pompey in the north. Pompey's claim of the credit for completing the war soured relations permanently between him and Crassus; the two men went on to hold the consulship together in 70.

*I suppose . . . to Sicily*: cf. Sallust, *Histories* 4 fr. 32 Maurenbrecher 'Gaius Verres strengthened the coastline close to Italy.'

7 *there have been slave wars in Sicily in the past*: the First (135–132 BC) and Second (104–100) Sicilian Slave Wars, the second of which was ended by Manius Aquillius (first note on § 3 above).

*Lucius Domitius*: Lucius Domitius Ahenobarbus, governor of Sicily in c.97, consul in 94. His severity is understandable in view of the fact that the Second Sicilian Slave War was only just over, but on the other hand the Domitii Ahenobarbi were a notably cruel family, later to produce the emperor Nero (Suetonius, *Nero* 1–5).

8 *Gaius Norbanus*: a 'new man'; governor of Sicily at some point during the Social War (91–87, the war between Rome and her Italian allies); consul in 83 (after him, Cicero was the next new man to attain the consulship). He was not as inactive as Cicero implies: he defeated an Italian attack on Regium. Cicero speaks disparagingly of him because Verres' trial took place before Sullan jurors: Norbanus was a prominent Marian, committing suicide in 82 to avoid falling into Sulla's hands.

9 *he himself would like to be aired*: because they back up his case regarding the reality of the danger of slave risings.

10 *at an earlier date*: 104 BC, at the beginning of the Second Sicilian Slave War.

*some act of theft or looting*: i.e. committed by Verres.

*Verres . . . summoned him to appear*: Leonidas would have been anxious for his slaves not to be convicted, because, if they were, they would be executed, and he would suffer financial loss.

10  *tied to the post*: for flogging, prior to crucifixion.

13  *people of the popular or the aristocratic faction*: Cicero is using Roman terms but is thinking of Greek situations, i.e. of democrats and oligarchs. He will be thinking particularly of the amnesty at Athens which followed the disastrous defeat at Aegospotami in 405 BC, at the end of the Peloponnesian War.

14  *Paullus, Scipio, and Marius*: Lucius Aemilius Paullus (consul in 182 and 168 BC, censor in 164), who defeated Perseus of Macedon at Pydna (168); his son Publius Cornelius Scipio Aemilianus Africanus (consul in 147 and 134, censor in 142), the destroyer of Carthage (146) and Numantia (133); and the new man Gaius Marius (consul in 107, 104–100, 86), victor over Jugurtha (105), the Teutoni (102), and the Cimbri (101). Cicero's argument at this point seems particularly unfair.

15  *Gaius Matrinius*: mentioned at *Ver.* 2.3.60 as having been imprisoned for two days at Leontini by Verres' crony Apronius. The amount Verres took from him, 600,000 sesterces, was a vast sum: the property qualification for equestrian rank was 400,000 sesterces.

*Lucius Flavius*: also an *eques* (§ 155; also *Ver.* 2.1.14).

*Gnaeus Lentulus*: Gnaeus Cornelius Lentulus Clodianus, consul of 72 and censor in 70. As consul he proposed a motion in the senate to protect the Sicilians from Verres (*Ver.* 2.2.94–8); in the same year he was twice defeated by Spartacus, and withdrawn from his command. As censor with Lucius Gellius Publicola (who had been his colleague as consul), he expelled sixty-four men from the senate as being unworthy. Later, in 67, he served as one of Pompey's legates against the pirates. Cicero says that he looked intelligent, but was not, and was an indifferent orator (*Brut.* 234).

16  *(Apollonius' aged father . . . for some time.)*: Cicero adds this information to explain why Apollonius' father did not come too.

22  *rods of office*: the *fasces* (see Glossary).

25  *there is a general lack of fine soldiers*: ironic. We are expected to think of Pompey and Crassus (who had recently crushed Spartacus' revolt), and compare Verres unfavourably with them.

*Quintus Maximus . . . Gaius Marius*: Quintus Fabius Maximus Verrucosus (consul in 233, 228, 215, 214, and 209, censor in 230, dictator in 221 and 217) was one of the leading generals in the Second Punic War (218–201 BC), noted for his successful policy of avoiding direct confrontation with Hannibal (hence his nickname 'Cunctator', 'Delayer'). The elder Africanus (Publius Cornelius Scipio Africanus, consul in 205 and 194, censor in 199) was the conqueror of Hannibal (202). For the others, see note on § 14 above.

27  *the first roses*: i.e. decorating his dining room (since he allegedly spent his

days eating and seldom ventured out of doors). Dining rooms were strewn with rose petals at Roman banquets.

28  *Cannae*: 216 BC, the battle during the Second Punic War at which Hannibal inflicted on the Romans their worst-ever defeat, killing almost 80,000 men.

29  *because that is when the slaves . . . stand in their way*: this long parenthesis gives a list of reasons why the slaves were more likely to revolt at harvest time, and therefore why the governor needed to keep a close eye on them.

30  *where the gulf . . . towards the city*: i.e. on the tip of Ortygia, an island (though connected to the mainland by a bridge) projecting across, and so serving to narrow, the natural mouth of the Great Harbour. I have preserved the slight obscurity of Cicero's description in the translation.

*King Hiero*: Hiero II, king of Syracuse (*c.*271–216 BC) at the peak of its prosperity.

*(and it is remarkable . . . in Syracuse)*: a criticism of the Syracusans. Cicero criticizes the Syracusans because some of them supported Verres against himself.

31  *separated . . . by violence and trickery*: Verres had obtained his mistress Tertia by forcibly taking her from her partner, the piper, and marrying her to his friend Docimus, who then allowed him to pursue his relationship with her (*Ver.* 2.3.78).

*The aristocratic wife of Cleomenes . . . and the wife of Aeschrio*: named Nice and Pipa respectively (§§ 81–2).

*But this Hannibal . . . not by birth*: in the Second Punic War, Hannibal offered Carthaginian citizenship to anyone who killed an enemy of Carthage, regardless of their birth. The reference would have been familiar from Ennius' *Annales* (234–5 Skutsch). To Cicero its value consists largely in the scope it provides for contrasting Verres with a famous general, in order to ridicule Verres' claim to have been a fine general himself.

32  *that old oratorical trick . . . the first to use*: see § 3 above.

33  *pulled out of the forum . . . pulled in it*: i.e. hired out to a male customer by a pimp, rather than, as a free agent, persuaded to submit to another man's sexual desires without payment (the latter being less disgraceful). This meaning (which is either misunderstood or obfuscated by earlier scholarship) is confirmed by the last sentence of this section, which again refers (again obliquely) to the young Verres being prostituted for cash.

*the gambler from Placentia*: identity unknown. Placentia was in Cisalpine Gaul; today the place is Piacenza, and the outline of the Roman camp is still visible in the modern street layout.

34  *the consulship of Lucius Lucullus and Marcus Cotta*: Lucius Licinius Lucullus and Marcus Aurelius Cotta were consuls in 74, the year when Verres held the city praetorship.

*he used to have himself carried back inside the city*: thus technically resigning his command (cf. note on *Ver.* 45 above) and invalidating the vows that had been made—a serious matter.

35 *When I was elected to the quaestorship*: in 76, the office being held in 75.

36 *the holy games for Ceres . . . described as 'Roman'*: Cicero describes here, in calendar order, the games which he was required to put on the following year as plebeian aedile (that this passage shows him to have been plebeian, not curule, aedile is demonstrated by L. R. Taylor, *AJP* 60 (1939), 194–202). Ceres (goddess of growth, i.e. of crops, the Greek Demeter), Liber Pater ('Father Liber', god of fertility and wine, the Greek Dionysus), and Libera (the Greek Kore or Persephone) were the Aventine triad, introduced to Rome in 493 BC; their temple was supervised by the plebeian aediles, who put on the *ludi Ceriales* (Cerial Games) in April. Flora was an Italian goddess of flowering plants, especially cereals; her games, the Floralia, dated to 240, and had been celebrated annually since 173, later in April. Jupiter (Zeus), Juno (Hera), and Minerva (Athena) were the Capitoline triad; their temple was dedicated in 509. Their games that Cicero refers to here were the Plebeian Games (4–17 November), held by the plebeian aediles, not the Roman Games (4–18 September), which were held by the curule aediles; misunderstanding on this point led to the belief, disproved by Taylor, that it was the curule aedileship which Cicero held.

*the purple-bordered toga . . . a portrait mask of myself to posterity*: these benefits are normally associated only with curule magistracies, but, as Taylor argues (see previous note), must have been extended to plebeian aediles by this date, no doubt by Sulla.

38 *your election as praetor*: in 75, for office in 74.

*When time after time . . . with that office*: the centuriate assembly, by which the praetors were elected, consisted of 193 centuries. Eighty-five of the centuries consisted of seniors, men over 45, and eighty-five consisted of juniors, men under 46 (the juniors were liable to active service). The crier announced the choice of each century as it was made, so a successful candidate would hear his name announced many times before his election was confirmed (never, however, 193 times: the process was stopped once the required number of magistrates had obtained a majority). See further second note on *Phil.* 2.82 below.

*the job of city praetor*: the most prestigious and important of the praetorships.

39 *those rods and axes*: the *fasces* (see Glossary).

*to take refuge in a war against fugitives*: in this translation *fugitivi* is normally rendered 'runaway slaves', but here 'fugitives' is preferred in order to preserve Cicero's (very characteristic) play on words.

*the setback at Tempsa*: nothing is known about this incident beyond what Cicero goes on to say in §§ 40–1. Clearly there was a minor slave rising in 71 at Tempsa in Bruttium (on the west coast of Italy in the extreme south), and Verres rejected the request of the people of Vibo Valentia (30 miles south of Tempsa) to take military action against the slaves.

40 *you wore a workman's smock and a Greek cloak*: he should of course have been wearing a toga. The suggestion is that he had gone native in Sicily and so disgraced his office by appearing in Greek dress; moreover, the casual and banausic nature of his outfit compounded the offence. Cicero's audience would have been shocked that Roman culture and authority should be compromised in this way. Cf. the governor Lucius Metellus' rebuke to Cicero for addressing the Syracusans in their native Greek (*Ver.* 2.4.147).

*his behaviour when he was leaving for his province*: see the penultimate sentence of § 34.

*for the sake of something*: i.e. wearing clothes of his own preference.

41 *the temple of Bellona*: Bellona was the goddess of war, and her temple was situated in the Campus Martius. Since it was outside the city boundary, the senate often met there when it needed to consult with generals, whose command would be forfeited if they entered the city (cf. note on *Ver.* 45 above). Note that Cicero's argument here undermines his earlier view (implied at §§ 39 and 40) that Verres should have acceded to the request made of him by the people of Vibo Valentia. Given that it was not the wish of the senate that Verres take action against the slaves, he clearly did right in refusing to do so (in any case it would have involved exceeding his powers, which did not extend outside his province).

44 *Velia*: 20 miles south of Paestum, roughly halfway between Sicily and Rome.

45 *The laws which forbid this*: the *lex Claudia* (218 BC) restricted the size of ship which a senator or his son might own to a maximum capacity of 300 amphorae. The purpose was to prevent senators engaging in trade, an activity considered unworthy of their status. The law was carried despite near-unanimous opposition from the senate, and it is doubtful whether it was ever observed.

*you are not permitted to travel anywhere at all*: senators were not permitted to leave Italy except on public service. In practice, however, if they wished to travel abroad, they invented an excuse (such as the necessity to fulfil a vow), and obtained an unrestricted legateship (*legatio libera*). This allowed them to travel as they pleased, at public expense.

48 *Even the temple on the Capitol*: for this temple, see first note on § 36 above. It had originally been built in 509 BC, but was destroyed by fire in 83. At the time of Verres' trial the rebuilding (to which Cicero refers in this sentence) was almost complete; the new temple was dedicated the following year.

49 *the fetials*: a college of twenty priests who represented Rome in its dealings with other nations, particularly with regard to treaties and declarations of war.

50 *impaired the defences of the state*: Cicero conveniently overlooks the fact that, though Messana had been let off having to provide a ship, Tauromenium, which did not normally provide one, had been made to do so, and so the overall defences of the state were in fact unchanged.

   *the strait*: i.e. of Messina, separating Sicily from Italy.

51 *they had recently done us good service*: in 264 BC Messana appealed to Rome for help against Carthage and Syracuse, thus starting the process by which Rome became master of Sicily (the First Punic War, 264–241 BC). The treaty was agreed after 241.

52 *a senatorial decree and the Terentian-Cassian law*: the decree was passed at the beginning of each year, and laid down what the funds allotted to provincial governors were to be spent on. The *lex Terentia Cassia*, on the other hand, was a law carried by the consuls of 73, Marcus Terentius Varro Lucullus and Gaius Cassius Longinus. This provided for the compulsory purchase of grain from Sicily each year, since the tribute (a tithe, i.e. 10 per cent of their produce) which was demanded of most of the Sicilian states (all those without independent status or a treaty exempting them) was inadequate to Rome's needs.

53 *stipulated in the censors' law*: land that was classed as public land (typically land originally taken in war) belonged to the Roman people and was let to tenants on terms laid down by the censors.

   *stipulated by the law of Hiero*: when the Romans gained control of Sicily in 241 BC, they saw no need to alter the existing system of tax collection, that of Hiero II of Syracuse (c.271–216 BC), based on tithes. In the first century BC the same system was still in operation.

   *the law*: not the *lex Terentia Cassia*, since that dated only from 73, but an earlier one which made similar provision.

54 *taken from his own notebook*: it is questionable whether Cicero really had access to such a document; he may be inventing evidence for the published speech that he could not have used in the trial.

55 *Here are our interpreters . . . in religion!*: the implied contrast is with the fetials (see note on § 49 above).

   *Gaius Sacerdos and Sextus Peducaeus*: Verres' two immediate predecessors, Gaius Licinius Sacerdos (governor in 74) and Sextus Peducaeus (governor in 76–75).

60 *in the days when they provided us with auxiliary troops*: i.e. before they were granted Roman citizenship under the *lex Iulia* in 90 BC, during the Social War. Once they had Roman citizenship, they served in the legions and not the auxiliary units.

63 *Publius Caesetius and Publius Tadius*: Caesetius was Verres' quaestor at Lilybaeum in 72 and 71, Tadius one of his legates (they are referred to as 'his quaestor and his legate' below). Both were senators.

   *very good looking young men*: to be sold as domestic slaves, and worth a great deal of money.

*Megaris*: i.e. the site of Megara Hyblaea, a city destroyed by Marcus Claudius Marcellus in 213 BC, but at this date still with some inhabitants.

66 *Publius Servilius*: Publius Servilius Vatia Isauricus, consul of 79, governor of Cilicia in 78–74, and later censor in 55. As governor he suppressed the Cilician pirates before going on to fight against the mountain tribes; he was rewarded with a triumph in 74 and the *cognomen* 'Isauricus' (from his capture of Isaura Vetus, where an inscription naming him has been found). He was one of the jurors in this trial, so Cicero takes the opportunity to praise him.

68 *the quarries at Syracuse*: most famous as the place where the Syracusans imprisoned their 7,000 Athenian and allied captives after the defeat of the Athenian expedition against Sicily in 413 BC, as memorably described by Thucydides (7.87). It is slightly surprising that Cicero should claim that most of the jury had seen the quarries; probably he is simply flattering them as well-travelled and educated men.

69 *this man who was only masquerading as the pirate captain*: the subject of Verres' substitution of the fake pirate in place of the real one had already cropped up in the first hearing (§ 73).

70 *Centuripae*: a hill town 17 miles south-west of Mt Etna. Verres might well counter that a remote town well away from the sea was an eminently sensible place to imprison a pirate. But Cicero ingeniously argues that the man he imprisoned was not the real pirate, and that he chose an inland place of imprisonment only because the people there would have no knowledge of what the real pirate looked like, and so would not detect his substitution of a different person.

*Apronius*: Quintus Apronius, a tithe-collector, and crony of Verres.

71 *tied all the remaining pirates to the post*: for flogging, prior to crucifixion (as at § 10).

72 *soldiers from the army of Sertorius*: Quintus Sertorius was a Marian who held Spain against the central government from 82 BC; he used pirates for naval support. Pompey was appointed to the command against him in 77, and arrived in Spain in 76; but progress was slow until Sertorius was assassinated by his jealous ally Marcus Perperna Veiento in 72. Perperna was then defeated and executed by Pompey in the same year.

73 *Marcus Annius*: a Roman *eques* resident at Syracuse.

*two pirate captains*: we hear nothing elsewhere about this second pirate captain—an uncharacteristic loose end. Even more than usual, one senses here that more was going on than Cicero chooses to tell us about.

74 *the necessary measures for their own safety*: Verres was a danger to the Roman people, having illegally executed Roman citizens.

76 *Manius Glabrio*: Manius Acilius Glabrio, the presiding magistrate (see note on *Ver.* 4 above).

79 *Publius Servilius*: see note on § 66 above. Nico is otherwise unknown.

79 *a separate court*: the treason court. It was an act of treason to harbour or release a public enemy.

80 *that might have resulted in more plunder for himself*: because he might have captured some more pirate ships.

*his own royal residence*: the governor's residence had formerly been the palace of Hiero II of Syracuse, as Cicero has told us at § 30 (the same information is repeated in the manuscripts here, spoiling the effect of 'royal'; this must be an interpolation, and is therefore not translated).

*the Island at Syracuse*: Ortygia; see first note on § 30 (the passage to which Cicero has just referred) above. The spring of Arethusa was (and still is) about two-thirds of the way along the island on the side facing inside the harbour, so a point which was 'beyond the spring' would be towards the extremity of the island, at the mouth of the Great Harbour.

81 *the freedman Timarchides*: a freedman who looked after Verres' financial affairs and connived in his thefts.

*the daughter of Isidorus the pantomime actor*: Tertia (see first note on § 31 above).

83 *what about the legates*: after this the manuscripts add, 'what about the grain valued at three denarii a measure [a reference to Verres' swindling of the Sicilian farmers, whom he forced to pay him for the privilege of not being required to sell him grain at an inflated price], what about the mules, what about the tents, what about the plentiful and varied equipment authorized and entrusted to the magistrates and legates by the senate and people of Rome.' I have omitted these words as an interpolation: Cicero cannot be suggesting that Verres should have put mules and tents in charge of the fleet in preference to Cleomenes.

*their kinship with us*: Segesta was traditionally said to have been founded by Aeneas, in myth the original founder of Rome, on his journey from Carthage to Italy. We know nothing of any supposed kinship between Centuripae and Rome.

84 *Marcus Marcellus*: Marcus Claudius Marcellus (consul in 222, 215, 214, 210, and 208), one of the leading generals during the Second Punic War, most famous for his capture of Syracuse from the Carthaginians after a two-and-a-half-year siege in 211. Despite what Cicero goes on to say, the city was looted and its artistic treasures shipped to Italy.

86 *Herbita*: location unknown.

87 *the short distance to Pachynum*: the distance was 30 miles, and should have taken less than a day.

*wild palms*: the plant is now known as the dwarf palm, and is still common in Sicily.

88 *Cleomenes ... to tell the others to follow*: we naturally assume that Cleomenes is heading to Odysseae to attack the pirates; but it will quickly

become apparent that he has in fact fled in the opposite direction, towards Helorus (back in the direction of Syracuse).

89  *But their crew were men of courage*: the Sicilian allies were Cicero's clients, and he is careful to place all the blame for the disaster on Verres and Cleomenes.

90  *Locri*: i.e. Epizephyrian Locri in Bruttium (on the east coast of the toe of Italy). We do not know why the people of Locri did this; Phylarchus must have had some connection with the place.

92  *What a miserable, sickening moment for the province of Sicily!*: there is an excellent discussion of this passage (down to § 95)—one of the finest passages of narrative in Latin literature—by R. G. M. Nisbet in A. J. Woodman and J. G. F. Powell (eds.), *Author and Audience in Latin Literature* (Cambridge, 1992), 1–17.

93  *The crowd then made a full onslaught on his residence*: this crowd consisted of Roman citizens (as is made clear at the end of the paragraph), the only people allowed to live on Ortygia (§§ 84–5, 98).

94  *the danger he had faced at Lampsacus*: at *Ver.* 2.1.63–9 Cicero recounted how in 80 BC Verres, while passing through Lampsacus on his way to Asia to serve as a legate under Gnaeus Cornelius Dolabella, had nearly been burnt alive by an outraged mob in the house in which he was staying

   *the precedent . . . with Hadrianus*: in *c*.83 BC the repressive governor of Africa, Gaius Fabius Hadrianus, was burnt alive in his residence at Utica by the Roman citizens of the province (*Ver.* 2.1.70).

97  *throughout a great many Punic and Sicilian wars*: only two, in fact: the First and Second Punic Wars. There is a great deal of exaggeration for rhetorical effect in this paragraph.

   *the Syracusans saw the enemy . . . in the harbour*: when the city was taken by Marcus Marcellus, entirely from land, in 211 BC.

98  *the Athenian fleet of 300 ships*: during the disastrous Athenian expedition against Sicily during the Peloponnesian War (415–413 BC). The figure 300 is a gross exaggeration. A hundred and thirty-four ships set out on the expedition, they were reinforced after losses by a further 73, and 75 and 110 Athenian ships respectively took part in the two battles in the Great Harbour.

99  *the island of Ceres*: Ceres (the Greek Demeter) was the goddess of growth, i.e. of crops. Her daughter Proserpina (Persephone) was believed to have been raped by Dis (Pluto) at Henna, a town in the centre of Sicily.

108  *Gaius Sacerdos*: the governor before Verres (see second note on § 55 above).

109  *Sthenius of Thermae*: one of Verres' most prominent victims (and a client of Pompey's); his story is told at *Ver.* 2.2.83–118. He did not protest when Verres stole his works of art, but did do so when he proceeded to

remove the public statues of Thermae. Verres then had him prosecuted on a false charge of forgery. Sthenius fled to Rome where the consuls of 72 gave him their support by proposing a decree that no one in the provinces should be tried in absence on a capital charge; but the decree was talked out by Verres' father and friends, and Sthenius was condemned in absence. The tribunes of 71 then carried a resolution in his favour, enabling him to remain in Rome; he did not return to Sicily. He later assisted Cicero in mounting his prosecution of Verres.

112 *(yes, some of these people do have Latin names!)*: the jury would take crimes committed against Romans much more seriously than crimes committed against Greeks, and so Cicero draws attention to Furius' nationality.

114 *Titus Vettius*: Verres' brother-in-law and his quaestor at Syracuse in 72 and 71.

*Publius Cervius*: not elsewhere mentioned. On the rejection of jurors see first note on *Ver.* 10 above.

116 *this frightened him . . . to Timarchides*: Cicero assumes that the money went into Verres' pocket; but Verres may have known nothing about the transaction (still less about the transactions related in the next paragraph).

117 *The condemned men were shut up inside the prison*: this paragraph was famous in antiquity, and is cited by Quintilian no fewer than nine times.

124 *Publius Africanus*: i.e. Publius Cornelius Scipio Aemilianus Africanus, the destroyer of Carthage (146); see note on *Ver.* 14 above. The references to Scipio and Africanus later in the paragraph are also to him.

*the seventeen peoples of Sicily*: i.e. the seventeen who stayed loyal to Rome during the Second Punic War.

125 *Once upon a time Scipio led your sailors*: Cicero is now addressing the people of Tyndaris.

*Segesta's kinship with us*: see second note on § 83 above.

128 *look at the filth and rags of our allies!*: they are dressed in mourning (i.e. with shabby clothing, with the hair untended, and unshaven), to emphasize their wretched condition and their dependence on the favour of the jury. It was normal for the defendant to present himself in this way (the jury would take it amiss if he did not), and it may also have been normal (though evidence is lacking) for those associated with the prosecution to do so.

*Sthenius of Thermae*: see note on § 109 above.

132 *it is not Mars but Venus . . . determined the outcome*: Mars (god of war) was often said to be indiscriminate; but in this case, Cicero says, it was Venus (goddess of sex) who was indiscriminate, because she allowed Nice (Cleomenes' wife) to be shared between Cleomenes and Verres. This then determined the subsequent course of events (Cleomenes' appointment as commander of the fleet, and the fleet's capture by the pirates).

141 *he ordered Servilius . . . a slave of Venus*: Cicero will now relate how Verres
abused legal procedures to destroy Servilius. First he summoned him
away from his home town of Panhormus, where he would have local
support, to reply to a spurious civil action at Lilybaeum. The plaintiff
was allegedly a 'slave of Venus', i.e. a slave of the temple of Venus Erycina
on Mt Eryx, the most important religious centre in Sicily (since Cicero
does not make the obvious point that slaves could not bring lawsuits, this
'slave' was more probably a temple official of free status, perhaps of
relatively high standing). However, the plaintiff, if he ever existed, did
not turn up, leaving Servilius with no charge to answer. But Verres had
got him where he wanted him, in Lilybaeum, and now attempted to force
him to accept a kind of legal wager which would require Servilius to
defend his reputation, by demonstrating that he 'was not making a profit
by theft' (some scholars wrongly take this as referring to Verres). A sum
of 2,000 sesterces (a substantial but not enormous amount) would be
awarded against the challenger, one of Verres' lictors, if Servilius successfully convinced a board of arbitrators that the allegation was groundless;
but if he failed to convince them, the sum would be awarded against him.
The arbitrators would be appointed by Verres from his staff, and in the
event would inevitably find against Servilius, who would therefore be
declared a criminal and punished. Naturally Servilius wanted to have
nothing to do with this absurd wager, so Verres had him beaten until he
accepted it. He died afterwards; Cicero leaves us with the impression,
though does not explicitly state, that this was as a result of his beating.
Then we have the unexpected ending to the story: Verres took a silver
statue of Cupid from Servilius' property (which was presumably all confiscated) and deposited it in the temple of Venus, in fulfilment, Cicero
says, of some discreditable erotic vow. This behaviour of Verres appears
uncharacteristic: normally we find him removing valuable items from
temples, not depositing them there. His deposition of the Cupid is presumably connected in some way with the temple official and the original
threatened action against Servilius. Perhaps the accusation was that
Servilius had cheated the temple in some transaction, and Verres then
provided the Cupid as a way of reimbursing the temple for its loss. The
vow must surely be Cicero's invention. At all events, we receive the
impression here, not for the first time, that Cicero is not allowing us to
know the full story.

143 *Take the famous prison . . . the cruel tyrant Dionysius*: i.e. by Dionysius I,
tyrant of Syracuse from 405 to 367 BC; the historical detail is supplied
because Cicero wishes to compare Verres with a tyrant. Immediately after
these words the Latin text has 'which is called the quarries' (*quae lautumiae vocantur*). These words are objectionable on two counts. First, it is
not strictly accurate to say that the prison was *called* the quarries. It *was*
the quarries: the quarries existed first (the Athenian and allied captives
were imprisoned in them in 413 BC, prior to Dionysius; cf. note on § 68
above), and only later did Dionysius, on the evidence of this passage,

make regular use of them as a formal prison. Secondly, the words assume that the reader is ignorant of the quarries, yet Cicero has already given us a highly memorable description of them at § 68. I would therefore delete the words as an interpolation (with § 68 the source of the information supplied), and have not translated them.

145 *those people we have read about in the poets*: most obviously the Laestrygonians in Homer, *Odyssey* 10.80–132.

*Phalaris*: of Acragas (Agrigentum), the first major Sicilian tyrant (*c.*570–*c.*549 BC). He was traditionally famous for his cruelty, and was said to have roasted his enemies alive in a brazen bull.

146 *Charybdis or Scylla*: further hazards encountered by Odysseus in the *Odyssey* (12.73–126, 234–59). Charybdis was a treacherous whirlpool in a narrow strait, Scylla a man-eating monster with six heads and twelve feet, who lived in a cave above Charybdis. In later mythology Scylla acquired a series of dogs' heads round her waist, and other unusual attributes. The strait was traditionally identified as the Strait of Messina between Sicily and Italy; there is nothing resembling a whirlpool there.

*Cyclops*: in the *Odyssey* (9.105–542), the Cyclopes were a race of one-eyed giants living in a distant land; Odysseus was taken prisoner by one of them, Polyphemus ('the Cyclops', the son of Poseidon), and succeeded in escaping by blinding him. In Theocritus, *Idyll* 11, the Cyclops has become an ugly, rustic lover, and is located in Sicily.

*soldiers . . . fled from Dianium*: on Sertorius, see note on § 72 above. Dianium was his naval base, halfway down the east coast of Spain.

147 *Lucius Suettius*: probably a banker, and perhaps also a merchant.

148 *Even if that were a possible line of defence*: it was not, because the Syracusan records stated that some of the prisoners were executed.

*'Edikaiōthēsan,' it says . . . 'punished by execution'*: in standard Greek, 'edikaiōthēsan' could mean 'they were sentenced' or 'they were punished'. We only have Cicero's word for it that in Sicily it referred exclusively to execution; but it seems unlikely that he could have got away with a false statement on this important point (which the defence could have quickly disproved were it untrue). It also seems quite plausible that Verres should have been unaware that the word was used in Sicily with a more specialized meaning than elsewhere. (But at *Ver.* 2.4.127 Cicero is obviously exaggerating when he claims that Verres knew no Greek at all.)

150 *entwined . . . completely netted*: the extensive hunting imagery in this paragraph is especially appropriate in view of the fact that 'verres', as well as being the name of Cicero's adversary, is also the Latin word for 'boar'.

151 *from a more commanding position*: the rostra. Cicero is hinting that if Verres is acquitted he will prosecute him before the plebeian assembly as aedile in 69.

152 *fugitives from Spain*: i.e. from Sertorius' army (defeated by Pompey in 72).

152 *that type of men*: i.e. men who fought for Sertorius in Spain and then returned to Rome after their defeat—and, more generally, men who fought for Marius against Sulla a decade earlier (Cicero is starting to shift his ground, to prepare for a false argument: see next note but one).

*(a man who . . . embezzled public money)*: on Verres' desertion of Carbo, whose quaestor he had been, see *Ver.* 2 and 11 (with third note on *Ver.* 2 and note on *Ver.* 11, above). (Cicero is not referring to Dolabella here.)

*he would have inflicted . . . in any part of Sicily*: i.e. Verres would have executed all the surviving Marians in Rome and throughout the empire if they had chanced to come to Sicily while he was governor. Cicero's argument in this (very complex) sentence is false: it does not by any means follow that, because Verres' policy was to execute men who had just come from Sertorius' army, he would also have been willing to execute men who had fought for Marius ten years earlier and had been peaceful since then.

153 *Perperna*: see note on § 72 above.

*that type of men*: i.e. former Sertorian rebels.

*a new proscription*: a large-scale programme of legalized murder accompanied by confiscation of property, on the model of the original proscription of the dictator Sulla (in 82–81 BC), which was likewise directed against former Marians.

154 *But it is not open to me . . . it is not open to me*: in this paragraph Cicero continues to assume (absurdly) that it would help his case if Verres' victims really were former Sertorian rebels rather than innocent merchants.

*Puteoli*: the most important port on the west coast of Italy south of Rome; it was 7 miles west of Naples. Ships bound for Puteoli would often come via Sicily.

*Publius Granius*: otherwise unknown; presumably not an *eques*, otherwise Cicero would have said so (as he does in the case of Flavius below).

155 *Lucius Flavius*: mentioned earlier at § 15.

*Lepcis*: i.e. Lepcis Magna, on the north African coast, due south of Cape Pachynum.

156 *Marcus Annius*: mentioned earlier at §§ 73–4.

158 *Consa*: better known as Compsa, a town in central southern Italy, in Samnium but close to the border with Lucania, 57 miles due east of Naples. (It was where Milo was killed in 48 BC.)

161 *Lucius Raecius*: otherwise unknown.

163 *the Porcian law and the Sempronian laws*: there appear to have been three *leges Porciae* (Porcian laws) in the second century BC, designed to protect Roman citizens from summary justice by magistrates. One abolished the

flogging of citizens; another extended beyond the city of Rome a citizen's right of appeal (*provocatio*) to the people. The *lex Sempronia* (Sempronian law), on the other hand, was a law of Gaius Sempronius Gracchus (123 or 122 BC) prohibiting the execution of citizens except after trial before the people or in a court sanctioned by the people. So Roman citizens in the provinces who were considered by the governor to be potentially guilty of a criminal offence had a right to be sent under guard to Rome to have their case heard there (like St Paul), whether before the people directly at an assembly or in one of the permanent courts (which had been sanctioned by the people). Verres' treatment of Gavius would have been legal only if Gavius' claim to be a Roman citizen was (as Verres maintained) false.

163 *the tribunician power . . . restored to them*: see first note on *Ver.* 44 above.

*Gaius Numitorius*: otherwise unknown.

169 *since Messana was founded*: in *c.*725 BC.

173 *since they have given me . . . before them*: by electing him aedile for 69 BC.

*breaking the law themselves*: the jurors, by accepting his bribes.

*jurors that I myself have chosen and approved*: Cicero did not in fact choose any jurors, though he did approve them in the sense that he did not reject them (on the rejection of jurors see first note on *Ver.* 10 above).

*smeared not so much with wax as with mud*: the voting-tablets were coated with wax; cf. *Ver.* 17 and 40 above, with notes.

175 *your and your friends' tyrannical domination of the courts*: i.e. the exclusively senatorial juries imposed by Sulla in 81 BC.

*on the day . . . tribunes of the plebs back*: see first note on *Ver.* 44 above.

176 *Quintus*: for Cicero to address Hortensius by his first name in this way is presumptuous, very unusual, and very striking.

177 *the text of a bill on new courts and juries has been published*: i.e. the *lex Aurelia*, put forward by the praetor Lucius Aurelius Cotta, which Cicero speaks of as if it were going to prescribe exclusively equestrian juries (cf. 'a different order'), but which in the event enacted a compromise, making juries effectively two-thirds equestrian and one-third senatorial.

178 *the Roman people will put that juror on trial*: i.e. at an assembly. Both of the alternatives proposed by Cicero in this sentence assume that the *lex Aurelia* will have been passed (and that it will have prescribed exclusively equestrian juries). A juror who has taken bribes will either be tried before the people, who will have voted for the *lex Aurelia* and whose hostility to senatorial jurors can therefore be assumed, or in the new court staffed by jurors from 'a different order' (§ 177): in either case, his conviction will be a foregone conclusion.

180 *without them even having to get out of bed*: elections began at the crack of dawn. Cicero was an early riser, doing much of his correspondence and his literary work in the early hours. In the passage which begins here,

Cicero expresses the resentment felt by 'new men' such as himself towards the 'nobles' (for these terms, see Glossary); his aim is of course to convince the jury that he is serious in his threat to prosecute any jurors who accept bribes.

*Marcus Cato*: Marcus Porcius Cato the elder (234–149 BC), the new man from Tusculum who became consul in 195 and censor in 184. He was forever prosecuting his enemies, such as the Scipios and their friends, and was unusually severe in his revision of the senate. He may have been the author of the Porcian laws mentioned at § 163.

181  *Quintus Pompeius*: another new man, the consul of 141 and, in 131, the first plebeian censor.

*Gaius Fimbria, Gaius Marius, and Gaius Coelius*: a further three new men who reached the consulship, Gaius Flavius Fimbria in 104, Gaius Marius (the enemy of Metellus Numidicus and Sulla) in 107, 104–100, and 86, and Gaius Coelius Caldus in 94.

182  *It is impossible . . . we might perform*: though Cicero did not know it, his subsequent career was to demonstrate the falsity of this statement.

184  *whose royal offering*: the reference is to a jewelled candelabrum which the two sons of Antiochus, king of Syria, had had specially made and were keeping ready to dedicate in the temple of Jupiter on the Capitol once its rebuilding (see note on § 48 above) was complete; Verres made the elder prince lend it to him, and then kept it. The sentence which begins here continues until the close of the speech (I was wrong in *Defence Speeches* to say in my second note on *Mil.* 72 that *Mil.* 72–5 is the longest sentence in Cicero: this is longer). In this translation I have stopped the sentence (not before time, some might feel) in the middle of § 188.

*whose holy and beautiful image*: a statue of Zeus Ourios (sender of favouring winds), stolen from a temple at Syracuse.

*Melita and Samos*: in this list Cicero will include acts of sacrilege from Verres' whole career, particularly from the period of his legateship under Gnaeus Cornelius Dolabella in 80–79. Melita is the modern Malta.

*at Syracuse . . . roof and walls*: Verres allegedly removed the ancient paintings of battle scenes with which the temple was decorated, and placed them in a brothel.

185  *Latona . . . Delos*: Latona (Leto) gave birth to the twins Apollo and Diana (Artemis) at Delos. Verres stole some statues from the famous temple to Apollo there, but they were recovered when his ship was wrecked in a storm.

*Perga*: in Pamphylia.

*Publius Africanus*: i.e. Publius Cornelius Scipio Aemilianus Africanus, in the Third Punic War (149–146 BC).

*Mercury . . . Tyndaris*: Verres persuaded the senate of Tyndaris to give him their statue of Mercury (Hermes) only after binding their chief magistrate naked to a bronze statue in the forum of Tyndaris in freezing weather. Hermes was the patron god of athletics and his statue was often placed in public exercise-grounds.

186 *he attempted to . . . carry away*: the attempt was unsuccessful: the slaves were driven off by the townspeople.

*holy mother of Ida*: Rhea, mother of Jupiter (Zeus), who bore him on Crete and gave him to the Curetes (to whom the Engyium temple was dedicated) on Mount Ida in Crete to look after.

*except for the name of Africanus*: Verres removed some bronze urns and armour which Scipio Aemilianus had dedicated, but left the dedicatory inscription behind.

*from whose temple . . . profit and plunder*: when he was city praetor in 74, Verres profited from having an imaginary defect in the columns of the temple of Castor and Pollux corrected (the temple was at the south-west corner of the forum, and the senate often met there—hence 'the great deliberations').

*whose route . . . for his own profit*: also during his praetorship, but we do not know the details; on the face of it, this hardly seems something to offend the gods. If Verres had instead neglected the road, Cicero would no doubt have criticized him at least as strongly.

187 *Ceres and Libera . . . grandeur and mystery*: a reference to the Eleusinian mysteries, held at Eleusis near Athens in honour of Demeter (Ceres) and Persephone (Libera); on these gods, see first note on § 36 above. The omission of Liber (Bacchus, Dionysus), the third member of the Aventine triad, is striking. Cicero does not claim that Verres outraged Liber (or indeed Venus), for obvious reasons; cf. §§ 27 'he concluded that he owed the rest of his time to Venus and to Bacchus', 142 'a devotee of Venus'.

*its rightful home at Henna*: see note on § 99 above.

## DE IMPERIO CN. POMPEI

1 *the spot where I am now standing*: the rostra.

*to defending my friends in their hour of need*: i.e. speaking for his friends in court as their advocate. The prosecution of Verres need not be seen as an exception to this pattern, since that could be represented as a defence of Cicero's friends the Sicilians. Note the play on words, 'time . . . hour'.

2 *because of successive reruns . . . the votes of all the centuries*: for the procedure for the election of praetors by the centuriate assembly, see second note on *Ver.* 2.5.38 above. Cicero was the choice of each century until he had obtained the support of sufficient centuries (97 out of 193) to be declared elected; he obtained a majority of the centuries before any of the other candidates did; and although the election was held all over again twice (because of postponements we otherwise know nothing about, no doubt caused by violence), he achieved the same result each time.

4 *Asia*: references to 'Asia' denote the Roman province of Asia, i.e. the western end of Asia Minor, the former kingdom of Attalus III of Pergamum, bequeathed to Rome in 133 BC.

5 *Bithynia, which is now a province of yours*: since it was bequeathed to Rome by Nicomedes IV in late 75 or early 74.

   *the kingdom of Ariobarzanes*: Cappadocia. It bordered with the Roman province of Cilicia.

   *his successor*: Manius Acilius Glabrio, the consul of 67, appointed as commander in Bithynia and Pontus in 66. See note on *Ver.* 4 above.

7 *that man*: Mithridates. Cicero refers to his 'Asiatic vespers' of 88 BC.

8 *Lucius Sulla . . . and so did Lucius Murena*: both triumphs were held in 81, Sulla's having been delayed as a result of the civil war with the Marians.

   *and Murena by Sulla*: I suspect there is just a hint of criticism of Sulla here, for not allowing Murena to complete the job. Criticism of Sulla would be appropriate before a popular audience (cf. note on § 47 below).

9 *the kingdom of the Bosporus*: i.e. the Cimmerian Bosporus, the kingdom immediately to the east of the Crimea.

   *to the chiefs*: in fact to one Roman commander, the rebel Sertorius (for whom see note on *Ver.* 2.5.72 above). Cicero's choice of the word 'chief' denies Sertorius the privilege of being considered a Roman; the rhetorical plural makes the reference still vaguer. An equally colourful account of Mithridates' dealings with Sertorius is given at *Mur.* 32: 'This king, after spending some years making the necessary plans and preparing his forces for war, had such high hopes for himself that he fully expected to link the Atlantic Ocean with the Black Sea and the forces of Sertorius with his own.' The topic was clearly a gift to any orator with imagination.

11 *your forefathers wanted Corinth . . . extinguished*: in 146 BC four Roman envoys addressing an assembly of the Achaean League at Corinth were insulted and perhaps treated with violence. The Romans under Lucius Mummius then destroyed the city, one of the richest and most historic in Greece, as an example to the other Greek states. Cicero expresses his disapproval of this action at *Off.* 3.46 (and less unequivocally at 1.35).

   *who put a legate of the Roman people . . . and then killed him*: Manius Aquillius, the consul of 101, had led the commission to Asia which restored Nicomedes IV to his throne in Bithynia, but had then forced him to invade Pontus, thus precipitating the First Mithridatic War (88–85 BC). Upon Aquillius' capture by Mithridates in 88, he was tied to a donkey and paraded around wearing a placard; afterwards he was executed by having molten gold poured down his throat. Mithridates then proceeded to his next atrocity, the 'Asiatic vespers', referred to twice in this paragraph.

12 *two kings*: Mithridates and Tigranes.

*especially seeing that you have already sent someone else*: i.e. Glabrio (whom Cicero refrains from complimenting).

13 *even though it is for a naval war that he has come*: the war against the pirates, now completed.

14 *wars against Antiochus, Philip, the Aetolians, and the Carthaginians*: i.e. the Antiochean War (192–189 BC) against Antiochus III of Syria and the Aetolians, the First and Second Macedonian Wars (214–205, 200–197) against Philip V of Macedon, and the three Punic Wars (264–241, 218–201, 149–146) against the Carthaginians. All these wars were undertaken at least nominally in defence of allies.

15 *the harbour duty, the tithes, and the grazing tax*: the harbour duty (*porto-rium*) was a 2½ per cent duty levied on imports and exports at the borders of provinces (cf. 'the size of its exports', § 14 above); the tithe (*decuma*) was a 10 per cent tax on crops, fruit, and wine (cf. 'the productiveness of its soil, the variety of its crops'); and the grazing tax (*scriptura*) was a charge imposed for grazing cattle on public land (cf. 'the extent of its pasturage').

16 *in the guard-posts*: probably lookout posts designed to prevent goods being smuggled into or out of the province without the harbour duty being paid.

19 *at the beginning of our hostilities with him*: in 88 BC, after the 'Asiatic vespers'.

21 *A large and well-equipped fleet . . . by this same commander*: Sertorius (see second note on § 9 above) had sent Mithridates a representative, Marcus Marius (a senator), whom the king had put in charge of a part of his fleet; in 72 Lucullus destroyed this fleet at Lemnos and executed Marius. On the reading 'puffed up' (*inflata*) for the manuscripts' 'set on fire' (*inflammata*), see my note at *CQ*, NS 55 (2005), 309–10.

*Sinope and Amisus . . . his approach and arrival*: both in fact withstood long sieges before being taken. Sinope was the capital of Pontus and the birthplace of Mithridates.

*with other kings in other countries*: with Tigranes, with his son Machares, ruler of the kingdom of the Bosporus, and with Arsaces, king of Parthia.

22 *the famous Medea*: in myth, Medea was the daughter of Aeëtes, the king of Colchis. She fell in love with Jason, the leader of the Argonauts, helped him to obtain the golden fleece, and ran away with him in his ship. Her father pursued them, and to prevent him catching them up, Medea murdered her brother Absyrtus and scattered his limbs in the sea for her father to collect.

*in the earlier war*: the first.

23 *a certain extremely wealthy . . . temple*: probably the temple of Nanaea of Anaïtis in Elymais (between Susa and the Persian Gulf), previously the object of raids by Parthian and Syrian kings. It was in fact much too far away for Lucullus to think of going to. His ultimate goal was Artaxata, in the opposite direction.

*one city from Tigranes' kingdom*: Tigranocerta. Cicero's wording contains a veiled criticism, that Lucullus only succeeded in capturing one city out of many.

24  *to them the name of king is something great and venerated*: to the Romans, on the other hand, it was detested. They were proud of having expelled their last king, Tarquinius Superbus, in 509 BC.

25  *our disaster*: Triarius' defeat at Zela (67 BC). This was Mithridates' greatest success against the Romans: 7,000 Romans were killed and their camp was taken.

28  *to his father's army . . . against formidable enemies*: Pompey (born 106 BC) served in the Social War under his father the consul Gnaeus Pompeius Strabo at Asculum in 89.

*at the end of his childhood . . . of a great commander*: he continued to serve under his father during the civil war of 87.

*at the beginning of his youth . . . of a great army*: during 83–81, when he fought for Sulla in Italy, Sicily, and Africa. His father had died in 87.

*Civil, African, Transalpine, Spanish . . . slave, and naval wars*: Pompey fought civil wars against the Marian consul Gnaeus Papirius Carbo in Sicily (82) and against the anti-Sullan rebel Marcus Aemilius Lepidus in Etruria (77); he fought against Cinna's son-in-law the Marian Gnaeus Domitius Ahenobarbus and King Iarbas in Africa (81); against Gallic tribes while on his way to Spain (77–76); against the Marian rebel Sertorius in Spain (76–72); against the remnants of Spartacus' slave revolt (71); and against the pirates (67).

32  *you*: the Roman people.

*how many cities of your allies . . . captured by the pirates?*: Plutarch (at *Pomp.* 24, a fascinating account of the extent of piracy before 67 BC and the Romans' utter powerlessness in the face of it) says that the pirates captured 400 cities.

*the crossing from Brundisium*: to Greece.

*twelve axes*: i.e. two praetors, with their twelve lictors ('axes' refers to the *fasces*: see Glossary). Plutarch (*Pomp.* 24) gives the praetors' names as Sextilius and Bellienus; we do not know their year of office.

33  *Can you be unaware . . . by pirates at Misenum?*: nothing is known about the incident at Caieta (a port in Latium close to Campania); the praetor was certainly not Marcus Antonius Creticus, as is sometimes suggested. The general whose child was kidnapped at Misenum (at the tip of the northern headland of the Bay of Naples) is known from Plut. *Pomp.* 24 to have been Marcus Antonius, the orator (see second note on *Ver.* 2.5.3 above). Antonius was praetor in 102 and fought a war against the Cilician pirates, triumphing at the end of 100; he was then consul in 99. Plutarch says that it was Antonius' daughter that was kidnapped ('as she was taking a trip into the countryside'), whereas Cicero says 'the children'; but in Latin 'children' was sometimes written for 'child', as at *S. Rosc.* 96

(cf. Aulus Gellius 2.13). Plutarch adds that the daughter 'fetched a very rich ransom'.

33    *that setback at Ostia*: Dio also mentions this (36.22.2), but gives no date and says nothing about a consul (Dio's account of the problem of piracy, less informative than Plutarch's but still useful, is at 36.20–3). Ostia, the port of Rome, was 'virtually under your very eyes' because it was only 15 miles from Rome, at the mouth of the Tiber.

      *within the mouth of Ocean*: i.e. in the Mediterranean, the mouth of Ocean being the Strait of Gibraltar.

35    *people from as far away as Crete*: Quintus Caecilius Metellus (afterwards 'Creticus'), the consul of 69, had been engaged in conquering Crete, with great cruelty, since 68, and the Cretans were anxious to surrender to Pompey so as to secure better terms than they would obtain from Metellus. Metellus and Pompey fell out over the incident. Metellus organized Crete as a Roman province in 66.

      *completed by midsummer*: 67 BC. Pompey cleared the western Mediterranean in forty days and then the eastern Mediterranean in forty-nine days.

36    *more from a comparison with others*: the passage which follows contains strong criticism of other, unnamed contemporary generals. Cicero must mean his audience to think first of Lucullus: had he not intended this, he would have excluded him explicitly.

40    *statues, paintings, and other works of art . . . theirs for the taking*: Lucullus was a great art collector (Plut. *Luc.* 39); this reference of Cicero's is an indication that he is thinking of Lucullus throughout this passage.

44    *in a war that affected all peoples*: the war against the pirates. Cicero is referring to the day on which the *lex Gabinia* was passed.

45    *after the catastrophic defeat . . . a short while ago*: at Zela, referred to at § 25.

      *the province*: Asia.

46    *the enemies of the Roman people*: the pirates.

      *and when envoys . . . wished to surrender!*: on this incident, see first note on § 35 above. Pompey was in Pamphylia at the time (§ 35); Cicero greatly exaggerates the distance involved, which was only about 400 miles. It is also misleading of him to suggest that the Cretans offered their surrender to Pompey rather than to Metellus because his authority was greater: they were hoping for more favourable terms.

      *And did not Mithridates . . . to Gnaeus Pompeius?*: we know about Mithridates' negotiations with Sertorius in Spain (§ 9), but hear nothing anywhere else about any approach he may have made to Pompey at that time. Such an approach seems on the face of it highly improbable.

      *those who resented . . . expressly to Pompeius*: the reference will be to Quintus Caecilius Metellus Pius (first cousin once removed of Metellus

Creticus, the 'commander of ours' referred to above). Metellus Pius had been consul with Sulla in 80, and had then fought unsuccessfully against Sertorius in Spain until being joined by Pompey in 76. It would not have been unnatural if he felt resentment towards Pompey, who was not even yet a senator, but he did in fact co-operate fully with him in the campaign against Sertorius.

*those kings*: Mithridates and Tigranes.

47   *Maximus, Marcellus, Scipio, Marius*: see notes above on *Ver.* 2.5.25 (Quintus Fabius Maximus Verrucosus), 2.5.84 (Marcellus), and 2.5.14 (Scipio Aemilianus and Marius). Sulla, though famed for his luck, is not mentioned, since Cicero is speaking before the people (who, generally speaking, had been well disposed to Marius and had hated Sulla; cf. second note on § 8 above).

48   *as indeed you do*: a reminder that in this speech Cicero is preaching to the converted.

51   *Quintus Catulus . . . Quintus Hortensius*: Quintus Lutatius Catulus (the consul of 78) and Quintus Hortensius Hortalus (the consul of 69), the chief opponents of the bill. Both were prominent conservatives; Hortensius was married to Catulus' sister. On Catulus, see second note on *Ver.* 44 above. Hortensius was Rome's most foremost orator until defeated by Cicero in the Verres trial in 70; the complimentary reference to his 'talent', below, is to his oratorical ability. After Cicero attained the consulship, he and Hortensius worked together as partners in the courts; but they were never close friends. The people had a great respect for Catulus; Hortensius, by contrast, was not popular.

52   *Aulus Gabinius*: the tribune of 67 who proposed the *lex Gabinia* giving Pompey his command against the pirates. He was later to become consul in the year that Cicero was exiled (58); declining to support him, he thereby earned his undying hatred and became a target of his invective. He was convicted of extortion in 54 or 53, after Pompey had forced Cicero to defend him—one case Cicero was happy to lose. See further second note on *Phil.* 2.48 below.

55   *King Antiochus and King Perseus*: Rome fought the Antiochean War against Antiochus III of Syria in 192–189 BC; there were naval victories at Corycus in 191 and at Myonnesus in 190. Perseus of Macedon was defeated in a land battle at Pydna in 168, in the Third Macedonian War (172–167). His fleet in fact defeated the Roman fleet in 170, and then surrendered to the Romans after Pydna without fighting; but Cicero's audience would no doubt be unaware of this.

*and defeated the Carthaginians*: in the First Punic War (264–241 BC).

*The island of Delos*: a great commercial centre, particularly after the destruction of Corinth in 146 BC, and the centre of the slave trade in the eastern Mediterranean. It was sacked in 69 by the pirates, who enslaved the inhabitants; Mithridates had also sacked it in 88.

55 *the Appian Way*: the road from Rome to Capua; it follows the coast, and so no doubt was vulnerable to pirates. If Cicero is referring to a specific incident, it is unknown.

*this very platform*: the rostra. It was adorned with bronze prows taken from warships of Antium (in Latium) captured in 338 BC.

56 *you*: the Roman people. Latin has singular and plural forms of personal pronouns, so the ambiguity in the English is not present in the Latin.

57 *opposition to the request . . . appointed as his legate*: sponsors of laws were not allowed to hold any office created by their own law, and therefore Gabinius was unable to serve as a legate of Pompey's in the campaign against the pirates; Cicero affects to consider this merely a technicality (cf. § 58 below, 'So are people going to insist on the letter of the law . . . ?'). Once the *lex Manilia* was passed, however, Pompey's command no longer derived from the *lex Gabinia*, and at this point Gabinius could, and did, take a position as one of his legates.

58 *Gaius Falcidius, Quintus Metellus, Quintus Coelius Latiniensis, and Gnaeus Lentulus*: all were presumably still alive, since the phrase 'whose names I mention with the greatest respect' is only used by Cicero with reference to the living. T. P. Wiseman argues (*CQ*, NS 14 (1964), 122–3) that this list must be in order of seniority, and suggests that (i) Falcidius was tribune and legate in the 80s; (ii) Metellus is probably Metellus Creticus (see first note on *Ver.* 26 above), presumably tribune in 82 and legate in 81; (iii) Coelius was perhaps tribune and legate in the 70s ('Latiniensis' may be a geographical description, 'of the *ager Latiniensis*', not a *cognomen*); and (iv) Lentulus is Gnaeus Cornelius Lentulus Marcellinus, tribune in 69, legate in 68, and later consul in 56. R. Syme (*JRS* 53 (1963), 55–60), on the other hand, takes Quintus Metellus as Celer (consul in 60), not Creticus, and makes all four tribune in 68 and legate in 67. This is surely ruled out by Cicero's order, which places the obscure Falcidius first; but Marcellinus' tribunate should probably be dated, with Syme, to 68.

60 *two very serious wars . . . by the same man, Scipio*: Cicero here says the same thing twice over (while claiming not to be saying it at all), that one man, Scipio Aemilianus, ended the Third Punic War by destroying Carthage in 146, and then went on the end the war in Spain by destroying Numantia in 133. (Here 'the Spanish war' refers to the Numantine War; at § 28 it referred to the war against Sertorius.)

*against Jugurtha . . . against the Teutoni*: see note on *Ver.* 2.5.14 above.

61 *for a mere youth . . . at a time of national crisis*: when, in 83 (aged 23), he raised three legions from his father's veterans in Picenum and went to join Sulla on his return to Italy. After that he went on to fight Carbo in Sicily and Domitius and Iarbas in Africa (see fourth note on § 28 above), before returning to Rome for a triumph in 81 (or possibly 80).

*much too young to qualify for senatorial rank*: quaestors joined the senate at the end of their year of office, and, under a law of Sulla's of 81, no one could become a quaestor before the age of 30 (or praetor before 39 or consul before 42). Pompey omitted all the junior magistracies, and remained an *eques* until 70, when he became consul at the age of 35.

62 *two illustrious and valiant consuls*: Decimus Junius Brutus and Mamercus Aemilius Lepidus Livianus, consuls in 77 when Pompey was sent to fight Sertorius in Spain. The consuls had refused to go to Spain themselves, probably because they knew they were not capable of undertaking such a difficult war (which took even Pompey a full five years).

*Lucius Philippus ... but with that of both the consuls!*: Lucius Marcius Philippus was consul in 91 and censor in 86; he conquered Sardinia for Sulla in 82. The oldest consular still active in politics, he was a man of considerable influence in the post-Sullan era. He was noted for his witticisms, of which this one, which Cicero quotes again at *Phil.* 11.18, is the most famous. It is (naturally) snappier in Latin than in English, *non ... pro consule sed pro consulibus*.

*at an age ... any curule office*: i.e. when he became consul in 70, he was not even old enough to hold the praetorship (see second note on § 61 above). He could, however, have held the curule aedileship, to which Sulla seems not to have attached any age qualification. (*curulem*, 'curule', is the conjecture of D. R. Shackleton Bailey, and is absolutely necessary to the sense, since Pompey was of course old enough to hold the non-curule office of quaestor; see *Harvard Studies in Classical Philology*, 83 (1979), 254.)

*a second triumph by senatorial decree*: in 71, for his victory over Sertorius (see note on *Ver.* 45 above). The first triumph (in 81 or 80) was actually granted by Sulla, but was no doubt rubber-stamped by the senate.

63 *with the full endorsement ... of equal standing*: Catulus and the other senators had of course opposed Pompey's appointment to the pirate command, which is why Cicero omits that departure from precedent from his list.

65 *the greed and corruption ... in recent years*: Cicero's prosecution of Gaius Verres four years earlier allows him to speak on this subject with some authority.

66 *they know well ... their lamentations*: yet Hortensius had defended Verres

67 *as if we did not see that Gnaeus Pompeius is 'great'*: a reference to Pompey's *cognomen* Magnus ('Great'), adopted in imitation of Alexander the Great in 81. (This is the only such reference in this speech: in this translation the English word 'great' is used to translate other Latin words besides *magnus*.)

68 *Publius Servilius*: Publius Servilius Vatia Isauricus, the consul of 79; see note on *Ver.* 2.5.66 above.

*Gaius Curio*: Gaius Scribonius Curio, the consul of 76; see note on *Ver.* 18 above.

68    *Gnaeus Lentulus*: Gnaeus Cornelius Lentulus Clodianus, the consul of
      72; see third note on *Ver.* 2.5.15 above.

      *Gaius Cassius*: Gaius Cassius Longinus, the consul of 73. In 72 he was
      governor of Cisalpine Gaul, where he was defeated by Spartacus.

70    *help in attaining office*: i.e. in attaining the consulship. This is one of
      Cicero's more disingenuous sentences.

      *the career I have been following*: i.e. forensic advocacy.

71    *this high office*: the praetorship.


## IN CATILINAM I

1    *How far, I ask you*: *Quo usque tandem*, a highly dramatic and effective
     opening to the speech (and one of the two or three most famous quota-
     tions from Latin literature). The expression is used nowhere else by
     Cicero, but occurs in Sallust (*Cat.* 20.9) in an address given by Catiline to
     his followers a year before Cicero delivered the *First Catilinarian*.
     Scholars have debated why Sallust should make Catiline echo the words
     with which Cicero began his famous denunciation of him. The problem
     was solved, in my view, by D. A. Malcolm (*CQ*, NS 29 (1979), 219–20),
     who proposed that *quo usque tandem* was a demagogic phrase favoured by
     Catiline, which Cicero then mockingly threw back at him. Sallust would
     therefore be accurately characterizing Catiline's language in the speech
     he attributed to him—and incidentally explaining to his readers the
     significance of Cicero's famous words.

     *what you were up to yesterday evening, what you were up to last night*:
     scholars are uncertain what the Latin means, and unfortunately the date
     of the *First Catilinarian*, *Second Catilinarian* (one day after the *First
     Catilinarian*), and the SCU (eighteen or seventeen days before the *First
     Catilinarian*, depending on whether Asconius (6 C) has used inclusive
     reckoning) depend on it. The passage is normally held to mean, 'what
     you were up to last night, what you were up to the night before': in that
     case, the events of 'last night' would be unknown, the events of 'the night
     before' would refer to the meeting at Laeca's house (since the same
     phrase is used to refer to it below at § 8), the date of the *First Catilinarian*
     would be 8 November (since we know from Cic. *Sul.* 52 that the meeting
     at Laeca's house was on the night of 6–7 November), and Cicero would
     have delayed twenty-four hours after the assassination attempt on the
     morning of 7 November before summoning the senate. In our passage,
     however, it is difficult to see how 'where you were, whom you collected
     together, and what plan of action you decided upon' can apply to two
     different nights: the conspirators were summoned and plans made,
     surely, on just one night, that of the meeting at Laeca's house on 6–7
     November. I therefore prefer to translate the passage in such a way as to
     refer to a single night, 'what you were up to yesterday evening, what you
     were up to last night', and allow Cicero to say the same thing twice over

for rhetorical effect (as he commonly does, by the figure known as 'pleon-asm'). It is possible that different times of the same night are being described, as was suggested by T. Crane (*CJ* 61 (1965–6), 264–7). If we accept that Cicero is referring to a single night, the date of the *First Catilinarian* becomes 7 November, there is no second night to explain away, and Cicero no longer hesitates for twenty-four hours before sum-moning the senate. The date of the *Second Catilinarian* accordingly becomes 8 November, and the date of the SCU 20 October (or 21 October if Asconius used inclusive reckoning). Since this is the solution I have adopted, I have translated all references to the meeting at Laeca's house as 'last night' in the *First Catilinarian* and as 'the night before last' in the *Second Catilinarian* (studies of the relevant Latin terms suggest that their meaning varied according to the context—hence the uncertainty).

3 *Publius Scipio ... killed Tiberius Gracchus*: Tiberius Sempronius Gracchus was the tribune of 133 BC whose controversial agrarian bill and unprecedented attempt to secure re-election to office led to his murder and that of his supporters at the hands of the *pontifex maximus* Publius Cornelius Scipio Nasica Serapio (the former consul of 138), in 133. Cicero's remark below about Gracchus causing a 'mild disturbance' is an extreme understatement, and well illustrates Z. Yavetz's observation that 'Cicero was extremely tolerant of all dead *populares*' (*Historia*, 12 (1963), 493). Similar understatement is used at § 4 and at *Cat.* 4.13.

*Gaius Servilius Ahala ... killed Spurius Maelius*: Maelius was a wealthy plebeian who used his own means to relieve a corn shortage in 439 BC, was suspected of aiming at tyranny, and was killed by Ahala.

*a decree of the senate*: the SCU, although it was passed in response to Manlius' rising, and not specifically against Catiline.

4 *the consul Lucius Opimius ... came to no harm*: in 121 BC the consul Opimius secured the passage of the first-ever SCU (the wording of which Cicero quotes here; it mentions only one consul because the other one, Quintus Fabius Maximus, was away in Gaul fighting the Allobroges). He then immediately proceeded to massacre the supporters of the reformer Gaius Sempronius Gracchus (the tribune of 123 and 122, and younger brother of Tiberius); Gracchus himself committed suicide to avoid capture. (Gracchus' father, mentioned below, was Tiberius Sempronius Gracchus, consul in 177 and 163 and censor in 169, and his maternal grandfather was Publius Cornelius Scipio Africanus, the con-queror of Hannibal (202), consul in 205 and 194, and censor in 199.) Marcus Fulvius Flaccus, the consul of 125, and his two sons were among the 3,000 Gracchans who lost their lives (see first note on *Cat.* 4.13 below).

*A similar senatorial decree ... Lucius Valerius*: when the SCU was passed for the second ever time in 100 BC, the consuls Gaius Marius and Lucius Valerius Flaccus took action against the violent activities of Marius' former allies the tribune Lucius Appuleius Saturninus and the praetor Gaius Servilius Glaucia, both of whom were seeking further office for 99. Saturninus had been elected to his third tribunate (after 103 and 100), and Glaucia was standing for the consulship (illegally, so soon after the praetorship); on election day, Saturninus' men murdered Glaucia's principal rival, Gaius Memmius. Marius shut Saturninus and his supporters inside the senate-house, hoping to save their lives; but the people broke through the roof and stoned them to death with the roof-tiles. Glaucia was captured and killed in a separate incident.

4 *for twenty days now*: Asconius (6 C) claims that this is a round figure, and that it was in fact only eighteen days since the SCU had been passed. He says that it was Cicero's regular practice in his speeches to talk in round figures.

*my only wish is to be compassionate*: passages like this are often suspected of having been added after the event, since at the time when Cicero spoke the conspirators had not yet been executed. (I translate *clemens* as 'compassionate' in the *Catilinarians*, but prefer to render *clementia* as 'clemency' in the very different context of *Pro Marcello*.)

8 *Praeneste*: in the hills 20 miles south-east of Rome. It had been a Marian stronghold; Sulla sacked it in 82 and settled a colony of his veterans there.

*Marcus Laeca*: Marcus Porcius Laeca, a senator (his career is unknown), chiefly remembered as the owner of the house where the meeting of the conspirators took place on the night of 6–7 November. He was convicted and went into exile in 62.

9 *I am not even wounding . . . with my words*: because he has not named them.

*Two Roman equestrians*: Gaius Cornelius and Lucius Vargunteius.

11 *Jupiter Stator*: Jupiter the Stayer (of troops in battle); he was said to have stayed the flight of Romulus' army from the Sabines at the point where the temple was later built (in an uncertain location close to the Palatine). The senate was meeting in this temple (we know of no other occasion when it met there); we should imagine Cicero as turning towards the statue of the god. On the significance of the choice of venue, see A. Vasaly, *Representations: Images of the World in Ciceronian Oratory* (Berkeley etc., 1993), 41–59.

*the last consular elections*: in July 63.

14 *Or again . . . with yet another that is quite incredible?*: Cicero alleges that Catiline murdered his penultimate wife in order to secure his marriage to his last wife, Aurelia Orestilla (who in *In toga candida* (Asc. 91 C) he goes so far as to claim was actually Catiline's daughter). He then alludes to a further, unspecified crime, explained by Sallust (*Cat.* 15.2) and later authors: that Catiline also murdered his own son, again in order to facilitate his marriage to Orestilla. The brevity with which Cicero touches

upon these mysterious allegations is a sure sign that they could not be substantiated. Nevertheless, they were repeated and enlarged upon by later authors with relish.

14   *on the 13th of this month*: literally, 'on the coming Ides'—the Ides being the 13th or the 15th day of the month (depending on the month), and the day on which debtors were required to pay interest.

15   *Can this light of day . . . the good luck of the Roman people?*: this allegation is one of the bases of the myth of the 'first Catilinarian conspiracy' (the only such basis in the *Catilinarians*, in fact—one indication that it is indeed a myth). The reference to Catiline appearing armed in the place of assembly (*comitium*) in front of the senate-house on the last day (29th) of December 66 (the consulship of Manius Aemilius Lepidus and Lucius Volcacius Tullus) appears to have the status of a historical fact. But the statement that his purpose was to kill the consuls and other prominent men can be no more than a conjecture, since no one was attacked, or prosecuted afterwards. It is hard to see why Catiline might have wanted to kill outgoing consuls; but if Cicero is referring to the incoming ones (who would not, however, enter office until 1 January), the statement is even less plausible, because one of them, Lucius Manlius Torquatus, went on to support Catiline at his extortion trial in 65 (a difficulty Cicero attempts to explain away at *Sul.* 81). Catiline's appearance in the forum can more plausibly be explained as being connected in some way with the impending trial of Gaius Manilius for extortion.

16   *left the area of benches . . . you took your seat*: see third note on *Cat.* 4.3 below.

18   *while escaping punishment and remaining free*: a reference to two occasions when Catiline was acquitted in court: in 64, when he had been charged with murders committed during the Sullan proscriptions, and in 65, when he had been charged with extortion committed while he was governor of Africa.

19   *Manius Lepidus' house*: Manius Aemilius Lepidus, the consul of 66 and a fellow patrician. Catiline had made the offer only a few days previously, when Lucius Aemilius Paullus had threatened to prosecute him for violence.

     *Quintus Metellus*: Quintus Caecilius Metellus Celer, the praetor who had been assigned the governorship of Cisalpine Gaul for 62, and who was to block off Catiline's escape before the battle of Pistoria. He afterwards became consul in 60.

     *Marcus Metellus*: the identity of this man is unknown, but he may be Marcus Caecilius Metellus, the praetor of 69 (on whom see second note on *Ver.* 21 above). Cicero treats him as a friend of Catiline's who could not be trusted to keep him under guard.

20   *it would not be my practice to do so*: more to the point, it would not be within the senate's powers to order a citizen into exile.

21  *Publius Sestius*: one of the quaestors, attached to the staff of Antonius. He helped Cicero at Capua, returned to Rome, and then joined Antonius against Catiline in Etruria. As tribune in 57 he opposed Clodius and worked tirelessly for Cicero's recall from exile, sustaining injuries in the process; in return, Cicero (together with Hortensius and Crassus) secured his unanimous acquittal on a charge of violence the following year. Cicero's defence, *Pro Sestio*, survives.

*Marcus Marcellus*: Marcus Claudius Marcellus, the future consul of 51 and subject of Cicero's *Pro Marcello*. He had been quaestor in 64.

24  *Forum Aurelium*: a small town near the coast of Etruria, about 60 miles north of Rome on the Via Aurelia (the road to Massilia by which Catiline was to leave Rome).

*that silver eagle*: a military standard reputedly used by Marius in the war against the Cimbri in 102–101 (Sal. *Cat.* 59.3).

26  *Those physical powers of yours*: Sallust also comments on Catiline's physical powers in a passage closely resembling this one, and no doubt based on it (*Cat.* 5.1–5). For Sallust, Catiline's physical strength would have been a positive quality, had his character not been corrupt; for Cicero, on the other hand, it merely reinforces the impression of brutality. Similar passages occur below at *Cat.* 2.9 and 3.16.

27  *When I prevented you from attaining the consulship*: at the consular elections of July 63, when Cicero deterred Catiline from using violence to secure his election.

*the mobilizer of slaves*: Cicero cleverly slips this allegation, which was untrue, into an imaginary speech, rather than have it come directly from himself. See further second note on *Cat.* 4.4 below.

28  *the laws . . . relating to the punishment of Roman citizens*: particularly the *lex Sempronia* of 123 or 122 BC; see first note on *Ver.* 2.5.163 above. The view which Cicero puts forward in the next sentence, that citizens' rights could be forfeited in certain circumstances, had no legal basis; it is significant that this view, too, is placed within the imaginary speech.

29  *Saturninus, the Gracchi, Flaccus*: see §§ 3–4 above, with notes.

32  *thronging round the tribunal of the city praetor*: i.e. to secure judgements in legal disputes with creditors. The city praetor in 63 was Lucius Valerius Flaccus, Cicero's future client. In Sallust (*Cat.* 33.1; 33.5), Manlius is made to complain to Quintus Marcius Rex that the praetor and the moneylenders have not treated his men fairly.

33  *And you, Jupiter . . . whom we rightly call the 'Stayer'*: see first note on § 11 above. Cicero is again turning towards the statue.


## IN CATILINAM II

1  *Lucius Catilina*: where Cicero writes simply 'Catilina', without *praenomen* (first name), as he does throughout the *First*, *Third*, and *Fourth*

*Catilinarians*, I translate this as 'Catiline', since that is the familiar form of the name in English. But where he dignifies Catiline by the inclusion of his *praenomen*, as here (and at §§ 3 (twice), 14, and 15, only), I prefer to keep the Roman form of the name, and hope that readers will not object to the inconsistency.

1 *He has gone, departed, cleared off, escaped*: whether to Manlius' army or, as he himself claimed, into exile was not yet known. Hence the scepticism which Cicero has to counter in this speech.

4 *Tongilius*: otherwise unknown, as are Publicius and Minucius. Presumably they must have been familiar to at least a significant part of Cicero's audience; no doubt they were well known to the sort of people who frequented the forum.

5 *Quintus Metellus*: see second note on *Cat.* 1.19 above. The reference Cicero has just made to Gaul is to Cisalpine Gaul.

*the praetor's edict*: the edict published by the city praetor at the beginning of each year; it set out how he intended to administer the civil law during his period of office, including the policy he would follow in cases involving debt (cf. note on *Cat.* 1.32 above).

8 *Some of them . . . sexual impulses*: i.e. he penetrated some and was penetrated by others, the latter activity being much the more disreputable.

*the death of their parents*: this might be desired by young men with large debts impatient to receive their inheritance.

9 *no actor*: actors, with rare exceptions, were of very low social standing at Rome, and were thought of as having low moral standards.

11 *one man's valour*: Pompey had just completed the Third Mithridatic War (73–63), having previously cleared the Mediterranean of pirates (67). Mithridates himself had committed suicide earlier in the year (hence 'no king capable of making war on the Roman people').

12 *yesterday*: refers grammatically to Cicero's summoning of the senate, not to his escape from assassination; therefore this sentence cannot prove that the *First Catilinarian* was delivered on 7 November (though in my view it was; see second note on *Cat.* 1.1 above).

*the leading senators . . . empty and unoccupied*: see third note on *Cat.* 4.3 below.

13 *axes, rods of office*: the *fasces* (see Glossary).

*that silver eagle*: see second note on *Cat.* 1.24 above.

14 *Manlius . . . declared war on the Roman people*: some modern scholars have in fact believed this to be the case; one argument against it is that Manlius' veteran colonists came to Rome to support Catiline in the election campaign of 63 (*Mur.* 49). It is interesting that Cicero needs to explain to his audience who Manlius was; presumably the general public would have known of the rising in Etruria, but not necessarily the name of the leader (since he was not otherwise a person of any prominence).

The SCU had been passed against Manlius (not Catiline) on 20 October.

15 *within three days*: in the event, Catiline spent some days at Arretium before joining Manlius (Sal. *Cat.* 36.1), and so the news must have taken a week or so to reach Rome.

18 *New books*: the standard term for a general cancellation of debts (the term would normally be translated 'cancellation of debts', but a literal translation has to be used here because of the play on words which follows).

20 *the plundering of former times*: i.e. when under Sulla's confiscations and proscriptions (82–81) property was taken from Sulla's enemies (including perhaps the 'poor and needy farmers' just mentioned) and given to the veterans. This whole passage is savage in its hostility to the Sullan veterans and the Sullan period.

21 *in dishonourable circumstances*: fighting against their country.

22 *the prison*: the state prison, between the temple of Concord and the senate-house, used for executions only. Besides the five conspirators executed on 5 December, Jugurtha and Vercingetorix also met their ends there. The building still exists, although nowadays one enters the lower of the two chambers (the execution chamber or 'Tullianum') by a staircase, not a rope—and leaves.

26 *Quintus Metellus*: see second note on *Cat.* 1.19 above.

27 *and it has a prison*: Cicero is referring to execution, not imprisonment (see note on § 22 above).

29 *now that all the forces ... on land and sea*: a reference to the recent completion of the Third Mithridatic War (see note on § 11 above).

## IN CATILINAM III

2 *the founder of this city*: Romulus.

3 *some days ago*: in fact nearly a month ago.

4 *I spent all my time ... they were planning*: not strictly true, since his defence of Murena must have taken up a good deal of his time.

*Publius Lentulus*: Publius Cornelius Lentulus Sura, a patrician and the most distinguished of Catiline's followers (more so than Catiline himself); his wife Julia was the sister of another patrician, Lucius Julius Caesar, the consul of 64. Lentulus had been praetor in charge of the extortion court in 74, and then consul in 71, but had been expelled from the senate the following year by the censors; to secure his readmission, he had become praetor a second time in 63. At *Cat.* 4.10, Cicero gives an interesting hint that Lentulus had been lavish in his generosity to the Roman people and was viewed as a 'popular' politician. No doubt his generosity had placed him heavily in debt, and he was now looking to Catiline for at least a second consulship and a lucrative provincial governorship; but the remarks attributed to him at § 9 imply an even larger ambition.

4  *Titus Volturcius*: G. Forsythe has demonstrated that Volturcius must have been a native of Cortona in Etruria (14 miles south of Arretium), and not of Croton in Bruttium, as Sallust maintains at *Cat.* 44.3 (see *AJP* 113 (1992), 407–12).

5  *Lucius Flaccus and Gaius Pomptinus*: Lucius Valerius Flaccus and Gaius Pomptinus, praetors of 63 (like Lentulus). Both were military men (as is implied by the term 'valiant'). Flaccus, a patrician, had served in Transalpine Gaul, Cilicia, Spain, Crete, and Achaea before becoming city praetor in 63; in 62 he was governor of Asia, being successfully defended on a charge of extortion by Hortensius and Cicero in 59 (Cicero's defence, *Pro Flacco*, survives). Pomptinus had served under Crassus against Spartacus in 71; he went on to be governor of Transalpine Gaul in 62–59, suppressing a rising of the Allobroges (62–61), and later served under Cicero in Cilicia in 51–50.

*from the prefecture of Reate*: a small town in the hills in the Sabine territory 45 miles north-east of Rome; Cicero was a patron of the place. It is interesting to learn that he, like other politicians, had his own gang of armed supporters. Reate was later to become famous for being the birthplace of the emperor Vespasian.

6  *Towards the end of the third watch*: there were four watches of the night, so the time indicated will be between 3.00 and 3.30 a.m.

*and their entourage*: the envoys would have been some of the most high-ranking men of their tribe, and no doubt brought a considerable staff with them to Rome.

*Cimber Gabinius*: Publius Gabinius Capito; he came from a senatorial family, but he himself was only an *eques*. 'Cimber' may have been a nickname (the Cimbri were a German tribe defeated by Marius in 101).

*Lucius Statilius*: another *eques*, not known to have had senatorial relatives.

*Gaius Cethegus*: Gaius Cornelius Cethegus, a patrician senator. All we know of his life prior to 63 was that he apparently went to Spain in the 70s, intending to assassinate Quintus Caecilius Metellus Pius (see fourth note on *Imp.* 46 above), but succeeded only in wounding him.

*he had stayed up . . . writing letters*: ironic; for the length of his letter to Catiline, see § 12. Cicero implies that Lentulus was a late riser—a lazy patrician. He specifically mentions his laziness at § 16 below.

8  *Gaius Sulpicius*: not otherwise known, but he must have been a military man, like Flaccus and Pomptinus, since he too is described as 'valiant'. Plutarch adds the detail (an important one, in view of Cethegus' defence at § 10) that the weapons he discovered were all newly sharpened (*Cic.* 19.2).

9  *Lucius Cassius*: Lucius Cassius Longinus, a praetor (in charge of the treason court) with Cicero in 66 and, like Catiline himself, one of the

unsuccessful candidates for the consulship of 63. Asconius calls him stupid (82 C); but he was intelligent enough not to give the Allobroges a letter.

9   *according to the Sibylline books . . . Cinna and Sulla*: the three Sibylline books were a collection of ancient prophecies purchased, according to legend, by Rome's fifth king, Tarquinius Priscus, from the Cumaean Sibyl. They were kept underground in a stone chest in the temple of Jupiter on the Capitol, but were destroyed in the (accidental) burning of the Capitol in 83; their contents were afterwards reconstructed. Lucius Cornelius Cinna (consul in 87–84) controlled Rome from the death of Marius until his own death in 84; his opponent Lucius Cornelius Sulla Felix was consul in 88, dictator (responsible for the proscriptions) in 82–81, and consul again in 80 (see further first note on § 24 below).

  *the acquittal of the Vestal virgins*: we know of two such trials, one, of the Vestal Licinia, for adultery with Crassus, and one, of the Vestal Fabia (a half-sister or cousin of Cicero's wife Terentia), for adultery with Catiline. On the assumption that these are the trials Cicero is referring to, both trials are conventionally dated to 73. The six Vestal virgins were priestesses of Vesta, the goddess of the hearth fire; they were of high social status and enjoyed various privileges, such as reserved seats at the games. The temple of Vesta was a circular building near the south-western corner of the forum, and contained the sacred fire, the Palladium (the sacred guardian-statue of Pallas Athena), and an erect phallus. If a Vestal allowed the fire to go out, this was taken as evidence of her impurity; if convicted, she would be buried alive. Vestals were allowed to retire after thirty years.

10   *during the Saturnalia*: 17–23 December. At this festival, a precursor of the modern Christmas, presents were exchanged, there was much eating and drinking, and slaves were allowed to speak and do as they pleased.

  *your illustrious grandfather*: Publius Cornelius Lentulus, suffect consul in 162 and *princeps senatus* (leader of the senate) from 125 until after 120. In 121 he was seriously wounded while participating in the suppression of Gaius Gracchus (cf. *Cat.* 4.13).

11   *through whom*: i.e. Umbrenus and Gabinius.

  *he confessed that it was true*: Cicero does not make it clear exactly what it was that Lentulus confessed to.

  *the oratorical skill in which he has always excelled*: at *Brut.* 235, however, Cicero tells us that Lentulus delivered his speeches well, but was otherwise an indifferent orator. (In view of the fact that Cicero executed him, it is a little surprising to find Lentulus popping up in the *Brutus* (also at 230); perhaps this shows that Cicero did not view himself as responsible for his death.)

12   *'The person I have sent to you . . . however lowly'*: there is little doubt that Cicero quotes the letter accurately; Sallust recasts it and removes two

colloquialisms (*Cat.* 44.5). It would have been obvious to Catiline, from the seal and handwriting, who had sent the letter; and the contents, with the advice to accept the help of slaves, were entirely superfluous. The purpose of the letter must therefore have been to demonstrate to Catiline that Volturcius, whom he had not met, was a genuine conspirator, and not a government infiltrator. An alternative explanation of the letter, that Lentulus was not previously a member of the conspiracy, should be rejected (as by E. J. Phillips, *Historia*, 25 (1976), 446–7).

14 *my valiant colleague*: Antonius. The senate acknowledged that he had been a friend of Catiline, but had put his duty to his country above his duty to his friend.

*Marcus Caeparius*: Marcus Caeparius (alternatively Ceparius) of Tarracina (the former Volscian town of Anxur, on the coast 57 miles south of Rome). He had already left for Apulia, but appears to have been brought back to Rome at the end of the day. Nothing is known about him; one wonders how he could have hoped to start a slave rising on his own (particularly in view of the presence of Metellus Creticus in the area), and what he expected to get out of the conspiracy.

*Publius Furius*: a Sullan veteran (like Manlius), otherwise unknown. It is possible that he was the man from Faesulae whom Sallust says commanded the left wing of Catiline's army at Pistoria (*Cat.* 59.3).

*Quintus Annius Chilo*: a senator; his career is unknown.

*Publius Umbrenus*: a man with business interests in Gaul, who knew many of the leaders of the Gallic tribes. He made the first approach to the Allobroges.

*Moreover, citizens . . . to their senses*: it would be difficult to argue that this sentence is not an addition made after the executions, at a time when Cicero needed to justify the action he had taken (in my view, every mention of leniency, compassion, or mercy should arouse suspicion).

15 *Although the senate . . . to resign his office*: constitutionally, however, the senate was not empowered to strip a citizen of his legal rights. This paragraph also looks like a later addition (Lentulus' resignation has already been covered in § 14). See J. Barlow in C. Deroux (ed.), *Studies in Latin Literature and Roman History*, 7 (Brussels, 1994), 180–9, who argues that Cicero has added this passage in order to counter accusations that he had committed sacrilege by executing a praetor in office (a Roman magistracy was considered sacred).

*Gaius Glaucia*: see second note on *Cat.* 1.4 above. The precedent is a weak one because Marius was not directly responsible for Glaucia's death.

19 *the consulship of Cotta and Torquatus*: Lucius Aurelius Cotta and Lucius Manlius Torquatus were consuls in 65.

*you will remember it*: it is interesting that Cicero needs to describe the statue. It looks as if he is addressing himself to people who were familiar with the statue but were not aware that it was of Romulus.

19   *every corner of Etruria*: haruspicy had always been an Etruscan
      science. Whenever disquieting natural phenomena occurred, the senate
      summoned the soothsayers from Etruria to explain their meaning.

20   *until this very day!*: scholars assume that Cicero timed the erection of the
      statue to coincide with this speech. But at the height of the conspiracy,
      was Cicero really sending messages to the workmen to ask them to speed
      up or delay their work so that its completion would coincide with his
      discovery of incriminating evidence, should he happen to discover any—
      merely in order that he could make a point in a speech which he might or
      might not then happen to give? It is surely more likely that he made use
      of a lucky coincidence (as is in any case implied by *De divinatione* 2.46–7
      (44 BC), where he ridicules the idea that the statue was erected on the day
      in question by divine purpose rather than by chance). The passage which
      follows gives a good impression of the superstitious credulity of ordinary
      Romans, and the ease with which a more sophisticated person could
      exploit it—i.e., of the gulf between uneducated and educated Romans.

21   *the temple of Concord*: at the northern end of the forum, at the foot of the
      Capitol. It was built in 121 BC by the consul Lucius Opimius after his
      brutal suppression of the supporters of Gaius Gracchus (see first note on
      *Cat.* 1.4 above), and was often used for meetings of the senate in times of
      civil disorder.

24   *Lucius Sulla crushed Publius Sulpicius*: Cicero now gives a résumé of the
      civil wars between 88 and 77 BC (when he himself was aged 18 to 29); the
      passage presents these wars from the point of view of his audience (hence
      the respect for Marius and disapproval of Sulla), but I suspect that it
      accurately reflects Cicero's own point of view as well (particularly in the
      reference to the victims of Cinna and Marius). In 88 the tribune Publius
      Sulpicius Rufus carried a bill to replace the consul Sulla with Marius in
      the Mithridatic command; Sulla occupied Rome and annulled Sulpicius'
      laws, killing Sulpicius and killing or exiling his other opponents. Marius
      ('the guardian of this city', i.e. victor against the Teutoni and Cimbri in
      102–101) escaped to his veterans in Africa, and Sulla went east to fight
      Mithridates. The next year, the consuls were Gnaeus Octavius and
      Lucius Cornelius Cinna, respectively a supporter and an opponent of
      Sulla. Cinna attempted to recall Marius and the other exiles, but was
      expelled from Rome by Octavius. Cinna then joined forces with Marius,
      who had meanwhile returned to Italy, and the two men seized Rome,
      inaugurating a reign of terror in which Octavius and the orator Marcus
      Antonius, the consul of 99 (and father of Cicero's colleague), were mur-
      dered, and Quintus Lutatius Catulus, the consul of 102, committed sui-
      cide (cf. 'our most illustrious citizens'). In 82, Sulla, who had returned
      to Italy the previous year, defeated the Marians (Marius himself having
      died in 86 and Cinna in 84), captured Rome, had himself made dictator,
      and instituted the proscriptions. Upon his death in 78 the consuls
      Marcus Aemilius Lepidus and Quintus Lutatius Catulus (son of the
      consul of 102), respectively an opponent and a supporter of Sulla,

quarrelled; Lepidus started a rising and was crushed the following year
by Catulus and Pompey, dying soon afterwards (on Catulus, see second
note on *Ver.* 44 above). With hindsight, all these conflicts can be seen as a
single civil war starting with the attempt by Marius to seize the command
against Mithridates in 88 and ending with the final defeat of the Marians
(principally Sertorius) in Spain in 72. By 63, the wounds had not healed.

*Lepidus' death . . . those of the others*: 'the others' is more likely to refer, in
my view, to those who died with Lepidus than to the victims of the civil
wars just mentioned. We must assume that the point was not ambiguous
to Cicero's audience.

26   *In return for this great service . . . this day for ever*: this is another passage
(§§ 26–29a) that looks as if it was written later than the dramatic date of
the speech. The content of §§ 26–7 is closely similar to that of *Cat.* 4.22–3,
which was probably added on publication in 60 BC (see first note on *Cat.*
4.18).

*one of whom*: i.e. Pompey, who had just completed the Third Mithridatic
War (73–63) and added Bithynia, Pontus, Syria, and Judaea to the
empire.

28   *But if the attacks of internal enemies*: Cicero is not thinking any longer of
the conspirators, but of people like Metellus Nepos who were to attack
him for executing the conspirators.


## IN CATILINAM IV

1   *I see, conscript fathers . . . about the danger to me*: from the outset Cicero
focuses his discussion not simply on what should be done about the
conspirators, but on the consequences of their punishment for himself.
This is generally taken as an indication that the speech has been revised,
and reflects his position in 60 BC rather than on 5 December 63. M.
Winterbottom (in B. Vickers (ed.), *Rhetoric Revalued* (New York, 1982),
61–2) points to the note of personal concern in the speech, and argues
that the speech has been recast, particularly at the beginning and end
(i.e. §§ 1–3 and 19–24, 'hardly conceivable in the original senatorial
speech'), in ways which bring it close to a forensic speech, one written
in his own defence ('the arguments for execution become, as well,
arguments for Cicero's correctness in desiring and carrying out that
execution'). He goes on to suggest that Cicero did this partly for self-
justification, but partly also because his readership of young aspiring
orators was more interested in reading forensic speeches than deliberative
ones. See further R. G. M. Nisbet in T. A. Dorey (ed.), *Cicero* (London,
1964), 62–3.

2   *the home of all justice*: trials were held in the forum (hence the term
'forensic').

*nor the bed*: an allusion to the attempt to assassinate Cicero on the morning after the meeting at Laeca's house; cf. *Cat.* 1.9 'they gave their word

that they would assassinate me in my bed the very same night, just before dawn'.

2 *much that I have forfeited*: for example his province, Macedonia, to Antonius.

*the Vestal virgins*: see third note on *Cat.* 3.9 above. The reference is a little odd unless Cicero is thinking of Catiline's trial for adultery with the Vestal Fabia in 73.

*Publius Lentulus . . . destruction for our country*: cf. *Cat.* 3.9.

3 *for a man who has reached the consulship, it cannot be untimely*: Cicero was to recall this remark nineteen years later at *Phil.* 2.119.

*my dear beloved brother*: Quintus was now a praetor-elect.

*all these men you can see surrounding me*: in the senate, senators moved around so as to sit near those whose opinions they agreed with or apart from those whose opinions they disagreed with (hence the empty benches around Catiline at the meeting of 7 November: see *Cat.* 1.16, 2.12); this was a convenient way in which those not senior enough to be called to speak could make their views known. In this debate there must have been considerable movement around the temple as senators changed their minds.

*my wife . . . my . . . daughter, my baby son . . . my son-in-law*: Terentia; Tullia, now about 16; Marcus, now 2; and Gaius Calpurnius Piso Frugi, not yet a member of the senate (he became quaestor in 58 and died the following year). Plutarch (*Cic.* 20.2) tells us that the day before the debate Terentia, prompted by an omen, had urged Cicero to take strong action against the conspirators.

*but only to make me wish . . . the destruction of our country*: i.e. if strong action is taken against the conspirators, Cicero may possibly be assassinated as a result—but at least his family and the senate will have been saved; if inadequate action is taken, then he, his family, and the senate will inevitably be massacred by the victorious conspirators.

4 *This is not Tiberius Gracchus . . . he killed Gaius Memmius*: see first note on *Cat.* 1.3 (Tiberius Gracchus), first note on *Cat.* 1.4 (Gaius Gracchus), and second note on *Cat.* 1.4 (Saturninus) above.

*the slaves are roused to revolt*: this allegation relates (as the next clause confirms) to the conspirators in the city, not to Catiline. In his letter to Catiline, Lentulus had urged him to enlist slaves (*Cat.* 3.8), and Caeparius had intended to start a slave rising in Apulia (*Cat.* 3.14).

7 *Decimus Silanus*: Decimus Junius Silanus, consul-elect of 62 and the husband of Cato's half-sister Servilia. We know little about him. In view of the importance placed by Murena's jury on there being two consuls in place on 1 January 62 (*Flac.* 98), he is unlikely to have been a military man; and in view of his change of mind in the debate, it is possible that he was not a natural leader. He had made a previous attempt at the consulship in 65.

8  *someone*: i.e. a chief magistrate in an Italian town. Cicero is explaining why a request to the Italian towns would be 'problematic': the towns would most likely refuse to have conspirators from Rome foisted on them for life.

9  *his own standing and the distinction of his ancestors*: Caesar was a patrician, claimed descent from Venus and Aeneas, was related by marriage to Marius (hence the popular credentials), and had just been elected *pontifex maximus* for life (defeating Catulus) and praetor for 62 (along with Quintus Cicero).

   *demagogues*: such as Quintus Caecilius Metellus Nepos and Lucius Calpurnius Bestia, who were to attack Cicero for the executions.

10  *one of those . . . popular politicians*: Crassus.

   *the Sempronian law*: on the law, see first note on *Ver.* 2.5.163 above; and on the validity of Cicero's argument, note on *Cat.* 1.28 above. We do not know exactly what Caesar said, but it looks as if Cicero is making inferences about his views (in his presence!) rather than simply reporting them. The passage is well discussed by A. W. Lintott, *Violence in Republican Rome*[2] (Oxford, 1999), 170 ('This passage shows Cicero placing ideas in Caesar's mind, when Caesar himself had refused to express them').

11  *to the public meeting*: i.e. the meeting at which Cicero would announce the senate's decision to the people in the forum. In the event, no such meeting appears to have taken place. It is interesting that Cicero clearly anticipates trouble in justifying either course of action to the people: the difficulty was that both courses were illegal, and would be opposed by the tribunes Nepos and Bestia.

12  *as he told us himself . . . to hope*: cf. *Cat.* 3.9.

   *Vestal virgins being raped*: see fourth note on § 2 above.

13  *Lucius Caesar*: Lucius Julius Caesar, the consul of 64. His sister Julia was married to Lentulus (they were all patricians), and his maternal grandfather was Marcus Fulvius Flaccus, the consul of 125 who was killed in 121 along with his elder son and the other followers of Gaius Gracchus (see first note on *Cat.* 1.4 above). Fulvius' younger son (the uncle of Lucius Caesar), to whom Cicero refers in the next sentence, had been sent by his father to discuss terms with the consul, Lucius Opimius, but was thrown into prison where he was either executed or allowed to commit suicide. The Scholiasta Gronovianus (290 Stangl) gives further details of the incident which Cicero is about to relate. He says that Lucius Caesar made his remarks in the senate, and that his actual words (though he no doubt gives a shortened paraphrase) were: 'This man lives, and has my sister for his wife! My grandfather was killed on a consul's order—and does this man live?' Lucius Caesar's words would have had a greater poignancy in that they were spoken in the temple of Concord, which Opimius had built after carrying out the killings referred to (see note on *Cat.* 3.21 above).

13　*a desire . . . an element of factional strife*: Cicero refers to Gaius Gracchus' controversial scheme to provide subsidized grain (cf. *Off.* 2.72), the first time this had been provided at Rome. As at *Cat.* 1.3–4, he uses extreme understatement in referring to the violence and political turmoil of the Gracchan period.

　　*Lentulus' illustrious grandfather*: the man depicted on Lentulus' seal; see second note on *Cat.* 3.10 above.

15　*of all people*: the family from which Cicero came was equestrian, not senatorial, and rather than trying to conceal this, he frequently goes out of his way to draw attention to his special status as the senior senator with the closest ties to the equestrian order. See further D. H. Berry, *CQ*, NS 53 (2003), 222–34.

　　*Now . . . harmony with this order*: the long-standing conflict between the senators and the *equites* had in fact been substantially put to rest in 70 by the *lex Aurelia*, which resolved the question of who should control the courts by making juries effectively two-thirds equestrian and one-third senatorial. Mindful of his own special status and connections, Cicero was anxious to promote 'harmony between the orders' (*concordia ordinum*), and he viewed the unanimity between the senate (most of it), *equites*, and people over the Catilinarian question as evidence that this was being achieved. Conflict was to break out again in 60, however, when a company of *equites* demanded renegotiation of their contract for tax-farming in Asia.

　　*the entire body of scribes*: a body (technically an 'order') of officials attached to the various magistracies; those attached to the quaestors dealt with financial matters and enjoyed the highest status (the poet Horace was one for a time). The scribes had come to the treasury (adjacent to the temple of Concord) because this was the day on which they drew lots for their posts for the year ahead (as did the new quaestors, who assumed office on 5 December). According to the Scholiasta Gronovianus (290 Stangl), when they saw the conspirators being taken to the senate, they left off what they were doing and offered themselves as guards.

18　*that is how the matter stands*: it is likely that this paragraph was the ending of the original speech, and that §§ 19–24 were added on publication in 60 BC: see H. Fuchs, *Hermes*, 87 (1959), 463–9. Fuchs draws attention to the verbal repetitions between § 18 and §§ 19+24, and suggests that when §§ 19–24 were added in 60 BC the copyists failed to suppress § 18, with the result that we now have both of the alternative endings of the speech. See further second note on § 21 below.

　　*yonder eternal fire of Vesta*: see third note on *Cat.* 3.9 above. Cicero gestures in the direction of the temple, at the other end of the forum.

19　*a single night*: that of 2–3 December.

21　*Let Scipio have his fame*: on the generals mentioned in this paragraph, see second note on *Ver.* 2.5.25 (the elder Scipio), note on *Ver.* 2.5.14 (the younger Scipio, Aemilius Paullus, Marius), and second note on *Cat.* 3.26 (Pompey), above.

*unless perhaps . . . return in triumph*: Cicero compares Pompey's achievement unfavourably with his own, arguing that Pompey merely extended the empire, whereas he saved Rome (the argument is rhetorically neat but faulty in logic, since he has just said that Pompey's achievement was greater than that of Marius, who saved Rome twice). On the face of it, Cicero's remarks would seem needlessly and inappropriately insulting to Pompey. But *Off.* 1.78 shows that he is in fact paraphrasing (and reminding his readership of) a gracious compliment that Pompey had paid him: 'Gnaeus Pompeius, in many people's hearing, paid me this compliment: he said that he would have brought home his third triumph in vain were it not for the fact that my service to the state had ensured that there was a home to which he could bring it.' This compliment cannot of course have been paid by Pompey in the east and reported at Rome in time to be included in the original *Fourth Catilinarian*: news could not travel from Rome to Pontus (where Pompey was spending the winter) and back again between 3 and 5 December. The compliment will obviously have been made on or after Pompey's return to Italy at the end of 62 (he paid Cicero a similar compliment immediately on his return: see *Phil.* 2.12). Our passage cannot therefore have been included in the original speech, and so must date from its publication in 60—a point which gives powerful support to Fuchs's thesis (first note on § 18 above). This conclusion is supported by the letter which provides our evidence for the publication of the *Catilinarians*. In that letter (*Att.* 2.1), after discussing the publication of his consular corpus, Cicero goes on to say (§ 6) that Pompey has been eulogizing his achievements, and has declared that whereas he had merely given the state good service, Cicero had saved it. Cicero was clearly flattered by these compliments, and it would seem that when he published his speech he could not resist slipping an allusion to one of them into his new ending—taking care, however, not to attribute it directly to Pompey, in order to avoid an anachronism.

22  *are admitted*: i.e. to friendship and alliance with the Roman people.

23  *instead of the province I have given up*: Macedonia. This sacrifice was also alluded to in § 2.

 *my little son*: also mentioned at § 3. Cicero is already thinking of the absolute necessity, for the maintenance of his own reputation and standing, of his 2-year-old son attaining the consulship (as did indeed happen, in 30 BC).

# PRO MARCELLO

1  *out of a mixture of grief and diffidence*: cf. *Fam.* 4.4.4, where Cicero tells Sulpicius that he had made his decision to refrain from speaking because he no longer enjoyed the standing that had formerly been his.

2  *in my work*: i.e. at the bar.

   *to raise a standard*: the military metaphor is chosen as a compliment to the
   addressee. For similar care taken in the choice of a metaphor relating to
   Caesar, cf. 'laid the foundations' at § 25 below (where see note).

3  *after reminding us . . . had wronged you*: Caesar had complained of
   Marcellus' 'bitterness' (*acerbitas*) towards him when Marcellus was
   consul (*Fam.* 4.4.3).

4  *but even to record them*: of course, Caesar wrote his *Gallic War* and *Civil
   War*, which were greatly admired for their purity of style. Those who
   consider Cicero's flattery excessive may like to reflect on the fact that
   Caesar told Cicero around this time that it was a greater achievement to
   have advanced the frontiers of the Roman genius than to have advanced
   those of the Roman empire (Plin. *Nat.* 7.117).

5  *the speed . . . your conquests*: the speed of Caesar's conquests is famously
   illustrated by his remark *veni, vidi, vici* ('I came, I saw, I conquered'),
   originally made in a letter to a friend after his victory over Pharnaces, the
   son of Mithridates, at Zela in 47 (Plut. *Caes.* 50.3).

10 *that great personage*: Marcellus.

   *the excellent Gaius Marcellus*: the consul of 50 and cousin of Marcus
   Marcellus (not to be confused with Marcus' brother Gaius, who by this
   time was dead).

11 *the countless major thanksgivings*: these were decreed in 57 for successes in
   Gaul, in 55 for the success in Britain, in 52 for successes in Gaul, and
   earlier in 46 for the victory at Thapsus.

14 *the toga*: the toga, the formal garment of a Roman civilian, was a symbol
   of peace (cf. second note on *Phil.* 2.20 below).

   *a particular individual*: Pompey.

16 *How often . . . in victory!*: cf. two letters of Cicero to Marcellus from this
   same time, *Fam.* 4.7.2 'I also saw your dissatisfaction, the utter lack of
   confidence you always felt in the way the civil war was conducted, in
   Gnaeus Pompeius' forces, in the type of army he led. I think you remember that I held the same views. Accordingly, you took little part in the
   conduct of operations, and I was always careful to take none'; 4.9.3 'Did
   you not see as I did how cruel that other victory would have proved?'
   (It is coincidences like this of the speech with Cicero's private correspondence which lead us to conclude that the speech is likely to be
   sincere and not ironic.)

18 *his physical location*: cf. *Att.* 11.6.6 (27 November 48) 'Everyone who had
   stayed in Italy was counted as an enemy.'

21 *that awful suspicion that you have expressed*: i.e. that there are people who
   are plotting to assassinate him. Cicero does not mention this complaint of
   Caesar's in his letter to Sulpicius (*Fam.* 4.4). The fact that he feels free
   to refer to such a delicate and personal matter in his speech should be

seen as a compliment to Caesar, not a threat. (It is easy for us, with our knowledge that Caesar would indeed be assassinated, to make too much of this passage.)

*have either . . . through their own stubbornness*: Cato springs to mind.

23 *Courts must be established . . . the birth-rate raised*: in 46 Caesar altered juries from being effectively one-third senatorial and two-thirds equestrian to being half senatorial and half equestrian; in 47 he had carried measures to stabilize the economy; earlier in 46 he had carried a sumptuary law and granted himself a three-year 'prefecture of morals'; and in 46 or later he legislated to provide payments for large families. To this programme Cicero here 'promises his support with woolly generalizations' (R. G. M. Nisbet in T. A. Dorey (ed.), *Cicero* (London, 1964), 74).

24 *ornaments of its prestige*: including revenues and public buildings.

25 *'I have lived long enough for nature, or for glory'*: Caesar had recently turned 54. Cicero makes the same remark with reference to himself (aged 62) at *Phil.* 1.38.

*laid the foundations*: the building metaphor is especially appropriate in view of Caesar's many proposed construction projects (cf. the metaphor 'to raise a standard', used of Caesar, at § 2 above). The most important of these projects, the Forum Iulium and the temple of Venus Genetrix, had been dedicated earlier in 46, but were not completed until after Caesar's death.

28 *the Rhine, the Ocean, the Nile*: Caesar reached the Rhine in 57 and bridged it in 55 and again in 53; he crossed the Ocean and invaded Britain in 55 and 54; and he won the Alexandrine War against Ptolemy XIII of Egypt in 47.

29 *Among those yet to be born . . . find something missing*: an extraordinarily accurate prediction of the conclusions of nineteenth- and twentieth-century scholarship on Caesar.

30 *us some mistakenly believe*: i.e. the Epicureans. Cicero was always hostile to their teachings. Cf. *Arch.* 30 'And whether I shall have no awareness, after I have died, of the world's memory of me, or whether, as the wisest men have maintained, that recollection will indeed touch some part of my being, I do at least derive pleasure at this moment from the thought and hope that my achievements will be remembered.'

31 *Ungrateful and unjust . . . is better*: i.e. those who have accepted Caesar's pardon but remain secretly hostile to him are worse even than those who continued to resist him after Pharsalus, and fell at Thapsus.

34 *his excellent and devoted cousin Gaius Marcellus*: see second note on § 10 above.

## PHILIPPIC II

1 *over the past twenty years*: i.e. since his suppression of Catiline in 63 (according to the Roman system of inclusive reckoning, 63 to 44 BC gives twenty years).

2 *but in my case alone that I saved it*: the decree was passed on 3 December 63; cf. *Cat.* 3.15, 4.20.

3 *in opposition to . . . an extremely close friend*: the details of the case, a civil hearing, are obscure. The stranger may have been Fadius, mentioned below, and the friend someone named Sicca, who appears in Cicero's letters (*Att.* 16.11.1).

*he*: Antony.

*Quintus Fadius*: Cicero claims that Antony had fathered children from this man's daughter; but if 'son-in-law' is not meant literally, as seems likely (cf. first note on § 20 below), he does not actually claim that he had been married to her.

*Gaius Curio*: Cicero is referring to the 60s when, he claims (§§ 44–6), Gaius Scribonius Curio was Antony's lover. Curio was a friend of Clodius', and after his death married his widow Fulvia. As tribune in 50, he transferred his allegiance from Pompey and the senate to Caesar in return for a massive bribe. He was killed in Africa in 49; Fulvia then (in 47 or 46) married Antony.

4 *to stand for the augurate*: Cicero was elected to the augurate in 53 (or 52), filling the vacancy created by the death at Carrhae of Crassus' son Publius. Antony was then elected in 50, in succession to the orator Hortensius (on whom see note on *Imp.* 51 above).

5 *That you did not kill me at Brundisium?*: when Cicero gave up the republican cause after Pharsalus (48), Caesar (referred to below as 'the victor himself') asked Dolabella, Cicero's son-in-law (later consul with Antony in 44), to write to Cicero ordering him to return to Italy; Cicero therefore crossed over to Brundisium. But afterwards Caesar instructed Antony (whom he had made 'the chief of his band of brigands', i.e. his Master of the Horse) to expel all the ex-Pompeians from Italy on pain of outlawry. Antony therefore asked Cicero to leave; but when Cicero showed him Dolabella's letter, he publicly exempted him by name from the expulsion order.

*the man who had saved them*: i.e. Caesar. Many of Caesar's assassins, such as Brutus and Cassius, were ex-Pompeians whom he had pardoned.

6 *that complaint*: the *First Philippic*, delivered in the senate on 2 September.

*at your house . . . most disgraceful of markets*: on 17 March the senate had voted to ratify all Caesar's acts, including those that had not yet been made public. Antony, who had already taken custody of Caesar's private papers, soon began producing forged documents in Caesar's name, often in return for massive bribes.

*you admitted that . . . in your own interest*: the reference is to the passage on 2 or 3 June of the law which extended his and Dolabella's governorships of Macedonia and Syria respectively from two to five years. It was illegal for the proposer of a law, or his colleagues or relatives, to receive any commission or power from the law which he had proposed.

*you were going around with an armed escort*: he did this from the time of his return to Rome from Campania on *c.*18 May. It was illegal to bear arms within the city boundary.

7 *Marcus Crassus*: Cicero always disliked Marcus Licinius Crassus (the consul of 70 and 55 and member of the 'first triumvirate'), and had a stormy relationship with him. Crassus had suspected that Cicero was behind the attempt to incriminate him in the Catilinarian conspiracy (Sal. *Cat.* 48.8–9).

*a letter*: Antony had written to Cicero in April to ask him to agree to the recall from exile of Sextus Cloelius (in the 50s the leader of Clodius' gang, convicted in 52 for his part in the violent disturbances following Clodius' death); Cicero had readily agreed. Both letters survive (*Att.* 14.13A, 14.13B). Antony's is respectful but menacing, Cicero's fulsome and insincere.

8 *Mustela Seius and Tiro Numisius*: the commanders of Antony's guard. Their names were actually Seius Mustela and Numisius Tiro; the inversion is a sign of contempt.

*your knowledge of which has been so lucrative*: see second note on § 6 above.

*your teacher*: the rhetorician Sextus Clodius, from Sicily. Cicero will reveal the fee he was paid at § 43 ('two thousand *iugera* of arable land at Leontini').

10 *Of course . . . to be mine*: ironic.

*in the manner of his appointment*: he was appointed by Caesar rather than elected by the Roman people in the normal way.

11 *For what decision . . . vote of this order?*: Cicero had held a debate and vote in the senate before executing the captured Catilinarian conspirators on 5 December 63.

*the thing which did for both of them*: i.e. Fulvia, the wife in turn of Clodius, Curio, and Antony (see fourth note on § 3 above). She hated Cicero, not without reason, and is said to have insulted and mutilated his head and tongue after his murder (Dio 47.8.4). On Clodius' death, see first note on § 21 below.

12 *Publius Servilius*: Publius Servilius Vatia Isauricus, the consul of 79, who had died earlier in the year. Cicero will now go on to name the other consulars of 63, now dead, who expressed their approval of his consulship by voting a thanksgiving in his honour on 3 December (that this is the meeting which Cicero refers to is shown by § 13 below, 'Lucius Cotta proposed a thanksgiving . . . , and the consulars I have just named . . . accepted the proposal'; it cannot be the meeting of 5 December because

Crassus was absent from that (*Cat.* 4.10) but is named here). The consulars named are: Quintus Lutatius Catulus (consul in 78), Lucius Licinius Lucullus (consul in 74), his brother Marcus Terentius Varro Lucullus (consul in 73), Marcus Licinius Crassus (consul in 70), Quintus Hortensius Hortalus (consul in 69), Gaius Scribonius Curio (consul in 76—his name is out of order), Gaius Calpurnius Piso and Manius Acilius Glabrio (consuls in 67), Manius Aemilius Lepidus and Lucius Volcacius Tullus (consuls in 66), and Gaius Marcius Figulus (consul in 64). The meeting referred to took place, of course, two days prior to the executions—but it would have been the executions, not the arrest of the conspirators, for which Antony had criticized Cicero. This passage, therefore, impressive as it is, fails to answer Antony's charge.

12 *Decimus Silanus and Lucius Murena*: Decimus Junius Silanus and Lucius Licinius Murena, the consuls of 62 (the latter of whom owed his consulship to Cicero's *Pro Murena*).

*Marcus Cato*: Marcus Porcius Cato, the tribune-elect whose speech on 5 December persuaded the senate to vote for execution. A committed Stoic, he committed suicide after Thapsus (46) rather than submit to Caesar, thereby winning undying fame as a republican martyr.

*Gnaeus Pompeius*: Pompey was away from Rome in 63, settling the east after concluding the Third Mithridatic War (73–63). He returned to Italy at the end of 62. See further second note on *Cat.* 4.21 above.

*A packed senate approved my consulship*: on 3 December.

13 *Lucius Cotta*: Lucius Aurelius Cotta, the consul of 65. It was he who in 70 had carried the *lex Aurelia*, which altered the composition of juries, making them effectively two-thirds equestrian and one-third senatorial (hence his description here as 'judicious'). He was a relative of Caesar's mother.

14 *Lucius Caesar*: Lucius Julius Caesar, the consul of 64 (and a distant relative of Caesar's). In the debate of 5 December he spoke in favour of the execution of Publius Cornelius Lentulus Sura; for his words, see first note on *Cat.* 4.13 above. His sister Julia, Lentulus' wife, had previously been married to Marcus Antonius Creticus; Antony was their son.

15 *Phormio ... Gnatho ... Ballio*: low types from Roman comedy, representing Antony's hangers-on. The first two are parasites from Terence's *Phormio* and *Eunuchus* respectively, the third a pimp from Plautus' *Pseudolus*.

*in the very temple*: the temple of Concord; see note on *Cat.* 3.21 above.

16 *the Capitoline path*: a path which wound its way from the forum up to the Capitol, starting outside the temple of Concord and then running alongside the temple of Saturn.

*Did anyone fail to give in his name?*: i.e. to volunteer for military service in defence of the city.

17 *the sort of leader*: i.e. Cicero himself.

18  *For I arrested the guilty men, but the senate punished them*: technically, Cicero as consul was solely responsible for the executions (the senate was merely an advisory body, and was not a court); but in practice, having consulted the senate, it would have been difficult or impossible for him not to carry out its wishes.

19  *which at that time was united with the senate*: on Cicero's cherished 'harmony between the orders' (*concordia ordinum*) in 63, see second note on *Cat.* 4.15 above.

   *Ituraeans*: Arabs troops from the territory south of Syria, famous as archers. Pompey had conquered the region in 63.

20  *your actress wife*: Volumnia Cytheris, a mime actress, Antony's mistress. She was a freedwoman of Volumnius Eutrapelus, and is probably to be identified with 'Lycoris', the mistress of the poet Gallus. In referring to her as Antony's wife, Cicero uses the same freedom that he used at § 3 when he claimed that Antony was the son-in-law of the freedman Quintus Fadius.

   *'Let arms to the toga yield'*: Antony had ridiculed a verse from the epic poem Cicero wrote in 60 on the subject of his consulship. The verse ran, 'Let arms to the toga yield, and the laurel give way to praise' (*Cedant arma togae, concedat laurea laudi*, fr. 12 Courtney), i.e. 'Let war yield to peace' (uncontroversial enough) 'and the laurel granted to a general give way to the praise granted to a civilian magistrate' (more controversial, suggesting that Cicero's civilian suppression of Catiline represented a greater achievement than the military victories of—most obviously—Pompey).

21  *the killing of Publius Clodius*: Clodius was murdered on the Appian Way by his enemy Titus Annius Milo in 52, apparently without any premeditation on either side. In response to that event and to the violent scenes which followed it, Pompey, who was sole consul, carried a new law, the *lex Pompeia de vi* (Pompeian law concerning violence), under which Milo was prosecuted (by Antony, among others), defended by Cicero, and convicted. Some time later (perhaps at the beginning of 51), Cicero revised the defence he had made and published it as *Pro Milone*, the rhetorical tour de force which, together with this speech, is traditionally regarded as his masterpiece.

   *Now what would people think . . . halted your attack*: this incident, dating from the latter part of 53, is described more colourfully at *Mil.* 40: 'And recently, when Marcus Antonius had given all loyal citizens the strongest grounds for confidence in our future salvation, when that young man of the highest rank had bravely taken on an important public duty and had netted the monster Clodius as he recoiled from the meshes of a trial, what a chance there was, immortal gods, what an opportunity! When Clodius had fled and taken refuge in a dark hidey-hole beneath the stairs, would it have been a difficult job for Milo just to finish off that pestilential villain, incurring no blame whatsoever for himself but bestowing the greatest glory on Marcus Antonius?' See also § 49 below.

22 *an inquiry*: i.e. the trial of Milo, held under the *lex Pompeia*. Cicero considered the *lex Pompeia* an unnecessary and vindictive law; he felt that the existing law, the *lex Plautia* (70 BC?), under which he had successfully defended Publius Sulla (62), Sestius (56), Caelius (56), and others, would have been perfectly adequate.

*the allegation . . . while the trial was taking place*: Cicero may not have been accused of having instigated the murder of Clodius while Milo was actually on trial, but he was in fact accused of it while the *lex Pompeia* was being proposed: see *Mil.* 47.

23 *In the consulship of . . . Marcus Bibulus*: Marcus Calpurnius Bibulus and Caesar were consuls in 59 (Cicero pointedly omits Caesar's name when designating the year). Bibulus opposed the 'first triumvirate' (a private arrangement between Caesar, Pompey, and Crassus), and spent his year of office at his house watching for unfavourable omens, thus technically invalidating Caesar's entire legislative programme.

24 *The first was . . . to stand for office in absence*: i.e. (1) in 55, when Pompey and Crassus, as consuls, carried a law to extend Caesar's command in Gaul until 1 March 50, and (2) in 52, when all ten tribunes carried a law giving Caesar the right to stand for the consulship in absence, thus enabling him to avoid prosecution for the illegalities of his consulship in 59. In reality, it is unlikely that Cicero attempted to dissuade Pompey from either of these courses of action.

*But after Pompeius had handed over . . . to Caesar*: an exaggeration. Pompey had lent Caesar a legion during the winter of 54–53; but he took it back again in 50.

25 *For who ever heard . . . that glorious deed?*: Cicero was not let into the plot against Caesar: he was thought too old and timorous. His innocence is proved by letters (*Fam.* 10.28 and 12.4, both of *c.*2 February 43) that he later wrote to two of the conspirators, Trebonius and Cassius, in which he said that he wished they had invited him to the feast on the Ides of March, because then there would have been no leftovers (i.e. he would have insisted on Antony's assassination as well).

26 *the Bruti . . . that of Ahala*: two of the leading conspirators were called Brutus, Marcus Junius Brutus, a committed republican and ex-Pompeian (and the dedicatee of many of Cicero's treatises, including the *Brutus*, 46), and his cousin Decimus Junius Brutus Albinus, a disaffected Caesarian. Both claimed descent from Lucius Junius Brutus, who had expelled Tarquinius Superbus and become one of the first two consuls in 509 BC; Marcus was in addition descended through his mother from Gaius Servilius Ahala, who had freed Rome from the threat of tyranny in 439 by killing Spurius Maelius. Wax portrait-masks (*imagines*) of ancestors who had held curule office were kept in cupboards within the *atria* of the houses of the leading families; they were a sign of high social status.

*Gaius Cassius*: Gaius Cassius Longinus, an ex-Pompeian pardoned by Caesar in 47 and then promoted by him to a praetorship in 44; he and

Marcus Brutus (to whose half-sister he was married) were the leaders of the conspiracy. In the next sentence, Cicero probably alludes to Spurius Cassius Vicellinus (consul in 502, 496, and 486), who was said to have executed his son for aspiring, like Spurius Maelius, to tyranny.

26  *he would have finished the job off in Cilicia*: we have no other evidence for this alleged assassination attempt, which would date from 47.

27  *Gnaeus Domitius*: his father was Lucius Domitius Ahenobarbus, the former consul of 54 who was killed while trying to escape from Pharsalus, and his uncle was Cato, who committed suicide after Thapsus (see third note on § 12 above). After being pardoned by Caesar in 46, he declined to enter public life; later he became consul in 32. He was the great-grandfather of the emperor Nero.

*Gaius Trebonius*: a 'new man' who owed his entire career to Caesar and rose to become suffect consul in 45; he was the most senior Caesarian to join the conspiracy. He drew Antony away from Caesar immediately before the assassination took place (cf. note on § 25 above).

*Lucius Tillius Cimber*: another friend of Caesar. At the assassination, he approached Caesar on the pretext of petitioning him on behalf of his brother, and thereby allowed him to be surrounded. Afterwards he immediately departed for Bithynia-Pontus, where he had been appointed governor.

*the two Servilii—Cascas . . . or Ahalas*: Publius Servilius Casca Longus struck the first blow, and called out to his brother to help him. Cicero again refers to the tyrannicide Gaius Servilius Ahala (see first note on § 26 above), playing on the fact that the Cascas and Ahala shared the same *nomen* (clan name).

28  *what I myself had done*: i.e. in suppressing the Catilinarian conspiracy.

31  *the parent of one's country*. Caesar was given this title in 45 (or perhaps 44).

*Why was Marcus Brutus . . . for more than ten days?*: Brutus was city praetor, and therefore prevented by law from being absent from Rome for more than ten days at a time (he was expected to be available to litigants). He left Rome on *c.* 12 April, never to return.

*the Apollinarian Games*: held on 6–13 July at Brutus' expense, though Brutus himself did not dare attend. A popular demonstration took place in his favour.

*Why were provinces given . . . the number of legates increased?*: Brutus was given Crete and Cassius Cyrene, perhaps on *c.* 1 August. On 5 June they had both been given a grain commission, and so when they were assigned their new provinces (the grain commission also counted as a province) quaestors had to be assigned to them and their legates increased probably from one to three.

32  *you*: i.e. Antony.

34 *that pen*: not a quill for writing on papyrus, but a sharp metal instrument for inscribing letters on wax tablets. Such pens could be used to wound or kill; so Cicero's metaphor is well chosen. The sentiment expressed here is echoed in the famous letter to Trebonius (see note on § 25 above).

*you and Gaius Trebonius . . . at Narbo*: we have no independent evidence for this plot. If it ever happened, it would date either from the winter of 46–45, when Antony was attempting to reach Caesar in Spain (§§ 75–6), or from the summer of 45, when Antony went to meet him on his return (§ 78). Narbo (Narbonne) was on the southern coast of Gaul, near the Pyrenees.

35 *Cassius' famous test, 'Who stood to gain?'*: Lucius Cassius Longinus Ravilla (the consul of 127 and censor of 125), whose strictness was proverbial, was famous for his use of this question (in Latin, *cui bono?*). Cicero applies it in his forensic speeches at *S. Rosc.* 84 and *Mil.* 32.

*You freed yourself . . . at the temple of Ops*: either Antony stole money from the temple, or else he falsified account books, held at the temple, in which his debts were recorded (cf. § 93a). Ops was a goddess of plenty; her temple was on the Capitol.

*You had a large part . . . transferred to yours*: cf. § 109 'The statues and paintings which, together with his gardens, Caesar bequeathed to the Roman people, Antonius had carted off, some to Pompeius' house outside the city and some to Scipio's villa.'

*a highly profitable factory . . . notebooks and memoranda*: see second note on § 6 above.

37 *Pompeius' camp . . . and that whole period*: i.e. the period between the outbreak of the Civil War and Pompey's defeat at Pharsalus. In 49, Cicero delayed in Italy until June, when he crossed over to join Pompey at Dyrrachium (in northern Greece, across the Adriatic from Brundisium). But having arrived in Pompey's camp, he was disgusted by the truculent attitude of the Pompeian leaders, whom he seems to have annoyed with his sarcastic comments and untimely wit. When Pompey moved south to Pharsalus in 48, Cicero stayed at Dyrrachium owing to ill health, and so was not present at the Pompeians' defeat.

*as I have already said*: at § 24.

*once saved by your efforts and mine*: on 5 December 63.

38 *This was indeed 'great'*: probably a pun; Pompey was known as 'Magnus' ('Great') from 81 BC (cf. *Imp.* 67).

39 *Paphos*: on the western coast of Cyprus. This was the last place at which Pompey stopped before arriving in Egypt, where he was murdered (48).

*the purchaser of his property*: Pompey's property was confiscated and sold at auction in 47. Antony was the sole bidder (§ 64); after purchasing the property, he broke it up and sold it on to others.

40 *Lucius Rubrius of Casinum*: otherwise unknown. Casinum (modern Cassino) was in southern Latium, halfway between Rome and Naples.

41  *his brother Quintus Fufius*: otherwise unknown. Because his name was
Fufius, not Rubrius, he cannot have been a full brother of Lucius
Rubrius, but must have been his half-brother or his cousin (*frater*, the
Latin word for 'brother', may also denote a cousin).

*Lucius Turselius*: otherwise unknown.

42  *after you yourself . . . that of your father*: if an estate was encumbered with
debts, as Cicero implies Antony's father's was, an heir could decline to
accept it, though this would bring disgrace on the family. Antony's
father, Marcus Antonius Creticus, had a reputation as a spendthrift; he
died in *c.*71, when Antony was 11 or 12 years old.

*you spent day after day . . . to someone else*: Antony spent seventeen days
preparing his attack on Cicero at his villa at Tibur, formerly the property
of Pompey's father-in-law Quintus Caecilius Metellus Pius Scipio Nasica
(who had committed suicide after Thapsus); the speech was then
delivered in the senate on 19 September (*Phil.* 5.19).

*a rhetorician*: Sextus Clodius from Sicily, referred to already at § 8.
'Master' above means both 'master of ceremonies' at Antony's parties
and 'teacher of rhetoric', i.e. the coach who helped him prepare his
speech against Cicero.

*your grandfather*: Marcus Antonius the orator (see second note on *Ver.*
2.5.3 above).

43  *two thousand iugera*: about 1,250 acres (nearly 2 square miles). (A *iugerum*
was about five-eighths of an acre.) This gift of public land to Sextus
Clodius deprived the Roman people of the revenue that would otherwise
have been paid from it.

*I shall be talking later*: at §§ 101–2.

44  *Do you remember . . . you went bankrupt?*: see first note on § 42 above.

*the Roscian law*: i.e. the *lex Roscia theatralis*, a law carried in 67 by the
tribune Lucius Roscius Otho. It reserved the first fourteen rows in the
theatre for the *equites* (senators sat in the orchestra).

*Then you assumed . . . a toga of womanhood*: Roman boys wore the purple-
bordered toga of boyhood until their mid-teens, when they formally
changed it for the unbordered toga of manhood; but togas were also worn
by female prostitutes. Cicero says that no sooner had Antony assumed
the toga of manhood than he prostituted himself to other men, taking the
dishonourable passive (female) role.

*Curio*: see fourth note on § 3 above.

45  *his father*: Gaius Scribonius Curio, the consul of 76 and censor of 61. See
note on *Ver.* 18 above.

46  *to pay off his son's debts*: i.e. to pay off Antony's creditors, after the
younger Curio had been foolish enough to stand surety for him.

*such promising . . . abilities*: Curio had a natural gift for oratory (*Brut.*
279–80).

47 *you . . . know more about this than I do*: Cicero is alluding to his absences
from Rome during the Civil War and in the months prior to the dramatic
date of the speech (cf. second note on § 57 below).

48 *he knows very well what I am talking about*: Cicero insinuates that, during
Clodius' tribunate in 58, Antony committed adultery with Clodius' wife
Fulvia (whom he was much later to marry).

*Then he marched off . . . divine prohibition*: in 57–54 Antony served as a
cavalry commander under the governor of Syria, Aulus Gabinius (the
consul of 58, whom Cicero hated for having done nothing to prevent
his exile). In 55 Gabinius, assisted by Antony, restored the deposed king
of Egypt, Ptolemy XII Auletes, to his throne at Alexandria, in return
for a bribe. This was contrary to the senate's orders, to law (a governor
could not leave his province or start a war without permission), and
to a Sibylline oracle; Gabinius was therefore prosecuted on his return
to Rome and, though acquitted on a charge of treason, was ultimately
convicted of extortion. See further note on *Imp.* 52 above.

*to Furthest Gaul*: in 54 Antony joined Caesar in Gaul (Furthest Gaul, the
part Caesar was occupied in conquering). He would no doubt have been
anxious not to become involved in Gabinius' trials at Rome.

*In those days . . . you had none*: i.e. before the Civil War, during which
many properties were confiscated or seized. Antony's bankruptcy would
appear to have entailed the loss of his family home.

*some sort of Sisapo*: a mining area (for cinnabar) in central southern
Spain, owned by Roman shareholders. Antony did not own his property
at Misenum outright because it was mortgaged to creditors.

49 *You returned . . . to stand for the quaestorship*: he stood for election in the
autumn of 53; was elected in 52; and then immediately returned to
Caesar in Gaul, serving his year of office (51) under him. See J. Linderski
and A. Kaminska-Linderski, *Phoenix*, 28 (1974), 213–23.

*your mother*: Julia, daughter of Lucius Julius Caesar, the consul of 90, and
brother of Lucius Julius Caesar, the consul of 64 (see note on § 14 above).

*It was then . . . eyes of the Roman people*: see § 21 above.

*the wrongs you had done me*: i.e. Antony's support for Clodius in 58, when
Cicero was exiled (§ 48).

50 *all of a sudden . . . you ran off to Caesar*: normally quaestors drew lots for
their provinces. What seems to have happened in this case is that Caesar
put in a special request for Antony, which was then approved by the
senate, but not before Antony had departed. His haste would be
explained by the revolt of Vercingetorix: he participated in the siege of
Alesia (52).

*you flew . . . just as your husband had*: Antony was elected tribune for 49.
As a magistrate in office, he would be immune from prosecution, and
therefore safe, for the time being, from his creditors. Cicero says that he

intended to behave as Curio had done in his tribunate in 50: Curio had gone over to Caesar in return for a bribe (see fourth note on § 3 above).

51  *the consulship of Lucius Lentulus and Gaius Marcellus*: Lucius Cornelius Lentulus Crus and Gaius Claudius Marcellus (the brother of the subject of *Pro Marcello*) were consuls in 49. On 1 January, Curio arrived in Rome with a letter from Caesar in which Caesar offered to give up his army and provinces if Pompey would give up the two Spains and his forces there; if this proposal were not accepted, Caesar would resort to force. The proposal was not put to a vote; instead, Pompey's father-in-law, Metellus Scipio, proposed that if Caesar did not lay down his arms by a certain date, he should be declared a public enemy. This proposal was carried, but was then vetoed by Antony and his fellow-tribune Quintus Cassius Longinus (who was probably a cousin of Caesar's assassin). A number of further meetings took place, and on 7 January the senate finally passed the emergency decree (*senatus consultum ultimum* or 'SCU'); Antony and Cassius fled to Caesar that night. On 10 or 11 January Caesar then invaded Italy.

*that axe*: referring literally to the consul's *fasces*, but metaphorically to the SCU.

*the saviour of the state*: cf. § 2.

52  *a single youth*: Cicero ignores Cassius.

*that stroke which fell on few before you*: yet at § 51 Cicero said, 'that axe which has come down on many others'.

*from which none had escaped unscathed*: yet the SCU had been passed against Quintus Caecilius Metellus Nepos and Caesar in 62, and both had gone on to become consul within five years

55  *three armies of the Roman people were slaughtered*: at Pharsalus (48), Thapsus (46), and Munda (45).

56  *his own uncle*: i.e. Gaius Antonius Hybrida, Cicero's consular colleague whom in 59 he had unsuccessfully defended on a charge, probably extortion, relating to Antonius' governorship of Macedonia (62–60), and who in 49 was still in exile in Cephallenia (he had, however, been restored by 44). The reason Antony did not recall him was not, as Cicero implies, because of a lack of family loyalty, but because his law on the restoration of convicted persons was concerned primarily with those who had been convicted under Pompey's *lex Pompeia de ambitu* (Pompeian law concerning electoral malpractice) of 52.

*Licinius Lenticula*: otherwise unknown. Gambling (with dice) was illegal, except at the Saturnalia. Those convicted were deprived of their civic rights until their debts were paid, not exiled (as we can tell from 'as if it were really the case . . .!', below); hence 'restored', not 'recalled'.

57  *Caesar . . . handed Italy over to this man here*: Caesar left Antony in charge of Italy during his Spanish campaign (early summer 49).

*than to me who was not*: Cicero is trying to cover up the fact that he delayed in Italy until 7 June before joining Pompey in Greece: he actually had two months to observe Antony's administration of Italy for himself.

58  *Lictors . . . marched in front of him*: tribunes were not entitled to lictors; but Antony in fact had been given the status of a praetor, and therefore was entitled to them. The laurels would have been awarded for Caesar's victories in Gaul.

*an actress*: Antony's mistress Volumnia Cytheris, a mime actress (see first note on § 20 above). The townspeople (below) addressed her as 'Volumnia', rather than by her stage name 'Cytheris', because that name was more respectable.

*such disastrous offspring*: she was also the mother of Antony's brothers Gaius and Lucius Antonius (praetor and tribune in 44 respectively).

59  *dangerous*: i.e. because of the risk of giving offence to Caesar's veterans (as Cicero explains below).

*He took part in the war*: he commanded Caesar's left wing at Pharsalus.

*And there you did not kill me*: see § 5.

62  *he was appointed . . . Master of the Horse*: Caesar reached Alexandria at the beginning of October 48. Later in the month, he was named dictator at Rome, with Antony as his Master of the Horse. Caesar was not in direct communication with Rome at this time, but had no doubt left instructions.

*to live with Hippias . . . with Sergius the actor*: Plutarch (*Ant.* 9.6–7) informs us that Hippias was an actor at whose wedding Antony got disgracefully drunk, and Sergius, another actor, was someone who had considerable influence over him. The reason Cicero brings in these characters at this point is to make a play with 'Master of the Horse', Hippias (which means 'horsey' in Greek), and then the reference to hired horses. There is a further subtlety in that the Greek for 'Master of the Horse' is *hipparchos*: Hipparchus and Hippias were the sons of the sixth-century Athenian tyrant Pisistratus.

*not the house . . . but that of Marcus Piso*: the former house was that of Pompey, which Antony had purchased in 47 (§ 64), but which at the time of writing was claimed by Pompey's son Sextus Pompeius, who was in Spain with an army. Marcus Piso was probably the son of Marcus Pupius Piso Frugi Calpurnianus, the consul of 61; he was presumably on the Pompeian side at Pharsalus, although he was praetor in 44.

*Lucius Rubrius . . . Lucius Turselius*: see §§ 40–1.

*an instant heir*: he bought their property, which had been confiscated, at auction in 47.

64  *Caesar returned from Alexandria*: in October 47. On his way back to Rome he had defeated Pharnaces, the son of Mithridates, at Zela in August (the victory referred to in the slogan *veni, vidi, vici*, 'I came, I saw, I conquered'; cf. Plut. *Caes.* 50.3).

*A spear was planted ... Jupiter Stator*: a spear planted in the ground denoted a public auction. On the temple of Jupiter Stator, see first note on *Cat.* 1.11 above.

65 *'rags to riches'*: possibly the title of a mime.

*some poet*: Naevius (third century BC), as Cicero was of course aware. In his speeches he avoids alienating his audience by displaying literary erudition.

67 *Charybdis*: see first note on *Ver.* 2.5.146 above.

*one man's patrimony*: i.e. that of Sextus Pompeius.

68 *those naval trophies*: captured by Pompey in the war against the pirates (67).

69 *He has told that woman ... as the Twelve Tables prescribe*: i.e. he has divorced her (the Twelve Tables were the first collection of Roman statutes, compiled in 451–450 BC). The woman Cicero is referring to is of course Cytheris (see first note on § 20 above), not Fulvia.

70 *'both consul and Antonius'*: i.e. both consul and (unlike Cicero) an aristocrat in his own right. Antony may have made the remark (not necessarily more than once) in his speech of 19 September.

*your grandfather*: Marcus Antonius the orator (see second note on *Ver.* 2.5.3 above).

*My colleague, your uncle*: Gaius Antonius Hybrida, the consul of 63 (see first note on § 56 above).

71 *At this point*: i.e. at the end of 47, the point Cicero has reached. Caesar departed for Africa in December 47, but Antony stayed in Rome throughout the campaign. J. T. Ramsey (*CQ*, NS 54 (2004), 161–73) has shown that Antony must have failed to accompany Caesar not because he had fallen out with him, as was traditionally assumed, but because Caesar needed him for the vital task of breaking up and disposing of Pompey's property in order to raise money for his troops.

*Lucius Domitius*: Lucius Domitius Ahenobarbus, the consul of 54 and the only consular killed at Pharsalus. He was a relentless enemy of Caesar; his son was one of the conspirators (§§ 27, 30).

*after his return from Africa*: Caesar returned to Rome on 25 July 46, having defeated the republicans at Thapsus in February.

*quaestor*: in 51 (§ 50). On the special bond between a quaestor and the magistrate under whom he served, see note on *Ver.* 11 above.

*Master of the Horse*: from October 48 until late in 47 (§ 62).

*under the terms of his will ... his son*: in fact Antony was named in Caesar's will only among the heirs in the second degree. No doubt he had hoped for greater recognition.

73 *that place at Misenum*: see § 48.

74 *Lucius Rubrius*: see §§ 40–1. We know nothing about the decree referred to.

74  *Caesar . . . complained about it in the senate*: Cicero does not actually claim that Caesar accused Antony of the attempt (and the next sentence makes it pretty clear that Caesar did not consider him responsible).

*Then he set out for Spain*: at the end of 46, to fight the sons of Pompey (the elder of whom, Gnaeus Pompeius, would be executed after Munda (45), leaving only Sextus Pompeius surviving).

*for his own self-interest*: since Antony had an interest in ensuring that Pompey's sons did not return to Rome to claim their inheritance.

75  *Dolabella*: Publius Cornelius Dolabella, Antony's colleague as consul in 44. No doubt he was able to reach Spain without difficulty because he travelled with Caesar, whereas Antony, leaving later, may have encountered bad weather.

*in Thessaly, Africa, and Spain*: i.e. at Pharsalus (49), Thapsus (46), and Munda (45).

76  *Narbo*: Narbo was as far as Antony got before he gave up the attempt to reach Spain and turned back to Rome (cf. second note on § 34 above). He arrived at Rome at the beginning of March 45.

*why I had returned . . . I had undertaken*: Cicero returned to Rome on 1 September 44, and explained his reasons for doing so at *Phil.* 1.7–10, delivered in the senate on 2 September.

*slippers*: literally, 'Gallic sandals'. In popular imagination, the Romans went everywhere in sandals; but in fact the wearing of sandals in public was regarded as a social crime.

*you supposed yourself . . . Master of the Horse*: Cicero implies that his appointment was invalid (cf. § 62).

77  *Saxa Rubra*: 'Red Rocks' (modern Grotta Rossa), about 9 miles north of Rome on the Via Flaminia.

*the woman he had come to see*: Fulvia.

*you subjected Rome . . . to many days of uneasiness*: it must have been Antony's return in itself which Cicero claims gave rise to these feelings, not the fact of Antony's having assumed a disguise. Italy and Rome were most likely afraid that he had been sent back from Spain by Caesar to initiate a purge.

78  *Lucius Plancus*: Lucius Munatius Plancus, one of the city prefects responsible for managing the city of Rome during Caesar's absence (no praetors had yet been elected). He went on to become consul in 42.

*you gave rise to . . . jokes at your own expense*: because 'private affairs' may denote both business matters and sexual ones.

*When Gaius Caesar came back from Spain*: in midsummer 45. Antony went back to Narbo to meet him.

79  *for you to be elected consul*: i.e. for 44.

*Dolabella . . . than I am doing now*: Dolabella would have been objecting to

Antony's opposition to Caesar's proposal to make him suffect consul when Caesar departed for his Parthian campaign (§§ 80–1)—not to Antony's alleged persuasion of Caesar to take for himself the consulship which he had been promised (the final sentence of the previous paragraph, a fiction of Cicero's).

80  *before he himself left Rome*: for the east. Caesar was intending to set out in the spring on a three-year war against the Parthians, to avenge the defeat of Crassus at Carrhae in 53. In the event, his assassination prevented him from undertaking this.

*our fine augur here*: see note on § 4 above.

81  *many months before this*: i.e. in the autumn of 45, when Caesar must first have told him of his intention to make Dolabella suffect consul.

*what in the event he did*: he let the election take place, but then adjourned the meeting (§§ 82–3).

82  *his colleague's litter*: i.e. Caesar's. Antony is pictured as walking obediently behind Caesar's litter.

*Lots were drawn . . . the first to vote*: Cicero now briefly describes the voting procedure in the centuriate assembly, which elected the consuls; cf. second note on *Ver.* 2.5.38 above. (On this occasion, Dolabella seems to have been the only candidate; but the procedures still had to be gone through.) There were 193 centuries, their choices were announced serially, and a simple majority (97 centuries) was needed for a candidate to be elected. The century which obtained the privilege of voting first (the *praerogativa*: see second note on *Ver.* 26 above) was chosen by lot; and after that the centuries voted within census classes (with the six equestrian centuries voting immediately after the first class).

*The result was announced*: i.e. it was announced that the first century had chosen Dolabella.

83  *Gaius Laelius*: the consul of 140, a famous augur and a friend of Scipio Aemilianus. He is given the leading part in Cicero's *De amicitia*, written at about the same time as this speech.

*As augur . . . a consul*: i.e. he obstructed Caesar, his colleague as both augur and consul (Caesar had been an augur since *c*.47).

*to our college*: the College of Augurs, which would need to rule on the validity of Dolabella's election (Antony's fabricated auspices were taken seriously; cf. § 88).

84  *but the moment . . . in order*: in the senate on 17 March Antony had recognized Dolabella as his colleague, in spite of his own objection.

*the Lupercalia*: the Lupercalia was a festival celebrated annually on 15 February. The priests (Luperci) sacrificed goats and a dog at the cave (the Lupercal) where Romulus and Remus were supposed to have been suckled by a she-wolf; then they dressed in goatskin girdles and ran around the Palatine whipping any women they encountered with goatskin thongs in order to encourage their fertility. In 44, during this ceremony, Antony, who was one of the Luperci, offered Caesar a royal diadem. What his motive was, and what Caesar's was if he had pre-arranged the gesture (as would seem likely), are questions which have naturally invited considerable speculation. The festival survived until AD 494, when it was turned into the feast of the Purification of the Virgin.

84 *what he did at the Porticus Minucia*: cf. § 63 'at a gathering of the Roman people, while conducting public business, as Master of the Horse, when a mere belch would have been shocking, he vomited, filling his lap and the whole platform with morsels of food stinking of wine'. The Porticus Minucia was in the Campus Martius.

*the point at which . . . comes into view*: i.e. whether Antony's teacher the rhetorician Sextus Clodius has earned his fee (cf. §§ 43, 101).

85 *Your colleague*: Caesar.

*(you were indeed a Lupercus . . . also a consul)*: it was indecorous for a consul to appear (almost) naked (cf. Dio 45.30.1–5).

86 *You should have requested . . . happily accept servitude*: see §§ 44–6.

*to jab you with cattle-prods*: a punishment inflicted on slaves.

*our greatest heroes*: Caesar's assassins.

87 *he*: Caesar, according to Dio (44.11.3); but Cicero, by not specifying the subject, allows the casual reader to infer that Antony was responsible.

*dictator for life*: Caesar had assumed this title (*dictator perpetuo*) at some point after 26 January 44.

*by order of the people*: cf. § 86 'You certainly had no right to make the request on our behalf, or on that of the Roman people.'

*Lucius Tarquinius . . . Marcus Manlius*: Tarquinius Superbus was Rome's last king, expelled by Lucius Junius Brutus in 509 BC. On Cassius, see second note on § 26 above; and on Maelius, second note on *Cat.* 1.3 above. Marcus Manlius Capitolinus, the consul of 392, saved the Capitol from the Gauls in 390, but was later charged with aiming at tyranny (for attempting to alleviate debt) and thrown from the Tarpeian Rock in 384.

88 *But surely . . . your view on the auspices?*: see first note on § 84 above.

89 *on that day or the next*: i.e. on 15 or 16 March.

*Two days later . . . the temple of Tellus*: on 17 March. The temple was on the west slope of the Esquiline; it was chosen for this meeting of the senate because it was close to Antony's house.

90 *peace made through a hostage . . . Marcus Bambalio!*: the boy was Marcus Antonius Antyllus, the infant son of Antony (hence his noble birth) and Fulvia (whose father Marcus Fulvius Bambalio, Cicero implies, was of inferior birth; he insults him further at *Phil.* 3.16). After the meeting on 17 March, Antyllus was sent as a hostage to the conspirators on the Capitol to persuade them that it was safe for them to come down.

*if funeral is what it was*: Caesar's body was meant to be taken to the Campus Martius (outside the city boundary, as the law prescribed) for formal cremation, but Antony's funeral oration in the forum so inflamed the crowd that they burned the body on their own initiative then and there. The date was *c.*20 March.

91  *Lucius Bellienus*: identity unknown. He was presumably sympathetic to the conspirators.

*no tablet granting exemption*: i.e. from taxation. The decree from which Cicero quotes probably did not block Caesar's acts outright, but merely made them subject to review by the consuls; see J. T. Ramsey, *CQ*, NS 44 (1994), 130–45.

92  *to whole communities*: in Crete (§ 97).

*to entire provinces*: only in fact to Sicily, much of which already possessed Roman citizenship.

93b  *from persons close to you*: the reference is to Fulvia (§ 95 'in the women's quarters'; *Att.* 14.12.1).

*King Deiotarus*: the ruler of Galatia in central Asia Minor. In return for his services to Rome during the Mithridatic Wars, Pompey had granted him extensions of his territory into Pontus and Armenia Minor, and the title of king; accordingly he supported Pompey in the Civil War. After Pharsalus, at which he was present with his cavalry, he received Caesar's pardon, but was deprived of Armenia Minor. He was then accused in 45 of having attempted to poison Caesar, but was defended by Cicero (whom he had helped in Cilicia in 52); the case was unresolved at the time of Caesar's death. (Cicero's *Pro rege Deiotaro*, delivered before the dictator in a private audience, but in Deiotarus' absence, survives.) After Caesar's death, Deiotarus immediately retook Armenia Minor and bribed Fulvia to be granted official recognition as its king.

94  *Massilia*: modern Marseilles. It refused to open its gates to Caesar in April 49 and was therefore besieged, forced to surrender, and punished.

*Caesar . . . enjoying his hospitality*: Caesar visited Deiotarus after his victory over Pharnaces at Zela in 47. This was the occasion on which Deiotarus was later alleged to have attempted to poison Caesar.

*a Greek he had brought with him*: Mithridates of Pergamum, who had served Caesar well in the Alexandrine War. He claimed to be an illegitimate son of the famous Mithridates VI Eupator.

95  *in the women's quarters*: see first note on § 93b above.

96  *whenever a tyrant is killed . . . get it back again*: Ramsey well comments that, according to this rule, Pompey's property ought to have been taken from Antony and handed over to Sextus Pompeius, who was claiming it.

*that person*: possibly someone up-and-coming such as Publius Alfenus Varus, a pupil of Servius Sulpicius Rufus who later oversaw the land confiscations for the triumvirs in 41.

96   *we hate the author but defend his acts*: see second note on § 6 above.

93a  *Where are . . . the temple of Ops?*: see second note on § 35 above.

     *with a sad provenance*: because it consisted, in part, of proceeds from the sales of the property of the defeated Pompeians.

     *to save us from having to pay tribute*: since 167 BC Roman citizens had not had to pay tribute; but they would have to do so again in 43, to meet the cost of the war against Antony. Either Cicero is here showing great foresight, or the possibility of raising tribute from citizens was in the air at this time.

97   *notebooks . . . memoranda*: see second note on § 6 above.

     *Marcus Brutus' term as governor*: see fourth note on § 31 above. Crete had been a province only since 66 (first note on *Ver.* 26 above).

98   *And was it Caesar . . . regarding exiles?*: Caesar had recalled some exiles in 49 (through Antony as tribune; cf. § 56) and then a second batch in 46 or 45; but Antony's law, which he passed off as Caesar's, recalled further individuals whom Caesar, Cicero maintains, had deliberately chosen not to recall, because of their bad characters.

     *the way you treated your uncle*: Gaius Antonius Hybrida, in 49; see first note on § 56 above.

     *you even made him stand for the censorship*: in 44; nothing came of it. It was indeed inappropriate for him to stand, given that he had been expelled from the senate in 70 and then convicted and exiled in 59. He was, however, to become censor in 42.

99   *thunder on the left*: thunder from any direction caused an assembly to be dissolved. However, thunder on the left was a good omen; perhaps Cicero's point is that Antony's augural knowledge is not strong (cf. § 81).

     *the Board of Seven*: this was set up in mid-June to distribute public land in Italy among Caesar's veterans and the poor.

     *if you said no . . . in jeopardy*: ironic. With the exception of Antony, his brother Lucius Antonius, and Dolabella, the members of the Board were all nonentities.

     *your surrogate father*: on Antony's natural father, who died in *c*.71, see first note on § 42 above.

     *His daughter, your cousin*: Antonia, to whom Antony had been married before he married Fulvia. Cicero implies at the end of this sentence that Antony had been unfaithful to Antonia prior to divorcing her in 47 (cf. first note on § 48 above).

     *wicked of you . . . Dolabella*: Dolabella was in fact a notorious womanizer.

100  *Did you ever invite anyone to sit on it?*: the commission is in fact known to have met at least once (*Att.* 16.16C.2).

     *your tour of the veterans' colonies*: Antony spent April–May settling Caesar's veterans in Campania. Hitherto they had been staying in Rome, a source of fear and unrest, and the senate wanted them out of the way.

*you even attempted to found a colony at Capua*: as Cicero explains at § 102, Antony could not legally do this, since Capua was already a colony (founded by Caesar in 59). In the event, he and his would-be colonists were driven out by the Capuans (*Phil.* 12.7).

101  *to the soldiers*: to Pompey's Mithridatic veterans in 59 and to Caesar's veterans in 45.

*To his rhetorician*: Sextus Clodius. Three thousand *iugera* is about 1,875 acres (nearly 3 square miles) and two thousand is about 1,250 (nearly 2 square miles).

102  *Casilinum*: 3 miles north-west of Capua, where the Appian Way crosses the Volturnus. Caesar had founded a colony there in 59.

*You wrote to me asking my opinion*: because Cicero was an expert in augury.

103  *Marcus Varro*: Marcus Terentius Varro (116–27 BC), Rome's greatest scholar and the author of an estimated 620 books (parts of his work on the Latin language, dedicated to Cicero, and his treatise on farming are all that have survived). He pursued a military career under Pompey, who appointed him governor of Further Spain from (probably) 55 to 49. Caesar pardoned him at some point after Pharsalus, and in 45 asked him to form Rome's first public library; nothing came of this. Casinum (see note on § 40 above) was on Antony's way back from Capua to Rome.

*Lucius Rubrius' heirs . . . Lucius Turselius' heirs*: see §§ 40–1.

*the spear in the ground*: see second note on § 64 above.

104  *'how different a master'*: a quotation from an unknown tragedy. A. R. Dyck (on *Off.* 1.139) suggests Accius' *Erigona* as the source, in which case the original reference would be to Clytemnestra and Aegisthus in Agamemnon's palace.

105  *the laws of the Roman people, the records of our ancestors*: i.e. Varro's fifteen books on civil law and forty-one on 'human and divine antiquities', all now lost.

*Aquinum, and Interamna*: nearby towns. Aquinum was the next town after Casinum on the Via Latina in the direction of Rome. It was only 12 miles from Arpinum: one can sense Cicero's local knowledge in this passage.

106  *Anagnia*: a hill town about halfway between Aquinum and Rome, on a ridge overlooking the Via Latina (the 'main road' just referred to).

*just as though he were a consul*: cf. § 10 'he cannot in any sense be regarded as a consul, either in his private life, or in his administration of the state, or in the manner of his appointment'.

*Mustela and Laco*: Seius Mustela (§ 8), the swordsman, was a commander of Antony's guard; Laco is unknown.

107  *the Sidicini . . . the people of Puteoli*: the Sidicini were a people of northern Campania (their chief city was Teanum); Antony would have passed through their territory when he travelled from Casilinum to Casinum. For Puteoli, see second note on *Ver.* 2.5.154 above.

107   *Gaius Cassius and the Bruti*: see first two notes on § 26 above.

*Basilus*: Lucius Minucius Basilus, patron of the Picene and Sabine territories (*Off.* 3.74, where he is again criticized); presumably not the man of the same name who was one of Caesar's assassins.

*when he demolished that tomb*: in early April, Caesar's supporters had erected an altar and column over the place in the forum where the dictator's body had been cremated, and had began to worship him as a god (in referring to this monument as a tomb, Cicero implicitly denies Caesar's divinity). Later in the month, after Antony and the soldiers had left for Campania, Dolabella demolished the monument, executed the worshippers, and arranged for the site to be paved over—much to Cicero's delight.

*I suppose fear . . . must have prevailed*: in fact Antony bought Dolabella off with money from the temple of Ops.

108   *We remembered . . . the monarchy of Caesar*: an eloquent and impressive statement. On Cinna and Sulla, see second note on *Cat.* 3.9 above.

*barbarian*: Antony made use of archers from Ituraea (§§ 19, 112).

109   *He extended . . . provincial governorships*: Caesar had limited this to two years for proconsular appointments and one year for propraetorian appointments. On 2 or 3 June Antony extended his and Dolabella's prospective governorships (of Macedonia and Syria respectively) from two to five years.

*A will he made null and void*: technically, Antony did not make Caesar's will null and void, although he did block Octavian's inheritance and the payment of legacies to the Roman people.

*Scipio's villa*: see second note on § 42 above.

110   *a couch, a sacred image, a pediment on his house, a priest*: all divine honours voted to Caesar in the last months of his life—and of course a major cause of his assassination. (He was not technically declared a god, however, until 42.) The sacred images of the gods were placed on couches at thanksgivings. Antony had been appointed Caesar's priest, but was not formally inaugurated until 40.

*your colleagues*: i.e. your fellow augurs.

*the fourth day of the Roman Games in the circus*: i.e. 18 September. The Roman Games lasted from 4 to 18 September (see first note on *Ver.* 31 above), but only the last four days (15–18 September), devoted to chariot racing, were held in the Circus Maximus.

*Can you have allowed . . . similarly polluted?*: Cicero's point is obscure. He seems to mean: why has Antony added an extra day to all the thanksgivings to the gods in Caesar's honour (the proposal, made on 1 September, seems not to have been specific to the Roman Games; cf. *Phil.* 1.13), and yet not have been prepared to go so far as to display his image on a couch with those of the gods?

111 *your grandfather*: Marcus Antonius the orator (see second note on *Ver.* 2.5.3 above).

*he never addressed . . . in the nude*: in (stark, of course) contrast to Antony at the Lupercalia (§ 86).

112 *Why are the doors . . . not standing open?*: when the senate met, the doors of the building were normally kept open so that passers-by could listen to what was being said inside.

113 *owed her third instalment*: Fulvia's first two husbands, Clodius and Curio, had both met violent deaths (cf. § 11).

*The Roman people have men*: such as Brutus and Cassius. Brutus was in Greece, Cassius at sea off Sicily.

*young men*: Brutus and Cassius were both a little over 40. But Cicero probably means young in comparison with himself.

114 *Brutus made war on Tarquinius*: on this example and the three which follow, see fourth note on § 87 above.

115 *you abolished the dictatorship*: cf. § 91. The date will have been around the end of March.

*persons close to you*: a reference to Fulvia, as at § 93b.

*something else . . . afraid of*: i.e. assassination.

116 *And if you are not afraid . . . tolerate you for long*: i.e. even if you are not afraid of being assassinated by patriots, because you have your henchmen to keep them at bay, you ought still to be afraid of being assassinated by your own supporters (as happened to Caesar).

119 *If nearly twenty years ago . . . reached the consulship*: on 5 December 63, in the debate on the Catilinarian conspirators, cf. *Cat.* 4.3 'For a man of courage, death cannot be shameful; for a man who has reached the consulship, it cannot be untimely; and for a wise man, it cannot be pitiable.' Cicero's words also recall the first sentence of this speech.

# GLOSSARY

**aedile** the third of the annual magistrates, below consul and praetor. There were four aediles, two curule and two plebeian; they were responsible for city administration, the corn supply, and for putting on public games. Cicero was plebeian aedile in 69 BC, and gave three sets of games.

**allies** the *socii* or 'federate states', native communities, in Italy or overseas (e.g. in Sicily), linked to Rome by treaties of alliance; they provided Rome with troops and received certain benefits in return. In 91–87 BC the Italian allies rebelled against Rome in the Social War (the war against the *socii*) and won their goal of Roman citizenship and incorporation within the Roman state.

**augur** a member of the College of Augurs, the official interpreters of religious auspices (sacred signs or omens revealing the gods' approval or disapproval of an action contemplated or in progress). When an augur announced that an omen was unfavourable, the action that was in progress (e.g. the passage of a law, or an election) would be suspended. As with the College of Pontiffs, there were fifteen members, all high-ranking aristocrats. Cicero was elected to membership in 53 (or 52) BC.

**auspices**, *see* **augur**.

**Campus Martius** the 'Plain of Mars', a flood plain to the north-west of the city, between the Capitol and the Tiber. It was used for military training, for elections, and as the place where the census was taken. In Cicero's time it was already starting to be built over.

**censor** one of two magistrates elected every five years for a maximum period of eighteen months. They conducted the census (register of names, ages, and property of all adult male citizens), and revised the list of senators and *equites* by excluding the unworthy; they also leased out the right to collect taxes and acted as guardians of public morals. The office was of great importance and prestige, and was normally held by ex-consuls.

**centuriate assembly** the *comitia centuriata*, an assembly consisting of all Roman citizens divided into 193 'centuries' (military units), grouped into five census classes based on wealth; it elected the consuls, praetors, and censors, and occasionally passed legislation (it passed the law recalling Cicero from exile in 57 BC). The centuries were unequally composed so as to give greater voting power to the rich, and the voting system also favoured the rich. A result was usually declared before the poorest citizens had had the opportunity to vote.

**century**, *see* **centuriate assembly**.

*cognomen* the third component of a Roman's name, serving to differentiate different branches of a clan (*gens*), and usually hereditary; the *cognomen* of Marcus Tullius Cicero is 'Cicero'. It tended to be only the grander Romans (originally, the patricians) who had a *cognomen*; very grand Romans might have several, e.g. Quintus Caecilius Metellus Pius Scipio Nasica (four *cognomina*). The actual meaning of a *cognomen* (where it had one) might be not at all complimentary (*brutus* and *crassus* mean 'stupid'; *calvus*, 'bald'; *strabo*, 'cross-eyed'; *verrucosus*, 'covered with warts'). *Cognomina* were sometimes adopted by generals to commemorate their conquests (e.g. Publius Cornelius Scipio Aemilianus Africanus Numantinus). Some prominent Romans had no *cognomen*: Marcus Antonius (Mark Antony) did not, though his father was Marcus Antonius Creticus. Gnaeus Pompeius (Pompey) started off without one, but became Gnaeus Pompeius Magnus ('Great') in 81 BC.

**colony** a town, usually in Italy, founded by official authority (for example, by Sulla in 81) and settled by Roman citizens.

**conscript fathers** the ancient term for senators, which senators used formally in the senate.

**consul** the most senior of the annual magistrates. The two consuls held office for the calendar year, which (in the absence of any numerical system) was named after them. Ex-consuls were called 'consulars' and were influential in the senate. Cicero was consul in 63 BC.

**curule magistrates** consuls, praetors, censors, and curule aediles were known as curule magistrates and enjoyed special privileges, including the right to sit on an ivory 'curule' chair (*sella curulis*). (Plebeian aediles, such as Cicero, also enjoyed these privileges by 70 BC.)

**dictator** in the early republic, an extraordinary magistrate with supreme powers appointed in an emergency for a maximum of six months. He appointed a deputy who was called Master of the Horse. In the later republic, Sulla and Caesar revived the office for their own ends, Caesar taking it for life. In some other communities, the dictator was simply the chief magistrate.

*eques*, *see* *equites*.

**equestrian**, *see* *equites*.

*equites* the members of the Roman upper class who were not senators (originally, the *equites* were the cavalry); there was a property qualification of 400,000 sesterces. Unlike senators, *equites* were permitted to engage in trade, and some were involved in tax-farming in the provinces. The singular is *eques* ('an *eques*'), the plural *equites*; it is often translated 'knight', but in this translation 'equestrian' is preferred ('an equestrian', 'the equestrians', 'the equestrian order'). Cicero came from an equestrian, not senatorial, family, and viewed himself as a representative of the *equites* and defender of their interests; but, as a senator, he wished to minimize conflict between the two groups and promote 'harmony between the orders' (*concordia ordinum*).

*fasces*, *see* **lictors**.

**federate states**, *see* **allies**.

**freedman** an ex-slave. A freedman/freedwoman would normally remain a dependant of his/her former master.

**legate** a senator serving as an assistant to a general or provincial governor.

**lictors** attendants of senior magistrates. A consul had twelve, a praetor six. Each lictor carried *fasces*, a bundle consisting of an axe and some long rods tied together with red straps; the axe and the rods symbolized the right to inflict capital and corporal punishment respectively (though the axe was omitted within Rome, in recognition of Roman citizens' right of appeal).

**magistrate** the holder of a public office (technically, however, tribunes of the plebs were not magistrates). They are listed in T. R. S. Broughton's *The Magistrates of the Roman Republic* (*see* Select Bibliography).

**Master of the Horse**, *see* **dictator**.

**military tribune** a senior officer in the legions. The tribunes of the first four legions recruited each year were elected by the tribal assembly and enjoyed considerable prestige; those in the other legions were appointed by their commander, and were not necessarily military men.

**new man** a *novus homo*, the first man of a family to reach the senate. Cicero was therefore a new man, but Lucius Licinius Murena, being descended from praetors, was not. The senate contained many new men, but few rose high (in the first half of the first century BC, only four besides Cicero reached the consulship).

**noble** a direct descendant of a consul through the male line. Plebeians as well as patricians might be noble. Cicero was not a noble; his son was.

**optimate** an aristocrat of conservative opinions, at the opposite end of the political spectrum from 'popular' politicians. Sulla was an optimate, but Marius and Caesar were popular politicians. In the 50s, Cicero wished to broaden the term 'optimate' to include all citizens who were concerned for the welfare of their country.

**patricians** members of a select group of Roman clans (*gentes*). The distinction dated back to the regal period: it was believed that the patricians were descended from the 100 fathers (*patres*) chosen by Romulus to form the original senate. In early Rome, the patricians monopolized the priesthoods and the political offices, but by the late republic the offices had long been opened up to the plebeians (i.e. non-patricians) and, from a practical point of view, patrician birth brought more disadvantages than advantages (patricians were ineligible for the offices of tribune of the plebs and plebeian aedile: Clodius had to be adopted into a plebeian family to become tribune). At the end of the republic, only fourteen patrician clans were still in existence. Cicero was not a patrician.

**plebeian assembly** the *concilium plebis* (council of the plebs), an assembly consisting of plebeians only and organized on tribal lines (*see* **tribal assembly**). It elected tribunes of the plebs and plebeian aediles, and passed plebiscites (which had the force of law from 287 BC).

**plebeians,** *see* **patricians**.

*pontifex* a member of the College of Pontiffs in charge of Rome's religious affairs. There were fifteen members, holding office for life, and their head was called the *pontifex maximus* ('chief pontiff'). Caesar was *pontifex maximus* from 63 BC until his death. The office of *pontifex maximus* still exists: it is held by the Pope.

**popular politician** a politican who set out to win the favour of the people in ways that more conservative politicans (optimates) would consider controversial or objectionable, for example by proposing land redistribution or cheaper grain. The tribunate, with its powers to initiate and veto legislation, was a natural ambition for aspiring popular politicians (e.g. Tiberius Gracchus in 133, Gaius Gracchus in 123 and 122, Saturninus in 103 and 100, and Clodius in 58). The civil conflict which resulted from the growth of popular politics was a major cause of the fall of the republic. Before he reached the consulship Cicero sometimes backed popular causes, for example the appointment of Pompey to the Mithridatic command in 66, but he was always opposed to the more extreme manifestations of popular politics.

**praetor** the second most senior of the annual magistrates. In the late republic there were eight praetors each year. The city praetor (*praetor urbanus*) handled civil suits between citizens and the foreign praetor (*praetor peregrinus*) civil suits between citizens and non-citizens; the remaining six praetors presided over the permanent criminal courts (not all the criminal courts were presided over by a praetor). Cicero was praetor in 66 BC, and presided over the extortion court. After their year of office, praetors regularly went out to govern a province as propraetors (consuls did the same as proconsuls).

**prefecture** a district of Italy governed by a magistrate sent out annually from Rome.

**private citizen** a Roman citizen not holding a civil or military public office.

**proconsul** a magistrate who was not a consul but was given a consul's authority in order to command an army or govern a province. Similarly, a propraetor was a magistrate who was not a praetor but was given a praetor's authority, for the same reasons. A proquaestor was an acting quaestor, appointed by a provincial governor to fill a vacancy in the quaestorship.

**propraetor,** *see* **proconsul**.

**proquaestor,** *see* **proconsul**.

**quaestor** the most junior of the annual magistrates and the first stage in the 'sequence of offices' (*cursus honorum*); ex-quaestors automatically became members of the senate. Twenty quaestors were elected annually (their year of office began on 5 December, not 1 January); the two city quaestors were in charge of the treasury, while the rest were officials, mainly dealing with financial matters, in Italy and the provinces. Cicero was quaestor in 75 BC, in western Sicily.

**rostra** the speaker's platform in front of the senate-house in the forum. It was named after the *rostra*, the bronze prows which adorned it, taken from warships of Antium (in Latium) captured in 338 BC.

**SCU,** *see* **senate**.

**senate** the supreme council of the Roman state, consisting of all ex-magistrates (except those expelled as unworthy by the censors). The senate passed decrees, advised the magistrates, assigned provinces, negotiated with foreign embassies, and voted funds, but could not legislate. Its most famous (and controversial) decree was the emergency decree (*senatus consultum ultimum*, 'ultimate decree of the senate' or 'SCU'), passed at moments of civil crisis. The 600 or so senators enjoyed a very high social status (and were forbidden to engage in trade), but only a minority were influential in politics: a small number of families predominated. The senate-house was at the north-east corner of the forum, but the senate sometimes met elsewhere.

**sesterce** a silver coin, the equivalent of four *asses*.

**tax-farmers** *publicani*, private businessmen of equestrian rank whose companies leased from the state the right to collect taxes in the provinces. The system varied from province to province. For the most lucrative one, Asia, the state auctioned the right to collect taxes for a period of five years. The company which submitted the highest bid would be awarded the contract: it would pay the agreed amount up-front, and then set about recouping its outlay, plus an element of profit, from the province; the companies had no power, however, to alter the rates of tax, which were set by the state. If a company overestimated the likely revenue and bid too high, as happened towards the end of the Third Mithridatic War (perhaps in 65 BC), its members could end up heavily out of pocket; in that particular case, the company was, exceptionally, refunded one-third of what it had paid, in 59.

**tribal assembly** the *comitia tributa*, an assembly consisting of all Roman citizens divided into thirty-five largely territorial 'tribes' (four urban and thirty-one rural); it elected the curule aediles, quaestors, and military tribunes, and passed some legislation.

**tribe**, *see* **tribal assembly**.

**tribune (of the plebs)** one of ten annual officers (their year of office began on 10 December, not 1 January) elected to protect the interests of plebeians (the office was closed to patricians). A tribune could initiate legislation, exercise some jurisdiction, and veto any law, senatorial decree, election, or other act of a magistrate—powers which gave the office great political importance. In 81 Sulla removed or curtailed all these powers, and in addition disqualified tribunes from further public office; but the disqualification was removed in 75, and the other powers restored in 70. Tribunes of the plebs are not to be confused with military tribunes or with *tribuni aerarii*.

*tribuni aerarii* 'treasury tribunes', originally treasury officials, but from 70 to 46 BC one of the three classes of jurors, after senators and *equites*. They may be considered as *equites*; there may have been a lower property qualification.

A SELECTION OF     OXFORD WORLD'S CLASSICS

Classical Literary Criticism

The First Philosophers: The Presocratics
and the Sophists

Greek Lyric Poetry

Myths from Mesopotamia

APOLLODORUS     The Library of Greek Mythology

APOLLONIUS OF RHODES     Jason and the Golden Fleece

APULEIUS     The Golden Ass

ARISTOPHANES     Birds and Other Plays

ARISTOTLE     The Nicomachean Ethics
Physics
Politics

BOETHIUS     The Consolation of Philosophy

CAESAR     The Civil War
The Gallic War

CATULLUS     The Poems of Catullus

CICERO     Defence Speeches
The Nature of the Gods
On Obligations
The Republic and The Laws

EURIPIDES     Bacchae and Other Plays
Medea and Other Plays
Orestes and Other Plays
The Trojan Women and Other Plays

GALEN     Selected Works

HERODOTUS     The Histories

HOMER     The Iliad
The Odyssey

A SELECTION OF **OXFORD WORLD'S CLASSICS**

| | |
|---|---|
| THOMAS AQUINAS | **Selected Philosophical Writings** |
| FRANCIS BACON | **The Essays** |
| WALTER BAGEHOT | **The English Constitution** |
| GEORGE BERKELEY | **Principles of Human Knowledge** and **Three Dialogues** |
| EDMUND BURKE | **A Philosophical Enquiry into the Origin of Our Ideas of the Sublime and Beautiful** **Reflections on the Revolution in France** |
| CONFUCIUS | **The Analects** |
| ÉMILE DURKHEIM | **The Elementary Forms of Religious Life** |
| FRIEDRICH ENGELS | **The Condition of the Working Class in England** |
| JAMES GEORGE FRAZER | **The Golden Bough** |
| SIGMUND FREUD | **The Interpretation of Dreams** |
| THOMAS HOBBES | **Human Nature** and **De Corpore Politico** **Leviathan** |
| DAVID HUME | **Selected Essays** |
| NICCOLO MACHIAVELLI | **The Prince** |
| THOMAS MALTHUS | **An Essay on the Principle of Population** |
| KARL MARX | **Capital** **The Communist Manifesto** |
| J. S. MILL | **On Liberty and Other Essays** **Principles of Political Economy** and **Chapters on Socialism** |
| FRIEDRICH NIETZSCHE | **Beyond Good and Evil** **The Birth of Tragedy** **On the Genealogy of Morals** **Twilight of the Idols** |

A SELECTION OF    **OXFORD WORLD'S CLASSICS**

The Anglo-Saxon World

Beowulf

Lancelot of the Lake

The Paston Letters

Sir Gawain and the Green Knight

Tales of the Elders of Ireland

York Mystery Plays

GEOFFREY CHAUCER    **The Canterbury Tales**
**Troilus and Criseyde**

HENRY OF HUNTINGDON    **The History of the English People**
**1000–1154**

JOCELIN OF BRAKELOND    **Chronicle of the Abbey of Bury**
**St Edmunds**

GUILLAUME DE LORRIS    **The Romance of the Rose**
and JEAN DE MEUN

WILLIAM LANGLAND    **Piers Plowman**

SIR THOMAS MALORY    **Le Morte Darthur**

An Anthology of Elizabethan Prose Fiction

An Anthology of Seventeenth-Century
Fiction

Early Modern Women's Writing

Three Early Modern Utopias (Utopia; New
Atlantis; The Isle of Pines)

FRANCIS BACON    Essays

APHRA BEHN    Oroonoko and Other Writings
The Rover and Other Plays

JOHN BUNYAN    Grace Abounding
The Pilgrim's Progress

JOHN DONNE    The Major Works
Selected Poetry

BEN JONSON    The Alchemist and Other Plays
The Devil is an Ass and Other Plays
Five Plays

JOHN MILTON    Selected Poetry

SIR PHILIP SIDNEY    The Old Arcadia

IZAAK WALTON    The Compleat Angler

A SELECTION OF    **OXFORD WORLD'S CLASSICS**

---

**Women's Writing 1778–1838**

WILLIAM BECKFORD    **Vathek**

JAMES BOSWELL    **Life of Johnson**

FRANCES BURNEY    **Camilla**
**Cecilia**
**Evelina**
**The Wanderer**

LORD CHESTERFIELD    **Lord Chesterfield's Letters**

JOHN CLELAND    **Memoirs of a Woman of Pleasure**

DANIEL DEFOE    **A Journal of the Plague Year**
**Moll Flanders**
**Robinson Crusoe**
**Roxana**

HENRY FIELDING    **Joseph Andrews and Shamela**
**A Journey from This World to the Next and
The Journal of a Voyage to Lisbon**
**Tom Jones**

WILLIAM GODWIN    **Caleb Williams**

OLIVER GOLDSMITH    **The Vicar of Wakefield**

MARY HAYS    **Memoirs of Emma Courtney**

ELIZABETH HAYWOOD    **The History of Miss Betsy Thoughtless**

ELIZABETH INCHBALD    **A Simple Story**

SAMUEL JOHNSON    **The History of Rasselas**
**The Major Works**

CHARLOTTE LENNOX    **The Female Quixote**

MATTHEW LEWIS    **Journal of a West India Proprietor**
**The Monk**

HENRY MACKENZIE    **The Man of Feeling**

ALEXANDER POPE    **Selected Poetry**

A SELECTION OF     **OXFORD WORLD'S CLASSICS**

| | |
|---|---|
| ANN RADCLIFFE | **The Italian** |
| | **The Mysteries of Udolpho** |
| | **The Romance of the Forest** |
| | **A Sicilian Romance** |
| SAMUEL RICHARDSON | **Pamela** |
| FRANCES SHERIDAN | **Memoirs of Miss Sidney Bidulph** |
| RICHARD BRINSLEY SHERIDAN | **The School for Scandal and Other Plays** |
| TOBIAS SMOLLETT | **The Adventures of Roderick Random** |
| | **The Expedition of Humphry Clinker** |
| | **Travels through France and Italy** |
| LAURENCE STERNE | **The Life and Opinions of Tristram Shandy, Gentleman** |
| | **A Sentimental Journey** |
| JONATHAN SWIFT | **Gulliver's Travels** |
| | **A Tale of a Tub and Other Works** |
| HORACE WALPOLE | **The Castle of Otranto** |
| MARY WOLLSTONECRAFT | **Mary and The Wrongs of Woman** |
| | **A Vindication of the Rights of Woman** |

A SELECTION OF    **OXFORD WORLD'S CLASSICS**

JANE AUSTEN
**Emma**
**Persuasion**
**Pride and Prejudice**
**Sense and Sensibility**

MRS BEETON
**Book of Household Management**

ANNE BRONTË
**The Tenant of Wildfell Hall**

CHARLOTTE BRONTË
**Jane Eyre**

EMILY BRONTË
**Wuthering Heights**

WILKIE COLLINS
**The Moonstone**
**The Woman in White**

JOSEPH CONRAD
**Heart of Darkness and Other Tales**
**Nostromo**

CHARLES DARWIN
**The Origin of Species**

CHARLES DICKENS
**Bleak House**
**David Copperfield**
**Great Expectations**
**Hard Times**

GEORGE ELIOT
**Middlemarch**
**The Mill on the Floss**

ELIZABETH GASKELL
**Cranford**

THOMAS HARDY
**Jude the Obscure**
**Tess of the d'Urbervilles**

WALTER SCOTT
**Ivanhoe**

MARY SHELLEY
**Frankenstein**

ROBERT LOUIS
STEVENSON
**Treasure Island**

BRAM STOKER
**Dracula**

WILLIAM MAKEPEACE
THACKERAY
**Vanity Fair**

OSCAR WILDE
**The Picture of Dorian Gray**

A SELECTION OF  **OXFORD WORLD'S CLASSICS**

LUDOVICO ARIOSTO  **Orlando Furioso**

GIOVANNI BOCCACCIO  **The Decameron**

MATTEO MARIA BOIARDO  **Orlando Innamorato**

LUÍS VAZ DE CAMÕES  **The Lusíads**

MIGUEL DE CERVANTES  **Don Quixote de la Mancha**
**Exemplary Stories**

DANTE ALIGHIERI  **The Divine Comedy**
**Vita Nuova**

BENITO PÉREZ GALDÓS  **Nazarín**

LEONARDO DA VINCI  **Selections from the Notebooks**

NICCOLÒ MACHIAVELLI  **Discourses on Livy**
**The Prince**

MICHELANGELO  **Life, Letters, and Poetry**

PETRARCH  **Selections from the *Canzoniere* and**
**Other Works**

GIORGIO VASARI  **The Lives of the Artists**

*The
Oxford
World's
Classics
Website*

**www.worldsclassics.co.uk**

- Information about new titles
- Explore the full range of Oxford World's Classics
- Links to other literary sites and the main OUP webpage
- Imaginative competitions, with bookish prizes
- Peruse the Oxford World's Classics Magazine
- Articles by editors
- Extracts from Introductions
- A forum for discussion and feedback on the series
- Special information for teachers and lecturers

**www.worldsclassics.co.uk**

American Literature

British and Irish Literature

Children's Literature

Classics and Ancient Literature

Colonial Literature

Eastern Literature

European Literature

History

Medieval Literature

Oxford English Drama

Poetry

Philosophy

Politics

Religion

The Oxford Shakespeare

A complete list of Oxford Paperbacks, including Oxford World's Classics, Oxford Shakespeare, Oxford Drama, and Oxford Paperback Reference, is available in the UK from the Academic Division Publicity Department, Oxford University Press, Great Clarendon Street, Oxford OX2 6DP.

In the USA, complete lists are available from the Paperbacks Marketing Manager, Oxford University Press, 198 Madison Avenue, New York, NY 10016.

Oxford Paperbacks are available from all good bookshops. In case of difficulty, customers in the UK can order direct from Oxford University Press Bookshop, Freepost, 116 High Street, Oxford OX1 4BR, enclosing full payment. Please add 10 per cent of published price for postage and packing.